MW00808366

Speculative Poetry and the Modern Alliterative Revival

The shield of Thorskegga Thorn. Photograph by Math Jones, 2022.

Speculative Poetry and the Modern Alliterative Revival

A Critical Anthology

Edited by
Dennis Wilson Wise

FAIRLEIGH DICKINSON UNIVERSITY PRESS
Vancouver • Madison • Teaneck • Wroxton

Published by Fairleigh Dickinson University Press
Copublished by The Rowman & Littlefield Publishing Group, Inc.
4501 Forbes Boulevard, Suite 200, Lanham, Maryland 20706
www.rowman.com

86-90 Paul Street, London EC2A 4NE, United Kingdom

*Fairleigh Dickinson University Press gratefully acknowledges the support received
for scholarly publishing from the Friends of FDU Press.*

British Library Cataloguing in Publication Information Available

Library of Congress Cataloging-in-Publication Data

Names: Wise, Dennis Wilson, 1979– editor.
Title: Speculative poetry and the modern alliterative revival : a critical anthology / edited
    by Dennis Wilson Wise.
Description: Vancouver ; Madison : Fairleigh Dickinson University Press, 2024. |
    Includes bibliographical references. | Summary: "In Speculative Poetry and the
    Modern Alliterative Revival, editor Dennis Wilson Wise argues that speculative poets
    over the last century have initiated a long unrecognized revival of medieval alliterative
    poetics. This anthology collects for the first time those poets-C. S. Lewis, Poul
    Anderson, and others-who have fomented this revival"—Provided by publisher.
Identifiers: LCCN 2023039169 (print) | LCCN 2023039170 (ebook) | ISBN
    9781683933298 (cloth) | ISBN 9781683933304 (epub)
Subjects: LCSH: Speculative poetry. | Speculative poetry—History and criticism. |
    Alliteration. | LCGFT: Poetry. | Literary criticism.
Classification: LCC PN6110.S64 S64 2024 (print) | LCC PN6110.S64 (ebook) | DDC
    809.1—dc23/eng/20230918
LC record available at https://lccn.loc.gov/2023039169
LC ebook record available at https://lccn.loc.gov/2023039170

To Martina

Contents

APPENDICES

Preface

Historians may know this feeling well: that arresting moment when, reading an otherwise unremarkable passage of text, you suddenly encounter a statement so unexpected, so bizarre, yet so mundanely expressed, that nothing remains but to spend the next two years chasing that rabbit down its rabbit hole. For literary critics without the privilege of working often with archival materials, such throat-catching moments are rare, but such is how *Speculative Poetry and the Modern Alliterative Revival* began. In late 2017, a few months after defending my dissertation on Tolkien and yearning for something different, I turned my sights on Paul Edwin Zimmer, a little-known fantasy writer whose two-volume novel *The Dark Border* has long mesmerized me. With my newly available free time and the magic of interlibrary loan, I devoted myself to researching Zimmer's obscure other works, including his short stories, poems, and one quasi-academic article about Tolkien's verse published in *Mythlore* in 1993. So far as I know, this article has never been cited. Still, I hoped it might articulate something about Zimmer's own poetics, and it did not disappoint. One remark stopped me in particular. As Zimmer was discussing alliterative poetry, a topic on which I then knew nearly nothing, he ascribed all his success in the meter to two "masters," Tolkien and Poul Anderson. Furthermore, claims Zimmer, these two masters inspired the "perhaps half-dozen younger writers I know of who have experimented with this form."

Questions arose immediately. First, what alliterative poetry *had* Zimmer written? Second, Poul *Anderson*? Although every Inklings scholar knows that Tolkien wrote alliterative-style poetry—a fact recently reinforced by the publications of *The Legend of Sigurd and Gudrún* (2009) and *The Fall of Arthur* (2014)—I'd never seen any Tolkienist ever mention Anderson. At that time, my own experience with Anderson was limited to *Tau Zero*, a masterpiece of hard SF, and *The Broken Sword*, a renowned example of sword and sorcery. (Tellingly, I completely overlooked the numerous alliterative poems in the latter book—an oversight not uncommon, I later discovered, among readers untrained in medieval literature.) Still, why weren't fantasy scholars talking about Anderson, even in passing, and who *were* those "half-dozen younger writers" mentioned by Zimmer?

These questions might have faded in time if, about a year later, I hadn't chanced upon a call for applications to *Science Fiction Studies*'s R. D. Mullen Postdoctoral Research Fellowship, which funded original archival research by contingent scholars on SF topics unrelated to their dissertations. Well, that certainly described my Anderson project, so I applied, got the fellowship, and in August 2019 visited UC Riverside for a ten-day research trip to the Eaton Collection of Science Fiction & Fantasy. There, I delved into a host of fanzines and pulp mags—*Amra, Star*Line, Wyrd, Owlflight, Fantasy Book, Unknown*—hoping to find Zimmer's "half-dozen younger writers," but although I gathered a few new names, I ultimately left disappointed. Only after returning home did the light bulb flash: the Society of Creative Anachronism. Because the ISFDB does not catalogue things like *Tournaments Illuminated*, that venue originally never occurred to me. Luckily, the SCA is nothing if not meticulous about online record-keeping. I soon found a bibliography of old issues and, again assisted by the magic of librarians and interlibrary loan, discovered a small cornucopia of alliterative verse by individuals with names like Mistress Keilyn FitzWarin, Anne of Briar Ditch, Duke Cariadoc of the Bow, Ana Areces, and Brynhildr Kormáksdóttir. It was only after discovering the *drápur* of Geirr Bassi Haraldsson, however, that I realized that *Speculative Poetry and the Modern Alliterative Revival* might someday be possible.

The only problem?

I had absolutely no idea who any of these people—including Bassi—were.

Discovering his identity took another month of digging, and now I must acknowledge the generosity of two people in particular: Beth Tanner Morris and Sandra B. Straubhaar. I first contacted Beth because, under her maiden name, she'd edited a booklet called *Ars Poetica Societatis* (1993), and it was Beth who told me about Bassi—Jere Fleck—with whom she had taken classes. Beth also introduced me to Sandra, whose first reply to me was accompanied by a pdf with *sixty* pages of alliterative verse by multiple poets. In one way or another, the kindness of these two people led me to most Society poets in this anthology, and without them Part II would not have been possible.

Locating other texts in the Modern Revival has been a lesson in perseverance and good fortune. Paul Douglas Deane's website *Forgotten Ground Regained* was an important initial resource, and although I discovered Heathenism distressingly late in the game, Michaela Macha's website *Odin's*

Gift offered another boon. Several poets in Part III were found through the Science Fiction and Fantasy Poetry Association's Facebook page. Other discoveries were plain dumb luck. A random Google search led me to John D. Niles and his *Mosaic* article—a piece he himself had half-forgotten—and I only thought to tackle James Blish after reading a review that mentioned his pseudonym, William Atheling Jr., whose surname is a word in Old English. A reverse Google Scholar search for citations of "Auden and the Inklings" by Carl Phelpstead led me to Rahul Gupta. My amazement at accidentally finding a contemporary scholar *and* poet so dedicated to reviving the alliterative meter in Modern English is hard to express.

My sincere and deep appreciation also goes to every contributor and/or estate representative with whom I've interacted during this long process. Without their willingness to answer questions, this anthology's editorial apparatus would have been much the poorer. Interviews with Bruce Blackistone, Frederick Hollander, Melissa Snow, and Eva Fleck provided significant details and facts discoverable no other way. David O'Neil offered valuable assistance with this anthology's texts in Old English, and B. S. W. Barootes did the same for some highly specific questions on Middle English meter. Fi Boon lent me her expertise in Latin, and Rahul Gupta provided another set of eyes—much appreciated—on my metrical appendix. My footnotes on Blish's "The Coming Forth" owe much to the knowledge of Jim Clarke. The SFWA Estates-Legacy Program guided me to several estates difficult to find. Of course, *Science Fiction Studies* again deserves special mention for sponsoring the R. D. Mullen Postdoctoral Research Fellowship; it literally made this project possible. Two early teachers, Susan Elberty and Charlotte Owens-Cummings, helped set me down this academic path, and two *later* teachers helped see me through it: my dissertation director and personal model of the ideal academic, Dr. David Lavery, who passed away six months before my defense, and Dr. Rebecca King, who graciously took over. Tracy Blackstone, Diana L. Paxson, and Pat Yarrow all contributed time, energy, and knowledge to answering queries or providing valuable resources. My appreciation goes to editor James Gifford at Fairleigh Dickinson University Press as well as to Zachary Nycum and the entire publishing staff for believing in this project and guiding it through the process. I would also like to mention this volume's anonymous peer reviewer. All too often, reviewing is a thankless task, but even thanks are insufficient for truly great reviewers—people sympathetic toward your larger project, yet also meticulous, critical, and unwilling to pull punches. Such academics are pure gold. Finally, nothing about this book would have been possible without my beloved wife, Martina, who supported me through this process and so much more.

Introduction

Speculative Poetry and the Modern Alliterative Revival

Connections Missed

"Hwaet."

If someone heard this word spoken quietly, in context, they might have been guesting at an early English mead hall sometime during the centuries after Rome withdrew from Britain but before William of Normandy, fatefully, landed at Pevensey in Sussex in 1066. In this mead hall, plucking a lyre, a *scop* would have just begun one of two classic poems in Old English, *The Dream of the Rood* or *Beowulf*; or, had this one word been declaimed in thundering tones (as contemporary medievalists believed it spoken until only recently), the listener might have been an Oxford undergraduate attending a lecture by a young, lean professor of Anglo-Saxon, J. R. R. Tolkien. Despite a tendency to mumble, Tolkien often began his *Beowulf* lectures with this resounding call for attention; it certainly impressed the young W. H. Auden, who many years later confessed how Tolkien's lecture left him "spellbound" (41). Unfortunately, we don't know how much of Tolkien's own alliterative verse Auden ever read. He certainly knew *The Lord of the Rings* (1954–1955) and "To W.H.A.," a poem Tolkien presented to Auden on the latter's sixtieth birthday, but otherwise the professor's lectures were what drove Auden into experimenting with archaic medieval meters. His most famous alliterative poem is *The Age of Anxiety* (1947), but he also penned a powerful—if relatively free—translation of the *Poetic Edda*. These manifold efforts led one prominent British medievalist in 1977, Thorlac Turville-Petre, to lament how among contemporary poets only Auden has "made a serious attempt . . . [at] a second alliterative revival" (128).

1

In retrospect, this remark seems brash and overly flippant. For one thing, Turville-Petre unequivocally believes in a *first* alliterative revival, specifically between the mid-fourteenth and mid-fifteenth centuries, a hypothesis now challenged by many medievalists. More crucially, Turville-Petre clearly but silently excludes Tolkien from the ranks of "serious" poets, turning a cold shoulder to Auden's major inspiration in Old English meter. Admittedly, few of Tolkien's alliterative poems were widely known by 1977, mainly just those in *The Lord of the Rings*, but Turville-Petre probably knew of others by reputation if nothing else. After all, Tolkien's name was hardly unknown to the Turville-Petre family. Both of Thorlac's parents, Gabriel and Joan, studied under Tolkien's supervision at Oxford; they likely met there, and Tolkien would attend their wedding with his wife (Scull and Hammond 1064–65). In due time Gabriel ("E. O. G.") Turville-Petre became an eminent scholar of Ancient Icelandic literature; in a twist of fate, he supervised the BLitt thesis of Tolkien's own son Christopher, who then wrote an introduction to Gabriel's scholarly edition of *Hervarar saga ok Heiðreks* (1956) before publishing an annotated translation of this text in 1960. Along similar lines, Joan Turville-Petre paid posthumous tribute to her former supervisor by editing *The Old English Exodus: Text, Translation, and Commentary by J. R. R. Tolkien* (1981). Despite these connections, however, the younger Turville-Petre apparently saw no need or reason to mention Tolkien in the same breath as Auden. We can only guess his reasons today, but I suspect they involve Tolkien's strong public association with fantasy and children's literature, two popular literary forms then viewed with deep suspicion—if not outright hostility—by the academics of Turville-Petre's generation.[1]

Yet herein lies the tale, the main story of the Modern Alliterative Revival— a tale of opportunities overlooked, of connections missed; a story of blind spots both scholarly and literary, of poets and scholars on both sides of the Atlantic working in circles that only barely (or never quite) managed to overlap. In a way, *Speculative Poetry and the Modern Alliterative Revival* answers the literary equivalent of the philosopher's problem: "If a tree falls in the forest, and no one is around to hear, does it make a sound?" In this analogy, the Modern Revival is the tree, and the forest represents those multiple zones of alliterative activity sprawling across decades and continents without anyone in the twentieth century seeming to notice. Since 1954 especially, a newfound fascination with alliterative style has lent a uniquely medieval flavor to several popular subcultures and trends. These include pulp magazines; genre fandom; historical reenactment societies; the San Francisco Renaissance; the American Counterculture; speculative poetry; alternative spiritual movements such as Wicca, Asatru, and Neo-Paganism; and an explosion in mass-market fantasy literature that continues to inspire a deep and abiding fascination with the Middle Ages extending well beyond academic conferences and academia's Ivory Tower.

Historically, though, these subcultures and trends have interacted only on their outer margins. Although none are fully isolated, few overlap to any significant degree—and most revivalist texts, to be honest, are obscure enough that even critics favorably disposed toward popular culture have missed the Modern Revival. Still, opportunities did exist. One golden moment—a tantalizing trifecta of missed chances—spanned one twelve-month period running from 1977 through 1978. About a year after Turville-Petre expressed hope for a second alliterative revival, another young medievalist, an American this time, wrote a provocative article for the interdisciplinary journal *Mosaic*. This article analyzes several contemporary poets working in alliterative styles. Nonetheless, although John D. Niles touches upon a wider range of writers than his British colleague, including the Inklings and Richard Wilbur, he reaches a virtually identical conclusion: there did not *yet* exist any true revival in alliterative poetry. As he says,

> To judge from the current little magazines, there exists no campaign among the young to revive alliterative poetry in [Modern] English, if only in the spirit of irrelevance, escapism, and just plain fun which one sees overflowing like mead from a goblet in the various chapter meetings of the Society for Creative Anachronism. (30)

Yet this eloquent passage teases readers with untapped possibility: two dropped threads that, in hindsight, could have led decades sooner to critical awareness of the Modern Revival. First, Niles admits to searching for alliterative poetry in the "current little magazines," and, as a strategy, this move makes sense. After all, it was the little magazines that famously launched American modernism. In the 1920s, for instance, *The Dial* published important early work by Hart Crane, Ezra Pound, and Wallace Stevens, not to mention the American edition of T. S. Eliot's "The Waste Land." As it happens, though, the little magazines were precisely the *wrong* place to have searched for a contemporary alliterative revival. During the late 1970s, the poems Niles actually wanted were to be found in cheap paperbacks with lurid covers; in disposable magazines dedicated to the sub-literary genres of science fiction and fantasy (SFF); and in amateur fanzines produced on mimeograph and circulated by mail by fans. Not the sorts of places, granted, where one might reasonably suspect a revival in archaic medieval poetics, but so it was.

Niles's other dropped thread involves the Society for Creative Anachronism (SCA), an organization dedicated to historical reenactment. Although Niles clearly approves of their activities, he also clearly overlooks—a near miss now particularly painful to see—its official magazine, *Tournaments*

Illuminated. During the late 1970s, the local SCA consisted mainly of Bay Area history buffs and SFF enthusiasts who saw themselves as playfully re-creating medieval life, chivalry, and culture—even if, as Michael A. Cramer notes, they often romanticized the Middle Ages through the lens of Victorian medievalism (xi). Still, their official magazine, a quarterly, was a grab bag of content on medieval history, lifestyle, and material culture. A typical issue might include articles ranging from arms and armor to music and metalwork-ing. Had Niles browsed a few issues, though, or at least a few of the *right* issues, he would have noticed a small but astonishing cadre of poets using the Old Norse and Old English alliterative meters. Perhaps Niles lacked any contacts in the SCA who knew *Tournaments Illuminated* sufficiently well—or who, if they did, could recognize an alliterative poem. It is also possible that Niles's own aversion to San Francisco's careless bohemianism of the late 1970s, an attitude deftly conveyed by his own fine poem "Fair Day," prevented any closer ties with the group. Yet it was precisely this perpetual Bay Area carnivalesque, a second flowering of the literary renaissance from the Beats a generation earlier, that launched the SCA and stimulated its early alliterative windfall.

After Turville-Petre's book and Niles's article, one more incident com-pletes our tantalizing trifecta of missed opportunities. This time, the event centers around an author and editor of speculative fiction, a future winner of the World Fantasy Award. Like our two medievalists, Steve Rasnic Tem was just then starting his career, and in May 1978 he issued a provocative letter to the editor of *Star*Line*, a fledgling publication serving an organization just launched a few months earlier, the Science Fiction Poetry Association (SFPA). For Tem, the SFPA could not have arrived at a better time. His own speculative fanzine, *Umbral*, which lasted five issues up through 1981, had just begun, and Tem's 1978 letter expresses his wish for a supplement to *Umbral.* He specifically wants

> formal verse, but formal verse which really makes use of the form—for exam-ple, Pound's imitation of the Anglo-Saxon in his first, "Greek," canto. In other words, using the formal verse pattern AND diction AND imagery to draw paral-lels, analogues between different cultures and periods of history. . . . The idea of verse parallels between the future and a past culture excites me. (Rasnic 5)

In other words, Tem sought the kind of poetry that might have jump-started a second alliterative revival more quickly. His call went unanswered, though, and why is hard to say. Poul Anderson, granted, was by then an established professional writer who reserved his poetry for his novels, but Paul Edwin Zimmer—a young firebrand brimming with self-confidence and primed for a revolution in poetics—should have found Tem's call a lightning rod. We also know Zimmer read early issues of *Star*Line*. Still, Tem reports never receiving any appropriate submissions, nor did he unearth any suitable material to reprint ("Re: New Message"). When he published his *Umbral Anthology of Science Fiction Poetry* a few years later, this landmark anthology would contain nothing directly influenced by medieval alliterative poetics.

Despite this triad of golden opportunities, then, nobody ever quite managed to connect the dots. Despite a small yet widespread alliterative revival in speculative verse, nobody ever quite managed to see the phenomenon as a whole. Sparks were being set, but the kindling never caught. Two different issues are involved. The first is disciplinarity: the way literary studies organizes itself as a field. Because the alliterative meter belongs to a niche branch of metrical history, namely medieval poetics, specialized training is necessary for anyone even to recognize the form. Unfortunately, few scholars receive such training in graduate school; I certainly never did. Conversely, the scholars who *do* sometimes receive this training, medievalists, rarely have any reason to comb through obscure pulp magazines or unpublished fan poetry. Yet even if more critics did possess the right skill sets, the Modern Revival's other major issue—communication—has been just as problematic. Historically, neither mainstream literary critics nor the SFF community have paid one another much attention. The editors, poets, reviewers, scholars, and critics potentially most interested in the Revival simply run in different circles. Worse, revivalists can be divided into two distinct subgroups. Poets in the "university branch" include writers like Tolkien, Lewis, Auden, and Pound: people who discovered and developed their alliterative poetics through formal education. In contrast, although poets in the "demotic branch"—Anderson, Zimmer, folks in the SCA—may or may not have studied medieval literature at college (if they went at all), they overwhelmingly shared their work in amateur or semi-professional venues, such as SFF magazines, novels, fanzines, newsletters, public poetry readings, *Tournaments Illuminated*, and more. All these sites, notably, operate far below the horizons usually scoured by academic medievalists—the one group best positioned to appreciate their efforts.

Still, even the better-known university poets have rarely received proper credit. As we've seen, Turville-Petre dismisses Tolkien with silence, but although such outright hauteur has grown rare, other critics have simply traded silence for puzzlement. Writing for *The Old English Newsletter* in 1992, Hugh Magennis praises Pound, Wilbur, and Seamus Heaney—three mainstream poets—for their alliterative styles, but he seems unsure of Tolkien, whom he calls "interesting, and eccentric" (17). Yet such hesitation is far less damaging than the assumption, almost reflexive by some, that genre writing simply counts for less than "real" literature. Heather O'Donoghue falls into this trap when she observes—her ambivalence clear—that the *Poetic Edda* has influenced contemporary culture mainly through "texts in different ways marginal to the literary canon." What texts does she consider "marginal"? Video games, children's literature, and modern fantasy (363). This perception perhaps explains why her major reception study, *English Poetry and Old Norse Myth* (2014), never once mentions the two most important poets in either branch of the Modern Revival, Tolkien and Anderson. Similarly, Tolkien is given only a brief mention in Chris Jones's major reception study, *Strange Likeness* (2006). This book focuses on four mainstream poets from the twentieth century—Pound, Auden, Heaney, and Edwin Morgan—but, explicitly and tellingly, not the progenitor of modern fantasy. As Jones explains, Tolkien's influence as a "poet on other writers is negligible, and having to justify his inclusion alongside more 'serious' poets would unbalance the book" (13).

No matter how sincerely Jones means his scare quotes around "serious," however, a word used also by Turville-Petre, this word performs a hefty amount of hidden ideological labor. One paragon of the New Weird, Jeff VanderMeer, provides a relevant anecdote. In an interview from 2018, he explains that academic conversations surrounding his novels changed dramatically once he "switched to a mainstream literary publisher in the US" (53). His earlier work hailed from places like Tor Books, a prolific publisher of genre fantasy, but when Farrar, Straus and Giroux—a more prestigious firm—published the *Southern Reach* trilogy in 2014, that created an instant buzz never before matched by VanderMeer's earlier New Weird fiction. Unfortunately, critics are only human. All too often, they let place of publication serve as a quick index—an initial clue—to literary quality, but this rough heuristic has reinforced a cycle of obscurity that has kept the Modern Alliterative Revival within the shadows. Disarmingly, Hugh Magennis confesses that if other poets besides those he names are working with Old English materials, "I do not know about them" (17). Of course, there *were* such poets—it's just that they were genre.

This situation is what *Speculative Poetry and the Modern Alliterative Revival*, a book as much argument as anthology, seeks to remedy. Over the last ten decades, the Modern Revival has scratched out a cultural foothold on the outskirts of "serious" literature, producing a beguiling, semi-populist poetry flavored by medievalism and yet thriving beyond the strict confines of senior seminars and college-level survey courses. In what remains of this section, I'll outline how Modern Revival differs from its parallel phenomenon, the fourteenth-century Alliterative Revival. Next, in Part Two, I'll turn to the Modern Revival's university and demotic branches. Finally, my third part will comment briefly on the texts themselves, plus how we might best approach them.

Revivalism Redux: The Fourteenth Century and Now

The idea of literary revivalism can be a tricky one, not to mention contentious. Commonly, a revival implies the restoration or renewal of something diminished, absent, or faded. More strongly, revivals can imply certain metaphorical acts of necromantic power by a magician or magicians resurrecting the dead or moribund. When literary historians hear the term, it's often associated with the Alliterative Revival of the mid-fourteenth century, an apparent resurgence in Old English poetics after their seeming extinction three centuries prior. From roughly 1350 through 1450, texts like *Piers Plowman*, *Sir Gawain and the Green Knight*, and the *Alliterative Morte Arthure* arose that were heavy on structural alliteration, short on rhyme, and free from regular rhythm. In the three hundred years prior, our manuscript record preserves only various kinds of quasi-alliterative writing: the rhythmical prose of Ælfric and Wulfstan; poetic texts with more end-rhyme than front-rhyme; and Lawman's *Brut*, a late twelfth-century metrical anomaly. Otherwise, unrhymed alliterative verse simply does not appear. According to one estimate by Derek Pearsall, the seventy-five years prior to 1350 preserve only twenty-eight lines of such poetry; in contrast, the seventy-five years after 1350 preserve over forty thousand ("Origins" 1).

Since *Speculative Poetry and the Modern Alliterative Revival* clearly owes its titular thesis to the fourteenth-century phenomenon, it's worth examining the controversies that swirl around this purported event. My central claim is that, since the 1920s, multiple speculative poets have begun reviving various poetic traditions centered on an alliterative meter. Yet, even here, matters begin to grow complicated. Historically, all medieval Germanic languages—Old English, Old Norse, Old High German, and Old Saxon, plus probably Gothic and Old Frisian as well—used the alliterative meter as their primary poetic form. Until the end of the early English period, the meter's rules in the English-language tradition are relatively straightforward:

- a medial caesura between the *a*-verse and *b*-verse;
- four metrical positions per half-line comprised of two *lifts* (stressed syllables) and two *dips* (one or more consecutive unstressed syllables);
- alliteration usually in an *ax/ax* or *aa/ax* pattern across the line's four lifts; and
- verses using the five metrical rhythms in Old English poetry called "Sievers types."

For more details, see Appendix B. In addition to these rules, though, Old English was a language rich in synonyms and poetic compounds. The word for *man*, for instance, could be rendered *beorn, freca, guma, hæle, hæleth, rinc, scealc*, or *wer*, which helps make alliterations easier to find. Likewise, the unique compound phrases in Old English, many found only in verse, helped poets fulfill the Sievers types. Like other medieval Germanic languages, too, Old English is a tongue heavy in words beginning with stress-initial syllables, a feature that encourages front-rhyme (i.e., alliteration) and promotes a falling trochaic rhythm on initial verse positions. But as loanwords began entering the language from French and Latin, Old English's predominately trochaic rhythms became harder to maintain. Nor did it help that prepositions and auxiliary verbs gradually came to replace most inflected word endings. As a result, although the alliterative poets of the fourteenth century mostly retained the four-lift lines and the *aa/ax* alliterative patterns of their Old English forebears, the new linguistic realities of Middle English forced them to compose lines longer and looser than any permitted by Old English *scopas*.

Medievalists have proposed several explanations for why this new alliterative meter, however modified, reemerged so vigorously in the mid-fourteenth century. These explanations can be divided into three camps, and the oldest argues for *continuity*. According to this hypothesis, although alliterative poetry persisted throughout the three centuries following the Norman Conquest, it persisted within the oral vernacular tradition only. Properly speaking, then, the fourteenth-century Alliterative Revival is a revival of alliterative poetry in its *written* form. To this camp belong the Inklings, and their colleague R. W. Chambers, whom Tolkien once dubbed the "greatest of living Anglo-Saxon scholars" ("Beowulf" 68), articulated their generation's most famous statement on continuity:

> There can be few stranger things in the history of literature than this sudden disappearance and reappearance of [an alliterative] school of poetry. It was kept alive by oral tradition through nine generations, appearing in writing very rarely, and then usually in a corrupt form, till it suddenly came forth, correct, vigorous, and bearing with it a whole tide of national feeling. (lxvii)

As Chambers's final remark indicates, the continuity camp highly valued patriotism and a sense of English cultural identity. In a famous essay from 1931, for example, James R. Hulbert argues that the Alliterative Revival was politics by other means: the metrical expression of native baronial discontent against London's Anglo-Norman royal court (406). This folk romanticism affected the Inklings deeply. Late in the 1920s, Lewis could claim that while classical literature might furnish Modern English authors with subject matter, the English *spirit* came about through absorbing "our ancient alliterative poetry" (*Rehabilitations* 72). Old English was therefore the literary "tap-root" for literature in Modern English (92). A similar sentiment, although later abandoned, pervades Tolkien's early legendarium. As Tolkien writes, what initially drove him to invent a self-contained mythology wholesale was his youthful desire to forge a "body of more or less connected legend . . . which I could dedicate simply to: to England; to my country" (*Letters* 144).

In 1977 arose another camp that favored *discontinuity*. Here, the Alliterative Revival represents a true revival, a genuine return to long-moribund literary practices, and we've met its main proponent before: Thorlac Turville-Petre. Disturbed by the lack of hard evidence for an unbroken oral tradition, Turville-Petre proposed that an alliterative school must have arisen during the mid-fourteenth century that took its metrical cues from existing rhythmical prose texts and rhymed alliterative verse. This school, says Turville-Petre, had nearly no contact with Chaucer's accentual-syllabic school of poetics (36). These bold claims roiled the field of medieval studies almost immediately, and they just as quickly drew several fierce rejoinders, even among those who fundamentally agreed with Turville-Petre on the likelihood of discontinuity. Elizabeth Salter, for instance, saw the "thesis of continuity as a piece of romantic mystification" (Pearsall, "Alliterative" 42), but, in her view, nothing *except* meter united late medieval alliterative poetry. There was no school; rather, the Middle English alliterative poets operated along "several parallel, or overlapping, narratives" with quite different affiliations and circumstances (Salter, "Review" 464). Likewise, N. F. Blake argued for not "one alliterative revival but several" throughout the West Midlands and Scotland (207). This third camp arguing for disunity—a sort of null hypothesis—seems to enjoy leading status today. Randy P. Schiff, for example, blasts the entire notion of revivalism as a "monolithic narrative" that blinds medievalists to the firmly local contexts of the fourteenth century (2). Because continuitists and discontinuitists alike share an anachronistic modern notion of nationhood, Schiff argues, what separates them is only "superficial disagreement" (36).

For this anthology, I need not take a position on any of these three camps. However we view the fourteenth-century phenomenon, the Modern Revival has undeniably broken with all past alliterative traditions. One final wrinkle besets this anthology's thesis, however: the non-zero chance that every single rule of alliterative metrics just described—the thing speculative poets are allegedly trying to revive—is utterly, completely, and embarrassingly *wrong*. Sadly, the alliterative meters in English have never had their Snorri Sturluson. Everything we now know about them derives entirely from scholarship undertaken only since the late 1700s. In fact, outside a few tantalizing references, no medieval poet even directly mentions their unique poetic practices.[2] Even the term *alliteration* was unknown during the Middle Ages. According to Ian Cornelius, the Latin word *alliteratio* goes back to the 1490s, and the word doesn't enter English until the 1600s—long *after* English-language poets ceased to write alliterative poetry. In our earliest sixteenth-century commentaries, moreover, editors tended to conflate an initial likeness of sound with an initial likeness of spelling, describing the medieval meter as *"running upon a letter, playing with the letter, hunting the letter*, and *coursing a letter"* (Cornelius 29, emphasis original). Only much later did amateur antiquarians begin calling Old English and Middle English poetry "alliterative," and it took until the mid-nineteenth century before anyone began to recognize this meter as accentual. Then, once Eduard Sievers published *Altgermanische Metrik* in 1893, his work shaped and solidified our knowledge of alliterative metrics for roughly the next hundred years, especially in Old English.

In the mid-1980s, however, Hoyt N. Duggan and Thomas Cable independently discovered that certain hard rules did, in fact, govern the Middle English meter, or at least its *b*-verse, formerly viewed as an unregulated anarchy of lifts and dips. Shortly thereafter, Geoffrey Russom proposed eliminating a foundational principle of Sieversian metrics, the four-position principle, and replacing it with his "word-foot" theory. Even more radically, a doctoral student named Nicolay Yakovlev defended a D.Phil. thesis in 2008 that, although retaining and prizing Sievers's four-position principle, sought to overturn two other previously unquestioned Sieversian principles: that Old English poetry was accentual, and that alliteration held its lines together. As Ian Cornelius explains, Yakovlev describes the meter as *morphological*, based not on strong stresses but on the category membership of individual morphemes. Alliteration thereby arises only as an incidental or ornamental—*not* a structural—feature of the meter. Although Yakovlev's thesis remains unpublished, it quickly gained several influential adherents, including Eric Weiskott in *English Alliterative Verse* (2016) and Cornelius in *Reconstructing Alliterative Verse* (2017). Alongside further work by Thomas Cable, Donka Minkova, and others, this new research—much of it linguistic and phonological in nature—has given a much-needed jolt to the continuity thesis, albeit freed now from that camp's early association with English cultural nationalism.

Yet these exciting advances have barely touched the Modern Revival. For one thing, most revivalists lack access to university library research databases, so older models of alliterative poetics remain in use. In addition, while linguistic and phonological research can help explain why Middle English poetics evolved naturally from Old English poetics, this research has limited relevance for the Modern Revival. After all, in this latter-day movement, discontinuity reigns. Regardless of how *Sir Gawain*'s meter relates to the meter of *Beowulf*, the mid-sixteenth century oversaw a decisive break in English alliterative metrical history.[3] Moreover, when the meter finally reemerged in the nineteenth century, *we already know how it happened*. It reappeared not through fortuitous linguistic change or the sudden discovery of lost oral traditions, but through the careful and patient work of medievalists. When William Morris, Alfred Lord Tennyson, and Gerard Manley Hopkins began borrowing and adapting techniques from Old English poetry, they relied first and foremost on scholarly editions of medieval texts just recently established. The first original-language editions of *Beowulf* and *Sir Gawain* didn't see print, respectively, until 1815 and 1839. Furthermore, Victorian poets needed the help of professional medievalists to understand the metrical principles behind these texts' meters, and they gained all this knowledge during a time when the British university system was just beginning to recognize English literature as a serious and respectable subject of study.

Nonetheless, Rahul Gupta has argued that a "proper" alliterative revival could arise only *after* the Victorians. According to him, poets such as Tennyson and Morris lacked an "established working and convincing theory" of the alliterative meter (14). That theory came via Sievers in the 1880s and 1890s, but, just as importantly, the philologist Henry Sweet introduced Sieversian metrics to English-speaking audiences through his massively influential *An Anglo-Saxon Reader in Prose and Verse* (seventh edition, 1894). Accordingly, despite other competing non-Sieversian metrical models, nearly all modern alliterative poetry in the Old English tradition is essentially "*Sieversian verse*" (Gupta 20–21, emphasis original). In support of this view, Fred C. Robinson has shown how Ezra Pound used Sweet's *Reader* to prepare his famous translation of *The Seafarer* (248–56), and C. S. Lewis relied necessarily on Sweet because he lacked the skill in German to tackle Sievers in the original.[4] Likewise, later generations of poets such as Auden, Heaney, and Geoffrey Hill all profited from Sweet's volume (Atherton 3). This Sieversian legacy would continue alive and well even through the 1960s when Alan J. Bliss, a former student of Tolkien, updated and reaffirmed the Sievers system in several important works.

Still, four aspects of Gupta's argument run directly counter to the evidence gathered by this anthology. First, when Gupta invokes the "archetypically and quintessentially *English*" character of the alliterative meter (10, emphasis original), he signals his allegiance to the same cultural nationalism that marked the early continuity camp. Indeed, Gupta seems to accept an almost mystical sense of continuity between past and present when he writes that the "Inklingsian revival of alliterative metre constructs a poetics predicated upon the *chthonic leyline of the [English] language*, dowsing a subterranean mainstream continuous with the Anglo-Saxon source" (55, emphasis added). Yet, besides Gupta and the Inklings, few poets in this anthology demonstrate much interest in national identity. Even John Myers Myers, who lionizes the Western literary canon, instead seems to value the alliterative meter for how it recalls premodern heroism. Second, Gupta's training leads him to privilege

Old English alliterative poetics, but the Modern Revival embraces the Old Norse and Middle English traditions as well. Third, the mainstream obscurity of most demotic poets has left many important figures—Poul Anderson, Jere Fleck, the Greyhaven Circle—completely unknown to most medievalists, Gupta included. Finally, as his argument (and own poetry) shows, Gupta prioritizes a philologically "correct" revival of Old English meter. This attitude demonstrates a perfectly legitimate purist sensibility, but it also risks discounting—even disregarding—those poets who deviate from an imagined Platonic ideal of metrical perfection. What Eric Weiskott claims for alliterative verse in the fourteenth century, however, holds just as true for alliterative verse in the twentieth century. Never has there been just one "unvarying meter, which all alliterative poems reproduced like clockwork" (*English* 12). Arch-purists can thus recognize only half the Modern Revival—and not always the most interesting half.

Altogether, contemporary revivalists range across a wide spectrum of metrical fidelity. Personally, I picture this spectrum as a sliding scale between one and ten. On the leftward side, purists: poets who accurately imitate more known features of the alliterative meter than not. On the rightward side, impressionists. This latter group is less engaged with replicating a historical alliterative tradition and instead prefers medieval "flavoring" to one degree or another. Some texts approaching the "10" side of my scale can seem barely alliterative at all—for instance, Jo Walton's "In Death's Dark Halls, a Dog Howls." Such extreme impressionism can make it hard to decide whether a text properly belongs to the Modern Revival or not, and I explain my selection criteria in Part Three. Still, medievalists find themselves in a similar bind as well. Thomas Cable, for one, insists that strong metrical reasons exist for excluding *The Destruction of Troy*, the longest medieval poem with structural alliteration, from the main corpus of fourteenth-century alliterative verse (111–12), which leaves this anonymously written medieval text in a metrical world apart.

For the most part, though, modern revivalists enjoy much greater freedom than their medieval brethren. What metrical features should one replicate? Which ones abandon? A poet may even freely choose *between* alliterative traditions, and this freedom has been afforded them by the simple fact of discontinuity. The alliterative meter is no longer an inherited tradition; it is a poet's smorgasbord of options. If one revivalist prefers scholarly rigor, another might prefer a vague general sense of archaism. Still others might yearn for new applications entirely. A magnificent example hails from Edwin Morgan in "Spacepoem 3: Off Course," and Joshua Gage provides another in "Demetrius Yardley, Fire Nurse," a unique blend archaic poetics with steampunk aesthetics—a kind of metrical retro-futurism. Indeed, such diversity makes the Modern Alliterative Revival difficult to generalize. While many purists belong to the university branch, others like Sandra B. Staubhaar and Jere Fleck have only written for demotic contexts despite impeccable scholarly credentials. A few purists are even self-taught, such as Math Jones and Mary K. Savelli. Nonetheless, the following section will attempt to lay out the six strongest commonalities of the Modern Revival.

Major Features of the Modern Revival

A) Eclecticism

Many medievalists throughout the twentieth century, observes Eric Weiskott, have seen alliterative and non-alliterative poetry during the Middle Ages as two "mutually exclusive schools locked in zero-sum combat for control of the English literary field" ("Alliterative" 278). As we saw, Turville-Petre denied that alliterative poets ever interacted with Chaucerian poets, and James R. Hulbert read political import into this alleged separation. As early as the 1960s, though, Elizabeth Salter began questioning this separation, and few current medievalists now see any issue with medieval poets being equally at ease with both alliterative and accentual-syllabic poetics—indeed, the *Pearl*-poet deftly combines the two. Nevertheless, language is a barrier more formidable than metrics, and whatever the degree of historical contact between various Middle English poets, nothing directly links the *Beowulf*-poet with Egil Skallagrímsson, say, or William Langland with Eysteinn Ásgrímsson or Einarr Gilsson, two fourteenth-century Icelandic contemporaries. Although these poets all composed verse structured by alliteration, their work follows substantially different rules and cultural reference points. So, while nothing prohibits the *Pearl*-poet from combining rhyme with structural alliteration, we have no reason to suppose he had the ability or knowledge to construct a skaldic *drápa* or something in Old English meter.

In the Modern Revival, however, eclecticism prevails. Revivalists may prefer one tradition to another, but no absolute barrier precludes anyone from plundering the metrical tradition of their choice. Good models exist aplenty. Likewise, the internet makes researching any tradition's basic rules easier than ever. No longer do geography or the centuries present an insurmountable stumbling block. Many speculative poets therefore follow their archaic metrical passions wherever the Muse and natural inclination lead.

B) Speculative Poetry

When mainstream poets turn to an alliterative meter, it usually happens after encountering medieval literature at college. Granted, some speculative poets discover the meter this way as well, but genre fantasy, in particular *The Lord*

of the Rings, is another major guide. Although medieval meters don't neces-
sarily require a medieval subject, Tolkien's immense popularity has yoked
genre fantasy so firmly to the Middle Ages that other historical associations
have been hard to draw. It should come as no surprise, then, that fantasy
poetry (or at least fantasy-inflected poetry) dominates the Modern Revival.
Nonetheless, I'll continue using *speculative poetry* as my catch-all term. This
broader category embraces SF, horror, and the weird as well as fantasy, plus
other kinds of imaginative writing with a generic kinship to *fantastika*. Yet,
like the concept of revivalism, definitions can be tricksy things. As Nancy
Johnston observes, the names we choose underline what kinds of "historical
ties . . . critics and poets wish to encourage in the genre as a whole" (40). The
founder of the SFPA, Suzette Haden Elgin, prefers "SF poetry" because, in
her view, "speculative poetry" excludes science poems that focus on every-
day empirical reality (13). She thus willingly lays fantasy and horror on the
sacrificial altar because, she believes, SF poetry *must* include poems about
science. Nor is her choice entirely innocent. It reflects a deep-set division
between academic SF criticism and genre fantasy arising during the 1970s
and that continues to divide both fields to this day.[5]

In contrast, Steve Rasnic Tem specifically endorses "speculative poetry"
because, for him, it fulfills his Blakean, almost visionary understanding of
metered language; speculative poets engage fundamentally in "myth-writing
and dream-writing" (2). For my part, I'm guided by more pedestrian reasons.
Professional writers tend to be pragmatic, and they often switch genres at
will. Poul Anderson, Marcie Lynn Tentchoff, and Frida Westford all alternate
happily between SF and fantasy while poets such as Frank Coffman, Rahul
Gupta, and Darrell Schweitzer march bravely off into horror. Other poets
evade easy designations. At first glance, Paul Edwin Zimmer's *Logan* seems
like a straight historical poem, yet Zimmer twice published this long narra-
tive in speculative venues, first the fantasy fanzine *Wyrd,* then the SF anthol-
ogy *Armageddon!* Readers have therefore tended to view *Logan* through the
lens of genre. Something similar has happened with "The Death of Bowie
Gizzardsbane." When John Myers Myers first published *Silverlock* in 1949,
he had barely heard of genre fandom. As he wryly observes, his novel is as
"little concerned with science as Br'er Rabbit" (Myers 470). Nonetheless,
Silverlock found its initial (and only) audience among the early SF commu-
nity, a group uniquely poised to appreciate adventure stories set in unusual
secondary worlds. Most readers and scholars similarly code Mervyn Peake's
Gormenghast novels as fantasy even though they lack any magical elements,
and some critics like Gergely Nagy even read *The Lord of the Rings* as magic-
free. A broad term like *speculative* therefore recognizes the real fluidity that
exists among genre writers.

In addition, this broader term encompasses two movements vital to the Modern Revival: Neo-Paganism and the SCA. In terms of the first, it might seem odd to categorize sincerely held religious beliefs as speculative or fantastic, yet pagan themes resonate highly with genre fantasy. In *Blood of the Colyn Muir*, Zimmer and Jon DeCles end their sword-and-sorcery (S&S) novel with an extended coda on Goddess theology. Likewise, fantasist Diana L. Paxson has held several important leadership positions in The Troth, an inclusive international organization dedicated to Heathenry, Asatru, and Norse Paganism. As for the SCA, its poetry—much like Peake's *Gormenghast* novels—codes heavily as fantasy despite lacking any elements of the supernatural. For instance, in "Quest for Valhalla," Robert Cuthbert briefly refers to "Madylyne's magic" in line 29, but this is just a period-appropriate euphemism for Excedrin. Yet, traditionally, the SCA has drawn deeply from genre fantasy. As Paxson explains,

> everyone who wrote fantasy in the Bay Area [during the early days] spent some time in the SCA, improving their knowledge of medieval swordplay, until they discovered that they were spending more time on the SCA than they were writing. (Paxson, "Berkeley")

Paxson herself co-founded the SCA alongside several other speculative writers: Zimmer, DeCles, Poul Anderson, Marion Zimmer Bradley. Over the years, more fantasists have joined the SCA ranks, including Katherine Kurtz, Robert Lynn Aspirin, Debra Doyle, and Adrienne Martine-Barnes. The SCA has inspired an award-winning fantasy novel, Peter S. Beagle's *The Folk of the Air* (1986), and in the 1970s it provided a home to several large "barbarian households" inspired by Conan fandom and John Norman's *Gor* novels. Similarly, House Bloodguard in the East Kingdom owes its identity to the martial ascetics in Stephen R. Donaldson's *Chronicles of Thomas Covenant*. With connections such as these, reading SCA poetry as speculative requires little effort.[6]

C) The Two Branches: University and Demotic

By dividing the Modern Revival into two branches, I imply nothing about either branch's respective literary merits. My distinction simply indicates how each poet approaches their revivalism. Just as my titular thesis owes inspiration to the fourteenth-century phenomenon, my "two branches" distinction draws upon another source, Jamie Williamson's *The Evolution of Modern Fantasy* (2015). Williamson divides modern fantasy into two veins, one literary and the other popular. The literary fantasists include authors like Tolkien, Morris, Lord Dunsany, and Hope Mirrlees. Popular fantasists include pulp writers like Lin Carter, Fritz Leiber, and Robert E. Howard. What separates them is mainly literary technique, source material, and publication venue. Literary fantasists normally work with recognizable literary publishers, and, like Tolkien, many are trained scholars who adapt their medieval content directly from medieval texts in the hopes of reviving the "conventions of traditional 'faery, or romance literature'" (Williamson 36). In contrast, popular fantasists write quickly and for money. They sell their work to less-prestigious venues like pulp magazines and mass-market commercial publishers, and few have direct experience with medieval literature, borrowing their medieval content instead from contemporary books, translations, and other fantasy writers. Accordingly, most popular fantasists have no interest in—or capacity for—reviving the stylistic conventions of premodern literature. Generally and more modestly, they seek to write easily digestible but highly enjoyable adventure fiction with neo-medieval elements.

Williamson proposes a strict separation between his two veins, at least through the 1970s, not unlike how older medievalists once separated Chaucerian from alliterative poetics, but otherwise Williamson's thesis maps well onto the Modern Alliterative Revival. The university poets correspond closely to the literary fantasists. Tolkien, Lewis, Auden, and others studied the alliterative meter in its original languages, and they strove to maintain something historically authentic in their revivalism. This holds true even for impressionists. For instance, although Pound's translation of "The Seafarer" greatly loosened the Old English line, he famously retains an authentic-sounding Old English atmosphere and sense of poetic diction. The university poets also enjoy relatively decent mainstream recognition. First-rank poets such as Auden and Pound obviously submitted their work to venues likely to be noticed by reviewers and critics, but the scholar-poets discovered another key outlet as well: academia itself. When Tolkien first published "The Homecoming of Beorhtnoth Beorhthelm's Son" in 1953, his alliterative verse-drama appeared in *Essays and Studies*, and his friend C. S. Lewis similarly put "The Planets" into his essay collection *Rehabilitations* (1939). If nothing else, these academic venues guaranteed their work an audience of fellow medievalists. A similar path has been followed by John D. Niles, who included three poems in his 1978 academic article for *Mosaic*. Two appear in this anthology.

Conversely, the demotic poets of the Modern Revival strongly resemble Williamson's popular fantasists. A good test case is Poul Anderson. At first glance he would seem a prime candidate for the university branch. He read avidly in the Scandinavian Middle Ages and knew Old Norse well enough to translate dozens of Norse poems. Nonetheless, few writers are more deeply "pulp" than Anderson; he held the demotic branch in his bones. Despite at-

tending the University of Minnesota, he never took a single course in litera-
ture, medieval or otherwise, and he gained his knowledge of Norse history
entirely through independent reading. Furthermore, Anderson began his writ-
ing career with SF pulp magazines such as *Astounding Science Fiction* and
Planet Stories, and from these genre origins he never swerved. What poetry
he produced went mainly into his fiction, a model inadvertently replicated
by Tolkien with *The Lord of the Rings*. All told, the demotic branch has no
more prolific or widely read revivalist than Anderson, but his revivalism lies
in almost complete critical obscurity. Most SF scholars, like most readers in
general, lack the training necessary to appreciate texts composed in allitera-
tive style, especially given that SF as a genre postdates the Middle Ages. For
scholars engaged with Tolkien more specifically, the situation is somewhat
different since so many are medievalists themselves, yet Anderson's presence
has flown under their radar too. Except for Zimmer's essay "Another Opinion
of 'The Verse of J. R. R. Tolkien'" (1993), I've not encountered any article on
Tolkien that even acknowledges Anderson's existence.

Besides Anderson himself, some other poets in the demotic category might
be surprising. For example, Jere Fleck was a professor at the University of
Maryland, College Park, who disregarded popular culture almost completely;
he never even read *The Lord of the Rings*. According to his widow, Fleck "pre-
ferred the real thing": the literature and history of northern medieval Europe.
Despite this university background, though, Fleck composed his many skaldic
poems under the auspices of two demotic historical reenactment groups, the
SCA and the Markland Medieval Mercenary Militia. Indeed, although such
revivalists have sometimes sought publication in local newspapers, *Tourna-
ments Illuminated*, or the SCA's *Compleat Anachronist* booklet series, they
more often wrote simply to entertain their specific fan communities. This has
helped create an "underground" movement within the Modern Alliterative
Revival that, nevertheless, continues to thrive within speculative fandom.

D) Purists and Impressionists

As mentioned, metrical fidelity can vary greatly among revivalists. More-
over, my informal 1–10 sliding scale between arch-purists ("1") and extreme
impressionists ("10") bears little relation to whether someone belongs to the
demotic or university branch. In fact, thanks to the SCA, more purists prob-
ably belong to the demotic branch than not. A real corollary of my sliding
scale, however, is that the theories of decay that once purported to explain
why Old English meter declined now obviously no longer apply. When *all*
revivalists, regardless of their level of purism, chose to adopt a medieval po-
etics reconstructed centuries after the fact, biological metaphors like decay or

growth hardly matter. Nor can purism automatically confer any special liter-
ary boost. Some scholars familiar with the historical meters, of course, such
as Gupta, may naturally valorize a purist-leaning poetics, and even the more
indulgent medievalists, I suspect, will have their indulgence tested by certain
impressionists. My personal favorite example occurs in *The Wise Man's Fear*,
a fantasy novel whose author, Patrick Rothfuss, could not have flouted Old
English metrical rules more egregiously had he tried. The character who re-
cites this novel's two alliterative poems explicitly denies knowing "anything
about meter" (Rothfuss 247), and his two poems fully bear out this claim.
Still, while determining a poem's degree of fidelity can be useful, it can also
be distracting. Other fruitful questions can be asked, for instance why one
poet prefers some metrical features over others or why they might prefer one
alliterative tradition over another.

Among impressionists, Auden presents a stellar test case. According to one
estimate, barely a dozen lines in *The Age of Anxiety* conform to an historically
"acceptable pattern of stressed and unstressed syllables," even by loosened
Middle English standards (Thomas Cable; qtd. in Szarmach 330, n.6). Yet
Auden studied Old English at Oxford, and he knows his craft. His deviations
are not random. As Auden explains in two letters, he introduced syllable
counting and position-variable caesuras because, he believed, such things
suited Modern English better than did the classical rules (Jacobs 109). Most
lines in Rosetta's final soliloquy, for example, reprinted in Part IV, bear nine
or ten syllables. In addition, let us look at the following:

> My poor fat father. How appalling was
> Your taste in ties.

In the first line, Auden puts his caesura squarely in the middle, as one ought,
but his *a*-verse has three stressed syllables, not two, and his *b*-verse only one.
Yet he compensates for this license by transverse alliteration on *p* and *f*. The
line succeeds as poetry. As Carl Phelpstead astutely observes, Auden "de-
liberately adapted the meter, something not appreciated by critics who have
accused him of failing to understand or to comply with the principles of Old
English verse" (453). A similar point applies even to purist-leaning poets. In
"Guðrinc's Lament," M. Wendy Hennequin presents us with the following:

> Shining and splendid. Steadfast and strong,

As an Old English scholar, Hennequin knows Old English poets never allit-
erated the onsets *sh-*, *sp-*, or *st-*, and she knows that final lifts should never

alliterate.[7] Nonetheless, such niceties no longer much matter to contemporary readers, so Hennequin ignores the rules, confident her audience will find nothing amiss.

Even for arch-purists, however, fidelity is never simple. Tolkien's own credentials are unassailable. In an analysis of *The Fall of Arthur,* T. S. Sudell finds only two verses out of 1,907 that do not conform to a valid Sievers type (75). Barring a few complications, Tolkien "obeys the rules of the [Old English] meter more or less exactly" (88). Similarly, Nelson Goering reveals that Tolkien uses the same frequency of Sievers types as would an Old English *scop* (11–12).[8] Even the most dedicated purist, however, cannot outpace their generation's best scholarship. Roughly four decades after Tolkien finished translating *Sir Gawain and the Green Knight*, Thomas Cable and Hoyt N. Duggan independently discovered that several principles—previously unrecognized—govern the shape of *b*-verses in Middle English alliterative poetry.[9] According to one summary, four major rules apply:

> Rule 1. The *b*-verse must contain a long dip (two or more consecutive unstressed syllables);
> Rule 2. The *b*-verse must not contain *more* than one long dip;
> Rule 3. The *b*-verse must contain exactly two stressed syllables ("lifts"); and
> Rule 4. The *b*-verse must end on a trochaic constituent: a Sx pattern.

> (Russom, "Evolution" 279)

Tolkien clearly accepts the third rule, which he viewed as an inheritance from Old English, but everything else in Middle English style he considers fair game. By his own account, late medieval poets left their unstressed syllables uncounted, nor in "this medieval form was their placing strictly ordered" ("Appendix" 200–01). As such, in his view the Middle English *b*-verse sometimes legitimately foregoes a long dip (contra Rule 1) and sometimes legitimately ends on an iambic or anapestic constituent (contra Rule 4). Although Tolkien recognized the rarity of the latter, this lack of strict regulation made non-trochaic endings metrically possible.

This understanding suffuses Tolkien's own translation of *Gawain*, where his "main object . . . is to preserve the metres" ("Introduction" 3). Let us examine lines 1808–1810. For convenience, I've marked caesuras and provided a scansion for Tolkien's *b*-verses.

and I am here on an errand	in unknown lands,	xSxS
and have no bearers with baggage	and beautiful things	xSxxS
(unluckily, dear lady)	for your delight at this time.	xxxSxxS

> (Tolkien, *Gawain* 93)

Although all three *b*-verses contain two lifts (as per Rule 3), Russom's other rules fare less well. Line 1808 has no long dip, and line 1810 has one long dip too many. The middle line, at least, strikes a proper balance, but all three lines run starkly afoul of Rule 4. Still, medievalists of Tolkien's generation firmly believed that iambic "rising rhythms" carried over into the fourteenth-century Alliterative Revival. In Tolkien and E. V. Gordon's 1925 edition of *Sir Gawain and the Green Knight*, they present line 571b as an example where the *b*-verse ends on one such rising rhythm, "*of a dére tars*," or xxSxS (119). Such opinions would seemingly have found reinforcement in the work of J. P. Oakden, who, in 1930, argued for an "absolute continuity of rhythm" between Old and Middle English poetics (174). Notably, when Norman Davis revised *Gawain* for a second edition in 1967, his revised section on Middle English meter preserves Tolkien and Gordon's core theories. By occasionally closing out *b*-verses with an iambic constituent, then, Tolkien was simply following the best scholarship of his era. Later research would prove this wrong, but such is a perennial problem for any purist in the Modern Revival.

E) Short Poems, Short Narratives

For anyone familiar with fourteenth-century alliterative poetry, the sheer length of its many narrative texts surely stands out. The *Alliterative Morte Arthure*, *Piers Plowman*, and *Sir Gawain and the Green Knight* all regale their audiences with complex tales told over several thousand lines. The *Destruction of Troy* alone spans a monumental fourteen thousand. This wealth of long narrative poetry has led some medievalists to claim a special advantage for the alliterative meter at telling longer tales. Turville-Petre suggests that, if

> there is any future for long narrative verse, modern poets might do worse than to look back to the practices of the poets of the fourteenth-century Revival, for the alliterative line gives the scope and flexibility that many poets search for, and yet contains them within that framework of control which is so helpful for an easy, long-poem style. (128)

Phelpstead quotes this passage as well, citing the Inklings as proof, and Gupta issues an even stronger claim. For him, the form and style of alliterative meter is never lyric but always intrinsically "epic-mythopoeic" (10). It enables an "extensive, impersonal poetry" aimed at three modes: the heroic-epic, the gnomic-didactic, and the ethopoeic-elegiac (47). By contrasting lyric personalist poetry so starkly with alliterative poetry that is impersonal, mythopoeic, and epic in scope, Gupta continues a long tradition in thinking about this meter as highly suitable for long-form narrative content.

Yet, although personalist lyric poetry is exceedingly rare within the Modern Revival, long-form narrative poetry appears less often than one might suppose, particularly if we exclude Tolkien's unfinished projects. A few long poems certainly appear, for instance *The Age of Anxiety* and *Artorius*, but otherwise semi-long narratives like "The Westfarer" and "The Death of Bowie Gizzardsbane" are the rule, not the exception. Zimmer's *Logan* is genuinely long but isn't alliterative throughout, and to date Gupta has only completed the middle non-narrative interlude of his *Arthuriad*. So, given the meter's supposed facility with longer tales, why this anomaly?

The most likely answer involves the demands and costs of print publication. While medieval manuscripts were highly expensive in terms of labor and materials, such manuscripts accommodated long-form narrative poetry marvelously well. Today, however, magazine editors reflexively shy away from longer submissions—and the longer the submission, the shyer they become. Publications like the biannual *Long Poem Magazine*, a paperless online venue, are few and far between. Readers themselves seem allergic to long-form poetry too. In a letter exchange with C. S. Lewis about "The Queen of Drum," a long rhymed poem, John Masefield offers him a telling bit of advice: "I feel that your story, as it stands, is too long. . . . I always feel that modern audiences begin to squirm and shuffle after about forty minutes" (qtd. in Lewis, *Narrative* 178). Considering how many SCA texts are performance pieces, audience fidgeting is honestly a real issue. The widow of Ron Snow, for instance, attests that people requested her husband's short comic poem "Olaf's House" much more frequently than the narrative poem he considered his masterpiece, *Blardrengir Saga*. Likewise, Jere Fleck has indicated a poor reception for his twenty-stanza *drápa*, "Comparison of Kings."[10] Shorter poems, in contrast, rarely try the patience of audiences, and magazine editors always need filler. Indeed, Poul Anderson advertised his many skaldic translations in *Amra* as an "Introduction to a Series of Fillers" ("Introduction" 16).

Besides a talent at long narrative poems, the alliterative meter also enjoys a reputation for description, in particular battle-writing. The *Alliterative Morte Arthure* is highly combat-oriented, and even Chaucer's rare alliterative passages suggest the "suitability of alliterative clangour for battle-descriptions" (Pearsall, "Alliterative" 39). Despite the shortness of most poems in the Modern Revival, this descriptive tradition seems alive and well. Indeed, SCA poets deserve special credit for lovingly recounting their "wars," tournaments, and duels. Particularly rousing examples include *Blardrengir Saga* and Daniel Marsh's "Snowberg at the Bridge." Otherwise, alliterative battle-writing most often (and perhaps surprisingly) flourishes in prose fantasy. The Rohirrim chapters in *The Lord of the Rings* borrow heavily from an elevated style reminiscent of medieval romance, and Dernhelm's spoken proverb to

Merry, "Where will wants not, a way opens" (bk. 5, ch. 3, 787), appears in perfect Old English meter. In terms of rhythmical prose, however, Paul Edwin Zimmer goes even further. The following line is not untypical of his style:

> Istvan's sun-glared eyes peered through spark-scarred darkness at rock that rang with muffled shouts and chimes. (*Gathering* 57)

The brief flashes of alliteration are obvious, but Zimmer also deploys a high rate of compound words ("sun-glared," "spark-scarred"); a minimum of un-stressed syllables (in this example, only eight out of twenty-one total); and a general preference, though not quite apparent here, for multisyllabic words with trochaic rather than iambic rhythms. When applied to scenes of martial conflict, Zimmer's alliterative techniques convey vividly the harrowing crush of armed battle in eras before the invention of gunpowder.

F) Diffusion and "Alliterative Zones"

One final feature of the Modern Alliterative Revival is its geographical and chronological diffusion. As we've seen, a central debate among medieval-ists, at least in decades past, has been whether the alleged fourteenth-century revival represented a unified group of poets or several zones of independent alliterative activity throughout the West Midlands, northern England, and Scotland. No such mystery clouds the Modern Revival. There *is* no unified movement. Although Tolkien and Anderson each play central roles within their separate spheres, Anderson considered himself primarily an entertain-ment writer. Lofty literary aims did not interest him; writing verse was a hobby, nothing more. In contrast, Tolkien *did* have literary ambitions, but he hesitated to advertise them. To be sure, someone like Zimmer clearly yearned for a revolution in contemporary poetics, and his SFPA directory update from 1986 notably lists him as a "'leading figure' by 3 different Poetry Movements" (SFPA 8). Unfortunately, Zimmer's reputation as a poet never extended much further than the San Francisco Bay Area, although his essay defending Tolkien's skill and interest in formal verse, "Another Opinion of 'The Verse of J. R. R. Tolkien'" (1993), comes close to being a genuine mani-festo for modern alliterative poetry.

Other factors besides diffusion, of course, help explain why the Modern Revival has never reached full self-consciousness. Many have already been mentioned: the obscurity of many poems; the academy's historical disdain for genre work; the Modern Revival's high proportion of unpublished verse; the separation between university and demotic branches; and the inability of most untrained readers to recognize alliterative metrics. Just the same, even revival-ists have had a tough time finding one another. Despite the internet and social media, the value of close personal contact should never be underestimated for literary movements. Even within the Modern Revival, the Inklings and the second San Francisco Renaissance prove that. A good example is John Ruble, a SCA poet. In one of our email exchanges, he revealed—unprompted—that his image of the ideal poet comes from Diana L. Paxson's 1984 fantasy novel *Brisingamen*. The character of Michael Holst is a biker-poet who

> used alliteration, internal rhyme, and every other verbal trick he could in his stand-up poetry, recognizing that his audience were listeners, not readers, and he wanted to do what he could to hook them. That concept stuck with me and I have since eschewed pretty-on-the-page poetry for the kind of poetry that enters the ear and entwines about the brain stem. (Ruble)

Nonetheless, later exchanges indicated that Ruble never made a direct connection between Holst's poetic theories and the "Bardic Art" as practiced by the Greyhaven Circle. The irony, of course, is that Ruble is a poet active in an organization, the SCA, founded by several Greyhaven members. Nonetheless, the geographical distance between San Francisco and Oklahoma, Ruble's home state, has been prohibitive. Whereas the Greyhaven writers flourished within the vibrant atmosphere of Bay Area literary culture, Ruble laments that, living in the Midwest, such "things as public poetry performances do not happen" (Ruble). Whether strictly true or not, such a comment certainly indicates the isolation felt by a Midwestern poet working in an unusual meter. Similarly, most alliterative American poets are wholly oblivious to their European brethren, and vice versa.

PART 2: SOCIETY FOR CREATIVE ANACHRONISM

The University Branch

Much like epic poets, literary historians do well to avoid starting at the beginning. Still, before the Inklings ever began writing original poetry in an alliterative meter, there was translation—that, and dedicated scholarship. Throughout the nineteenth century, a host of antiquarians, philologists, and medievalists—people like Rasmus Rask, Walter Skeat, Eduard Sievers, Karl Luick, Bernard ten Brink—spent decades decoding the principles that lay behind Old English and Middle English alliterative poetics. They had no true guides; nothing with the same authority as Snorri Sturluson's *Prose Edda*. Still, those nineteenth-century scholars established reliable texts for academic study, and they presented an entire generation of Victorian poets with a beguiling literary oxymoron: a *new* archaic poetics. At the same time, these decades witnessed surprisingly few original poems in an alliterative meter, and the "assimilation of Old English into material unrelated to Anglo-Saxon subject matter is, on the whole, a twentieth-century development" (Jones 8).[11] Victorian translators, though, have benefited mightily. Tennyson translated "The Battle of Brunanburgh," and William Morris did *Beowulf*, even if Morris's infamously archaic translation is, as one more recent translator has remarked, "glitteringly bonkers" (Headley 138). Along the same lines, Ezra Pound offered the world his version of *The Seafarer* in the early 1900s. Not to be outdone, Old Norse scholars quickly followed suit. Arthur Gilchrist Brodeur translated the *Prose Edda* into Modern English in 1916; Henry Adams Bellows did the *Elder Edda* in 1923; and renowned fantasist E. R. Eddison put his hand to *Egil's Saga* in 1930. Somewhat later, Lee Hollander left a lasting impression on the young Poul Anderson through books like *Norse Poems* (1936) and *The Skalds* (1945).

From these waters emerged the Inklings. First as students, then as professional medievalists, Tolkien, Lewis, and to a lesser extent Nevill Coghill inherited four generations' worth of rigorous scholarship on alliterative prosody. Since Coghill mainly did translation, the bulk of original poetry belongs to Lewis and Tolkien. While at the University of Leeds from 1920 through 1925, Tolkien started—then abandoned—the alliterative "Lay of the Children of Húrin" and other fragments; Lewis's earliest surviving poem in the meter, "Artless and Ignorant Is Andvári," hails from June 1929. Yet their alliterative *anni mirabiles* truly began in the early 1930s. In August 1930 Lewis finished *The Nameless Isle*, and, over the next five years, he would complete all or most of his remaining poems in the meter.[12] After a six-year hiatus, Tolkien himself returned to alliterative poetry in late 1931, producing two long texts in Old Norse *fornyrðislag* (C. Tolkien, *Legend* 5). Tolkien then switched to Old English meter for *The Fall of Arthur*, which he abandoned by 1934, and wrote a different poem, "Doworst," in December 1933 using the *Piers Plowman* meter. Yet, by the later 1930s, the Inklings' alliterative output had slowed considerably. Lewis turned his attention to prose, and except for "King Sheave" in 1936 or 1937, Tolkien began devoting himself entirely to *The Lord of the Rings*, his sequel to *The Hobbit* (1937). Over the next few decades he would compose intermittently several short poems in the alliterative meter, including those found in *The Lord of the Rings*, but he never again attempted a long-form alliterative poem.[13]

This brief summary, though, tiptoes around a chronic issue for the Inklings: the sheer number of their poems left unfinished, unpublished, or both. Some texts, of course, circulated privately in manuscript, and not only among the Inklings. For instance, Tolkien's colleague R. W. Chambers praised *The Fall of Arthur* highly (C. Tolkien, *Fall* 10–11), but an even better anecdote concerns

"The Derelicts," a three-poem sequence by Tolkien in *dróttkvætt* meter. When a draft of this sequence fell into the hands of Eric Christiansen, a medieval historian, he had it typed and gave one copy to his graduate student, Roberta Frank, sometime in the 1970s. She held on to "The Derelicts" for over forty years until unobtrusively inserting a single stanza into an essay for *New Literary History* in 2019.[14] Generally speaking, however, unpublished poetry finds but a single fate. It disappears quietly into the void, unknown, unloved, and unremembered. However earnestly the Inklings may have hoped for a second alliterative revival—a hope suggested, if nothing else, by Lewis's prescriptive essay "The Alliterative Metre"—they lacked Ezra Pound's revolutionary zeal or sense of follow-through. When *Dymer* met a crushingly lukewarm reception in 1926, Lewis permanently disavowed his youthful ambitions for poetic fame, and Tolkien, always the more diffident Inkling by far, suffered from chronic insecurity over his literary efforts. With the notable exception of *The Lord of the Rings*, the Inklings' alliterative poetry almost never found its true audience, appearing either posthumously or in academic venues that encouraged fellow medievalists to see their work not *as* artistic productions but as scholarly addenda to more intellectual concerns.

Nevertheless, as two scholars teaching at a world-renowned university, Tolkien and Lewis wielded a considerable if subtle kind of power. Almost single-handedly, their pedagogical reforms at Oxford in the early 1930s accomplished what their individual literary efforts could not: a small-scale alliterative revival among young British poets. Tolkien in particular had a talent for curricular reform. While at Leeds he helped devise—nearly from scratch—an English syllabus focused heavily on his own specialty, philology. When Oxford hired Tolkien in 1925, the English School evidently hoped he would continue this work; Tolkien's application letter cites his prior curricular accomplishments (*Letters* 12–13). This process took time, of course, nearly six years, and Tolkien first had to acquire allies among the faculty, many of whom—Lewis, Coghill, Hugo Dyson—would later become key members of the Inklings. After much "hard fighting," as Lewis reports, the English faculty approved the new syllabus in 1931, and Lewis jokingly boasts that their group's conspiratorial "anti-junto is in the ascendent" (*Letters* 9). This new curriculum presented three options for anyone reading for English Final Schools. Course I emphasized what biographer Raymond Edwards calls "hard-core" philology, and Course II combined hard-core philology with literature from 1400 to 1800. The third course permitted students to study modern literature up through 1830, but even here students continued to have mandatory papers on Old English and Middle English. Students interested in literature *after* 1830, however, were mostly out of luck—such easy texts, it was believed, did not require a tutor's aid (Edward 150–51). Until Tolkien's retirement in 1959, this syllabus remained virtually unchanged, and even a subsequent reorganization left the philological component intact through 1970.

Yet, as Edwards notes, there was nothing inevitable about this new curriculum. While Tolkien was re-prioritizing medieval literature at Oxford, the English School at Cambridge was busily foisting its medieval content and Celtic languages off onto the Department of Archaeology and Anthropology (Edwards 152). Put another way by a less sympathetic scholar, while Cambridge was firmly taking literary studies in a modernist direction, Tolkien and Lewis were helping Oxford turn its back on modernity by emphasizing "medieval language and literature to the near exclusion of other periods in English literary history" (Cecire 99). Regardless of how one regards these institutional histories, though Oxford students for several decades finished their educations with impressively deep immersions in medieval literature and medieval poetics. Granted, other British universities successfully trained young poets fascinated by the Middle Ages. A few notables include Cambridge (Ted Hughes, Thom Gunn, Richard Eberhart); Queen's University Belfast (Seamus Heaney); and the University of Glasgow (Edwin Morgan). Yet, adapting a phrase from Nicholas Howe, many of these poets merely "encountered" Old English literature. They did not try reviving it. Although Hughes, Gunn, and Heaney all borrow elements from Old English diction, they avoid tell-tale features of alliterative poetics such as caesuras, structural alliteration, and the four-position principle. In contrast, Oxford has trained the majority of the Modern Revival's university-branch poets. This list includes Auden, John Heath-Stubbs, C. Day Lewis, and Carter Revard, an American who attended Oxford on a Rhodes Scholarship. Of these names, Auden would produce the most famous modern poem with structural alliteration, *The Age of Anxiety*. John Heath-Stubbs would produce the best: *Artorius*.

Unfortunately, little of this legacy has reflected much glory back onto the Inklings themselves. As we have seen, Turville-Petre names Auden as a "serious" revivalist but ignores Tolkien completely, and not until 2003 would another medievalist, Carl Phelpstead, analyze Auden alongside the Inklings in an article foundational for anyone interested in the Modern Revival. (Technically, Niles connects Auden with the Inklings much sooner, but his 1978 *Mosaic* article has gone overlooked; according to Google Scholar, it has been cited just three times, none substantial or especially relevant.) Meanwhile, something of a counternarrative—an alternate literary history—has arisen from the few medievalists interested in modern poetry's inheritance from the Middle Ages. The work of Fred C. Robinson is paramount here. In a series of influential essays in *The Tomb of Beowulf and Other Essays on Old English* (1993), Robinson positions Pound as the key figure in the "afterlife" of Old English verse. As Nicholas Howe explains, Robinson's literary history calls for a more complex process of influence in which poets and translators of the last two centuries mastered and then transformed Old English poetics through their own practice. The central figure in Robinson's vision of this afterlife is Ezra Pound, whose 'Seafarer' (1911) is undoubtedly the most famous Old English poem of its century. (295)

Neither Robinson nor Howe are far wrong, of course. Under one way of thinking, Pound *is* a central figure for contemporary alliterative poetics. His style of revivalism has influenced writers as diverse as Michael Alexander (translator), John D. Niles (medievalist), and James Blish (SF writer); the latter two appear in this anthology. So far as naming "key figures" goes, Pound is an obvious choice.

But the absence of speculative poetry from this counter-narrative constitutes a glaring omission, as does the absence of alliterative traditions beyond Old English. For the first point, we can blame pure habit. After all, narratives about literary history run partly on momentum, and academia has long had a tradition of discounting SFF. When discussing Chris Jones's exclusion of Tolkien from *Strange Likeness*, for example, Tom Shippey finds it heartening that an "academic in an English Literature department" would even mention Tolkien's poetry at all (Phelpstead, "For W.H.A." 52, n10). Still, even Tolkien scholars often find themselves at a loss when assessing Tolkien's contributions to modern poetry. As Michael Drout observes, while there "seems to be no end of personal testimony to the importance of *The Hobbit* and *The Lord of the Rings* in peoples' lives . . . love for Tolkien's poems is little discussed" (2–3). What this anthology hopes to demonstrate, then, is just how deeply admiration for Tolkien's poetry can (and does) run. During my correspondence, I found myself continually surprised at just how many contributors voluntarily offered Tolkien's name as a formative influence. Although Lewis and Poul Anderson have their place, *The Lord of the Rings* has continually drawn young speculative poets to medieval forms like a siren's call. In fact, years after his retirement and death, Tolkien remains as much teacher as model. Widely accessible essays such as "Appendix on Verse-forms" (Middle English style) and "On Translating *Beowulf*" (Old English style) continue to impart these alliteration traditions to new generations. The talented Pagan poet Math Jones, to name just one, specifically credits Tolkien's latter essay with teaching him Old English meter.

Tolkien's influence on the Modern Revival thus runs surprisingly deep. It has only become *dominant*, however, in the last few decades. If we go back further, we must turn to the Modern Revival's more populist side—the demotic branch.

The Demotic Branch

As we have seen, the careers of Tolkien and Lewis entwined closely within the British university system. Unlike many of their contemporaries, they profoundly admired "unfashionable" modes of popular literature, medieval and modern alike, but despite writing SF as well as fantasy—Lewis and his *Space Trilogy*, Tolkien and his aborted time-travel narrative *The Lost Road*—neither Inkling ever apparently considered publishing their creative work within the burgeoning genre-fiction market. Admittedly, pulp magazines were mainly an American phenomenon, not a British one, but they gave home to an emerging subculture of fans and writers devoted passionately to space-adventure stories, interplanetary romances, and weird tales. This new fandom was high fun rather than highbrow. It read stories written quickly by authors brashly uninterested in literary subtleties, but their stories explored radical new ideas made suddenly imaginable by the romance of scientific discovery. Although speculative poetry never enjoyed the same readership as speculative fiction, it found a home in the early pulps nonetheless. Two sets of writers shape this demotic branch. The first is Poul Anderson, a giant of Golden Age SF and, in his day, one of the most highly respected pro writers of his generation. The second is the Greyhaven Circle, a group whose work drew inspiration from genre fandom, historical reenactment, and alternative spiritual movements. Each will be taken in turn.

A) Poul Anderson

In the early days, full-time pulp poets were few. The standout names are Lilith Lorraine and Clark Ashton Smith, but H. P. Lovecraft, Dorothy Quick, Donald Wandrei, and Robert E. Howard wrote poetry prolifically as well. Still, despite audiences (and paying editors) who favored action-packed prose rife with dialogue, a surprisingly large number of speculative authors dabbled in verse. Up through the Second World War, it's probably fair to say that such authors came from a generation that still considered poetry almost as prestigious and as popular as prose. Even if writing verse would never pay the bills, they'd grown up reading it and enjoying it. Such was certainly true for Poul Anderson, whose early career coincided with a budding fandom whose outstanding virtue was its pragmatic willingness to read any and everything it deemed remotely fascinating. Mystery, fantasy, scientific romance, picaresque, Westerns, mainstream realism: it didn't matter. As Karen Anderson explains, in those days any "work of interest would be talked about in the SF community, both in person and in fanzines, widely and at length" (13). Despite SFF's mainstream reputation as sub-literary, early fandom attracted people with eclectic arrays of literary interests. Into this open atmosphere walked Poul Anderson, and he swiftly found a community who embraced his extensive literary and historical passions.

As a second-generation Danish American—mother born in Denmark, father raised there—Anderson spoke both his native languages fluently, which drastically expanded his reading pool. From an early age he loved the Icelandic sagas and the literature of northern medieval Europe, and he embraced ancient history as enthusiastically as the futuristic marvels of SF. Among his favorite authors are two Nobel laureates, Rudyard Kipling and Johannes V. Jensen; the former wrote two books, *Puck of Pook's Hill* (1906) and *Rewards and Fairies* (1910), that in particular link Britain's present with its distant past, and the latter was a prolific Danish journalist and mythographer whom Anderson ranks "among the giants" ("Johannes" 220). In fact, Jensen's influence on Anderson runs surprisingly deep; it even bookends his career. In the first solo-authored story published by Anderson, "Chain of Logic," he takes his epigraph from the English translation of *The Long Journey* (1908–1922), and the afterword to Anderson's final novel published during his lifetime, *Mother of Kings*, alludes to Jensen's book on Viking women, *Kvinden I Sagatiden* (1942). Anderson also draws frequently on Danish folklore and twelfth-century historian Saxo Grammaticus. All these passions, notably, were discovered by Anderson on his own; during college he never took a single elective in history or literature. In this regard, arguably, Anderson can be considered self-taught.

This voracious private reading helps explain why Anderson become the vanguard poet for the Modern Revival's demotic branch—a situation even more remarkable given how Anderson discovered the Middle Ages well before Tolkien ever arose as a light in the eyes of American genre fandom. Prior to Anderson, the pulps had published only a few spare instances of alliterative verse. For instance, in May 1940 a comic novella called "The Roaring Trumpet" appeared in *Unknown Fantasy Fiction*, and one of its co-authors, Fletcher Pratt, adapted several eddic poems without acknowledgment from previously existing translations. Similarly, Myers included "The Death of Bowie Gizzardsbane" in *Silverlock*, a novel Anderson helped to popularize. The year 1954, however, is the Modern Revival's true watershed moment. Not only did Tolkien publish *The Two Towers*, which includes several alliterative poems from the Ents and the Rohirrim, but Anderson unveiled his own fantasy masterpiece, *The Broken Sword*, a grim sword-and-sorcery romance harkening back to Norse sagas in form and style. Pervading the novel is a haunting sense of *wyrd*, and the plot revolves around elves, changelings, trolls, and human beings in tragic conflict. Like the sagas, too, *The Broken Sword* is prosimetric: it mixes poetry and prose. Unfortunately, the novel barely sold a single copy, and, until its 1971 reissue with the Ballantine Adult Fantasy Series,

Anderson's masterpiece suffered the same sad fate as *Silverlock*: each went unnoticed by anyone outside SFF fandom's small insular world.

This miserable reception taught Anderson a hard professional lesson. If he wanted to earn his living by the pen, he had to write for the current market. In the 1940s and 1950s, this meant SF, but adventure tales set in a far-distant futures left Anderson few chances to indulge his antiquarian interests. However, once Gnome Press began to reissue Robert E. Howard's Conan the Barbarian stories in the mid-1950s, the market for American fantasy slowly improved. Already a member of the Baker Street Irregulars (a Sherlock Holmes fandom), Anderson soon joined the Hyborian Legion, a Conan fandom. Their official fanzine *Amra* would go on to win two Hugo Awards and coin the phrase "sword and sorcery," but it also provided an unexpectedly robust home for alliterative poetry. The fanzine's publisher, the legendary George H. Scithers, believed *Amra*'s audience would gravitate naturally toward anything related to the Vikings, so Anderson obliged with a series of original translations of Old Norse skaldic poetry. Inspired by Lee Hollander, E. R. Eddison, and Johannes V. Jensen, who himself had translated Norse material into Danish, Anderson issued more than a dozen skaldic translations between 1960 and 1965. These texts he later recycled into his *Last Viking* trilogy (1980), but a more lasting legacy came through two semi-alliterative parodies of his work. Although neither Avram Davidson nor L. Sprague de Camp would ever again attempt poetry in an alliterative style, their two parodies in *Amra*—Davidson in 1961, de Camp in 1964—mark the first clear case of modern alliterative texts inspiring other revivalist texts.

As this story indicates, Anderson's involvement with fandom promoted alliterative poetics and medievalism as much as his actual writing did. More than anything else, though, Anderson strove to entertain. For anyone reading *Amra* today, the fanzine's sheer exuberance quickly shines through—its aura of folks coming together solely to share a niche passion. This same exuberance marks the early SFF community's response to *Silverlock*, too. What warmed fans like Poul and Karen Anderson to Myers's novel was, among other things, *Silverlock*'s inset songs and poems. These helped popularize a tradition at conventions called "filk singing"; people would perform preexisting poetry to musical accompaniment. Several poems in Anderson's novels inspired filk songs as well—a point attested elegantly by Frida Westford in in her poem "Poul Anderson's Lay." Still, by 1966, Anderson had slackened considerably in his activity for *Amra*. A new enthusiasm had captured his attention, a historical reenactment group, and in due time this group would become the single best conduit for original alliterative poetry in the Modern Revival. The story of the SCA, however, can only be told alongside the organization's other co-founders: the Greyhaven writers.

B) Greyhaven and the Later San Francisco Renaissance

Tucked away in the Claremont district of the Berkeley Hills is Greyhaven: a huge, gray-shingled, fifteen-room house collectively purchased in 1971 by Paxson, Zimmer, Jon DeCles, and Tracy Blackstone. Although not every writer associated with the location has lived there, Greyhaven for the past five decades has served the Bay Area as a focal point for literary soirees, writing workshops, parties, Bardic Circles, Pagan rituals, and (of course) more parties. Greyhaven has also been an intermittent waystation for dozens of itinerant young artists, poets, musicians, gamers, Neo-Pagans, witches, and more. As one friend recalls, "Greyhaven in its heyday was at the crossroads of half a dozen subcultures" (Byfield). Yet, strangely, Greyhaven has garnered little attention even from literary scholars focused on genre fantasy. Unquestionably, the group's best-known author is Marion Zimmer Bradley, once one of SFF's leading feminist lights for novels like *The Mists of Avalon* (1982) and her Darkover series.[15] Even so, Paxson and Zimmer have enjoyed significant writing careers of their own. For my part, I suspect Greyhaven's achievements have been swallowed within the critical crossfires dogging genre fantasy since the 1970s, a time when prominent SF critics like Fredric Jameson and Darko Suvin began castigating fantasy as inherently regressive and reactionary. Afterward, too, once critical and popular audiences alike began equating *all* fantasy with "Tolkien clones"—the massive, door-stopping epic-fantasy series that dominated bookstore shelves throughout the 1980s and 1990s—little chance remained for authors like Paxson or Zimmer to construct independent identities either for themselves or for their uniquely Neo-Pagan brand of heroic fantasy.

Arguably, though, Zimmer and Paxson have impacted the Modern Revival even more strongly than did Anderson, a close friend, or Tolkien, a frequent inspiration. Nor did the Greyhaven Circle arise within a vacuum. In addition to deep ties with the West Coast's SFF community, the group wrote with a wild bohemian energy absorbed from the Bay Area's vibrant arts scene: a second flowering of the San Francisco Renaissance. Today, when most critics reflect on this older era of the city, they invariably imagine the madcap carnivalesque years between 1955 and 1968, a dazzling period whose core events have entered into literary legend: the Six Gallery reading; Kerouac, Ginsberg, and Burroughs; the obscenity trial over *Howl*; surrealism; cut-up; City Lights Books and Lawrence Ferlinghetti; Haight-Ashbury and the hippies; North Beach and the Beats; poetry readings; Berkeley; Buddhism; and an almost manic throng of poets, authors, and dramatists from Jack Spicer and Gary Snyder to Michael McClure and Robert Duncan. As one literary historian remarks, these writers from San Francisco's postwar renaissance foregrounded "primitivist notions of community (the oral tradition, the role of the tribe, the divinity of nature) through which collective activity takes precedence over individual volition" (Davidson xi)—a stark countercultural contrast, it might be suggested, to the imagined bourgeois complacency of American consensus culture, the stultifying selfishness of WASPs seques-tered within their suburbs.

However, periodization can be limiting as well as useful. Although most scholars begin the San Francisco Renaissance at 1955, Timothy Gray ob-serves that Kenneth Rexroth and others were already reading verse to "jazz accompaniment, translating Chinese and Japanese poetry, and advocating left-wing political causes . . . long before the Beats became famous for do-ing the same things" (23). Likewise, the San Francisco Renaissance did not simply end in 1968. Granted, many famous Beat poets had departed town by then, and their departure left the city's literary culture in a moribund state. One editor from this period, Stephen Vincent, paints a bleak picture:

> The huge influx of people seeking Haight-Ashbury liberations, the huge con-sumption of drugs, combined with police and unsympathetic community reac-tion, had turned most 1965 visions on a downward spiral. Rapes, indiscriminate police street crackdowns on anybody who appeared to be under the influence, muggings, black anger at the apolitical and indulgent character of the hippies, the simple fact that many people freaked out behind the perceptions they expe-rienced on drugs—all contributed. (34)

Nonetheless, says Vincent, the early 1970s saw a revitalization of one of the San Francisco Renaissance's most famous legacies: the poetry reading. Be-tween 1972 and 1976 there passed barely a "day of the week free of a reading or poetry event somewhere," and Vincent attributes this second miniature renaissance to feminist authors and "writers of Latin, Asian, and black origin" (40, 38). He might just as easily have added SFF writers. Fandom gained a foothold in the city about a decade earlier when Bradley and Randall Gar-rett established themselves as powerhouses in genre fiction, and, in 1966, Zimmer and DeCles arrived at Berkeley just in time for the first SCA tour-nament. Afterward, the entire Greyhaven cohort thrived on San Francisco's heady arts-and-leisure vibrancy. They became steady fixtures at coffee shops such as Café International, La Salamandra, and Children of Paradise, and, as Paxson recalls, although their school of poetry "didn't really have a label . . . phrases like 'cult poetry' and 'the Bardic Art' appeared on fliers" ("Berke-ley"). Their poems were fiercely performative, and Greyhaven writers sought to evoke powerful emotional responses through the application of any and all aural devices, including alliteration. In Paxson's *Brisingamen*, notably, Michael Holst—in a passage already alluded to by John Ruble—passionately articulates the core Greyhaven aesthetic:

poetry is an oral art, and if people are going to listen to it, then the poet ought to use rhyme and meter and alliteration and any other damn device that will hit the ear. . . . But I bet you never got to memorize or read it aloud [in school]. That's the trouble—the teachers all thought it just had to look pretty on a page, and that free verse was ordained by God at that, and they killed poetry! (38–39)

A similar vision is articulated within "The True Critics" (see Appendix C), an impassioned *ars poetica* in which Zimmer fiercely denounces conventional attitudes in modern poetry, including literary modernism—a paradox, he continues, cracked only by the rawness and the energy of the Beats.

As that comment suggests, Zimmer firmly associates the Greyhaven aesthetic with the original San Francisco Renaissance. Similarities abound. Although the Greyhaven poets prefer Heathenry to Buddhism and ignore surrealism completely, they maintained the same bohemian lifestyle and strong communitarian ethic of the Beats—an inheritance witnessed, if nothing else, by their own communal household. Similarly, Greyhaven's insistence on oral poetry continues the tradition of Dionysian public readings, albeit with a twist. An aspect central to Greyhaven's Bardic Art are "Bardic Circles," events continuing alive and well to this day in venues such as MythCon, but differing in one important respect from traditional "coffeehouse events; there are *no* spectators" (Bradley 78, italics original). Everyone must participate, whether by reading their own work or another's. Abetted by a forceful personality and a deep booming voice, Zimmer acquired a formidable reputation as a leader of Bardic Circles, and the events hosted at Greyhaven attracted a wide range of skilled Bay Area poets, only some of whom were genre: Poul Anderson, Fritz Leiber, Julia Vinograd, Chris Trian, Deirdre Evans, Robert A. Cook, Michael Alan Kassel ("Vampyre Mike"), Paladin, and more.[16]

Yet even beyond the hurdles of academic critics' historical disregard for fantasy, one more roadblock has discouraged wider recognition for the Greyhaven poets. Although the fantasy *fiction* market began booming in the late 1970s, fantasy or speculative poetry has fared far less well. The journal *Star*Line* continued to focus exclusively on science poetry and SF, and few outlets consistently accepted verse in fantasy or horror. Paxson's poems (like Anderson's) appear mainly in novels, and Zimmer published fewer than a dozen stand-alone poems. Cook's work never saw print at all. Worse, Zimmer's partisanship in favor of formal verse swam hard against a rising zeitgeist among genre poets. Although the early pulps preferred formal poetry, Steve Sneyd notes that, for about a decade after the 1950s, genre poetry "effectively disappeared from the pulps and most fanzines" (1). When it began reappearing in the 1970s, free verse reigned supreme. Sneyd attributes this shift to Michael Moorcock's editorship of *New Worlds*, a key outlet for the British New Wave. These newer genre poets, most of them experimental, ignored the formal "tradition stemming from Poe" and overwhelmingly took their cues on form and content from surrealism and the Beats, especially Burroughs (Sneyd 13). Strangely enough, then, the Beats heavily impacted *two* separate veins of genre poetry, the Greyhaven Circle and the *New Worlds* poets, but from the Beats each group took radically different aesthetic lessons. As a result, despite the buzz created by Greyhaven's "Bardic Art" in San Francisco's crowded arts scene, a truly alliterative style never had much chance at making inroads with contemporary genre poetry—a situation that, perhaps, explains why Steve Rasnic Tem's provocative 1978 call for submissions to *Star*Line* went unanswered.

Still, the Greyhaven legacy prospers within two movements vital to the Modern Revival. The first legacy, the SCA, began as an informal tournament held in Paxson's backyard but now boasts over thirty thousand paid members across North America. Considering the SCA's firm ties to genre fantasy, the way it blends medieval nostalgia with modern irony has proven a fertile breeding ground for poetry in premodern forms. Yet, as one practitioner explains, SCA poets must constantly strive to balance "medieval, modern, and Society elements" in their work (Morris 66). In other words, the quest for historical authenticity is always under negotiation with the undeniable modernity of the SCA as an organization. For instance, one frequent subject for SCA poetry are "wars," but nobody ever dies in one, and most participants travel to the battlefield by car. Likewise, live-tweeting jousts is now a real thing. At the same time, the history, lore, and traditions of the SCA create a specialized interpretative community that affects every aspect of SCA poetry. Poets frequently make topical references and in-jokes that friends and fellow members will understand immediately, but this shared communal knowledge about monarchs, organizational structure, and history can also render these poems bewilderingly inaccessible to mundanes. Nonetheless, SCA texts can praise individuals, chronicle tournaments, mark festivals, celebrate personal achievements, and memorialize the friends who've passed away in real life. Greyhaven's legacy is thus a threefold mixture of orality, performance, and medievalism.[17]

The Greyhaven Circle is also heavily involved with modern Heathenry, the second major conduit for alliterative verse. Although this movement, which includes Asatru and other Pagan traditions, began gaining steam in the late 1980s, Bradley had already co-founded the Aquarian Order of the Restoration by 1964, whose mission lay in restoring "balance between the masculine and feminine in our image of the Divine, in other words, bringing back the Goddess" (Paxson, "Priestess" 32). Zimmer and DeCles were among the Order's first initiates, and Zimmer self-published a book of Pagan poems, many in alliterative style, called *The Wine of Kvasir* (1979). Paxson's relationship with

Neo-Paganism goes even further. After being consecrated as a priestess in 1982, she began teaching classes in Germanic runes, leading to her Berkeley-based kindred *Hrafnar*. This group is nationally affiliated with The Troth, an international organization based in the United States; Paxson became an Elder in 1993. Their membership is open to anyone regardless of personal ancestry or sexual orientation with spiritual experience with a Germanic Heathen tradition. This inclusivity helps distinguish The Troth from other groups such as the Asatru Folk Assembly, whom the Southern Poverty Law Center has categorized as a "neo-Völkisch" or white supremacist hate group. In 2016 The Troth, as an affirmation of its ideals, signed onto Declaration 127 asserting the "complete denunciation of, and disassociation from, the Asatru Folk Assembly [and similar groups]" ("Declaration"). Many independent Asatru communities have signed this declaration as well.

Whereas SCA poets usually discover the alliterative meter through their antiquarian love for the Middle Ages, Heathen poets often discover it through their spiritual training, especially as catalyzed by genre fantasy. In *Odin: Ecstasy, Runes, & Norse Magic*, Paxson notes that the two world wars had rendered Germanic history, lore, and myth into taboo subjects. Although she herself first encountered Odin through Anderson's *The Broken Sword*, for others "*The Lord of the Rings* . . . was their first exposure to Germanic culture" (17). As such, it should come as no surprise that Paxson's own fantasy includes many Germanic elements. Likewise, Asatru poet Michaela Macha specifically credits *The Mists of Avalon* with preparing her as a teenager for the idea that others might share her spiritual longings. Macha personally finds the "'geek percentage' . . . quite high within Asatru," and typical subculture crossovers include RPGs, languages, history, handcrafting, reenactment, heavy metal, graphic novels, runes, and tarot (Macha, "Original"). Yet, altogether, the Modern Heathen Revival considers itself a lore-based movement. Because spiritual practice goes hand in hand with personal study, Heathenism encourages adherents to dive deeply into the mythology, history, and literature of northern medieval Europe. Considering that many ceremonies employ poetry as a ritual aid, the alliterative meter constitutes an obvious metrical choice.

PART III: LATER REVIVALISTS

Speculative Poetry and the Modern Alliterative Revival comes in four parts. The meat of this anthology, the poetry itself, appears in Parts I–III. The fourth section is an addendum: poems that, while not speculative themselves, remain relevant to scholars interested in the Modern Revival. The SF author James

Blish, for instance, wrote a single alliterative poem under the auspices of Pound's modernism, and Auden and Heath-Stubbs each used an alliterative style learned at Oxford under a curriculum shaped by the Inklings. Among the first three parts, the Revival's main figures from earlier days—Lewis, Anderson, Myers, and more—appear in Part I. The lone exception is Tolkien; unfortunately, his estate does not grant anthologies permission to reprint his verse. Part II showcases poets from the SCA and the Markland Medieval Mercenary Militia. My third part covers more recent work in the Modern Revival; all these poets remain alive, well, and actively publishing. Unlike their predecessors, these contemporary revivalists have enjoyed relatively constant access to genre-friendly markets: *Star*Line*, of course, especially after it began accepting fantasy in 2017, but also *Eye to the Telescope* (the SFPA's online quarterly), *Uncanny*, *Strange Horizons*, and more. Each section arranges contributors according to a rough chronological period of their literary activity, although I've occasionally made exceptions to keep together poets with certain affinities—for instance, Canadian poets or Heathen poets.

Some readers might notice that relatively few selections in this anthology the 1980s or 1990s. Rather than a genuine scarcity, this dearth instead indicates an archival problem. Although *Tournaments Illuminated* published several amateur poets during the 1970s, it cut back significantly afterward, and no other venue stepped forward to fill the gap. Likewise, discovering new poets through word-of-mouth tactics like individual queries, social media, and scouring the internet works best only for authors active since the new millennium. Finding alliterative texts within that two decades-long gap, though, has been harder. A relevant story belongs to Ron Snow, a poet in the SCA who passed away in 1997. I only learned of his work because Robert Cuthbert mentions a Lion Skald in "Quest for Valhalla"; when asked, Cuthbert put me in touch with Snow's widow, Melissa, who kindly sent me a collection of her late husband's verse, none of it previously published. Even so, I've been forced to leave several SCA-specific allusions in *Blardrengir Saga* without a footnote. Neither Melissa Snow nor myself, sadly, could find anyone still living who remembered their meaning. Too much SCA poetry, I fear, has suffered a fate even unkinder than this—surviving, if it survives at all, only in damp basements, dusty attics, and long-forgotten old desk drawers.

In terms of inclusivity, I've gathered contributions from almost every speculative poet with an alliterative-style poem I could find. A slight majority have all or most of their revivalist texts represented. Yet since impressionism can make discerning the parameters of revivalist poetry difficult, I err on the side of generosity. Intention usually decides the matter. For example, although Patrick Rothfuss's two contributions break every known rule of Old

English poetics, he obviously means them to invoke the classic Old English meter. More difficult examples involve radically impressionistic texts like "In Death's Dark Halls, a Dog Howls." As Walton made clear during our correspondence, however, she explicitly intended to create cross-cultural echoes by retelling an old Greek myth in semi-alliterative style; she does the same with "Lew Rosson's Hall," a Celtic subject rendered in loose Old English meter. Moreover, once I ascertained that someone has written at least one alliterative poem in SFF or horror, I more willingly included their non-speculative alliterative texts; examples are Niles's "Fair Day" and Deane's "Freeway Dawn." Otherwise, non-speculative poems relevant to the Modern Revival appear in Part IV. Translations are avoided except when unusually appropriate for some reason—for instance, "The First Love" is a representative example of Anderson's translations for *Amra*.

As for the poems themselves, every author—or, barring that, a representative from their estate—has, whenever possible, personally approved the final text as it appears in *Speculative Poetry and the Modern Alliterative Revival*. On rare occasions, editorial suggestions have led to minor changes in wording from the original publication, but more frequently syntax has been added to clarify meaning, rhythm, or both—a virtual necessity given how few poems have appeared in professional venues. Indeed, some self-published texts like David Friedman's "Hildebrandslied" were never intended as anything more than mnemonic aids to performance; light editing for print publication has therefore been necessary. For older published texts, I've silently incorporated diacritical marks and non-standard letters such as thorn (þ) and eth (ð) when intent could be reasonably inferred; most such published poems were printed using older technologies unable to handle special characters. Otherwise, I have reproduced older texts exactly as found except for obvious typos and misprints. Headnotes and footnotes are all editorial. These, too, however, are, whenever possible, author or estate approved. Only one contributor, Adam Bolivar, a longtime advocate for traditional forms, has composed a text specifically for this anthology. Significantly and happily, this initial foray into Old English meter has since inspired Bolivar to write an entire collection of alliterative poems, *A Wheel of Ravens*, which he published with Jackanapes Press in September 2023. Otherwise, although many selections in *Speculative Poetry and the Modern Alliterative Revival* have never before seen print, all preexist this anthology. They are true discoveries.

Turning to a more subjective point, a matter of evaluation, some readers studying this anthology may be struck by a certain range in quality. Some contributors display great skill; others, less so. Such unevenness should be expected. In contrast to the professional poets gracing Part IV, comparatively few revivalists consider poetry their primary vocation. Especially in the early days of the Modern Revival, poets were self-professed amateurs or simple fans experimenting playfully with an archaic form. Rarely do literary ambitions run any deeper. An illustrative case concerns Jere Fleck, a scholar, and P. K. Page, one of Canada's foremost twentieth-century poets. For sheer linguistic dexterity, brilliance, and humor, none of Fleck's nearly one hundred stanzas in *dróttkvætt* meter come close to matching a single stanza from Page's "The Crow's Nest." Yet this is the wrong way to approach Fleck's work. In a way, his *drápur* show an ambition startling in their scope. They seek to revive a form of courtly praise poetry vanished these eight centuries past, gone with the last of the skalds; and each consecutive *drápa*, five over four years, shows Fleck methodically honing his craft as, for each new poem, he erects a new and carefully balanced narrative framework for best presenting his chosen theme. Had Fleck continued to refine his skills, there is no telling what might have been; alas.

Yet Fleck's situation speaks to something the late, great Ursula K. Le Guin once said. In *Always Coming Home* (1985), her quasi-utopian novel, Le Guin portrays a far-future people named the Kesh who have formed a non-industrial, post-apocalyptic society. In order to better portray their cultural life for readers, Le Guin incorporates several original Kesh poems into her novel. About this verse she writes:

> Most Kesh poetry was occasional—the highest form, according to Goethe—and much of it was made by what we call amateurs, people doing poetry as a common skill, the way people do sewing or cooking, as an ordinary and essential part of being alive. The quality of such poetry, sewing, and cooking of course varies enormously. We have been taught that only poetry of extremely high quality is poetry at all; that poetry is a big deal, and you have to be a pro to write it, or, in fact, to read it. This is what keeps a few poets and many, many English departments alive. That's fine, but I was after something else: the poem not as fancy pastry but as bread; the poem not as masterpiece but as life-work. (186–87)

Although the Modern Revival has its fair share of masterpieces, it has its life-works, too—poems by poets of varying talent who have, together, nevertheless formed a movement. This movement has largely survived underground beneath the notice of professional literary critics and medievalists, but it forms a vital avenue by which modern fandom engages with poetry in their everyday lives. Writing in 1978, John D. Niles believed that the "movement of English poetry away from the alliterative form . . . as natural and as irreversible as the movement of the English tongue away from its form in the time of King Alfred" (32). But Tolkien never believed this. Nor did Lewis, and neither do the many demotic-branch poets who love SF, fantasy, horror, and the weird and for whom the medieval world and its archaic poetics represent a continual source of fascination. What this anthology seeks to do, then, is bring such literary and cultural production—diffused widely across ten decades and two continents—to light: and, in the process, show new generations of speculative poets what the alliterative meter may achieve.

NOTES

1. Indeed, a consistent theme across the career of medievalist Tom Shippey has been how frequently the academic *literati* (to use his term) have failed to read Tolkien competently or well. This persistent failure Shippey attributes to an institutional conflict between "Lang. vs. Lit.," i.e. philology and literary studies, which plagued Tolkien even during his Oxford days. Nevertheless, Shippey doesn't discount the possibility of "simple snootiness . . . what Orwell called the 'automatic snigger' of the English-speaking Establishment intellectual" (308).

2. Of those tantalizing allusions, the most-often cited stems from Chaucer. In *The Canterbury Tales*, the Parson proclaims himself a "Southren man; I kan nat geeste 'rum, ram, ruf,' by lettre" (*ParsPro*, lines 42–43). Critics have traditionally understood this comment as Chaucer's dismissal of alliterative prosody. Throughout *The Canterbury Tales*, only a few spare instances of sustained alliterative phrasing arise—for instance, lines 2605–2616 from *The Knight's Tale*. Other medieval allusions are even less helpful. The *Gawain*-poet, for instance, briefly mentions "With lel letteres loken" in line 35 of that poem, but most medievalists consider this reference ambiguous at best. Some older scholars of Old English, furthermore, such as Frederick Klaeber, have thought verses 869b and 870a from *Beowulf—word óðer fand / sóðe gebunden*—refer directly to the alliterative meter, yet Tolkien has criticized this reading, suggesting that this passage instead refers to Old English diction and poetic synonyms, not linked front-rhyme; see Tolkien, *Beowulf: A Translation and Commentary*, pp. 280–84.

3. In fact, the alliterative meter has vanished from nearly *all* European literary traditions: Germany in the ninth century, the Nordic countries in the thirteenth century, and England in the sixteenth century. The only exception is Iceland. According to Ragnar Ingi Aðalsteinsson, this meter's standard rules have "survived over centuries in Iceland almost unchanged" (61). Aðalsteinsson attributes this continuity not only to Snorri Sturluson but to how Modern Icelandic, nearly alone among contemporary Germanic languages, maintains heavy initial word stress (141). In Iceland's alliterative history, its medieval and modern eras are distinguished merely by phonology, including the changing status of consonant *s*- clusters. Contemporary Icelandic alliterative poets include Þorsteinn frá Hamri (1938–2018) and the son of Iceland's former president, Þórarinn Eldjárn (b. 1949).

4. For a more thorough account of how Lewis came to the alliterative meter, see Wise, "Dating 'Sweet Desire,'" in *English Text Construction* (2023). In short, Lewis started learning Old English as a student at Oxford in 1922, but his first experiments with the meter did not happen until January 1927 at the earliest, which coincides with him joining the Coalbiters, an informal club begun by Tolkien for reading Norse

sagas in their original language. Tolkien himself, incidentally, read German perfectly well. As a young student, he composed a reading list marked "Books in Exeter Library useful," and this list contains nine works by Sievers (Cilli 260–61).

5. Notably, the SFPA excluded fantasy from its purview until 2017, and the Science Fiction Research Association *still* excludes fantasy scholars. In the mid-1980s, this legacy helped lead to the International Conference for the Fantastic in the Arts. Debates about genre boundaries, though, reflect early critical work by SF theorists such as Darko Suvin and Fredric Jameson, who each saw fantasy and the fantastic as anti-cognitive and reactionary. Nonetheless, SFF poetry suffers a double marginalization, even within genre circles. Unlike the Horror Writers Association, which permits published horror poetry to count for membership, the Science Fiction & Fantasy Writers Association still excludes published SFF poets from membership.

6. Michael A. Cramer also credits "mundanes"—the SCA term for non-members—to Piers Anthony's *Xanth* novels (34), but this is probably a false attribution; Poul Anderson uses *mundane* in a similar sense in his article "Richard the Lion Hearted Is Alive and Well in California" (1969), which appeared nine years before Anthony published his first *Xanth* novel. Still, even misattributions like this suggest how quickly SCA scholars can identify their organization with genre fantasy.

7. Technically, the surviving manuscript record shows several cases in Old English poetry of final-lift alliteration—the *Beowulf* manuscript contains four—but most scholars agree that "breaches of this constraint are symptoms of textual corruption"; thus, most modern editions of *Beowulf* amend their text accordingly (Terasawa 17).

8. Although Goering only scans half the poem, his percentages correspond closely with Sudell's full scansion (see Sudell 98). In both cases, A-types outnumber B-types, matching early English practice, and types A, B, and C significantly outnumber types D and E. Goering and Sudell each note that Tolkien uses more E-types than types Da or Db, but Goering attributes this reversal to linguistic differences between Old English and Modern English, particularly to the latter's comparatively fewer poetic compounds (12–13).

9. To be more specific, Scull and Hammond report that Tolkien completed his *Gawain* translation in 1947, but he'd translated lines 2000–2200 as early as 1923 (929). He also continued to tinker on this text until his death (932).

10. Although Bassi's core grievance against the monarch praised in "Comparison of Kings" centers around a real-world dispute concerning shared territory between the SCA and Markland, the seventh stanza of "Ravens' Rede" indicates a poor reception for his previous year's poem as well. According to a phone interview with Bruce Blackistone, now a retired civil servant from the National Park Service, *Marklandic* audiences greatly enjoyed Fleck's poetry; many members took courses with him and grasped his Norse references unusually well. In addition, Fleck often educated Militia members by providing quality resources based on real academic scholarship. While Blackistone doesn't remember the specific reception for "Comparison of Kings," he observes that performing for the SCA can be tricky. The SCA, notably, selects its royalty through combat-driven tournaments; some Marklanders dismissively call them "stick jockeys." This process creates a mixed bag of monarchs whose appreciation for historical authenticity can vary.

11. Among the few early original texts, Joseph Phelan selects William Morris's *Love Is Enough, or the Freeing of Pharamond* (1872) as organized by accentual meter; similarly, Gerard Manley Hopkins is known for having borrowed aspects of Old English prosody for his "sprung rhythm."

12. Lewis's alliterative poems all have firm dates except two. According to my own metrical analysis, "Sweet Desire" belongs to early 1930. Lewis's other poem in an alliterative meter, here given the title "*Viva Voce* Examination Session," would have been written before E. V. Gordon passed away unexpectedly in 1938.

13. One potential exception concerns *The Homecoming of Beorhtnoth Beorhthelm's Son*. Tolkien published this short play in 1953, but the earliest draft stems from between 1931? and 1933 (Scull and Hammond 407). Those initial drafts, however, appeared in heroic couplets, not the alliterative meter. Overall, Thomas Honegger counts twelve total versions of *Homecoming* among the Tolkien Papers at the Bodleian Library, which he labels α and versions A–K. Tolkien's switch to alliterative metrics happened in version E. Unfortunately, these "individual pieces cannot be dated definitively" (Honegger 190).

14. For Frank's account of this story, see "Dróttkvætt," footnote three. It's unclear if Tolkien lent Christiansen these stanzas intentionally. All three were typed onto a single loose-leaf page inserted into Tolkien's personal copy of *Heimskringla*, which he bought in 1922. At some point Tolkien (or possibly his son Christopher) lent this volume to Christiansen, who then discovered the loose-leaf page inside. Since book and poems now reside with the Tolkien Estate, Christiansen obviously returned both items. Interestingly, the Estate's relevant box file includes *two* versions of "The Derelicts"; Christiansen and Frank saw the earlier version. My appreciation goes to Douglas A. Anderson for information on the Tolkien Estate's holdings.

15. In 2014 deeply shocking allegations arose that Bradley engaged in acts of child abuse. Patrick Moran has since described Bradley's posthumous reputation as a "very rare instance of deliberate de-canonization" (58).

16. Unfortunately, I could not track down Paladin's real name. Many close friends, including Paxson herself, never heard it spoken. Within their group, Julia Vinograd—a street poet known for blowing bubbles in Berkeley's streets—achieved the most mainstream success.

17. Although far smaller and less poetry-driven than the SCA, the Markland Medieval Mercenary Militia deserves an honorable mention. This reenactment group began in 1969 as the *Maryland* Medieval Mercenary Militia, a student organization, but as students began graduating and community members wished to join, the group incorporated as "Markland" in 1974—technically, a loose confederation of different groups such as the Longship Company, the Order of the Lost Boys, and the original student group. Notably, the SCA founded the East Kingdom one year earlier in 1968, but neither organization initially knew about the other. A friendly rivalry developed in time; Marklanders refer to their counterparts as "Scadians," and Fleck, as part of a Marklandic "delegation" to the SCA, presented several *drápur* to their royal court. Overall, Markland reenacts an earlier and more Viking-centric era of medieval history. Tongue-in-cheek, Bruce Blackistone describes Scadians as "upper-class, chivalrous, and high medieval" but Marklanders as "lower-class, barbaric, and early medieval."

WORKS CITED

Aðalsteinsson, Ragnar Ingi. *Traditions & Continuities: Alliteration in Old and Modern Icelandic Verse.* Translated by Sigurlína Davíðsdóttir, U of Icelandic P, 2014.

Anderson, Karen. "A Book Like No Other." *Silverlock: Including the Silverlock Companion*, by John Myers Myers, edited by David G. Grubbs, Pam Fremon, and Fred Lerner, NSFA Press, 2004, pp. 9–16.

Anderson, Poul. "Introduction to a Series of Fillers." *Amra*, vol. 2, no. 10, April 1960, pp. 16–17.

———. "Johannes V. Jensen." *All One Universe*, Tor, 1996.

Atherton, Mark. "Priming the Poets: The Making of Henry Sweet's *Anglo-Saxon Reader*." *Anglo-Saxon Culture and the Modern Imagination*, edited by David Clark and Nicholas Perkins, D. S. Brewer, 2010, pp. 31–49.

Auden, W. H. "Making, Knowing, Judging." *The Dyer's Hand and Other Essays.* Random House, 1948, pp. 31–60.

Blake, N. F. "Middle English Alliterative Revivals." *Review*, vol, 1, 1979, pp. 205–14.

Bradley, Marion Zimmer. "The Bardic Revel." *Greyhaven: An Anthology of Fantasy*, edited by Bradley, DAW Books, 1983, pp. 79–80.

Byfield, Bruce. "Stopping by Greyhaven." *Off the Wall*, 18 Mar. 2007, www.brucebyfield.com/2007/03/18/stopping-by-greyhaven. Accessed 31 Aug. 2021.

Cable, Thomas. *The English Alliterative Tradition.* U of Pennsylvania P, 1991.

Cecire, Maria Sachiko. *Re-Enchanted: The Rise of Children's Fantasy Literature in the Twentieth Century.* U of Minnesota P, 2019.

Chambers, R. W. "On the Continuity of English Prose from Alfred to More and his School." *Harpsfield's Life of More.* 1932. Early English Text Society, Original Series no. 186, Oxford UP, 1963, pp. xlv–clxxiv.

Chaucer, Geoffrey. *The Riverside Chaucer.* Edited by F. N. Robinson, 3rd ed., Houghton Mifflin, 1987.

Cilli, Oronzo. *Tolkien's Library: A Checklist.* Luna Press, 2019.

Cornelius, Ian. *Reconstructing Alliterative Verse: The Pursuit of a Medieval Meter.* Cambridge UP, 2017.

Cramer, Michael A. *Medieval Fantasy as Performance: The Society for Creative Anachronism and the Current Middle Ages.* Scarecrow Press, 2010.

Davidson, Michael. *San Francisco Renaissance: Poetics and Community at Mid-Century.* Cambridge UP, 1989.

"Declaration 127." *Huginn's Heathen Hof: Blogs, Lore, and More*, www.declaration127.com. Accessed 12 Nov. 2021.

Drout, Michael D. C. "Introduction: Reading Tolkien's Poetry." *Tolkien's Poetry*, edited by Julian Eilmann and Allan Turner, Walking Tree Publishers, 2013, pp. 1–10.

Edwards, Raymond. *Tolkien.* Robert Hale, 2014.

Elgin, Suzette Haden. *The Science Fiction Poetry Handbook.* Edited by Mike Allen and Bud Webster, Sam's Dot Publishing, 2005.

Frank, Roberta. "Dróttkvætt." *New Literary History*, vol. 50, no. 3, 2019, pp. 393–98.

Goering, Nelson. "*The Fall of Arthur* and *The Legend of Sigurd and Gudrún*: A Metrical Review of Three Modern English Alliterative Poems." *Journal of Inklings Studies*, vol. 5, no. 2, 2015, pp. 3–56.

Gray, Timothy. *Gary Snyder and the Pacific Rim*. U of Iowa P, 2006.

Gupta, Rahul. *"The Tale of the Tribe": The Twentieth-Century Alliterative Revival*. 2014. University of York, PhD dissertation.

Headley, Maria Dahvana. "Acknowledgements." *Beowulf*, translated by Headley, Farrar, Strauss and Giroux, 2020, pp. 137–40.

Honegger, Thomas. "The Homecoming of Beorhtnoth: Philology and the Literary Muse." *Tolkien Studies*, vol. 4, 2007, pp. 189–99. *Project Muse*, doi:/10.1353/tks.2007.0021. Accessed 28 Sep. 2021

Howe, Nicholas. "Praise and Lament: The Afterlife of Old English Poetry in Auden, Hill, and Gunn." *Words and Works: Studies in Medieval English Language and Literature in Honour of Fred C. Robinson*, edited by Peter S. Baker and Nicholas Howe, U of Toronto P, 1998, pp. 293–310.

Hulbert, James R. "A Hypothesis Concerning the Alliterative Revival." *Modern Philology*, vol. 28, 1931, pp. 405–22.

Jacobs, Alan. "Appendix: Two Letters on Metrical Matters." *The Age of Anxiety: A Baroque Eclogue*, by W. H. Auden, edited by Jacobs, Princeton UP, 2011, pp. 109–12.

Johnston, Nancy. "'I would have swallowed the kiss': Reflections on Feminist Speculative Poetry." *Femspec*, vol. 2, no. 1, 2000, pp. 38–47.

Jones, Chris. *Strange Likeness: The Use of Old English in Twentieth-century Poetry*. Oxford UP, 2006.

Le Guin, Ursula K. "Text, Silence, Performance." *Dancing at the Edge of the World: Thoughts on Words, Women, Places*. Grove Press, 1989, pp. 179–87.

Lewis, C. S. "The Alliterative Metre." *Selected Literary Essays*, edited by Walter Hooper. 1969. Cambridge UP, 1980, pp. 15–26.

———. *The Collected Letters of C. S. Lewis: Volume 2: Books, Broadcasts, and the War, 1931–1949*. Edited by Walter Hooper, HarperSanFrancisco, 2004.

———. "The Idea of an 'English School.'" *Rehabilitations and Other Essays*. Oxford UP, 1939, pp. 59–77.

———. *Narrative Poems*. Edited by Walter Hooper, Geoffrey Bles, 1969.

Macha, Michaela. "Re: Original alliterative poetry?" Received by Dennis Wilson Wise, 7 Sep. 2021. E-mail.

Magennis, Hugh. "Some Modern Writers and Their *Fontes Anglo-Saxonici*." *The Old English Newsletter*, vol. 24, 1991, pp. 14–18.

Minkova, Donka. *Alliteration and Sound Change in Early English*. Cambridge UP, 2003.

Moran, Patrick. *The Canons of Fantasy: Lands of High Adventure*. Cambridge UP, 2019.

Morris, Elizabeth [Beth Morris Tanner], editor. *Ars Poetica Societatis. The Compleat Anachronist*, vol. 67, Society for Creative Anachronism, 1993.

Myers, John Myers. "The Inside Scoop on John Myers Myers." *Silverlock: Including the Silverlock Companion*, edited by David G. Grubbs, Pam Fremon, and Fred Lerner, NESFA Press, 2004, pp. 469–72.

Nagy, Gergely. "On No Magic in Tolkien: Resisting the Representational Criteria of Realism." *Sub-creating Arda: World-Building in J. R. R. Tolkien's Work, Its Precursors, and Its Legacies*, edited by Dimitra Fimi and Thomas Honegger, Walking Tree, 2019, pp. 153–76.

Niles, John D. "The Old Alliterative Verse Form as a Medium for Poetry." *Mosaic: An Interdisciplinary Critical Journal*, vol. 11, no. 4, Summer 1978, pp. 19–33. *JSTOR*, www.jstor.org/stable/24777593. Accessed 22 Apr. 2021.

Oakden, J. P. *Alliterative Poetry in Middle English*. Vol. 1, Manchester UP, 1930.

O'Donoghue, Heather. *English Poetry and Old Norse Myth: A History*. Oxford UP, 2014.

———. "The Reception of Eddic Poetry." *A Handbook to Eddic Poetry*, edited by Carolyne Larrington, Judy Quinn, and Brittany Schorn, Cambridge UP, 2016, pp. 349–65.

Paxson, Diana L. "The Berkeley Bardic Poetry scene.'" Received by Dennis Wilson Wise, 20 Aug. 2021. E-mail.

———. *Brisingamen*. Berkley Books, 1984.

———. *Odin: Ecstasy, Runes, & Norse Magic*. WeiserBooks, 2017.

———. "The Priestess of Avalon: A Remembrance of the Life of Marion Zimmer Bradley (1930–1999)." *SageWoman*, no. 48, 2000, pp. 31–34.

Pearsall, Derek. "The Alliterative Revival: Origins and Social Backgrounds." *Middle English Alliterative Poetry and its Literary Background: Seven Essays*, edited by David Lawton, D. S. Brewer, 1982, pp. 34–53.

———. "The Origins of the Alliterative Revival." *The Alliterative Tradition in the Fourteenth Century*, edited by Bernard S. Levy and Paul E. Szarmach, Kent State UP, 1981, pp. 1–24.

Phelan, Joseph. *The Music of Verse: Metrical Experiment in Nineteenth-Century Poetry*. Palgrave Macmillan, 2012.

Phelpstead, Carl. "Auden and the Inklings: An Alliterative Revival." *The Journal of English and Germanic Philology*, vol. 103, no. 4, 2004, pp. 433–57. *JSTOR*, www.jstor.org/stable/27712458. Accessed 18 May 2018.

———. "'For W. H. A.': Tolkien's Poem in Praise of Auden." *Tolkien's Poetry*, edited by Julian Eilmann and Allan Turner, Walking Tree Publishers, 2013, pp. 45–58.

Pratt, Fletcher, and L. Sprague de Camp. "The Roaring Trumpet." *Unknown Fantasy Fiction*, vol. 3, no. 3, May 1940, pp. 9–77.

Rasnic, Steve [Steve Rasnic Tem]. "Letters to the Editor." *Star*Line*, vol. 1, no. 5, May 1978, p. 5.

Robinson, Fred C. *The Tomb of Beowulf and Other Essays on Old English*. Blackwell, 1993.

Rothfuss, Patrick. *The Wise Man's Fear*. DAW Books, 2011.

Ruble, John. "Re: Contract to reprint 'Lutefisk and Yams.'" Received by Dennis Wilson Wise, 1 Apr. 2021. E-mail.

Russom, Geoffrey. *Beowulf and Old Germanic Metre*. Cambridge UP, 1998.

———. "The Evolution of Middle English Alliterative Meter." *Studies in the History of the English Language II: Unfolding Conversations*, edited by Anne Curzan and Kimberly Emmons, de Gruyter, 2004, pp. 279–304.

———. *Old English Meter and Linguistic Theory*. Cambridge UP, 1987.

Salter, Elizabeth. "The Alliterative Revival II." *Modern Philology*, vo. 64, no. 3, Feb. 1967, pp. 233–37. *JSTOR*, www.jstor.org/stable/436719. Accessed 12 Sep. 2021.

———. Review of *The Alliterative Revival*, by Thorlac Turville-Petre. *The Review of English Studies*, vol. 29, no. 116, 1978, pp. 462–64.

Schiff, Randy P. *Revivalist Fantasy: Alliterative Verse and Nationalist Literary History*. Ohio State UP, 2001.

Shippey, Tom. *J. R. R. Tolkien: Author of the Century*. Houghton Mifflin, 2002.

Scull, Christina, and Wayne G. Hammond. *The J. R. R. Tolkien Companion & Guide: Reader's Guide*. Houghton Mifflin, 2006.

SFPA directory update. *Star*Line*, vol. 9, no. 5, Sept./Oct. 1986, p. 8.

Sneyd, Steve. Introduction. *Time Grows Thin*, by Lilith Lorraine, edited by Sneyd, Hilltop Press, 2002, pp. 1–40.

Sudell, T. S. "The Alliterative Verse of *The Fall of Arthur*." *Tolkien Studies,* vol. 13, 2016, pp. 71–100.

Szarmach, Paul E. "*Anthem*: Auden's *Cædmon's Hymn*." *Medievalism in the Modern World: Essays in Honour of Leslie J. Workman*, edited by Richard Utz and Tom Shippey, Brepols, 1998, pp. 329–40.

Tem, Steve Rasnic. Afterword. "On Defining & Not Defining Speculative Poetry: A Preliminary Essay." *The Umbral Anthology of Science Fiction Poetry*, edited by Tem, Umbral Press, 1982, pp. 1–4.

Terasawa, Jun. *Old English Metre: An Introduction*. U of Toronto P, 2011.

Tolkien, Christopher, editor. *The Fall of Arthur*, by J. R. R. Tolkien. Mariner Books, 2014.

———. *The Legend of Sigurd & Gudrún,* by J. R. R. Tolkien. HarperCollins *Publishers*, 2009.

Tolkien, J. R. R. "Appendix on Verse-forms." *Sir Gawain and the Green Knight, Pearl, and Sir Orfeo*, translated by Tolkien, edited by Christopher Tolkien, Ballantine, 1975, pp. 199–212.

———. "'Beowulf' & The Critics (A)." *Beowulf and the Critics by J. R. R. Tolkien*, edited by Michael D. C. Drout. Rev. 2nd edition. ACMRS, 2011, pp. 67–112.

———. *Beowulf: A Translation and Commentary: Together with Sellic Spell*. Edited by Christopher Tolkien, Mariner Books, 2015.

———. Introduction. *Sir Gawain and the Green Knight, Pearl, and Sir Orfeo*, translated by Tolkien, edited by Christopher Tolkien, Ballantine, 1975, pp. 1–21.

———. *The Letters of J. R. R. Tolkien*. Edited by Humphrey Carpenter with the assistance of Christopher Tolkien. 1981. Houghton Mifflin, 2000.

———. *The Lord of the Rings*. 1954–1955. Houghton Mifflin, 1994.

———. "On Translating *Beowulf*." *The Monsters and the Critics and Other Essays*, edited by Christopher Tolkien. 1983. HarperCollins*Publishers*, 2006, pp. 49–71.

Tolkien, J. R. R., translator. *Sir Gawain and the Green Knight, Pearl, and Sir Orfeo*. Edited by Christopher Tolkien, Ballantine, 1975.

Tolkien, J. R. R., and E. V. Gordon, editors. *Sir Gawain and the Green Knight*. Clarendon Press, 1925. *HathiTrust*, https://catalog.hathitrust.org/Record/000433397.

Turville-Petre, Thorlac. *The Alliterative Revival*. D. S. Brewer, 1977.

VanderMeer, Jeff. "Birds, Bears, and Writing Humanimal Futures: An Interview with Jeff VanderMeer at the 75th Science Fiction WorldCon, Helsinki, August 2017." Interview with Beata Gubacsi. *Fafnir*, vol. 5, no. 1, 2018, pp. 45–55, www.journal.finfar.org/articles/1369.pdf. Accessed 8 Nov. 2021.

Vincent, Stephen. "Poetry Readings / Reading Poetry: San Francisco Bay Area, 1958–1980." *The Poetry Reading: A Contemporary Compendium on Language & Performance*, edited by Stephen Vincent and Ellen Zweig, Momo's Press, 1981, pp. 19–54.

Weiskott, Eric. "Alliterative Meter and English Literary History, 1700–2000." *ELH*, vol. 84, no. 1, Spring 2017, 259-85. *Project Muse*, doi.org/10.1353/elh.2017.0009.

———. *English Alliterative Verse: Poetic Tradition and Literary Tradition*. Cambridge, UP, 2016.

Williamson, Jamie. *The Evolution of Modern Fantasy: From Antiquarianism to the Ballantine Adult Fantasy Series*. Palgrave Macmillan, 2015.

Zimmer, Paul Edwin. "Another Opinion of 'The Verse of J. R. R. Tolkien.'" *Mythlore*, vol. 19, no. 2 (#72), 1993, pp. 16–23.

———. *A Gathering of Heroes*. Ace, 1987.

Part I

THE EARLY REVIVAL

C. S. Lewis

Although best known today as the author of the Narnia books and as a Christian apologist, C. S. Lewis (1898–1963) actually first began his literary career as a poet. He published his first book, *Spirits in Bondage* (1919), after returning from the First World War, and he had high hopes that his second volume, *Dymer* (1926), would establish his poetic reputation. This never happened, and thereafter Lewis wrote poetry—including alliterative poetry—mainly for private amusement. Stylistically, he dismissed the innovations of literary modernism, greatly preferring more traditional forms and meters, and he never lost his admiration for archaic diction and spelling. Nonetheless, Lewis's decision to revive the alliterative meter represents a genuine element of experimentation in his craft for which he is rarely given credit. Of the following texts, only "We Were Talking of Dragons" and "The Planets" saw publication during his lifetime; even then, they appeared merely as examples within a proscriptive yet perceptive essay on Old English prosody, "The Alliterative Metre" (1935/1939). Except where otherwise noted, all texts came from Don W. King's *The Collected Poems of C. S. Lewis: A Critical Edition* (2015).

We Were Talking of Dragons[1]

We were TALKing of DRAGONS,   ToLkien and I
In a BERKshire BAR.   The BIG WORKman
Who had SAT SILent   and SUCKED his PIPE
ALL the EVening,   from his EMPTY MUG
With GLEAMing EYE   GLANCED towards us;
"I SEEN 'em mySELF,"   he SAID FIERCEly.

Artless and Ignorant Is Andvāri[2]

Artless and ignorant is Andvāri
As a kneaded clod, if never he heard
Where is gold growing, the glory of Rhine!
    A second sun, under still water
(Can it be Odin's eye?) that upward shoots
Answering that other (or, from under earth,
Balder bringing the buried good?)
    Who knows the nature of that noble kind
Would not laugh lightly at the lover of it;
It holds inherent in it the heritage of nine worlds.   10
    None shall reave it from Rhine, nor to ring twist it
Till he unlearn the law whereby Love made him
And spill himself for the sake of the gold.
    Ignorant and artless is Andvāri—
Never dwarf but was dull, daring only in greed.

Viva Voce Examination Session[3]

Two at the table in their talk borrowed
Gargantua's mouth. Gordon and Tolkien
Had will to repeat well-nigh the whole
That they of Verner's law and of vowel sorrows,
Cares of consonants, and case endings,
Heard by hearsay.
    Never at board I heard
Viler vivas.[4]

The Nameless Isle[5]

In a spring season I sailed away
Early at evening of an April night.
Master mariner of the men was I,
Eighteen in all. And every day
We had weather at will. White-topped the seas
Rolled, and the rigging rang like music
While fast and fair the unfettered wind
Followed. Sometimes fine-sprinkling rain
Over our ship scudding sparkled for a moment
And was gone in a glance; then gleaming white   10
Of cloud-castles was unclosed, and the blue
Of bottomless heav'n, over the blowing waves

Blessed us returning. Half blind with her speed,
Foamy-throated, into the flash and salt
Of the seas rising our ship ran on
For ten days' time. Then came a turn of luck.
On the tenth evening too soon the light
Over working seas went beneath the sky line,
Darkness came dripping and the deafening storm
Upon wild waters, wet days and long,   20
Carried us, and caverned clouds immeasurable
Harried and hunted like a hare that ship
Too many days. Men were weary.
Then was a starless night when storm was worst,
The man of my mates whom most I loved
Cried "Lost!" and then he leaped. Alive no more
Nor dead either the dear-loved face
Was seen. But soon, after his strange going,
Worse than the weathers, came the word shouted,
"Breakers ahead of us," and out of black darkness,   30
Hell-white, appeared horrid torment
Of water at the walls of a wild country.
The cliffs were high, cluttered with splinters
Of basalt at the base, bare-toothed. We found
Sea-room too small; we must split for sure,
And I heeded not the helm. Their hearts broke there,
The men I loved. Mad-faced they ran
All ways at once, till the waves swallowed
Many a smart seaman. Myself, I leaped
And wondered as I went what-like was death,   40
Before the cold clasped me. But there came a sea
Lifting from under me, so large a wave
That far above the foam of the first rock-shelves
It bore me, and far above the spray,
Upward, upward, into the air's region,
Beyond the cliffs into a yawning dark.
Other echoes, earthlier sounding,
In closer space, shut out the clamorous waves.
Then backward drawn with a babble of stones,
Softly sounding, in its spent fury,   50
A dull, dragging, withdrawing sigh,
That wave returned into the wastes, its home,
And would have sucked me back as I sank wearied,
But that there was grass growing where I gripped the land,
And roots all rough: so that I wrestled, clinging,
Against the water's tug. The wave left me,

And I groveled on the ground, greatly wearied.
        How long I lay, lapped in my weariness,
Memory minds not. To me it seems
That for one full turn of the wheels above   60
I slept. Certainly when the sleep left me
There was calm and cool. No crashing of the sea,
But darkness all about. Dim-shadowed leaves
In mildest air moved above me,
And, over all, earth-scented smell
Sweetly stealing about the sea-worn man,
And faintly, as afar, fresh-water sounds,
Runnings and ripplings upon rocky stairs
Where moss grows most. Amidst it came,
Unearthly sweet, out of the air it seemed,   70
A voice singing to the vibrant string,
"Forget the grief upon the great water,
Card and compass and the cruel rain.
Leave that labour; lilies in the green wood
Toil not, toil not. Trouble were to weave them
Coats that come to them without care or toil.
Seek not the seas again; safer is the green wood,
Lilies that live there have labour not at all,
Spin not, spin not. Spent in vain the trouble were
Beauty to bring them that better comes by kind."   80
        Then I started up and stood, staring in the darkness,
After the closing strain. The clouds parted
Suddenly. The seemly, slow-gliding moon
Swam, as it were in shallows, of the silver cloud,
Out into the open, and with orb'd splendour
She gleamed upon the groves of a great forest.
There were trees taller than the topmost spire
Of some brave minster, a bishop's seat;
Their very roots so vast that in
Their mossy caves a man could hide   90
Under their gnarl'd windings. And nearer hand
Ferns fathoms high, flowers tall like trees,
Trees bright like flowers: trouble it is to me
To remember much of that mixed sweetness
The smell and the sight and the swaying plumes
Green and growing, all the gross riches,
Waste fecundity of a wanton earth,
—Gentle is the genius of that juicy wood—
Insatiable the soil. There stood, breast high,
In flowery foam, under the flame of moon,   100
One not far off, nobly fashioned.

Her beauty burned in my blood, that, as a fool,
Falling before her at her feet I prayed,
Dreaming of druery, and with many a dear craving
Wooed the woman under the wild forest.
She laughed when I told my love-business,
Witch-hearted queen. "A worthy thing,
Traveler, truly, my troth to plight
With the sea villain that smells of tar
Horny-handed, and hairy-cheeked."   110
Then I rose wrathfully; would have ravished the witch
In her empty isle, under that orb'd splendour.
        But she laughed louder, and a little way
She went back, beckoning with brows and eyes.
Like to lilies, when she loosed her robe
Under broad moonshine, her breasts appeared,
No maiden's breasts, but with milk swelling,
Like Rhea unrobed, rich in offspring.[6]
Her sign was not sent to the sea-wanderer:
Others answered. From the arch'd forest   120
Beasts came baying: the bearded ape,
The lion, the lamb, the long-sided,
Padding panther, and the purring cat,
The snake sliding, and the stepping horse,
Busy beaver, and the bear jog-trot,
The scurrying rat, and the squirrel leaping
On the branch above. Those beasts came all.
She grudged no grace to those grim ones. I
Saw how she suckled at her sweet fountains
The tribes that go dumb. Teeth she feared not,   130
Her nipple was not denied to the nosing worm.
I thought also that out of the thick foliage
I saw the branches bend towards her breast, thirsting,
Creepers climbing and the cups of flowers
Upward opening—all things that lived,
As for sap, sucking at her sweet fountains.
And as the wood milked her, witch-hearted queen,
I saw that she smiled, softly murmuring
As if she hushed a child. How long it was
These marvels stood, memory holds not,   140
—All was gone in a glance. Under the green forest
We two were alone, as from trance wakened.
She was far fairer than at first seeing.
Then she struck the string and sang clearly
Another lay. Earth stood silent.
"You are too young in years. My yesterdays

Left behind me, are a longer tale
Than your histories hold. Far hence she lies
Who would learn gladlier of your love-business.
Woven in wizardry, wearily she lingers,   150
Stiller and stiller, with the stone in her heart,
Crying; so cruelly creeps the bitter change on her,
—Happy the head is that shall harbour in that breast—
My dear daughter, that dieth away,
In the enchanter's chain. Who chooses best
Will adventure his life and advance far on
Into the cruel country. If he comes again
Bringing that beautiful one, out of bonds redeemed,
He shall win for reward a winsome love."
"This quarrel and quest, Queen," I answered,   160
"I will undertake though I earn my death
At the wizard's wiles. But of the way thither,
The councils, and the kind, of that crafty man,
Tell me truly." When she turned her face
Her teeth glittered. She tossed her head,
Nostrils widened, as a noble dame
In scorn, scoffing, at a shameful thing—
"Eastward in the island the old one stands
Working wonders in the woeful shade
Of a grim garden that is growing there   170
Newly planted. That was the navel once
Of a sweet country, stol'n now from me,
Where he would be called a king. But he is cold at heart
And he has wrought ruin in those rich pleasances,
He has felled forests, put to flight my beasts,
Chaining with enchantment many a changeful stream,
Putting into prison all that his power reaches;
Life is loathsome to that lord; and joy,
Abomination; and the bed of love
Eggs him with envy—outcast himself,   180
An old, ugly, ice-hearted wraith.
If I saw shaking the skin upon his throat,
Or the rheum dropping from his red eyelids,
Or his tongue mumbling in the toothless gums,
By loathing I should lose my life. Strong thief!
Once amid these waters, well was my country,
Living lonely in my land, a queen.
Truly, I cannot tell of a time before
I was ruling this realm. I am its right lady.
Ages after, that other came   190
Out of the ocean in an hour of storm,

Humble and homeless. At my hearth, kneeling,
Sweetly he besought me to save his life,
And grant him ground where he might grow his bread.
All that he asked for, ill-starred I gave,
Pleased with pity, that I have paid dearly,
And easily won. But for each acre
That my bounty gave to the beggar, soon
He stole a second, till as a strong tyrant
He holds in his hand one half the land. 200
My flute he has stolen. Flowers loved it well
And rose upright at the ripple of the note
Sound-drenched, as if they drank, after drought, sweet rain.
Grass was the greener for it, as at grey evening
After the sun's setting of a summer day,
When dusk comes near, and the drooping, crushed
Stalks stand once more in the still twilight.
That reed of delight he ravished away,
Stole it stealthily. In a strange prison
It lies unloved; and of my life one half 210
With the flute followed, and I am faded now,
Mute the music. But a mightier woe
Followed the first one; with his fine weavings,
Cobwebby, clinging, and his cruel, thin
Enchanter's chains, he has charmed away
My only child out of my own country,
Into the grim garden, and will give her to drink
Heart-changing draughts. He that tastes of them
Shall stand, a stone, till the stars crumble.
Of that drug drink not, lest, in his danger caught, 220
Moveless as marble thou remain. But take
This sword, seaman, and strike off his head.
Hasten, if haply, ere his hard threatenings
Or his lies' labyrinth, lapped about her,
Have driven her to drink that draught, in time,
You may redeem my dear."
                              Dawn was round me,
Cool and coloured, and there came a breeze
Brushing the grasses. Birds were chattering.
There was I only in the empty wood, 230
The woman away. One time I thought
It was a dream's burden; but, amid the dews sprinkled
At my feet, flashing, that fallow sword
Lay to my liking. Lingeringly I weighed it,
Bright and balanced. That was the best weapon
That ever I owned. I ate in that place

My full upon the fruits the forest bore.
Then, among still shadows, slow-paced I went
Always eastward into the arch'd forest.
It was at the fifth furlong, forth I issued   240
From the dreaming wood into a down country.
All the island opened like a picture
Before my feet. Far-off the hills,
Long and limber, as it were lean greyhounds,
With level chines, lay beneath the sunrise.
Chalk made them pale. Never a church nor a rick
Nor smoke, nor the smell of a small homestead,
Rose upon the ridges. The rolling land
Climbed to the eastward—there was the clearest sky—
Heaving ever hillward, until high moorland   250
Shut off my seeing. The sorcerer's home,
My goal, was there as I guessed. Thither
I held my way and my heart lightened.
          Over hedge, over ditch, over high, over low,
By waters and woods I went and ran,
And swung the sword as I swung my legs.
Laughing loudly, alone I walked,
Till many a mile was marched away.
          Half-way in heav'n to his highest throne
The gold sun glittering had gained above,   260
When I looked and lo! in the long grasses
By a brook's margin a bright thing lay,
Reflecting the flame of floating sun,
Drawing my glances. As in danger, aside
I swerved in my step: a serpent I thought
Basking its belly in the bright morning
Lay there below me. But when I looked again,
Lo it never moved. Nearer gazing,
I found it was a flute, fashioned delicately,
Purely golden. When I picked it up   270
I could make with my mouth no music at all
And with my five fingers, failing always
Whatever tune I tried, testing that instrument.
Almost, in anger—for it irked me so—
I had flung the flute among the flowers and grass,
Let it lie there by the lapping stream.
Presently I put it in the pouch I bear
Set on my shoulder. It was my second thoughts.
          Over hedge, over ditch, over high, over low,
By waters and woods I went and ran,   280
And swung the sword as I swung my legs.

Laughing loudly alone I walked
Till many a mile was marched away.
      Bright above me on the bridge of noon
Sun was standing, shadows dwindled,
Heat was hovering in a haze that danced
Upon rocks about my road. I raised my eyes.
On the green bosom of a grassy hill,
White, like wethers, in a wide circle,
Stones were standing; as on Salisbury Plain   290
Where wild men made for the worship sun
That old altar.[7] On thither I went
Marching right among them. Man-shaped they were,
Now that I was nearer and could know their kind,
—Awful images, as it were an earlier race,
Nearer neighbours of the noble gods,
They were so quiet and cold. Kingly faces
There hushed my heart from its hard knockings.
      As I walked, wondering, in their wide consistory,
Through and through them, for the throng was great,   300
Fear stopped my breath. I found sitting
Lonely among the lifeless, but alive, a man,
His head hanging, and his hands were clasped,
His arms knotted, and from his eyes there came,
Sadly, without ceasing, slow tears and large.
Hunched and hairy was his whole body,
Durned and dwindled. Dwarflike he seemed,
But his ears bigger than any other man's.
He was grubby as if he had grown from the ground, plantlike,
Big of belly, and with bandy legs.   310
Shrublike his shape, shock-headed too,
As if a great gooseberry could go upon legs,
Or a mangel be a man. Amazed, I spoke.
"What little wight then, weeping among the stonemen,
Lives alone here? What is the load of care
That has dwelled in you, dwarf, and dwined you thus?"
Then the little man lifted up his eyebrows
And he spoke sadly. "Sorrow it is to me
To remember my mates. Men they were born
Who are now stone-silenced in this circle here,   320
By wizard's wand. Once they beat me,
Captain kicked me, and cook also,
Bosun boxed me on both my ears,
Cabin-boy, carpenter—all the crew of the *Well Away*—
Before they fell—she foundered here—
Into the wizard's hand. He worked them into stone,

That they move no more, on the main or on the shore.
Able seaman of old were they all,
Ranting and roaring when the rum was in
Like true British sailors. Trouble it is to me   330
To remember my mates—the men that they were!
I shall not meet their match. When the mate was drunk
It took all ten of their toughest men
In a strange seaport to shut him up.
Now they are stones, standing. He stopped their life,
Made them into marble, and of more beauty,
Fairer faces, and their form nobler,
Proud and princely. But the price was death.
They have bought beauty. That broke my heart."
"I am an enemy to that old sorcerer,   340
Dwarf," I answered. "Dwelling in the greenwood
Where the waves westward wash the sea-cliff,
I found, fairest of all flesh, the Queen
Who should rule this realm, for she is its right lady.
I am sent on her side. I shall save the land
From the enchanter's chain; so my charge bids me.
Lead me loyally where that lord dwelleth
In his ill garden, ice-hearted man."
        The dwarf answered, "She who dwells in the wood
Is the second fear in this strange country.   350
She has a wand also, that woman there;
Whom she chooses to change, she'll choke the voice
In his throat. Thickly, like a thing without sense,
Growling and grunting, groveling four-foot,
He will pad upon paws. Pelt coats him round,
He is a brute beast then, once her bonds catch him.
The other half of my old shipmates
She bewitched in her wood. It is the way she deals.
Therefore I lurk alone in the land between
Twixt the devil and the deep. I am in dread of both,   360
Either the stone or the sty. But here I stay, hoping
Always, if ever such an hour should come,
To drink before I die out of the deep tankard,
And to eat ham and eggs in my home country
That is the weald of Kent. And I wish that I was there."
        Doubts came darkening and all grew dull within,
Cold and clouded with clinging dread,
At this new story. Noon was burning
Bright about us. I bade the dwarf
To lead me, though he was loth, to the lair of the mage.   370
Willingly he would not. But with words of threat,

With coaxings and with kicks, he must come at the last,
Following me; a faltering, faint-hearted guide.
        Over hedge, over ditch, over high, over low,
By waters and wood I went and ran
Till many a mile was marched away.
I swung no more my sword as I walked;
Little stomach to laugh had I,
And shuffling, and shaking on his shoulders his shaggy head,
    came the dwarf,
Cunningly catching all occasions to creep aside out of the way.   380
Every mile, he would be asking for another rest. If I had let him,
The task would have been interminable; the tale wanted an ending.
Day was dropping to the dazzling plain
Of the waves westward. Winging homeward
Came the flying flocks; flowers were closing,
Level light over the land was poured.
I looked to my left in a low valley
Among quiet flowers. Queen-like there stood
A marble maid, mild of countenance,
Her lips open, her limbs so lithe   390
Made for moving, that the marble death
Seemed but that moment to have swathed her round.
Her beauty made me bow as a brute to the earth.
To have won a word of her winsome mouth,
Scorn or sweetness, salutation,
Bidding or blessing, I would have borne great pain.
Longing bade me to lay my cheek
On the cool, carven countenance, and worshipping
To kiss the maid, if so she might come awake.
Awe forbade me, and her anger feared.   400
Then I was ware in a while of one behind;
There stood in stole that stately fell
And swept, beneath, the sward, a man.
The beard upon his bos'm, burnt-gold in hue
Grew to his girdle. That was the gravest man,
Of amplest brow, and his eye steadiest,
And his mien mightiest, that I have met in earth.
Then I gathered more sure my grip upon the sword,
And for clear arm-play I cast aside
From shoulder my sack. The silly dwarf   410
Caught and kept it. He was cold at heart,
Whimpering and woebegone. The wizard spoke:
        "Second counsels, my son, are best.
If my art aid not, in empty land,
Lonely and longing for a lifeless stone,

Here you may harbour. What help is that?
Marble minds not a man's desire,
Cold lips comfort him neither with kiss nor speech,
Nor will her arms open. Eager lover,
Not even the art of this old master   420
Can wake, as you want, this woman here.
Chaste, enchanted, till the change of the world,
In beauty she abides. Nor breath, nor death,
Touches nor troubles her. You can be turned and made
Nearer to her nature; not she to yours
Ever. Only your own changing,
Boy, can bring you, where your bride waits you,
If you are love-learnèd to so large a deed.
You think, being a thrall, that it is thorough death
To be made marble and to move no limb.   430
Wise men are wary. Once only fools
Look before leaping. Lies were told you.
Fear was informer; else you had freely craved,
If your master had been love, to be made even now
Like to the lady. It was your loins told you,
And your belly, and your blood, and your blind servants
Five, who are unfaithful. Fear had moved them.
Death they were in dread of. Death let them have;
For their fading and their fall is the first waking,
And their night the noon, of a new master,   440
Peace after pleasure. Passionless for the stonemen
Life stands limpid. Left far behind
Is that race rushing over its roar'd cataracts,
The murmuring, mixed, much thwarted stream
Of the flesh, flowing with confusèd noise,
Perishing perpetually. Had you proved one hour
Their blessed life whose blood is stilled,
—How they hearken to the heavens raining
Starry influence in the still of night,
Feel the fingers, far below them   450
Of the earth's archon in an ancient place
Moulding metals: how among them steals,
As the moon moves them when the month flows full,
Love and longing, that is unlike mortals'
Dreams of druery, drawn from further,
Nobler in nature—you would know 'tis small
Wonder if they will not to wander any more.
Life has left them, whoso looks without;
All things are other on their inner side.
This child that I have changed with the chalice of peace,   460

Was my own daughter. I, pondering much,
Gave her the greatest of gifts I knew.
Long she was in labour in a land of dread,
Tangled in torments. The toils had her,
And her wild mother, witch-hearted queen,
Delayed her in that lair. Long since it was
When the woman was my wife. Worse befell her
After, when she was evil. By arts she stole
The golden flute, that was a gift fashioned
For my dear daughter, and a daemon's work,   470
The earth's archon of old made it.
She took the toy. To touch the stops
Or to make with her mouth the music it held,
Art she had not. Envy moved her.
She was changed at heart. My child she stole,
Fled to the forests: found there comrades,
Beasts and brambles and brown shadows,
With whom she holds. Half this island
Wrongly she has ravished. I am its rightful lord.
Where she flung the flute as she fled thither,   480
No man knoweth. None the richer
Was the thief of her theft: but that she thinks it wealth
If another ail. She aches at heart.
Second counsels, oh son, are best.
All things are other on their inner side."
         He spoke those words. They sped so well,
What for the maiden's love and the man's wisdom,
Awed and eager, I asked him soon
For a draught of that drink. Drought parched my throat.
Cold and crystal in the cup it glanced,   490
White like water. In the west, scarlet,
Day was dying. Dark night apace
Over earth's eastern edge towards us
Came striding up. Stars, one or two,
Had lit their lamps. My lip was set
To the cold border of the cup. The dwarf
Cried out and crossed himself: "This is a crazy thing!
Dilly, dilly, as the duckwife said,
Come and let me kill you.[8] Catch younger trouts, Sir,
Tickling, tickling, with no trouble at all."[9]   500
         "What meddling mite," said the man of spells,
"Creeps in my country? Clod! Earth thou art,
Unworthy to be worked to a white glory
Of stable stone. But stay not long,
Base, mid thy betters! Or into boggy peats,

Slave, I'll sing thee." But he skipped away
Light and limber, though his limbs were crook'd.
Out of the bag that he bore on his brown shoulder
—He had caught it and kept when I cast it away—
The dwarf deftly drew the flute out,   510
Gold and glittering. Grinned while he spoke,
"All things, ogre, have another side.
I trust even now, by a trick I have learnt,
That I shall drink before I die out of a deep tankard
In the weald of Kent, will you, nill you!"
He laid his lip to the little flute.
Long and liquid,—light was waning—
The first note flowed. Then faster came,
Reedily, ripple-like, running as a watercourse,
Meddling of melodies, moulded in air,   520
Pure and proportional. Pattering as the rain-drops
Showers of it, scattering silverly, poured on us,
Charmed the enchanter that he was changed and wept,
At the pure, plashing, piping of the melody,
Coolly calling, clearer than a nightingale,
Defter and more delicate. Dainty the division of it,
True the trilling and the turns upon itself,
Sweet the descending. For it sang so well,
First he fluted off his flesh; away
The shaggy hair; and from his shoulders next   530
Heaved by harmonies the hump away;
Then he unbandied, with a burst of beauty, his legs,
Standing straighter as the strain loudened.
I saw that the skin was smoother on his face
Than a five-year boy's. He was the fairest thing
That ever was on earth. Either shoulder
Was swept with wings; swan's down they were,
Elf-bright his eyes. Evening darkened,
The sun had set. Over the sward he danced,
With arms open, as an eager boy   540
Leaps towards his lover. I looked whither.
Noble creatures were coming near, and more
Stirring, as I saw them, out of stone bondage,
Stirring, and descending from their still places,
And every image shook, as an egg trembles
Over the breaking beak. Through the broad garden
—The dew drenched it—drawn, ev'n as moths,
To that elf's glimmering, his old shipmates
Moved to meet him. There, among, was tears,
Clipping and kissing. King they hailed him,   550

Men, once marble, that were his mates of old,
Fair in feature and of form godlike,
For the stamp of the stone was still on them
Carved by the wizard. They kept, and lived,
The marble mien. They were men weeping,
Round the dwarf dancing to his deft fingers.
Then was the grey garden as if the gods of heaven
On the carol dancing had come and chos'n
The flowers folded, for their floor to dance.
Close beside me, as when a cloud brightens   560
When, mid thin vapours, through comes the sun,
The marble maid, under mask of stone,
Shook and shuddered. As a shadow streams
Over the wheat waving, over the woman's face
Life came lingering. Nor was it long after
Down its blue pathways, blood returning
Moved, and mounted to her maiden cheek.
Breathing broadened her breast. Then light
From her eyes' opening all that beauty
Worked into woman. So the wonder was complete,   570
Set, precipitate, and the seal taken,
Clear and crystal the alchemic change,
Bright and breathing. In my breast faltering
My spirit was spent. Speech none I found,
Standing by the stranger who was stone before.
But the wing'd wonder—wide rings they danced
Over the flowers folded to his fluting sweet—
Danced to my dear one. Druery he taught her,
Bent her, bowed her, bent never before,
Brought her, blushing as it were a bride mortal,   580
To hold to her heart my head as I kneeled,
Faint in that ferly: frail, mortal man,
Till I was love-learnëd both to learn and teach
Love with that lady. Nor was it long after
That the man of spells moved and started
As one that wakes. "Weary it is to me
To remember much. Miseries innumerable
Have ruled in this realm. I will run quickly
West to the woodland, to the wild city,
Haply my love lives yet. Long time I've borne   590
Hate and hungering. Now is harvest come,
Now is the hour striking, the ice melting,
The bond broken, and the bride waiting."
        All in order—the old one led—
On flowers folded, to flute music,

Forth we followed. No fays lightlier
Dance and double in their dew'd ringlet
On All Saints Eve.[10] Earth-breathing scents
On mildest breeze moved towards us.
Cobwebs caught us. Clear-voiced, an owl   600
To his kind calling clove the darkness,
The fox, further, was faint barking.
We came quickly to the country of downs
That lies so long between the land of dread
And the grim garden. Glory breaking
Unclosed the clouds. Clear and golden
Out into the open swam the orb'd splendour
Of a moon, marvellous. Magic called her.
Pale as paper, where she poured her ray
The downs lay drenched. Dark before us,   610
Stilly standing, was the stern frontier
Of the aisled forest. Out thence there came
Thunder, I thought it. Thick copses broke.
From dread darkness, with drumming hoofs,
Swept the centaurs, swift in onset,
Abreast, embattled, as a broad army,
To that elf's glimmering. They were his old shipmates,
Unenchanted, as those others were,
Bettered after beasthood. They had the brows of men,
Tongues to talk with, and, to touch the string,   620
Hands for harping. But the horse lingered,
And the mark of their might, as magic had wrought,
The stamp of that strength was still on them.
Hands for harping, hoofs for running,
Mighty stallions, that were men weeping
Round the dwarf dancing to his deft music.
First before them ran the fairest one,
Comeliest of the coursers; king-like his eye,
Proud his pawing and his pomp of speed,
Big and bearded. On his back riding—   630
Such courtesy he could—there came, so fair,
The lady of the land, lily-breasted,
Gentle and rejoicing. The magician's love
Made her beauty burn as a bright ruby
Or as a coal on fire, under cool moonlight,
And swam in her eyes till she swooned almost
Bending her body to his back on whom she rode.
And now full near those nations stood,
That king's courtiers whom he had carved in stone,

And the wide flung wings of the woman's horse,   640
Both as for battle; all the beauty of his,
The strength of hers. Straightway they fell
To talk, those two. Their tale was sweet
In all our ears. Earth stood silent.
Either answered other softly.

HIC: "My love's laughter is light falling
      Through broad branches in brown woodland,
      On a cold fountain, in a cave darkling,
      A mild sparkling in mossy gloom."

ILLA: "But my lord's wisdom is light breaking,   650
      And sound shaking, a sundered tomb."

HIC: "My love's looking is long dimness
      And stars' influence. In strange darkness
      Her eyes open their orb'd dreaming
      As a huge, gleaming mid-harvest moon."

ILLA: "But my lord's looking is the lance darted
      Through mists parted when morn comes soon."

HIC: "Thy dear bosom is a deep garden
      Between high hedges where heat burns not,
      Where no rains ruin and no rimes harden,   660
      A closed garden, where climbs no snake."

ILLA: "But thy dear valour is a deep, rolling,
      And a tower tolling strong towns awake."

HIC: "My friend's beauty is the free springing
      Of the world's welfare from the womb'd ploughland,
      The green growing, the great mothering,
      Her breast smothering with her brood unfurled."

ILLA: "But my friend's beauty is the form minted
      Above heav'n, printed on the holy world."

      So they were singing. The song was done.   670
When either in arms other folded
Fondly and fairly, fire-red was she,
Fire-white the sage. The fields of air
Beamed more brightly. About the moon
More than a myriad mazy weavings
Of fire flickered. Far off there rolled
Summer thunder. The sage all mild
For the maid and for me his mouth opened:
      "The air of earth this other two

Must breathe in breast. Now broad ocean   680
Smiles in sleeping and smoother winds
Favour, let us find them a ferry hence.
This elf also, even as he wished for,
Hoping, while he was helpless, for his home country,
Earth of England, unenchanted,
Let us send on the sea. He served us well,
MULTUM AMAVIT,[11] which is of most virtue,
In heav'n and here and in hell under us."
      Centaurs swiftly, when he said, were gone,
Glorying in gallop to the great forest.   690
Heaving hardily, whole trees they tore
From earth upward. Echoing ruin
Dinned in darkness. Down thence they hauled
Many an ancient oak. The orb'd splendour
Shone on their shoulders as they sweat naked
Under moon's mildness. Magic helped them,
The boat was built in the blink of an eye,
Long and limber, of line stately,
Fair in fashion. Out of the forest came
Spiders for spinning, speedily they footed,   700
Shooting like shuttles on the shadowy grass,
Backward and forward, brisk upon their spindle shanks,
And made for the mast a marvellous sail
Of shimmering web. That ship full soon
Over grass gliding, glorious stallions
With Heave! and Ho! hauled to the sea's rim,
A throng, dancing. They thrust her out
Into deep water. There was din of hoofs
In salt shallows and the spray cast up
Under moon, glancing. The maiden soon,   710
The elf also, I then, the third,
Were on board in the boat. Breathing mildly
Off the island—it arched our sail—
The breeze blew then, blest the fragrance
Of flower and fruit, floating seaward,
Land-laden air. I long even now
To remember more of that mixed sweetness.
But fast and fair into the foamless bay
Onward and outward, under the orb'd splendour,
Our boat was borne. Back oft I gazed   720
As the land lessened, lo! all that folk
Burned on the beaches as they were bright angels,
Light and lovely, and the long ridges
With their folds fleecy under the flame of moon

Swam in silver of swathing mist,
Elf-fair that isle. But on apace
We went on the wave. That wingèd boy
Held firm the helm. Ahead, far on,
Like floor unflawed, the flood, moon-bright,
Stretched forth the twinkling streets of ocean   730
To the rim of the world. No ripple at all
Nor foam was found, save the furrow we made,
The stir at our stern, and the strong cleaving
Of the throbbing prow. We thrust so swift,
Moved with magic, that a mighty curve
Upward arching from either bow
Rose, all rainbowed; as a rampart stood
Bright about us. As the book tells us,
Walls of water, and a way between,
Were reared and rose at the Red Sea ford,   740
On either hand, when Israel came
Out of Egypt to their own country.

The Planets[12]

Lady LUNA, in light canoe,
By friths and shallows of fretted cloudland
Cruises monthly; with chrism of dews
And drench of dream, a drizzling glamour,
Enchants us—the cheat! changing sometime
A mind to madness, melancholy pale,
Bleached with gazing on her blank count'nance
Orb'd and ageless. In earth's bosom
The shower of her rays, sharp-feathered light
Reaching downward, ripens silver,   10
Forming and fashioning female brightness,
—Metal maidenlike. Her moist circle
Is nearest earth. Next beyond her
MERCURY marches;—madcap rover,
Patron of pilf'rers. Pert quicksilver
His gaze begets, goblin mineral,
Merry multitude of meeting selves,
Same but sundered. From the soul's darkness,
With wreathèd wand, words he marshals,
Guides and gathers them——gay bellwether   20
Of flocking fancies. His flint has struck
The spark of speech from spirit's tinder,
Lord of language! He leads forever

The spangle and splendour, sport that mingles
Sound with senses, in subtle pattern,
Words in wedlock, and wedding also
Of thing with thought. In the third region
VENUS voyages . . . but my voice falters;
Rude rime-making wrongs her beauty,
Whose breasts and brow, and her breath's sweetness   30
Bewitch the worlds. Wide-spread the reign
Of her secret sceptre, in the sea's caverns,
In grass growing, and grain bursting,
Flower unfolding, and flesh longing,
And shower falling sharp in April.
The metal of copper in the mine reddens
With muffled brightness, like muted gold,
By her finger form'd. Far beyond her
The heaven's highway hums and trembles,
Drums and dwindles, to the driv'n thunder   40
Of SOL's chariot, whose sword of light
Hurts and humbles; beheld only
Of eagle's eye. When his arrow glances
Through mortal mind, mists are parted
And mild as morning the mellow wisdom
Breathes o'er the breast, broadening eastward
Clear and cloudless. In a clos'd garden
(Unbound her burden) his beams foster
Soul in secret, where the soil puts forth
Paradisal palm, and pure fountains   50
Turn and re-temper, touching coolly
The uncomely common to cordial gold;
Whose ore also, in earth's matrix,
Is print and pressure of his proud signet
On the wax of the world. He is the worshipp'd male,
The earth's husband, all-beholding,
Arch-chemic eye. But other country
Dark with discord dins beyond him,
With noise of nakers,[13] neighing of horses,
Hammering of harness. A haughty god   60
MARS mercenary, makes there his camp
And flies his flag; flaunts laughingly
The graceless beauty, grey-eyed and keen,
—Blond insolence—of his blithe visage
Which is hard and happy. He hews the act,
The indifferent deed with dint of his mallet
And his chisel of choice; achievement comes not

Unhelped by him;—hired gladiator
Of evil and good. All's one to Mars,
The wrong righted, rescued meekness,   70
Or trouble in trenches, with trees splintered
And birds banished, banks fill'd with gold
And the liar made lord. Like handiwork
He offers to all—earns his wages
And whistles the while. White-featured dread
Mars has mastered. His metal's iron
That was hammered through hands into holy cross,
Cruel carpentry. He is cold and strong,
Necessity's son. Soft breathes the air
Mild, and meadowy, as we mount further   80
Where rippled radiance rolls about us
Moved with music—measureless the waves'
Joy and jubilee. It is JOVE's orbit,
Filled and festal, faster turning
With arc ampler. From the Isles of Tin[14]
Tyrian traders, in trouble steering
Came with his cargoes; the Cornish treasure
That his ray ripens. Of wrath ended
And woes mended, of winter passed
And guilt forgiven, and good fortune   90
Jove is master; and of jocund revel,
Laughter of ladies. The lion-hearted,
The myriad-minded, men like the gods,
Helps and heroes, helms of nations
Just and gentle, are Jove's children,
Work his wonders. On his wide forehead
Calm and kingly, no care darkens
Nor wrath wrinkles: but righteous power
And leisure and largess their loose splendours
Have wrapped around him—a rich mantle   100
Of ease and empire. Up far beyond
Goes SATURN silent in the seventh region,
The skirts of the sky. Scant grows the light,
Sickly, uncertain (the Sun's finger
Daunted with darkness). Distance hurts us,
And the vault severe of vast silence;
Where fancy fails us, and fair language,
And love leaves us, and light fails us
And Mars fails us, and the mirth of Jove
Is as tin tinkling. In tattered garment,   110
Weak with winters, he walks forever

A weary way, wide round the heav'n,
Stoop'd and stumbling, with staff groping,
The lord of lead. He is the last planet
Old and ugly. His eye fathers
Pale pestilence, pain of envy,
Remorse and murder. Melancholy drink
(For bane or blessing) of bitter wisdom
He pours for his people, a perilous draught
That the lip loves not. We leave all things   120
To reach the rim of the round welkin,
Heaven's hermitage, high and lonely.

Sweet Desire[15]

These faint wavering far-travell'd gleams
Coming from your country, fill me with care. That scent,
That sweet stabbing, as at the song of thrush,
That leap of the heart—too like they seem
To another air; unlike as well
So that I am dazed with doubt. As a dungeoned man
Who has heard the hinge on the hook turning
Often. Always that opened door
Let new tormentors in. If now at last
It open again, but outward, offering free way,   10
(His kind one come, with comfort) he
Yet shrinks, in his straw, struggling backward,
From his dear, from his door, into the dark'st corner,
Furthest from freedom. So fearing, I
Taste not but with trembling. I was tricked before.
All the heraldry of heaven, holy monsters,
With hazardous and dim half-likeness taunt
Long-haunted men. The like is not the same.
Always evil was an ape. I know.
Who passes to paradise, within that pure border   20
Finds there, refashioned, all that he fled from here.
And yet . . .
         But what's the use? For yield I must,
Though long delayed, at last must dare
To give over, to be eased of my iron casing,
Molten at thy melody, as men of snow
In the solar smile. Slow-paced I come,
Yielding by inches. And yet, oh Lord, and yet,
—Oh Lord, let not likeness fool me again.

NOTES

1. Excluded from King's *The Collected Poems of C. S. Lewis*, "We were Talking of Dragons" appears only in Lewis's essay "The Alliterative Metre." He marked his heavily stressed syllables with small capitals in order to help students mark the lifts. For more details on meter, see Appendix B.

2. Lewis originally incorporated "Artless and Ignorant Is Andvāri," his earliest alliterative poem with a date, into a June 26th, 1929(?) letter asking Owen Barfield to comment on the meter. In Norse mythology, Andvāri is a dwarf condemned to spend his life as a pike, and taking his food from beneath a waterfall. The god Loki tricks away Andvāri's magic ring that enables great wealth. In retaliation, Andvāri puts a curse on the ring's gold, which plays a major role in Norse legend and later literature.

3. This short poem, whose title is editorial, appears only in Humphrey Carpenter's collective biography *The Inklings* (1978); King excludes it from *The Collected Poems*. A *viva voce* examination is an oral defense of one's thesis and graduate research; Lewis composed these lines to tease J. R. R. Tolkien and E. V. Gordon for speaking too much themselves in their role as examiners. In response to this verse, Tolkien told Carpenter that "during the sessions C. S. L.'s voice was the one most often heard" (qtd. *The Inklings* 55).

4. Gargantua is one of two giants in François Rabelais's *Gargantua and Pantagruel*; Verner's Law is a principle of historical sound change. The phrase *viler vivas* might be mistaken for Latin, but *viler* is just the comparative form of the English word *vile* (i.e., "more vile"), and "vivas" is the first word in *viva voce* but with an English plural.

5. The fair copy version of *The Nameless Isle*, dated August 1930 and originally untitled, was discovered in Lewis's notebooks after his death. Editor Walter Hooper provided the title for *Narrative Poems* (1969).

6. Daughter of Gaia (earth goddess) and Uranus (sky god), Rhea was the Titan who mothered several Olympian deities, including Zeus. She is thus often associated with fertility and motherhood.

7. The old altar, Stonehenge, lies on Salisbury Plain, a chalk plateau mostly in Wiltshire in southwest England. During the summer solstice, the monument is oriented toward the sunrise.

8. In colloquial usage, *dilly* is the name for a female duck. The phrase originated in a music-hall song about a cook, Mistress Bond, who asks her servants to fetch her some ducks by calling for them. Gradually, the phrase turned into a popular English nursery rhyme: "Dilly, dilly, dilly, dilly, come to be killed, / For you must be stuffed and my customers filled!" By Lewis's time, the phrase had come to suggest a lure to the unwary.

9. Trout tickling is an old poaching technique for catching trout by "tickling" them into a trance; Shakespeare mentions the practice in *Twelfth Night*, Act 2, scene v.

10. All Saints' Eve (or Halloween) is October 31st, a time of porous boundaries between the fairy Otherworld and ours. According to the *OED*, "ringlet" first appears with this sense in Shakespeare's *A Midsummer Night's Dream*. The Queen of the Faeries, Titania, says: "Met we on hill, in dale, forest or mead, / By paved fountain or

by rushy brook, / Or in the beached margent of the sea, / To dance our ringlets to the whistling wind" (in Act 2, scene i).

11. *Multum amavit*: "he loved much."

12. Lewis originally used "The Planets" as an example of Old English meter for his essay "The Alliterative Metre" (1935/1939); there, he claims the characters of the planets in medieval cosmology—the sun, the moon, plus Mercury, Venus, Mars, Jupiter (or Jove), and Saturn—retain "permanent value as spiritual symbols" (24).

13. *Naker* is a medieval term for kettledrums.

14. The Cassiterides, or Tin Islands, were an ancient Greek name for the geographical source of tin, usually thought to reside somewhere along Europe's western coast. Most ancient writers guessed them near northwest Iberia (modern-day Spain), but later geographers also attributed tin's source to Cornwall in southwest Britain. Lewis follows this latter attribution.

15. Lewis provides no date for this poem, which he left untitled, but editor Walter Hooper names it "Sweet Desire" in *Poems* (1964), most likely after Lewis's allegorical figure in *The Pilgrim's Regress* (1933) for the blissful ache of longed-for paradisal Joy.

John D. Niles

John D. Niles (b. 1945) is a prominent scholar of medieval literature, a professor emeritus at the University of Wisconsin–Madison and the University of California, Berkeley. Although known mainly as a scholar—his latest book, *God's Exiles and English Verse* (2019), analyzes the late tenth-century *Exeter Book*—Niles has also had lifelong interests in poetry, translation, and the continuum between scholarly and creative modes. His first book, *Beowulf: The Poem and Its Tradition* (1983), contains a prefatory poem called "The Seafarers," and he has written two collections of verse and translation: *Seven Songs of Guilhem IX: First of the Known Troubadours* (1978) and *Chapman's Pack* (2003). Among his early influences he counts Ezra Pound, on whom he did a bachelor's thesis, and J. R. R. Tolkien. Both led Niles into foreign-language studies, including English in its earliest recorded form. A major component of Niles's academic career has been the view that storytelling is a defining feature of the human species, a point presented in *Homo Narrans: The Poetics and Anthropology of Oral Literature* (1999) and other works. In the following two poems, Niles draws freely on Old English alliterative style. Each appeared in a 1978 article on modern poetry using an alliterative meter. The first features a werewolf, and the second is a powerful yet fictive distillation of several "fair days" that Niles remembers from Berkeley in the late 1970s.

Night Out

The children whispered as we checked the locks,
then sat in silence while we said goodbye.
"Goodnight, angels. Go to sleep early!
Turn off the TV when you're too tired to watch.

Don't answer the door if anyone knocks—
it might be the wolf!" we warned them, laughing,
then dashed for the door and drove away.
While we lunged into darkness, late for the party,
Jessica looked into Jonathon's eyes.
A flash of gray flared at her temples,   10
then the change came over her utter as night:
wolf eyes, wolf ears, and a wolf s gray body,
then she was gone like a rifle, running with the pack.
In the morning we found her five miles down the highway,
blood on her jaws, a bullet in her head.

Fair Day

On September the seventh, 1976,
the freaks held a free fair on Berkeley Common.
There were jugglers and Jesus freaks jostling for attention,
there were flutists and fiddlers fighting for spare change
while painters and pushers peddled their wares:
black, brown, and white, they all bought and sold there.
I saw big-bosomed belly-dancers oozing and swaying,
I saw long-legged lovers lying in the bushes,
I saw bare-bottomed babies and barefoot mommas,
from the smell of their foul feet I almost fell over.   10
I saw Chinese children eating chicken gumbo
while others ate herbs or the latest earth foods:
a wisp of wild watercress wound about with parsley
or a ground-up goat's gut garnished with guru's dung
I saw circus clowns and Cajun fiddlers,
I saw mimes and masseurs and a man who swallowed fire.
From sunup to sundown the freaks never stopped coming
till the sun sank slowly over the western rim.
The Golden Gate Bridge was glowing in the sunset
like a heavenly harp strung by God's own hand.   20
All the junkies joined hands in a giant circle
and we stood stock still, stunned by the beauty;
then the bagpipes began buzzing and bellowing again
and all blundered home, blessed and blessing,
while the sounds of the free fair faded and were gone.

Fletcher Pratt and L. Sprague de Camp

Together, Fletcher Pratt (1897–1956) and L. Sprague de Camp (1907–2000) are best known for their time-travel fantasy tales depicting the misadventures of Harold Shea, a psychologist, as he explores various parallel universes reflecting ancient myth and classic literary texts. In their first novella, "The Roaring Trumpet" (1940), Shea finds himself accidentally transported into a world shaped by Norse mythology; the text accordingly contains several poems in Norse style. De Camp later claimed that his mentor could read Old Norse in the original, thus implying Pratt wrote (or maybe translated) these poems himself, but, in fact, he adapted them from preexisting translations. In the following example, the first two lines hail from the 1923 translation of "Lokasenna" (in *The Elder Edda*) by Henry Adams Bellows; Pratt's only change is to remove the archaisms. The final two lines, however, are wholly original. He has them spoken by Loki the Trickster, and they pertain directly to Pratt and de Camp's plot. As such, this poem forms an early precursor to the more radical adaptive practices of Poul Anderson in *The Broken Sword*.

I Say to the Gods

I say to the gods and the sons of gods
The things that whet my thoughts;
By the wells of the world there is none with the might
To make me do his will.

John Myers Myers

John Myers Myers (1906–1988) was a prolific and highly respected poet and author now best remembered for his 1949 novel, *Silverlock*. In this madcap picaresque, its eponymous hero finds himself marooned on an island called the Commonwealth of Letters. Under the guidance of Golias, the archetypal wandering bard, Silverlock undergoes a series of adventures where he encounters familiar characters from the Western literary canon. Although little noticed by mainstream readers, *Silverlock* soon acquired an underground cult status among the SF fan community; the young Poul Anderson endorsed the novel heartily. Part of its popularity derived from its many in-set songs and poems. In the following selection, one of the best-known alliterative poems of the twentieth century, the bard Golias sings about a pivotal event in the Texas Revolution: the famous last stand of James Bowie at the Alamo. On March 6th, 1836, Mexican troops led by Antonio López de Santa Anna reclaimed the Alamo Mission near San Antonio de Béxar; in the process, they killed most of its inhabitants, including Bowie and American folk hero Davy Crockett. Here, in a virtuosic display of comic anachronism, the bard Golias sings this song at Hrothgar's hall Heorot shortly after Beowulf has defeated Grendel; hence the alliterative meter.

The Death of Bowie Gizzardsbane

Harsh that hearing for Houston the Raven:[1]
Fools had enfeebled the fortress at Bexar,
Leaving it lacking and looted the while
Hordes were sweeping swift on his land,
Hell-bent to crush him. The cunning old prince

Did not, though, despair at danger's onrushing;
Hardy with peril, he held it, perused it,
Reading each rune of it. Reaching the facts, he
Thumbed through his thanes and thought of the one
Whose guts and gray matter were grafted most neatly.   10
"Riders!" he rasped, "to race after Bowie!"
"Bowie," he barked when that bearcat of heroes
Bowed to his loved prince, "Bexar must be ours
Or no one must have it. So hightail, burn leather!
Hold me that fortress or fire it and raze it.
Do what you can or else do what you must."

Fame has its fosterlings, free of the limits
Boxing all others, and Bowie was one of them.
Who has not heard of the holmgang at Natchez?
Fifty were warriors, but he fought the best,   20
Wielding a long knife, a nonesuch of daggers
Worthy of Wayland.[2] That weapon had chewed
The entrails of dozens. In diverse pitched battles
That thane had been leader; by land and by sea
Winning such treasure that trolls, it is said,
Closed hills out of fear he'd frisk them of silver.
Racing now westward, he rode into Bexar,
Gathered the garrison, gave them his orders:
"Houston the Raven is raising a host;
Time's what he asks while he tempers an army.   30
Never give up this gate to our land.
Hold this door fast, though death comes against us."

The flood of the foemen flowed up to Bexar,
Beat on the dam braced there to contain it.
But Wyrd has no fosterlings, favors no clients;
Bowie, the war-wise winner of battles,
Laid out by fever, lost his first combat,
Melting with death.[3] Yet the might of his spirit
Kept a tight grip on the trust he'd been given.
"Buy time, my bucks," he told his companions.   40
"Be proud of the price; our prince is the gainer."
Bold thanes were with him, thirsty for honor,
Schooled well in battle and skilled in all weapons;
Avid for slaughter there, each against thirty,
They stood to the walls and struck for their chieftains,
Houston and Bowie, the bearcat of heroes.

Twelve days they ravaged the ranks of the foemen.
Tens, though, can't harrow the hundreds forever;

That tide had to turn. Tiredly the thanes
Blocked two wild stormings and bled them to death.   50
The third had the drive of Thor's mighty hammer,
Roared at the walls and rose to spill over,
Winning the fort. But the foemen must pay.
Heroes were waiting them, hardy at killing,
Shaken no whit, though sure they were lost.
Ten lives for one was the tariff for entry;
And no man got credit. Crushed and split skulls,
Blasted off limbs[4] and lathers of blood
Were the money they sought and minted themselves—
Worth every ounce of the weregild they asked.   60

Of every eleven, though, one was a hero
Turned to a corpse there.[5] Cornered and hopeless,
They strove while they yet stood, stabbing and throttling,
Meeting the bear's death, dying while fighting.
Chieftains of prowess, not chary of slaying,
Led and fell with them. Alone by the wall,
Travis, the red-maned, the truest of warriors,
Pierced through the pate and pouring out blood,
Kept death marking time, defied it until
His sword again sank, sucking blood from a foeman.   70
Content, then, he ended. So also died Crockett,
Who shaved with a star and stamped to make earthquakes,
Kimball, the leader of loyal riders,
Bonham whose vow was valor's own hallmark.

Crazed by their losses, the conquerors offered
No truce to cadavers; the corpses were stabbed
In hopes that life's spark would be spared to afford them
Seconds on killing. Then some, taking count,
Bawled out that Bowie was balking them still;
Like weasels in warrens they wound through the fort,   80
Hunting the hero they hated the most.
Least of the lucky, at last some found him,
Fettered to bed by the fever and dying,
Burnt up and shrunken, a shred of himself.
Gladly they rushed him, but glee became panic.
Up from the gripe of the grave, gripping weapons,
Gizzardsbane rose to wreak his last slaughter,
Killing, though killed. Conquered, he won.

In brief is the death lay of Bowie, the leader
Who laid down his life for his lord and ring giver,   90
Holding the doorway for Houston the Raven,
Pearl among princes, who paid in the sequel;
Never was vassal avenged with more slayings!

NOTES

1. Sam Houston (1793–1863) served two terms as president of the Republic of Texas; later, when the territory incorporated into the United States, he served as the state's senator. In 1836, knowing he lacked the forces to defend San Antonio de Béxar properly, Houston ordered James Bowie to take thirty men and evacuate the location's artillery. Once Bowie arrived on January 19th, however, he convinced himself of the site's strategic importance and decided to defend the Alamo Mission. According to Norse myth, ravens are traditionally associated with the god Odin.

2. A holmgang (from Old Norse *holmganga*) is a duel to the death, and the event Myers is referencing—the famous "Sandbar Fight" that earned James Bowie his reputation as a knife fighter—occurred nine years earlier on September 19th, 1827, in Natchez, Mississippi. Although neither original duelist came to harm, a brawl broke out among the onlookers, Bowie included. Despite being stabbed and shot in the hip, Bowie disemboweled a local sheriff, Norris Wright, with whom he had a prior history. Bowie's large sheath knife later became known as the Bowie knife. The allusion to Wayland is to the legendary master blacksmith who appears in several Old Norse and Old English texts—for instance, *Völundarkviða* and *Deor*.

3. Due to this unspecified illness, Bowie was confined to bed for most of the siege.

4. This reference to "blasted off limbs" is the closet Myers comes to acknowledging the presence of cannons or gunpowder at the battle; such anachronistic references would have confused the bard Golias's audience.

5. In this stanza, Myers names the famous fighters who died alongside Bowie at the Alamo. Lieutenant Colonel William B. "Buck" Travis had arrived on February 3rd, and Davy Crockett—the legendary frontiersman and former Tennessee Congressman—arrived on February 8th, or about two weeks before Santa Anna's troops. The others are George C. Kimball, who, on March 1st, brought a group of Texian reinforcements later eulogized as the "Immortal 32," and James Butler Bonham, a messenger tasked by LTC Travis (Bonham's second cousin) with finding reinforcements. When Bonham failed to find any more forces, he returned to the Alamo on March 3rd despite knowing the battle's likely outcome. Yet one major issue Myers excludes from his story concerns the confusion surrounding the issue of command. Technically, command belonged to Travis as the highest ranking regular-army officer present, but the troops—unenlisted men especially—gave greater weight to Bowie's orders, which led to several mishaps and miscommunications.

Poul Anderson

Poul Anderson (1926–2001) rose to prominence during the Golden Age of Science Fiction, and, throughout his long and varied career, he maintained the lessons he learned under the tutelage of editor John W. Campbell Jr.: rationalism, scientific plausibility, and competent male heroes who succeed in quick-paced adventure settings. Yet Anderson also loved ancient history. Growing up bilingual in English and Danish, he drew deeply for his work from the literature and folklore of medieval Scandinavia. For instance, he modeled his second published novel, *The Broken Sword* (1954), on Norse family sagas and their characteristic prosimetrum, and his many speculative writings often include in-set songs and poems. In 1993 Anderson collected his best poetry into a small booklet called *Staves*. As per his usual practice, Anderson took the opportunity to lightly revise his poems (though not always with noticeable improvement), but he also took the additional unusual step of combining several old poems into unified longer texts. Rather than reprint these unified versions, this anthology instead reprints the versions found in his more widely read novels; footnotes supply any necessary context. Except where noted, all titles are editorial.

from "CHAIN OF LOGIC" (1947) *and TWILIGHT WORLD* (1961)[1]

Epigraph to "Chain of Logic"

Brother bringeth
brother his bane,
and sons of sisters
split kinship's bonds.

Not ever a man
spareth another.
Hard is the world.
Whoredom waxeth.
Ax-time, sword-time,
—shields are cloven— 10
wind-time and wolf-time,
ere the world waneth.

—*Elder Edda*, verse 45/46

from "TIGER BY THE TAIL" (1951)[2]

The Scothan Queen

So I see you standing,
sorrowful in darkness.
But the moonlight's broken
by your eyes, tear-shining—
moonlight in the maiden's
magic net of tresses.
Gods gave many gifts, but,
Gunli, yours was greatest.

from THE BROKEN SWORD (1954)[3]

The Longships[4]

White-maned horses
(hear their neighing!),
gray and gaunt-flanked,
gallop westward.
Wild with winter
winds, they snort and
buck when bearing
burdens for me.

Swiftly Goes the Sword-Play (1)[5]

Swiftly goes the sword-play
singing in the mountains.
Clash of steel is calling,

clanging up to heaven:—
arrows flying angry;
axes lifting skyward,
banging down on byrnies,
breaking shields and helmets.

Swiftly goes the sword-play:
spears on hosts are raining;   10
men run forth in madness,
mowing ranks of foemen;
battle tumult bellows;
blood is red on ax-heads;
greedily the gray wolf
gorges with the raven.

The Strike at Trollheim

Elves come early
east to Trollheim,
spears and singing
swords their presents.
Good are gifts they
give, for troll-men:
sundered skulls and
splitted bellies.

Trolls shall tumble
(tumult rages),   10
fear of firebrands
freeing bowels.
Kin, be kind to
clamoring troll-men:
have they headaches,
hew the heads off.

Food Is Good for Friendship[6]

Food is good for friendship,
fairest one, and wine-cups.
Good it is to gladden
gullets in the morning.
But my eyes, bewildered
by the sight of Freda,
sate themselves on sun-bright
southern maiden's beauty.

Laughter from Your Lips

Laughter from your lips, dear,
lures me like a war-cry.
Bronze-red locks have bound me:
bonds more strong than iron.
Never have I nodded
neck beneath a yoke, but
wish I now the welcome
warmth of your arms' prison.

Life was made for laughter,
love, and eager heartbeat.
Could I but caress you,
came I to my heaven.
Sorceress, you see me
seek your love with pleading:
how can Skafloc help it
when you have ensnared him?

10

Fear of Fairest[7]

Fear of fairest
fay for chieftain
makes him merry—
means she loves him.
Girl, be gay now.
Gladly take I
gift you give me,
gold-bright woman.

**Swiftly Goes the Sword-Play (2):
Prelude to Battle**[8]

Swiftly goes the sword-play,
sweeping foemen backward
to the beach where tumult
talks with voice of metal:
belling of the brazen
beaks of cleaving axes,
smoking blood, where sea kings
sing the mass of lances.

Swiftly goes the sword-play,
storm-like in its madness: 10
shields are bloody shimmers,
shining moons of redness;
winds of arrows wailing,
wicked spearhead-lightning
lads will smite who lately
lay by lovely sweethearts.

Swiftly goes the sword-play!
Swinging bloodied weapons,
shields and helms to shatter,
shout the men their war-cry.   20
While the angry, whining,
whirring blades are sparking,
howl the wolves their hunger,
hawks stoop low for feasting.

Swiftly goes the sword-play!
Song of metal raises
din of blades for dancing
(death for eager partner).
Lur horns bray their laughter,
lads, and call to hosting.   30
Sweeter game was sleeping
softly with your leman.

Swiftly goes the sword-play.
Skald who lately chanted
gangs unto the game where
grim are stakes we play for.
Mock not at the mortal
may who is not dancing.
Better luck she brings me
by a kiss than magic.   40

Swiftly goes the sword-play.
Some must lose the gamble.
Norns alone are knowing
now who throws the dice best.
Winner in the wailing
weapon-game we know not,
but our foes will bitter
battle find in Alfheim.

Gravemound[9]

[*Skafloc speaks*]

Waken, chieftains,
fallen warriors!
Skafloc calls ye,
sings ye wakeful.
I conjure ye,
come on hell-road.
Rune-bound dead men,
rise and answer!

Grave shall open.
Gang forth, deathlings!   10
Fallen heroes,
fare to earth now.
Stand forth, bearing
swords all rusty,
broken shields, and
bloody lances.

[*Orm speaks*]

Who dares sunder
howe, and bid me
rise from death, by
runes and song-spells?   20
Flee the dead man's
fury, stranger!
Let the deathling
lie in the darkness.

[*Skafloc speaks*]

Terror shall not
turn my purpose.
Runes shall bind thee.
Rise and answer!
In thy ribs may
rats build nests, if   30
thou will give not
that I call for!

[*Orm speaks*]

Deep is dreamless
death-sleep, warlock.
Wakened dead are

wild with anger.
Ghosts will take a
gruesome vengeance
when their bones are
hailed from barrow.   40

[*Orm notices Freda, his daughter*]

Gladly see we
gold-decked woman.
Sun-bright maiden,
sister, welcome!
Ashy, frozen,
are our hollow
breasts with grave-cold.
But you warm us.

[*Orm turns to Aelfrida, his living wife*]

Dreamless was not
death, but frightful!   50
Tears of thine, dear,
tore my heart out.
Vipers dripped their
venom on me,
when in death I
heard thee weeping.

This I ask of
thee, beloved:
live in gladness,
laughing, singing.   60
Death is then the
dearest slumber,
wrapped in peace, with
roses round me.

[*Skafloc speaks to dead Ketil, son of Orm*]

Speak forth, deathling.
Say me whither
Bölverk giant
bides, the swordsmith.
Tell me further,
truly, warrior,   70
what will make him
hammer for me.

[*Ketil speaks*]

Ill thy questing
is, thou warlock!
Worst of evil
will it bring thee.
Seek not Bölverk.
Sorrow brings he.
Leave us now, while
life is left thee.   80

North in Jötunheim,
nigh to Utgard,
dwells the giant,
deep in mountain.
Sidhe will give thee
ship to find him.
Tell him Loki
talks of sword-play.

[*Asmund, son of Orm, addresses Skafloc and Freda*]

Bitter, cruel—
brother, sister—   90
fate the Norns let
fall upon ye.
Wakened dead men
wish ye had not
wrought the spell that
wrings the truth out.

Law of men is
laid on deathlings.
Hard it is to
hold unto it.   100
But the words must
bitter leave me:
Skafloc, Freda
is your sister.

Welcome, brother,
valiant warrior.
All unwitting
are you, sister.
But your love has
broken kinship.   110
Farewell, children,
fey and luckless!

[*Freda takes her leave of Skafloc in horror*]

Luckless Is the Lad

Luckless is the lad who
leaves without his dearest
sweetheart farewell saying
softly, in the morning.
Colder than her kisses
comes the blowing spindrift.
Heavy is my heart—but
how could I forget her?

Clear the Day Is, Coldly[10]

Clear the day is, coldly
calling with a wind-voice
to the sea, where tumbles
titan play of billows.
Stood you by my side now,
sweetheart, on the deck-planks,
life were full of laughter.
(Long you for me, Freda?)

Black and Cold, the Breakers

Black and cold, the breakers
bellow, thunder inboard.
Ropes are snapped, and rudders.
Roaring winds are sleet-cloaked.
Seamen weary stumble,
sick with cold and hunger.
Bitter is the brew here:
beer of waves is salty.

Late Will I the Lovely

Late will I the lovely
lost one be forgetting.
Ways that I must wander
will be cold and lonely.
Heavy is my heart now,
where she sang aforetime.
Greatest of the griefs she
gave me is her sorrow.

Skafloc Speaks to Bölverk

Asa-Loki,
angry, weary
with his prison,
wishes sword-play.
Here is weapon
which gives victory.
Bölverk, take the
bane of heroes.

Swiftly Goes the Sword-Play (3):
Tyrfing Re-Forged

Swiftly goes the sword-play!
Soon the foe shall hear the
wailing song of weapons.
Warlock blade is thirsty!
Howling in its hunger,
hews it through the iron,
sings in cloven skull-bones,
slakes itself in blood-streams.

The Daughters of Rán[11]

Cold and lustful
are the kisses
which Rán's daughters,
white-armed, give us.
Laughing, shouting,
shake they tresses
white and salt-sweet,
high breasts heaving.

Home Again the Howling

Home again the howling,
hail-streaked wind has borne me.
Now I stand here, nearing
ness of lovely England.
She dwells on these shores, but
Shall I ever see her?
Woe, the fair young woman
will not leave my thinking.

from THE GOLDEN SLAVE (1960)[12]

High Stood Our Helmets

High stood our helmets,
host-men gathered,
bows were blowing
bale-wind of arrows—

from AMRA (1960)[13]

The First Love

From my hill I followed
the faring, when on horseback
lightly did the lovely
let herself be out-borne.
And her shining eyes
did all my joy bereave me:
known it is, to no one
naught of sorrow happens.

Formerly in fairness,
filled with golden blossoms,   10
trees stood green and trembling,
tall above the jarldom.
Soon their leaves grew sallow,
silently, in Russia, —
gold alone now garlands
Ingigerdh's sweet forehead.

from THE PEOPLE OF THE WIND (1973)[14]

Route Song of the Winged Folk

Light that leaps from a sun still sunken
hails the hunter at hover,
washes his wings in molten morning,
startles the stars to cover.
Blue is the bell of hollow heaven,
rung by a risen blowing.
Wide lie woodlands and mountain meadows,

great and green with their growing.
    But—look, oh, look!—
    a red ray struck
    through tattered mist.
    A broadhorn buck
    stands traitor-kissed.
    The talons crook.

Tilt through tumult of wakened wind-noise,
whining, whickering, whirly;
slip down a slantwise course of currents.
Ha, but the hunt comes early!
Poise on the pinions, take the target
there in the then of swooping—
Thrust on through by a wind-wild wingbeat,
stark the stabber comes stooping.
    The buck may pose
    for one short breath
    before it runs
    from whistling death.
    The hammer stuns.
    The talons close.

Broad and bright is the nearing noontide.
Drawn to dreamily drowsing,
shut-eyed in shade he sits now, sated.
Suddenly sounds his rousing.
Cool as the kiss of a ghost, then gusty,
rinsed by the rainfall after,
breezes brawl, and their forest fleetness
lives in leafage like laughter.
    Among the trees
    the branches shout
    and groan and throw
    themselves about.
    It's time to go.
    The talons ease.

Beat from boughs up to row through rainstreams.
Thickly thutters the thunder.
Hailwinds harried by lash of lightning
roar as they rise from under.
Blind in the black of clawing cloudbanks,
wins he his way, though slowly,
breaks their barrier, soars in sunlight.

High is heaven and holy.   50
    The glow slants gold
    caressingly
    across and through
    immensity
    of silent blue.
    The talons fold.

from THE MERMAN'S CHILDREN (1979)[15]

Song of Returnings[16]

Here may I hail you, my homeland, my heartstrand.
Well for the wanderer's weal is the way's end.
Call up the clamor on conchs and on kettles!
Stories I'll strew from the silver-paved swanroad.
Gold the dawn glittered and glad wheeled the gulls,
when—

Song of Farewells[17]

Hard is the heartbeat when loves must take leave,
Dreary the dreeing, sundered in sorrow,
Unless they part lively, unweighted by weeping,
Gallantly going and boldly abiding,
Lightened by laughter, as oftentimes erstwhile.
Help me to hope that I'll see you right soon!
I'll lend you my luck, but back must you bring it—

Sea Burial[18]

Wide shall you wander, at one with the world,
Ever the all of you eagerly errant:
Spirit in sunlight and spindrift and sea-surge,
Flesh in the fleetness of fish and fowl,
Back to the Bearer your bone and your blood-salt.
Beloved:
The sky take you.
The sea take you.
And we will remember you in the wind.

Route Song of the Greenland Whales[19]

Lead bull: —All that is life did come out of the tides
That follow the moon, as in hollowness yonder
It circles this world, and the wake of its coursing
Lays hold on the seas, draws them upward in surges
More strong than the sun can arouse from remoteness—
The sun and the moon and this globe in a ring-dance
Through measureless deeps and a spindrift of stars.

Old cows: Yes, they circle, they circle,
Like the memory held
Of a calf that has died   10
When its mother cannot
Bring herself to the weaning
And release it to swim.

Young bulls: Heavy under heaven
Heaves the main in winter;
Warm are yet the wishes
Wakened by that rushing.
Summer also sees us
Seeking for each other.
Lustily may love go.   20
Laugh in your aliveness!

Young cows: Be you the quickening light,
Be you the wind and the rain
Begetting billows.
We are the ocean and moon,
We are the tides that for aye
Renew your mother.

Calves: Brightness of salt scud,
Wings overhead, scales beneath,
Milk-white foam—new, new!   30

Old bulls: The seasons come and the seasons go,
From the depths above to the depths below,
And time will crumble our pride and grief
As the waves wear even the hardest reef.
We cruise where grazing is found far-flung
And the orcas lurk to rip loose a tongue.
Though we are they whom the waters bless,
Our bones will sink into sunlessness.
The race is old, but the world more so,

And a day must come when the whales must go.   40
The world cannot forever abide,
But a day must come of the final tide.

Old cows: Yet we have lived.

Young bulls: Yet we do live.

Calves: Yet we will live.

Young cows: Yet we make live.

Old bulls: It is enough.

Lead bull: Fare onward.

from THE BOAT OF A MILLION YEARS (1989)[20]

Starkadh's Offering

Here shall wolves not hunger.
Harald fed the ravens.
Honor won we. Only
Odin overcame us.
Ale I lack, but offer
All these foes to Harald.
Never was he niggard.
Now I've shown I'm thankful.

Autumn

Slowly the moon
Slides aloft.
Keen is its edge,
Cutting the dark.
Stars and frost,
As still as the dead,
Warn of another
Waning year.

from "THE STAR OF THE SEA" (1991)

Veleda Speaks[21]

Hear me and heed ye, highborn or lowborn,
still in your strength or stumbling graveward,

doomed to death and dreeing the weird
boldly or badly. I bid ye hearken.
When life is lost, alone is left
for yourself and your sons, what is said of you.
Doughty deeds shall never die,
but in minds of men remain forever—
night and nothingness for the names of cravens!
No good the gods will give to traitors,   10
nor aught but anger unto the slothful.
Who fears to fight will lose his freedom,
will cringe and crawl to get moldy crusts,
his children chafing in chains and shame.
Hauled into whoredom, helplessly,
his women weep. These woes are his.
Better a brand should burn his home
while he, the hero, harvests foemen
till he falls defiant and fares on skyward.

Hoofs in heaven heavily ring.   20
Lightning leaps, blazing lances.
All the earth resounds with anger.
Seas in surges smite the shores.
Now will Nerha naught more suffer.
Wrathful she rides to bring down Rome,
the war gods with her, the wolves and ravens.

from WAR OF THE GODS (1997)[22]

Skuli's Shade's Warning[23]

[To Hardgreip]

You drew me from the dead.   Now doom shall fall on you
Who haled me out of hell.   Ill hap and woe be yours.
From the mold that was mine   has your magic most foul
And cruel now called me   to come from the shades
That I answer your asking   with all that I know
Of what shall fare whence   and go whither for you.
My word is of woe   that awaits you, and death.
Unwilling I wended here,   witch, and must speak,
My tongue bearing tidings   of terrible things.
Soon hence from my house   you will hasten your steps   10
Away to a wilderness,   wandering lost
Till horror shall have you,   a hideous end.

You will wretchedly rue   the wrong that you did
In dragging the dead   from the darkness up
By trollcraft to travel   the troublous road,
Bound to your bidding.   Abide now the time
When fearsome foes   take fell revenge.
You drew me from the dead.   Now doom shall fall on you
Who haled me out of hell.   Ill hap and woe be yours.

[To Hadding]

Yet know that as the net   of night pulls close about her,   20
The fishers thereon flensing   her flesh down to the heart,
Clutching with their claws   and cutting with their teeth,
Ripping, tearing, rending   the reddened stumps and rags,
Unshaken shall your luck   still shield you from them, Hadding,
Not hurling you to hell   but holding you alive
To walk and do your work   within this world a span.
The witch must pay the weregild   for wickedness she did.
She raised me from my rest,   she robbed me of my peace,
She dared make mock of death.   To dust she shall go down.

[To Hardgreip]

You drew me from the dead.   Now doom shall fall on you   30
Who haled me out of hell.   Ill hap and woe be yours.

The Elf-Woman's Curse[24]

Sailing the sea   or seeking the land,
Henceforth you have   the hate of the elves,
And wend where you will,   the worst shall befall you
Always on earth   and also on shipboard,
Where foul winds follow   your frozen sail.
Nor shall you find shelter   ashore below roofs.
Weather brings woe,   laying waste altogether
The holdings of him   who houses you,
Till, given no guesting,   you gang alone.
Anger you earned,   all ills must you suffer.   10
He was a high one,   in the hide of a beast
Decked for this day.   To death you brought him,
The goodly godling.   Now go to your ship.
The winds are wild   that wait for you.
Her hull they will harry,   their howls will raise,
To crush your craft,   the crashing waves,
Till you rue the wrong   you wrought on the elves
And give to their god   a gild of blood.

from MOTHER OF KINGS (2001)[25]

Give to Me Your Silence

Give to me your silence.
Suttung's mead I'm pouring
to tell how Eirik bloodied
the banks of River Dvina.
Hasty on the swan's road,
sea horses bore him thither.
soon the moons of bulwarks
beckoned to Valkyries.—

NOTES

1. Anderson uses this short text as his epigraph for "Chain of Logic" (1947), his first solo-authored story. It hails from A. G. Chater's English translation of *The Long Journey* (1908–1922), a novel by Johannes V. Jensen. This author, in turn, took the text from H. G. Møller's translation into Danish of the *Elder Edda*. Anderson, however, revises several of Chater's word choices, evidently with an eye toward improving accuracy. He made further revisions when reprinting "Chain of Logic" in *Twilight World* (1961), and this is the version used here.

2. The following poem, "The Scothan Queen," is the first original alliterative poem ever published by Anderson. Dominic Flandry is attempting to seduce the queen of a space-faring barbarian people, the Scothani, by using their native "bardic" form of verse.

3. Although Anderson revised *The Broken Sword* significantly for the Ballantine Adult Fantasy Series in 1971, scholars disagree on how much improvement these revisions represent. Since the original 1954 text applies Old Norse metrics with greater fidelity, however, my following selections derive from that edition. Poems are arranged according to their order of appearance. Overall, *The Broken Sword* tells the tragic tale of Skafloc, a human fosterling exchanged at birth for a changeling and then raised by elves. In the revised edition, Anderson names the broken sword as Tyrfing, a weapon of great power, but one that will confer terrible doom upon whoever wields it.

4. In *Staves*, this selection initiates a four-stanza sequence entitled "Of the Sea." The other three stanzas—also in *The Broken Sword*—are "Clear the Day Is, Coldly," "Black and Cold, the Breakers," and "The Daughters of Ran."

5. When preparing to meet the elvish Erlking, Skafloc sings these verses to celebrate his dwarf-wrought arms and armor made of iron, a metal deadly to the elves.

6. In *Staves*, this selection initiates a four-stanza sequence called "Of the Woman." The other three stanzas—also in *The Broken Sword*—are "Laughter from Your Lips," "Luckless Is the Lad," and "Home Again the Howling." The woman in question is Freda, whom Skafloc has just rescued from her captivity among the trolls. Unbeknownst to either, Freda and Skafloc are siblings; this poem initiates their unwitting romance.

7. As the Elves prepare for the trolls to invade their country, "Fear of Fairest" bespeaks Skafloc's appreciation that Freda should worry for his safety.

8. With invasion still imminent, the elves in Lord Imric's drinking-hall request this sword dance to gauge their omens. Serving as skald is Skafloc. In the penultimate stanza, the elf-woman Leea stumbles upon hearing Skafloc refer to Freda, the "mortal may" who, being human, refuses to participate in the sword dance. Although such a misstep betokens terrible ill, Skafloc will force his tone to remain cheerful.

9. The gravemound scene in *The Broken Sword* is an extended example of pro-simetrum; only the verse is reprinted here. It begins with Skafloc seeking answers on how to reforge Tyrfing by raising the ghost of Orm the Strong and his sons—he doesn't yet know they are his original human family. Freda accompanies him. While at the gravemound they also meet Orm's still-living wife, Aelfrida, Freda's (and Ska-floc's) mother.

10. Following Ketil's advice, Skafloc borrows a ship from the Sidhe at Tir-nam-Og. As he begins his quest for the giant Bölverk, Skafloc recites both "Clear the Day Is, Coldly" and "Black and Cold, the Breakers."

11. Rán is the Norse goddess of the sea. As Skafloc—with Tyrfing newly re-forged—leads his band of elves back to England, one of their ships capsizes and sinks.

12. *The Golden Slave* is a straight historical novel—a sword-and-sorcery plot without the sorcery. It follows the exploits of Eodan, war leader of the Cimbrians. This Germanic tribe from Jutland attempted to migrate into Roman-controlled terri-tory but was devastated at the Battle of Vercellae in 101 BC. Although captured and turned into a Roman slave, Eodan eventually fights his way into becoming king of the Rukh-Ansa. In the process he loses an eye "for wisdom," thus indicating that "Eodan" is the historical human source for the Norse god Odin. Earlier, when still a Roman slave, Eodan sings this four-line Cimbrian march using the native Germanic measure.

13. Throughout the 1960s, Anderson wrote a series of "fillers"—in short, transla-tions of Old Norse skaldic poetry—for the fanzine *Amra*. The following translation, "The First Love," was originally written by Olaf Haraldsson of Norway (995–1030), also known as St. Olaf, after encountering his former betrothed Ingigerdh as an old woman. Anderson reuses this text several times in slightly modified forms. For in-stance, it appears in two different versions in *The Last Viking* trilogy (1980) and once also in *Staves*.

14. Originally serialized in *Analog Science Fiction* in 1973, *The People of the Wind* focuses on a military conflict between the Terran Empire and the Domain in Ander-son's Technic Civilization series. The novel centers around the planet Avalon, which has a mixed population of humans and Ythrians, a sentient and high-technology—yet tribal and honor-driven—avian species who has evolved self-powered flight. The character Chris Holm, a human deeply attached to Ythrian culture, translates "Route Song of the Winged Folk" (a title provided in *Staves*) from a traditional Ythrian carol. Unusually for Anderson, this poem adapts the alliterative meter experimentally to represent a far-future alien species.

15. Anderson bases *The Merman's Children* off a late medieval Danish folk ballad called "Agnete and the Merman" (*Agnete og Havmanden*). The novel builds upon

two earlier novellas, "The Merman's Children" (1973) and "The Tupilak" (1977). As in *The People of the Wind*, the poetry in *The Merman's Children* shows Anderson experimenting with how he uses the alliterative meter.

16. Three merfolk, a faerie people without souls, are returning home to their kingdom just off the shores of Denmark, but their song cuts off abruptly when Christian priests suddenly perform an exorcism.

17. In *The Merman's Children*, the merman Tauno is being forced to fight a dangerous sea monster from Inuit folklore, a tupilak. "Song of Farewells" represents his leave-taking from Eyjan, his sister and his lover.

18. Sung by dolphins, "Sea Burial" mourns the death of Kennin, a merman killed by sailors in an act of treachery.

19. Sung originally by Greenland whales, "Route Song" is a fragment translated into human speech by the merman Tauno. Anderson includes it in *Staves* with minor revisions; that is the version used here.

20. *Boat of a Million Years* follows a group of immortals over the course of several thousand years. Chapter 5 represents something of an interlude as neither Starkadh nor Gest, two Norse immortals, appear elsewhere in the novel. Both figures appear in the sagas, but Anderson takes his specific vision of Gest from Johannes V. Jensen's *The Long Journey*. In the first poem, Starkadh—a man doomed to do ill deeds— slaughters several random people in an offering to King Harald Wartooth, recently fallen in the half-legendary Battle of Brávalla (c. 770). In the second poem, Gest, a widely traveled immortal, incorporates subject matter from Japanese haiku into Old Norse *fornyrðislag* meter. The title "Starkadh's Offering" is editorial; the title "Autumn" comes from *Staves*.

21. Originally appearing in Anderson's novella "Star of the Sea" from *The Time Patrol* (1991), this poem was originally a speech in prose by Veleda, a first-century AD Germanic seeress who prophesies doom for Rome; Anderson adds line breaks for his version in *Staves*. According to the novella, Veleda is granted her prophetic powers by Nerha (Niaerdh), a fertility goddess. This is the same figure as the goddess "Nerthus" mentioned in Tacitus and, possibly, a precursor to the male Norse deity Njörd. In "Star of the Sea," Nerha belongs to a pantheon known as the Anses (an etymologically earlier version of the Æsir).

22. *War of the Gods* reconstructs—primarily from Saxo Grammaticus—the half-legendary, half-mythical life of Hadding, an ancient Danish king sometimes conflated with Njörd. Unusually for Anderson, these selections follow the Old English—not the Old Norse—alliterative line. The two principal tribes of the novel, the Danes and Jutes, share a cultural background with the Angles and Saxons. Caesuras have been added for metrical clarity.

23. Plagued by ill omens as they set out on a journey, the giantess Hardgreip, Hadding's nurse-mother with whom he has a quasi-incestuous relationship, convinces him to let her raise the ghost of a man recently dead; theoretically, the shade's knowledge will prepare them for their future hardships.

24. While out journeying, Hadding and his men kill a seal-like animal, unaware of its divinity.

25. *Mother of Kings*, a historical fantasy, is the last novel published by Anderson during his lifetime. It tells the story of Gunnhild (c. 910–c. 980), the wife of Norwegian ruler Eirik Bloodax, and includes many translations of skaldic poems. Unlike Anderson's earlier translations for *Amra*, however, his afterword describes these ones as "pretty free" and "impressionistic." Only two poems are original; Anderson attributes both to a fictional skald, Dag Audunarson, and neither wins more than faint praise. The first, "Hearken, You Who Hear Me," which here is excluded, is a partial rough draft composed by Dag in anticipation (and the hope) of Eirik's homecoming from battle; the second praises Eirik for defeating an enemy in Bjarmaland (as told in *Egil's Saga*). This second poem is complete but judged only "middling good." The phrase "Suttung's mead" refers to the Mead of Poetry guarded by Suttung's daughter Gunnlöd.

Avram Davidson

A giant of American genre fiction, particularly SF and fantasy, Avram Davidson's (1923–1993) many awards include a Hugo Award, an *Ellery Queen's Mystery Magazine* short story award, and three separate World Fantasy Awards, including one for Lifetime Achievement. Alongside Poul Anderson and others, Davidson belonged to the Swordsmen and Sorcerers' Guild of America (SAGA), an informal association of heroic fantasy authors from the 1960s. As part of this activity, Davidson contributed often to *Amra* (1959–1982), an influential fanzine dedicated to Conan fandom. There he encountered Anderson's translations of skaldic verse. In response, Davidson wrote the following good-natured parody, an alliterative poem whose humor derives from its comic deflation of heroic norms.

Lines Written By, or To, or For, or Maybe Against,
That Ignoble Old Viking, Harald Hardass,
King of the Coney and Orkney Islands[1]

Woe is me, and wella-
day, that I set dreaming.
See, the steaming turn-spit
roast the ruptured roebuck.
Mingle men with mead-horns,
horns that hoist the highest,
held in horny hand-grips.

Often, o'er the Walrus-way
went the wicked Worm-ships.

Scoffing, skim'd past Scilly-land,   10
smote the smarmy strand-folk.
Leering, lop't their limbs loose.
Debauched their daughters, drooling.

Weary, over white-weave waves,
Calmly came to Norse-land.
For the captives, cards we cut.
Glittering gold did glut us,
limber lads 'neath larch-leaves.

Pass by me now the potent pot,
venison roasts vainly.   20
With rue and grue must guzzle gruel:
Harald has the heart-burn.

—translated from the original Old High Middle
Autochthonous, by Avram Aard-vark's son

NOTE

1. "Harald Hardass" refers to Harald Sigurdsson of Norway (c. 1015–1066), arguably the most famous king in Viking history; his moniker *Hardrada* roughly translates to "hard ruler" or "stern counsel." In addition to political acumen and warcraft, Hardrada was a gifted skald; the source texts for many of Poul Anderson's *Amra* translations are attributed to him. This Norse king was widely popular within the early SFF community, too. In the fantasy prozine *Wyrd* (1973–1980), for example, which first published Paul Edwin Zimmer's *Logan*, editor Greg Stafford announces in his issue 5 editorial (1975) that "we have adopted Harald Hardrada as our spiritual advisor" (31).

L. Sprague de Camp

L. Sprague de Camp (1907–2000) wore many hats during his long and energetic writing career. Best known for pulp fantasy, especially his five Harold Shea stories co-written with Fletcher Pratt, de Camp helped spark a small boom in heroic fantasy during the 1950s. Besides his own novels and short fiction, he edited several anthologies and reprinted several highly edited versions of Robert E. Howard's Conan the Barbarian stories for Gnome Press. Nor did de Camp stop there. He wrote biographies of Howard and H. P. Lovecraft, numerous nonfiction histories, plus one of the earliest book-length studies of modern fantasy, *Literary Swordsmen and Sorcerers* (1976). De Camp dabbled in poetry, too, excelling at lighthearted comic verse with elements of fantasy. In 1982 he collected these texts into *Heroes and Hobgoblins*. The following poem, "Heldendämmerung," first appeared in the 1964 issue of *Amra*; de Camp takes the opportunity to parody Poul Anderson's skaldic translations and, of course, the famous legend of Sigurd and the dragon Fáfnir.

Heldendämmerung

Hero Bigfeet, brave and brawny,
Seeks to slay the dragon Goofnir,
For he craves the golden gewgaws
Goofnir guards through endless eons.

Bigfeet bares his burnished broadsword,
Fearsome Nothing, forged by goblins,
Razor-sharp and rune-embellished;
Thumbs it, sheaths it, straps it to him.

To the garth of Goofnir goes he;
Builds a blind and lurks behind it;
Casts a stone into the cavern;
With it roars a rousing challenge:

"Come ye forth, O lazy lizard!
Come and fight, your weird to witness!"
With a Brobdingnagian bellow,
Goofnir from his sanctum shambles.

Fire from his nostrils flaring,
Left and right his leer is ranging,
For his saucy foeman searching;
'Neath his tread the earth is trembling.

Past the hero's blind he blunders.
Bigfeet hastens out from hiding,
Drawing forth his deadly Nothing,
Falls upon the flank of Goofnir.

But, though blade of brand is flawless—
Forged of finest fairy metal—
For the hilt, to hoard a ha'penny,
Bigfeet got a cut-rate goblin.

Hilt and blade now break asunder;
Hilt in hero's hand is brandished,
Whilst the blade, with runes bedighted,
Still abides, in scabbard sticking.

Doom of Bigfeet; dragon sated.
Back into his lair he lumbers;
Belches, bends his scaly body
Round his hoard, and sinks in slumber.

Edwin Morgan

A poet laureate of Glasglow in 1999, then of Scotland itself in 2004, Edwin Morgan (1920–2010) is one of his country's most renowned poets and translators. Among his numerous honors is a Queen's Gold Medal for Poetry. Despite his mainstream credentials, though, Morgan also had a powerful guiding interest in science fiction. He contributed two poems to the first major anthology of SF verse, *Holding Your Eight Hands* (1969), and a decade later he published *Star Gate: Science Fiction Poems* (1979). Yet Morgan's concurrent fascination with literary history lends an unusual inflection to his speculative poetry. The academic critic Chris Jones calls Morgan a "medievalist as well as a futurist," a distinction he shares with Poul Anderson, a more pulp-orientated writer. In the following poem, among the best short texts of the Modern Revival, Morgan explores the processes of time, change, and literary borrowing. Words from the poem's first stage reappear, recycled, in its latter stage, but the context shifts ever so slightly. All this happens via an alliterative meter (sans alliteration) that is, itself, a recycled form. In this regard, "Spacepoem 3" invites strong comparison to Richard Wilbur's poem "Junk."

Spacepoem 3: Off Course

the golden flood   the weightless seat
the cabin song   the pitch black
the growing beard   the floating crumb
the shining rendezvous   the orbit wisecrack
the hot spacesuit   the smuggled mouth-organ
the imaginary somersault   the visionary sunrise

the turning continents   the space debris
the golden lifeline   the space walk
the crawling deltas   the camera moon
the pitch velvet   the rough sleep   10
the crackling headphone   the space silence
the turning earth   the lifeline continents
the cabin sunrise   the hot flood
the shining spacesuit   the growing moon
      the crackling somersault   the smuggled orbit
      the rough moon   the visionary rendezvous
      the weightless headphone   the cabin debris
      the floating lifeline   the pitch sleep
      the crawling camera   the turning silence
      the space crumb   the crackling beard   20
      the orbit mouth-organ   the floating song

Darrell Schweitzer

Darrell Schweitzer (b. 1952) is a writer, editor, literary critic, and part-time literary agent active in horror and dark fantasy. Among his works are eleven collections of short stories, including two set within the Cthulhu Mythos; several non-fiction collections of criticism; and four novels. Yet Schweitzer's greater legacy might well rest on his award-winning work as an editor and anthologist. In 1992, along with George H. Scithers, Schweitzer won a World Fantasy Award for editing a rebooted version of the renowned genre magazine *Weird Tales*, and Schweitzer also worked as an editorial assistant on such magazines as *Amazing Stories* and *Isaac Asimov's SF Magazine*. The following poem, "The Outcast," which Schweitzer wrote for a graduate course in medieval literature at Villanova University, presents itself as the translation of an alliterative Old English elegy. That original version included a pseudo-scholarly gloss complete with Lovecraftian references, but by the time Schweitzer reprinted his poem in *Tom O'Bedlam's Night Out* (1985), the gloss had disappeared; accordingly, Schweitzer here supplies an Editor's Note to recreate some of that original pseudo-scholarly spirit. Given that he explicitly frames "The Outcast" as a corrupted text with several anachronistic interpolations, I have refrained from my usual practice of footnoting.

The Outcast

Editor's Note. Allegedly, this poem was found in the binding of a copy of John Dee's English translation of the *Necronomicon* of Abdul Alhazred. Sources are unclear on this point, since no printing of the Dee version has ever been recorded. Presumably a bound *manuscript* is what was meant, though if such a copy exists in the library of the British Museum, the proprietors have repeatedly denied it. The use of scraps of older and discarded documents in the binding process is commonplace in older books. Many items of interest have been discovered that way.

To make matters even more confusing, the following document is in an eighteenth-century hand, and seems to be an attempted translation from a text in Old English. Some of the specific references in the poem are problematic, though, and clearly anachronistic for the Anglo-Saxon period; presumably they come from the later fourteenth-century alliterative revival. All that can be said for certain is that, unlike as with the *Necronomicon*, no one has yet gone mad studying *this* version.

—D. S.

Let us hear now of the heroes of old,
of Constantine, the Christian king,
and Arthur, wielder of the wonder-sword.

Their flesh is dust; their bones are cold;
their ghosts are gathered on the fens.

Let us tell tales of brave warriors,
of Hnæf, who held the hall,
and Ælfric, master of the sea-steeds.

Their flesh is dust; their bones are cold;
their ghosts are gathered on the fens.   10

Let us sing of poets, recall the songs,
of Cædmon, who wrought the words of man's beginning,
and Eothere, who warned the world of future woe.

Their flesh is dust; their bones are cold;
their ghosts are gathered on the fens.

My lord lies slain, his stead is burnt;
his thanes are fallen on the field;
his people cast into the dark earth-cave.

Their flesh is dust; their bones are cold;
their ghosts are gathered on the fens.   20

Alone have I lived, to wend the ways of weary exile.
I sing of the past, while foreign lords rule the land.
There is no one to listen, none who knew the days that were.

Their flesh is dust; their bones are cold;
their ghosts are gathered on the fens.

I know this: that all men shall die,
Their lives shorn short, their deeds soon done.
Soon lords and folk shall sink into sleep;
soon great shall be gone, soon lowly lost;
soon shall my foemen fall before years.   30

Soon shall I be with my lord.

Paul Edwin Zimmer (A)

Though sometimes confused with American poet Paul Zimmer (b. 1934), the fantasist Paul Edwin Zimmer (1943–1997) lobbied consistently for a reformation in contemporary poetics. Part of the Greyhaven Circle, Zimmer began as a poet before turning to fiction; his two-volume novel, *The Dark Border*, belongs among the best heroic fantasy novels of all time. Among friends and associates, though, Zimmer was a larger-than-life personality. A swordmaster and bard as well as a fantasist, he advocated for the necessity of poetry in everyday life. He had a special talent for leading Bardic Circles, and he ardently promoted oral and formal verse, especially in alliterative and Welsh meters. In 1979 Zimmer self-published a collection of Pagan poetry, *The Wine of Kvasir*, but his most important poem is easily *Logan*. This long historical work recounts the tragedy of Logan the Orator (c. 1725–1780), a Cayuga diplomat and war leader whose sad fate earned him, on the eve of the American Revolution, the horror and empathy of many colonists, including Thomas Jefferson. A famous though possibly apocryphal speech, "Logan's Lament," circulated widely among newspapers at the time. Zimmer's poem might be considered a denunciation of such sentimentalized texts as Longfellow's *The Song of Hiawatha* (1855). The second long selection, "The Complaint of Agni," is one of the earliest fantasy texts to borrow heavily from Hindu mythology.

Invocation

ᚠ Invoking the aid of Odin our Father
ᛒ And Bragi the Bard-God, the brew of dwarves,
ᚲ Poetry we pour, the potent drink.
ᚦ Quaff now this cup of Kvasir's blood![1]

R Remember the roving Rider of Yggdrasil
h Stole the stuff, to bestow on men:[2]
X The Gallows-God, in Gunnlöd's womb
P Won the wondrous wine of bards,
P And in form of feathers flew with the gift,
M The magical mead, that men might sing!   10
X Give thanks for the gift to Gauta-Týr,
F And raise now the praise of the Raven-god!

Logan

We are met upon the gravesite
Of a million murdered children;
We are met beneath the shadow
Of slaughtered women, children.
But who can count a million,
Or can mourn a hundred thousand,
When the Earth we walk is made up
Of the bones of many millions?
A multitude is faceless, and one cannot mourn
A cipher.   10
All statistics of destruction are as empty
As the sorrow that is given by convention.
Yet—
Who is there to mourn for Logan?

Now listen, ye who established the Great League![3]
Now it has grown old.
Now it is nothing but wilderness.
Ye are in your graves,
Ye who established it.

Deganoweda and Hayenwatha   20
Comb the snakes
From Atotarho's hair.[4]
The Long House reaches
From the Great Lakes to the Hudson:
Five tribes shelter
Beneath the Great Peace.
The Senecas sit at the
Western Gate;
The Cayuga between them
And the fire.   30
At the Eastern Gate

The People of the Flint,
The Canienga,
Gaze towards the ocean
Over those who call them Mohawks.
Between them and the fire
The Oneida sit.
Between the Cayuga and the Oneida
The Onondaga keep the Council fire—⁵
That was the roll of you—   40
You that combined in the work,
You that completed the work,
The Great Peace.

But the sea has coughed up thirteen tribes,
White-skinned outlaws from beyond the dawn.
Heretics and traders, convicts and slavers,
They sit themselves down by the Eastern Gate.
They trade guns for beaverskins,
They bring beads and whiskey—
Whiskey! Whiskey!   50
They eat up the land
Of the lesser tribes
(Broken peoples flock to the Long House).
The forest echoes to the drum of their axes,
And trembles to the tale of toppling timber.
Dutchmen and English,
Puritans and rogues—
They trade guns for beaverskins,
They bring beads and whiskey—
Whiskey! Whiskey!   60
They prey on the lesser tribes
And quarrel among themselves.
Catholics in Maryland,
Puritans in Plymouth,
Quakers in Penn's Woods.
Dutch, Scots, and English,
Rich men and poor—
Convicts, landed gentry—
How they hate each other!

Etho! They have no Hayenwatha: 70
The serpent locks of hatred
Must writhe and hiss uncombed.
No Deganoweda speaks to still
The ancient feuds, covering old corpses;
Singing spilled blood to silence.

They quarrel over the land
Of the lesser tribes—
For *they* lock up land in little boxes,
Plowing up their Mother
With the labour of black brother.   80
They disagree about the nature
Of a single, distant, god.
Barbarous and bloody,
Divided by hatred;
They watch and wait
By the Eastern Gate.
No Council governs them,
Keeps peace between them,
No Council speaks for them all . . .
But—   90
They have a King across the sea . . .

The King he sits in London Town,
Planning his long French war:[6]
Saying: "Indian allies we must have
To defend the American Shore.
The Hurons with the French have joined
To drive us into the sea:
We must send gifts to the Iroquois
To bind their League to me."
Messengers now come to the Long House;   100
Bearers of gifts from the English King.
Old men listen to promises of peace,
While young men listen to words of war.
Ten pounds sterling for each Huron scalp;
Paid in bright cloth and beads,
In powder and in lead, and in sharp steel hatchets.
Huron scalps are better than beaverskins!

White belts are given to the English King,
And peace, and war both made.
Frenchmen are good in stew.   110
Huron scalps are better than beaverskins:
They bring guns and hatchets,
Woven cloth and beads,
Powder, lead, and whiskey
Whiskey! Whiskey!
The Hurons are broken,
Eries and Attiwandaronks crushed.
Broken bands fly westward,
And prisoners and orphans

Absorbed by the League,   120
Adopted into the Clans:
New sons and daughters
Swell the ranks of the Five Nations—
And the League stands
More strongly than before.

Up from the south
Tuscaroras come flying—
Slavers have been hunting them,
The supply of blacks is low.
Beaded wampum figures   130
On a white wampum belt
Link hands to hold up the tree.
The youngest brother
Takes his place by the fire
To live in peace upon Oneida land:
Six Nations now, instead of Five,
The League stands
More strongly than before.
Sheltered by their treaty
With the English King,   140
Rich and powerful, strongest
Of all the tribes,
Allies now with the white-skinned folk
Who trade guns for beaverskins
And bring beads and whiskey—
Sheltered by their treaty with the English King[7]
The League stands more strongly than before. . . .

The seasons came and went, the years whirled by;
Wind Keeper drove his creatures across the land.[8]
Dead leaves scattered: so did the foes of the League.   150
Into Ireokwa hands
The Northern nations give belts of peace,
To intercede with the English King,
And stand between the White Man and the Red.
Ojibway and Chippewa,
Delaware and Shawnee,
Miami and Illinois—
All listen in silence
When Six Nations meet.
The League forbids them war;   160
Bids them grow
Three Sisters,
Corn, Squash, and Beans.[9]

Nor may they sell their land to whites
Unless the League gives leave.

Between White Man and Red, the Great League stands:
The treaty belts for all the North gathered in their hands.

But listen, ye who established the Great League!
Now it has grown old.
Now it is nothing but wilderness.   170
Ye are in your graves,
Ye who established it!

Thus it began.
The Shawnee shelter in the shadow of the Long House;
Swatana is sent, the staunch Oneida,
Legate from the League to the lesser tribes
To represent as regent Ireokwa rule
And shield the Shawnee from shady dealings,
As accredited Ambassador to the English.[10]
With him his children came,   180
Cayugas, of their mother's clan and tribe:
Tagnegtoris was the eldest;
White men called him John Shikellamy.
Sagoheyata was the youngest;
John Petty was easier on the English tongue.
And thus their brother, Soyegtowa,
Was called James Logan,
The "White Man's friend."

Upon the Ohio, old and honored,
Worn out with work for White Man and Red,   190
The ageing Oneida his ancestors met:
Swatana sought strawberries on the skybound trail.
Sing the Karenna
White Man and Red![11]
Raise the praise
Of the honoured dead.
Sing to greet and thank the League,
Sing to greet and thank his kinsmen.
Thank the men and thank the women;
Lay the wampum on the grave.   200
Swatana's sons now sorrow with the Shawnee.

Wind Keeper's wind-creatures wander across the land,
Driving years before them in a whirl of leaves.
White Bear Wind breathes winter through the trees,
Harrying wolves and bobcats south with swirling snow.

Timid Fawn Wind from the South
Breathes Spring into the green buds.
Thus seasons pass, and the selfless brothers,
The Oneida exile's offspring among the Ohio Shawnee
Fulfill their father's mission freely for the League.[12]   210
But Logan is lonely: the League far distant.
From his Cayuga kinsmen he is cut off.
His youthful years filled with the usual yearnings
The lonesome Logan longs for love.

Unlock your legs to Logan, lovely maid.
Let the sachem's[13] seed inside you
Fill you full; feel not afraid
But widen your womb for the wise and true.

Lonely no longer, let the Cayuga
Conceive him kin in your kind embrace   220
Found a family, far from Ireokwa,
Rejoice in the renewal of his race.

Babies are born of the blood of Logan,
Lonely no longer along the Ohio;
Cherished by the chieftain, his children grow,
To play in the peace his prestige has brought—
For the father never falters in his fight for peace.

Though shrewdly shielding his Shawnee charges,
He wins White friends by the wisdom of his counsel:
Wars were averted, and once, when words failed,   230
And death and destruction by deaf ears wrought,
Calm in his cabin, the Cayuga chief
Sorrowed for the slaughter and sought for peace;[14]
Well was he famed as "the White Man's friend."

Where Logan dwells along the Ohio
Peace is preserved by his prestige alone.
Peacekeeper's prize is not praise from the Council,
But the laughter of little ones who live free from war.
The Cayuga keeps peace from his care for his children.
A fond father, he forges them joy   240
Telling old tales by the twilight fires;
A legacy of legend for Logan's children,
Of husk masks and false faces,
Of stonish giants and flying heads.
He tells how He-noh, the Thunderer
Fills thirsty fields,
How gladly the Three Sisters drink rain.

Of Wind Keeper's wind-creatures, and when and why they come,
Of Onestah, corn spirit, who feeds us all.
Closely clutching their cornhusk dolls,   250
Little ones listen, alight with joy
Their wondering faces watching their father.
Old Logan lives in his children.

Ohio River, flow with tears,
For after years the blow
Will fall, and Logan sorrow know.

White Bear Wind brings winter many times,
Stalking in snowstorms the silent ice river.
Winters have whitened the warrior's locks,
And long-lived Logan, who loves his children,   260
And shields the Shawnee on the shores of the Ohio,
Their gray-haired guardian: is a grandfather now.

The Virginia governor, Lord Dunmore,
Casts covetous eyes on Ohio land.[15]
The vastness of the West impells his dreams,
And bends his mind to Westward rulership.
To rule a tract stretching from sea to sea,
Would be a post more fit for belted Earl.
What though the King has treaties made with tribes
Of red-skinned savage pagans in the North?   270
His Colonials would gladly drive them forth,
And the Crown would gain thereby. These jailbirds
With whom the King had charged him were scarce fit
To be called men: disloyalty was rife.
Already tea was floating in Boston Harbour;
Rabble-rousers ranted in the taverns
And public streets of Williamsburg itself.
Indian war would keep them occupied.
Rebels and red niggers could kill each other.
The King would come to recognize his worth.   280

That scoundrel Greathouse was the tool to use,
And that fool, Cresap[16]—needless more to choose,
The common mob would follow common ways.

Long has Logan laboured for peace,
Following his father, fulfilling his work.
As age approaches, after thirty autumns
He seems to see success surrounding him.
With English aid, an era of peace appears:
Even the Iroquois's ancient enemy sends envoys,

Cherokee chieftains, whose champions have   290
Long scoured for scalps the southern trails
Come to the Council to cover the old feud,
Singing spilled blood to silence.

Since Iroquois slew Erie on the Ohio,
Crushing the Cat-people for the King,
The Shawnee's shelter in the shady forest
A bloody battleground has been, the border of warring tribes.
With English aid the old enmity ends,
In the Western wilderness no war-band prowls.
Worn out with work for White Man and Red,   300
The diplomat Logan dreams of a dawn of peace.

Greathouse; fat, nervous, a toady born.
Dunmore hides his sneer, thinking of return
And triumphant entry into London Town.
"I thought to buy land from the Shawnee, but—"
A civilized shrug of well-bred indifference,
"They cannot sell land: the League forbids it.
No matter. The charter of the Colony
Sets our borders to North and South, but West
Our claim runs to the shores of the Spanish sea.   310
The Shawnee are but squatters on our land,
Refugees, fled from slavers further south."

With trembling voice, Greathouse dares to demur.
"But the Council claims the land by conquest,
And both Crown and law support the League!
Royal edict forbids settling their land."

The vicious, low-born dog was insolent!
Nevertheless—the perfect instrument.

"The Crown will not prefer the League to me!
I am His Highness's rightful deputy—   320
But we speak not of the League, but the Shawnee.
If they rise to contend with us in war,
Then we must defend ourselves—no more
Is needed; for surely then, we must provide—
For our defence—forts by the riverside."

Greathouse's fat face swung denial back and forth.
"No war on Whites will the Shawnee wage while,
Loyal to the League, Logan keeps the peace.
He'll complain, through the Council, to the King.
His Majesty will take the Shawnee's part,   330
And end your war before it is begun."

"*If* Logan holds them back," Lord Dunmore said,
And laughed. Why such as this was simple sport!
He would yet return in triumph to the Court.

West through the mountains march the pioneers,
Despite Royal edicts and their own fears.
A flood of White Men on Allegheny trails,
Into the vast and virgin forest home
Of bears, wolves and Indians, dreaded vermin all.
Rifles ready, settlers watch each shadow,   340
Haunting the woods with ghosts of their fears.
Greathouse, with his wagonloads of whiskey,
And Michael Cresap with his militiamen,
And land-hungry settlers from Virginia,
Seek out and cross the ford of the Ohio.
Axes resound like thunder in the woods,
As they clear away the land for cornfields.

Ohio River, sing your song,
Nor right nor wrong you bring;
Water wants not any thing.   350

Men fell trees that have stood for a hundred years.
They fear the woods; its shadow haunts their dreams.
The devils in their minds take human form,
Red-skinned, and dressed in buckskins and war paint.
Greathouse feeds their fears with tales of torture;
Of captives writhing for hours at the stake.
The vastness of the West troubles their dreams,
Women and children grow gaunt and hollow-eyed;
In the vast and virgin forest they can hear
Wind Keeper's wind-creatures wander in the trees.   360

The East wind comes as a gigantic moose,
Crashing with his antlers through tangled trees.
Blowing in fury from the lands of the League.
Their eyes dart rapidly about the forest
Their fears have haunted with a thousand shapes;
Children start and sob at the slightest sound.
And even brave men remember tales of terror
When the black wind panther howls out of the West,
Eerily in the air among the endless trees.

Cornstalk[17] comes to the cabin of Logan,   370
Talking of treachery, and treaties broken.
(On the Cayuga's wise counsel, Cornstalk,
Chief of the Shawnee, charts his people's way.)

"When White Men come, they cut down the woods!
The deer decrease, driven from the land!
Deserted beaver dams dry up;
And the folk who fill the forest vanish too.
We slew many slavers in the South, yet
Were forced to flee and find homes here.
Must we now wander wearily into the West,   380
Hungry and homeless, our hunting-grounds destroyed?
Where, Logan, is the Law of the League?
Colonists have come across the Ohio,
To the North Shore treaties ensured as Shawnee land.
Surely the Shawnee are shielded by the League?
Let the League help its loyal allies,
To defend our domain and drive out the Whites!
Or does the Cayuga still call, like a coward, for peace?"

"Choose, Shawnee Chief, your words: Cherokee scalps
My bravery in battle show beyond question.   390
Calm yourself, Cornstalk: comfort your people.
Leave to Logan, and the League, these Whites.
The power of my people will prevent further inroads.
As for these ones—these woods are wide: White Men few.
Surely the Shawnee could share a *little* land?"

"With perfidy there is no peace," the proud Shawnee replied.
"But long has Logan, and the League,
Pursued peace for my people.
Visit the Whites, vanquish them with your voice.
Yet walk, wise one, warily among them."   400

"Who is that white-haired Indian, who stands,
Palm upraised in peace, by the palisade?"
"Surely, that is Logan, the 'White Man's Friend'?"
"Shouldn't we shoot him? He leads the Shawnee."
"Not yet, you fool! Let the Captain talk first!"[18]
"Welcome him with whiskey!" comes Greathouse's voice,
"A welcome with whiskey for the White Man's friend!"
With childish glee the chieftain takes the cup,
Drinking while he confers with the Captain,
Drowning his wisdom in welcome whiskey.   410
Nervous wide-eyed women watch, picturing
Their children scalped; their cabins smouldering ash;
Themselves tied screaming to the torture-stake.
Logan drinks, and babbles, and goes home sure
That the Whites are friendly, and there'll be no war.

Even the nervous, watchful women that winter became
Inured to Indians, as, again and again,
Logan returned; they learned to laugh, saying, "Look,
Back for another bottle!" Before long,
His wife comes with the wise one, wanting whiskey,   420
Bringing her younger boy beside her, and
Big with child, a baby on her back, Logan's daughter.
At last a time when Logan cannot come:
To his Shawnee charges the chief has duties:
Without the father, his family goes to the fort.
Hurrying off happily, knowing there'll be
A welcome with whiskey for the women of Logan.
Even the babe at the breast imbibes the liquor,
His mother's milk mingled with alcohol.
Dozing, drunk in a ditch, Death comes on them.   430
Greathouse has taken Lord Dunmore's bright gold,
And now his men to earn their pay are told.
Women and children lie helpless in mud,
Hatchets and skinning-knives are stained with blood.[19]

Ohio River, flow with tears,
For after years the blow
Has fallen. Who is the foe
Of children? Who knows why their death,
Their failing breath and cry
Should be a thing gold could buy?   440

While women's wailing wounded the silence,
Cornstalk called the Cayuga Peacemaker.
He came from his cabin, and questions died on his lips.
All Logan's loved ones were laid in a row:
Bloodied bodies of babes and women.
Cornstalk cursed Cresap while the Cayuga stared.
The Chieftain's face changed with his children's death.

Ohio River flow with blood!
A raging flood to show
What seed fear and greed can sow!   450

April, seventeen seventy-four.
The beginning of Dunmore's War.
The flowers that bloomed that Spring
Fed on the blood of Logan's children:
Fed on the blood of Red and White Men:
Blood of innocence, blood of guilt—
To the flowers it tasted the same.

Who could hold back the howling avengers
When Logan leads them; no longer the White Man's friend?
Well-loved is Logan along the Ohio: 460
To Cresap's camp the crazed Cayuga
Brings torch and torture—and triumph for Dunmore.

With all Virginia's power riding to war,
This is Lord Dunmore's hour! Proud and cocksure,
He leads his soldiers through the Western hills,
To the border, where Logan kills and kills,
Mourning in madness his murdered children,
Burying in butchery and blood his grief.
Colonel Cresap's tired troop finds no relief
On their grim retreat through the tangled wood.[20]   470
Six Nations meet in Council at Thendara:
Settlers writhe screaming at the torture-stake.
Lord Dunmore swells with pride. This day is his!
Naked savages must face cannon and steel:
(He thinks of the Charter, with its great seal,
And all the wealth he could expect to flow
As soon as the valley of the Ohio
Virginian land became—and *his* domain.)
Sweeping down on the bloodstained savage hordes,
The Virginian followers of Lord Dunmore   480
Bring sabre and musket and cannon's roar.

The flowers feasted well.
Rifles and roaring cannon wreak destruction
Among charging Shawnee, and shattered they retreat.
Fallen on the field, the father of Tecumseh
Leaves hate as legacy to a later generation:
The wailing of his widow much woe shall cause.[21]

Between White Man and Red, the Great League stands;
The treaty belts for all the North gathered in their hands.
The Onondaga call the Council at Thendara: 490
Wild Seneca come from the Western Gate,
With concerned Cayuga, the kin of Logan,
And the Youngest Brother, the Tuscarora.
From their rocky homes the Oneida bring
The hymns that settlers have taught them to sing:
And from the Great League's eastern wing
Come Anglican Mohawks, loyal to the King.
Messengers now leave the Long House,
Bearing belts of peace over forest trails.

Shattered by the shells, the Shawnee gather   500
Cheerless while their chieftains choose their path.
Cornstalk comes to the Cayuga peacemaker,
Lonely old Logan, lamenting his children,
Proposing a parley for peace.
"What purpose peace with perfidy?"
The chieftain's face changed at his children's death;
Now fiercely flashes fire in his eyes.
"*I* was not at war with the White Man!
Through thirty years their throne I served
Persuading to peace the peoples of the forest.   510
Now thirty scalps I've seized to soothe my heart's aching:
But thrice thirty scalps will not thaw out my hatred!
Let us fight on forever, until fear of us
Wakes in the White Man such wailing and terror
That they board their boats, and back over the ocean go.
There is no peace with perfidy. Let us paint for war."
Cornstalk confronts the Cayuga's raving eyes.
"What, Wise One, would you have us do?
The big knife is before us.
It can kill us all.   520
Shall we *all* kill
Our women and children,
And fight on till we fall?
          No.
I shall go make peace."[22]

Ohio River, flow with tears
For all the years that no
Child of Logan's line may know.

Now messengers from the Long House come running,
With White Men, agents of the English King.   530
White wampum belts of peace are in their hands.
Between White Man and Red the Great League stands.
The royal envoys seek out Lord Dunmore
To bid him cease his cruel and bloody war.
The League looks now to Logan peace to bring:
Along the blazing border war must cease
Because the League has treaties with the King.
All his life long Logan has served that peace.
White Men have come to bring the "White Man's Friend"
To Council, so their king may deal with these   540
Troubles, and bring all warfare to an end.
To treat with Lord Dunmore is Logan's task—

Such is the message that the Sachems send:
Terms of peace he must at the parley ask.
While White Men wait, the weary chief replies:
Like moaning wind they hear his voice arise.[23]

"I ask if ever any White Man
Hungry came to the cabin of Logan,
And found not food,
Or who came naked and cold, and clothing was denied him?   550
For the length of the last long and bloody war,
Logan calmly stayed in his cabin, calling for peace.
So loyal was Logan's love for the whites
That my people pointed as they passed,
Saying, 'See, there is the friend of the White Men.'
I had thought to have lived in friendship forever,
But for the cruel deed of one man. Colonel Cresap
This last spring, in cold blood and unprovoked,
Murdered *all* of the family of Logan;
Not even sparing my women and little children.   560

There runs not a drop of my blood
In the veins of any living creature.
This called on me for revenge.
I have sought it. I have killed many:
I have thoroughly glutted my thirst for vengeance.
For my people, I rejoice at the promise of peace:
But do not think my joy the joy of fear.
Logan never felt fear.
He will not turn on his heel
To save his life.   570
Who is there to mourn for Logan?
Not one!"

Some say
That Patrick Henry wept:
And that Thomas Jefferson dabbed at his eyes
Where he sat taking notes in a corner.
To have killed the Cayuga a kindness had been:
But lonely old Logan must live six more years.

But the deed went on.
Surly Shawnee gather,   580
Refusing belts of peace
When the Onondaga call the Council at Thendara:
Demanding with red belts
A hatchet to strike the English.

Angrily the Sachems
Hurl back their belts,
And bid them till the soil.
But the Shawnee defy the League;
To seek white scalps by the side of the river.
But now the White Man's war is blooming: 590
The settlers rise against the King in war.
Virginian rebels drive out Lord Dunmore,
Who leaves, as he flees from the rioting bands,
All his gold invested in Ohio lands—
And thus fade into nothing all his plots.
Lexington farmers fire their famous shots.
Between English settler and English King
The war-belt lies, to fill the land with pain;
Partisan cries across the land loud ring.
The Onondaga call for peace in vain.   600
The almost-English Canienga bring
The red belt of war sent them by the King.
Cayuga and Seneca stalk coldly from the Council,
Vowing vengeance for Logan.
Rebel preachers have taught the Oneida well:
Who stands for the King takes the road to Hell.
He who desires to become a saint
Must fight for the Congress in his warpaint.
Thus, torn apart by the partisan calls,
Drawn into a White Man's war;   610
The League is split, the Long House falls:
The Council shall meet at Thendara no more.[24]

A new Deganoweda and Hayenwatha,
Franklin and Jefferson,
Unite the Thirteen Tribes,
To build a second Great League,
In imitation of the first . . .
But listen, ye who established the Great League!
Now it has grown old.
Now it is nothing but wilderness.   620
Ye are in your graves,
Ye who established it!

We are met upon the gravesite
Of a million murdered children.
Unknown, unnamed, unnumbered,
Their bones make up our soil.
It is their flesh that fills our gardens,

We drink the tears shed for them:
The air we breathe—their laughter!
But who can mourn an abstract?　　　　　　　　　630
Truly sorrow for the nameless?
All statistics of destruction
Are as empty as the sorrow
That is given by convention.
A multitude is faceless,
One cannot mourn a cipher, yet—

Who are *we* that mourn for Logan?

Prayer

ᚺ　Hear us, Heimdall,　and Help us now:
ᚺ　Hear and Help us,　Holy gods!
ᛏ　Triumphant Týr,　who Tied the wolf:
ᚢ　All-Father Odin,　Aid us now;
ᚦ　Thor the Driver,　Drummer of Thunder,
ᚹ　Frey and Freya,　Vanir-kin,
ᚠ　We ask your Aid in　All we do!
ᚺ　Hear us. Help now　Heimdall's Children![25]

The Complaint of Agni[26]

I am flickering fire, fiercely flashing:
Glittering God of Glowing Glory.
Hot on the hearth, the home I bless,
I force the food to fuel your body;
I light the night with gleaming beams,
Yellow gold
And jeweled red—
See now! The Demon Cold
Has fled!
Agni—Fire-God am I!　　　　　　　　　10

Light, the lightest element
Illuminates the living world:
The logs I lick to light are turned!
The body I bless whose bones are burned
And the holy soul to the skies shall rise!
Sacred Fire
Flickers with mirth!

From the funeral pyre
Find rebirth!
Agni—Soul's friend am I!   20

Mindful of my might, ye men
In wonder worship him who warms you.
But with Royal Rama wroth am I,
For Sita's sorrow sorely grieved:
He heard my word yet she mourns forlorn!
Rama's wife
My fire faced:
I spared her life
And proved her chaste.
Rama! Rama! Dare you doubt my word!   30

King Ravan raided Rama's land;
As booty bore his bride away.
With stolen Sita south he fled
To lovely Lanka, lonely island.
The wise wife found ways to bedaze him;
Woman's wiles
Turned aside his lust
With gentle smiles.
She kept her trust!
Rama! Rama! I say your wife was chaste!   40

Hanumen's host the hero followed:
Stormed the stalwart Citadel.[27]
They laid the lords of Lanka low!
Rama slew Ravan, who'd robbed him.
This brave deed saved his pride. His bride?
Custom said
If Ravan forced
Her to his bed
That she must be divorced!
Rama! Rama! Beware injustice now!   50

Sita swore she'd slept not with him:
That the ruthless rogue had raped her not.
The hero of the Hindus held his peace.
Her verity and virtue she vowed she would prove
On the fiery pyre, my justice trusting;
In raging flame
She'd risk her life
To prove no shame
Had stained his wife!
Rama! Rama! Hark the outcome well!   60

The logs were lit. She leaped on them
And prayed the pyre would prove her story.
In a flash my flames had flesh become!
I bore the bride to her bold lover.
The crowd bowed before my glory
As I swore
To Rama's face
That she was pure,
Without disgrace.
Rama! Rama! A god had told you this!   70

Men marvelled at my miracle:
Divine defense all doubt dispelled,
And home the hero humbly took her.
Restored to Rama's royal bed
The bright delight of the queen was seen.
Slander woke
Up just the same
And whispers spoke
Of hidden shame!
Rama! Rama! Will you heed god—or man?   80

Rumours reached to Rama's ears that
"Cuckold" low-caste men had called him.
In fear of the furtive, faceless whisper,
His blameless bride he banishes.
Cowed by the crowd, fearing their jeers;
Sita's pain
Will hurt him less
Than lips that stain
His worthiness!
Rama! Rama! Who is ruling whom?   90

Thus mortal men his morals rule,
And falsehood's favoured over fairness:
Sita in sorrow was sent away
To live her life in longing vainly.
A loyal royal lady paid
A people's price
For an unstained king.
A woman's sacrifice
Is but a little thing . . .
Rama! Rama! Has truth no claim?   100

His people praised Propriety:
Their joy his judgement justifying.

But remember, King Rama, the raging flame?
Your folk shall fear my fires now.
Beware! Ye who dare to share the flame!
Divine fire
Shall speak no more!
Upon the pyre
I proved her pure.
Rama! Rama! Turn to the mob for justice now! 110

My form of fire folk shall know:
I'll heat your house, from hearth aglow—
But beware the Wildfire! Words move me not!
Until Man learns mercy, miracles come no more!
Beware! Your prayers I need not heed!
Home I'll warm
And bread I'll bake—
But human form
No more I'll take!
Rama! Rama! You've sundered God and man! 120

I am flickering fire, fiercely flashing
Glittering God of Glowing Glory.
With self-righteous Rama wroth I am;
For Sita's sorrow sorely grieved.
Until justice and truth return, I'll burn
Bright and pure
And deaf and blind,
And deal no more
With humankind!
Farewell! Mankind farewell! 130

Odin's Other Eye

ᛗ Mystic Odin's missing eye   in Mímir's Well gleams:[28]
ᛉ Glows in the gloom there,   glaring through
ᛈ Wisdom's deep waters,   watching the tides
ᛗ Of Mind that move   Men's dooms.

ᛈ In the Well of the Wise,   one eye sees
ᚺ Shadow shifting to   shape the world:
ᚲ The course of the currents   causing all things;
ᚱ Rightly thus reading   the Runes of Fate.

The Skald's Appeal

ᚠ   All-Father Odin, Ale-giving god:
ᚱ   Rune-winner, Rage-giver, Rider of Yggdrasil:
ᚺ   Heavy my heart is, from hoping too long,
ᚹ   Weary with waiting for work to bring guerdon.
ᛚ   Let soon my labour with luck be assisted,
ᛗ   That all my endeavors may earn their just wage.
ᚻ   Let the Skill of the Skald—the skoal that you gave me—
ᛉ   That draught of the dwarves'-drink that dream turns to tale—
ᚱ   Reap its reward in respect and in treasure
ᚹ   To win me my wage in the world of men.   10

NOTES

1. In Norse mythology, two dwarves created the Mead of Poetry by killing Kvasir, a being of incredible wisdom created by the combined spittle of the Æsir and Vanir; these dwarves then mixed Kvasir's blood with honey. The resultant brew then came into the guardianship of Gunnlöd, the giantess daughter of the jötun Suttung, but she permitted Odin three draughts after the god slept with her on three consecutive nights. Soon afterward, Odin escaped by flying away in eagle-form. Given this myth, many different poetic periphrases exist for the Mead of Poetry: *brew of dwarves, dwarves' drink, wine of Kvasir, Kvasir's life-spoor, Kvasir's blood, Suttung's mead,* and more. There are others as well, including *Gunnlöd's lust,* but the kenning used by Zimmer in line 7, "Gunnlöd's womb," is unusual. Rather than pure lust, Zimmer may be implying that the giantess's actions are motivated by maternal desire. The first skald to receive the Mead of Poetry was Bragi Boddason from the early ninth century.

2. The "Rider of Yggdrasil" is Odin. This god has many names, and each invokes something specific about Odin's extensive—though not always self-consistent—mythological history. For instance, Yggdrasil (literally, "Odin's steed") is the cosmic world-tree that structures the Nine Worlds. The god "rode" this tree by hanging himself from a branch for nine days and nine nights, after which Odin gained knowledge of the runic alphabet. Odin is thus also associated with the gallows (e.g., "Gallows-god") and runes (e.g., "Rune-winner"). Likewise, two ravens frequently accompany Odin, Hugin ("thought") and Munin ("memory"). In addition, several sources attest "Gauta-Týr" as one of Odin's names; *gautr* means "one from Gotland." Finally, Zimmer and Diana L. Paxson both name Odin as "Rage-giver" due to his association with berserkers.

3. Also known as the Iroquois Confederacy, the "Great League of Peace" (or *Haudenosaunee,* "People of the Longhouse") bought together five distinct Indigenous nations in the New York State area. Each had their own language and territory but shared perceived ties of kinship. Running west to east between the Great Lakes to the Hudson River, these five nations (in order) were the Senecas, the Cayugas, the Onondagas, the Oneidas, and the Caniengas or Mohawks. A sixth nation, the Tusca-

rora, joined the Great League after being displaced from the Carolinas by European settlement in the early eighteenth century.

4. The Great League was founded between 1450 and 1660 by two legendary organizers, Deganoweda and Hayenwatha (or Hiawatha); the latter is different from Longfellow's Hiawatha. According to oral tradition, the major barrier to permanent peace between the nations was Chief Atotarho of the Onondaga. His hair resembled snakes due to being so excessively matted and spiky. When Deganoweda and Hayenwatha healed Atotarho's grotesque appearance in a ceremony, however, he voluntarily joined the Great League.

5. Each nation had a special role. Since the Onondaga occupied the geographic center, they were officially the League's Fire Keepers; their central village served as capital where the Grand Council was held and the wampum records kept. A character in Zimmer's fantasy novel, *The Dark Border*, bears a phonetically similar name to Onondaga: Martos of Onantuga. The "Eastern Gates" were guarded by the Canienga, or People of the Flint, but whom the neighboring Algonquins called "Mohawks"— a name that means *man-eater*.

6. At this time the English king was George II, who reigned from 1727 until 1760. The next three stanzas cover the French and Indian War (1754–1763), which was sometimes considered—at least from a European perspective—the North American theater of the Seven Years' War. In 1763, Great Britain and its Native American allies, which included the Wyandot and the Catawba as well as the Iroquois, emerged victorious. This victory greatly strengthened the Great League, especially as the Iroquoian nations customarily adopted captives, sometimes even whole villages. Notably, Deganoweda and Hayenwatha were themselves both adopted by the Canienga (Mohawks).

7. This stanza incorrectly implies that the Tuscaroras joined the Great League *after* the French and Indian War. In fact, they joined four decades earlier in 1722. Nonetheless, the war brought one major political benefit to the Great League. In 1763 the British government, hoping to protect their alliance, forbade all white settlements beyond the Appalachian Mountains. Colonists mostly ignored the order.

8. The name "Wind Keeper" refers to Gă-oh, the personification of wind in Iroquois mythology. In addition, Gă-oh controls the four cardinal winds, each associated with a particular animal: a bear (north wind), a fawn (south wind), a panther (west wind), and a moose (east wind).

9. The "Three Sisters" are three major North American staple crops—corn, squash, and beans—planted closely together in a technique known as companion planting.

10. Swatana or Shikellamy (d. 1748) was the Oneida chief and diplomat overseeing the Shawnee and Lenape, two nations in central Pennsylvania who paid the Great League tribute. He also helped maintain close ties with the British. Today, Shikellamy State Park in Pennsylvania bears his name. Accounts differ on how many children Swatana had, but Zimmer here names three sons as John Shikellamy, James Logan, and John Petty. Considering that Swatana died well before the French and Indian War began, Zimmer—despite his phrase "thus it began"—is clearly jumping backward and forward in chronological time.

11. The Karenna (or "Orenda") is an indigenous name for a kind of spiritual energy thought to inhere within people and their environment.

12. Although not literally exiled from the Oneida, Swatana spent his last few decades living among the Shawnee; reportedly, he converted to Christianity just before his passing. James Logan, who acquired his English name in honor of Secretary James Logan of Pennsylvania (1674–1751), inherited his father's mission among the Shawnee. Sometime during the 1760s, Logan migrated westward to Ohio Country, where several Shawnee and Delaware groups had already resettled due to various pressures. Once there, Logan joined several Seneca and Cayuga remnants in forming a new Iroquoian-speaking tribe, the Mingo, but this new tribe—left unnamed by Zimmer—remained closely allied with the Algonquin-speaking Shawnee and Delaware (or Lenape).

13. A *sachem* is a tribe's paramount chief.

14. This is probably a reference to Pontiac's War (1763), not the French and Indian War (1754–1763), which had ended two months earlier. In both cases, the Shawnee fought against the British, but Pontiac's War—though short-lived and localized to the Great Lakes region—was particularly bloody.

15. John Murray, fourth Earl of Dunmore (1730–1809). Dunmore became the Royal Governor of Virginia in 1771, and he set in motion policies that led to Lord Dunmore's War (May–October 1774) against the Shawnee and the Mingo. His aggression specifically contravened the Royal Proclamation of 1763, which forbade all settlements west of a line drawn along the Appalachian Mountains.

16. Daniel Greathouse (c.1752—1775) and Captain Michael Cresap (1742–1775). Greathouse's role in the Yellow Creek massacre, for which Cresap was initially blamed, helped precipitate Lord Dunmore's War.

17. Cornstalk (d. 1777) was the Shawnee's primary war chief during Lord Dunmore's War. He previously led raids during Pontiac's War.

18. The "Captain" in this case is Captain Michael Cresap. Although glossed over by Zimmer, one reason people initially blamed Cresap for the Yellow Creek massacre was because, four days earlier, Cresap and others had killed and scalped two Native Americans in a canoe along the Ohio River.

19. The massacre at Yellow Creek occurred on April 30th, 1774. For the sake of simplicity, Zimmer lists the victims as Logan's wife, son, and pregnant daughter, who was accompanied by her own suckling child. In truth, the victims were Logan's younger brother, John Petty, plus two close female relations: one of them either Logan's wife or mother, the other almost certainly Logan's pregnant sister. This sister *was* accompanied by her baby, but its father obviously wasn't Logan himself but John Gibson, a prominent American trader known widely throughout the region. This infant was the only survivor of the Yellow Creek massacre, possibly due to being half-white.

20. As noted earlier, Cresap had the rank of captain, not colonel. However, many colonial newspapers—even Logan himself in "Logan's Lament"—incorrectly conflated Michael Cresap with his famous father, Colonel Thomas Cresap (c. 1702–c. 1790). Although Colonel Cresap participated in a Maryland–Pennsylvania boundary

dispute during the 1730s later known as Cresap's War, he had nothing to do with Yellow Creek. Thendara is a location in upstate New York.

21. Tecumseh's father, Puckeshinwau, was killed on October 10, 1774, at the Battle of Point Pleasant—the only major engagement of Dunmore's War. Although Michael Cresap participated in this battle, Logan did not. After the battle, Lord Dunmore marched his troops into Ohio Country and forced Cornstalk to sue for peace. These experiences led Cornstalk to advocate for Shawnee neutrality during the American Revolution, but his execution in 1777 left the way open for Tecumseh (c. 1768–1813) to become a major driving force in Shawnee resistance against American expansionism.

22. In the Treaty of Camp Charlotte, Cornstalk ceded all Shawnee claims to the lands south of the Ohio River, mainly in modern-day Kentucky and West Virginia. Although many Shawnee rejected the treaty, they were too decentralized to resist effectively.

23. The next two stanzas transcribe "Logan's Lament" almost word for word; Zimmer modifies the text only slightly to suit his meter. This speech quickly became famous throughout the colonies. Early in 1775, James Madison sent a copy to William Bradford, printer for the *Pennsylvania Journal*, which printed the speech on February 1, 1775. Within weeks, it was picked up by several major newspapers. Thomas Jefferson himself reprinted "Logan's Lament" in its entirety for *Notes on the State of Virginia* (1782).

24. This stanza succinctly summarizes the Great League's vexed situation during the American Revolution. Neutrality was unrealistic. After being lobbied by a missionary, Reverend Samuel Kirkland, the Oneida and the Tuscarora sided with the American colonists. Unfortunately, the Cayuga, Seneca, Canienga, and Onondaga all stayed allies with Great Britain. These divisions broke the Iroquois Confederacy apart.

25. "Heimdall's Children" is a kenning for humans; the *Rígsthula* names Heimdall, the god who watches for Ragnarök while guarding the Bifröst bridge, as the progenitor of humanity. The god Týr bound the great wolf Fenrir through subterfuge and the sacrifice of his right hand.

26. In Vedic literature, the fire-god Agni is a major deity. Zimmer takes the following story probably from the *Ramayana*, one of the ancient world's longest epics. Here, Sita voluntarily undergoes a "fire test" to prove her chastity after being kidnapped by Ravana, the king of Lanka. In some versions of the story, Rama accepts Agni's judgment; in other versions, as here, Rama does not.

27. Hanumen is Rama's divine companion, whom he sends to discover Sita's whereabouts following her abduction.

28. According to the *Poetic Edda*, Mímir's well is located beneath the roots of the world-tree Yggdrasil. Its water allegedly contains great wisdom, and for a draught Odin sacrificed one of his eyes.

Robert A. Cook

Despite a life cut tragically short by skin cancer, Robert A. Cook (1950–1981) developed a considerable local reputation in the Bay Area arts scene. A graduate of San Francisco State University, Cook excelled at dramatic readings, monologues, short-verse plays, and amateur theatrical work, and he also designed elaborate masquerade costumes. His best-remembered artistic endeavors include a poetry performance he organized in the late 1970s called "A Feast of Fools," plus a chilling monologue written about an assassin for a science-fiction costume competition in October 1980. Known as "Serpent" among his friends, as in "Your obedient humble Serpent," Cook resided at Greyhaven from 1975 until his marriage in 1978. He also became a fixture at SCA events and Renaissance Faires throughout northern and southern California, where he practiced writing Renaissance and medieval verse forms. By the time of his death, Cook left several short stories, poems, and unfinished drafts of novels. All his official publications have appeared posthumously. For instance, Marion Zimmer Bradley included "Morning Song" (poem) and "The Woodcarver's Song" (short story) in her 1983 anthology *Greyhaven*, and Diana L. Paxson included (with attribution) an alternate version of "Lightning, Lightning" in her 1984 novel *Brisingamen*.

Lightning, Lightning

Lightning, Lightning, lathe the sky
with fearful flails of flame on high!
Across the domed dimension smear
      your livid laths
      in flashing paths;

the ebon els of skyway sear!
    With years of depth and darkness broken,
    raging flanks of flame betoken
Lightning, Lightning, leering gold
in hoards of treasure, tempest told!   10
Assault with blinding arcs the air;
    its grottos frame
    with gilded flame
like vaults of gold volcanic glare!
    As Giants grim with frost appall, the
    angry Hosts of Heaven call the
Lightning, Lightning's lashing ridge
before the fabled Bifrost Bridge
to fling against the frozen fields
    of Demons dread   20
    to stay their stead
as Thor his Thunder-hammer wields!
    The sages sing their stories olden;
    words of wisdom warn of golden
Lightning, Lightning, lashing high,
betrays the shattered shards of sky
to startled stars and Thunder's din,
    and ere the eye
    can dark espy
the fabric's flailed with fire again!   30
    And, long as Earthen times are told, the
    awestruck eyes below behold the
Lightning, Lightning, lathe the sky
with fearful flails of flame on high!
Its fire flung in matchless might,
    it rapes the mind
    with flames that blind
and shears the sky with swords of Light!

Diana L. Paxson

A resident of Greyhaven since its inception, Diana L. Paxson (b. 1943) has been an underappreciated influence on multiple contemporary forms of cultural activity: heroic fantasy, genre fandom, modern Heathenry, and the SCA. She first encountered "northernness" after reading Poul Anderson's *The Broken Sword* in 1954, and nine years later she discovered Tolkien through a recommendation by her college mentor, the scholar and novelist Elizabeth Pope. In 1966 Paxson earned a MA in Comparative (Medieval) Literature from UC Berkeley. That same year, on May 1, she gathered a group of science-fiction fans and other friends for a "tournament" held in her backyard—the SCA's inaugural event. Paxson's writing career, however, developed more slowly. While working on environmental education and curriculum development for Native American students in 1971, Paxson began to write fiction seriously. A decade later, her first novel appeared, *Lady of Light* (1982), an alternate future history set in the northern Californian land of Westria. More novels followed thereafter, including several collaborations with sister-in-law Marion Zimmer Bradley. Starting in the late 1970s, Paxson began devoting more attention to her Pagan spiritual leanings. In 1986 she founded the Fellowship of the Spiritual Path, and, in 1993, Paxson was made an Elder in The Troth, where she has served in multiple capacities, including as editor of its journal *Idunna*. The last few decades have seen Paxson concentrating on writing nonfiction books about Pagan lore, rituals, and spiritual practices.

from THE LORD OF HORSES (1996)[1]

Gundohar's Death Song

Slain are the warriors, shields are shattered,
Bold heroes boast on bench no more,
Nor to the fray fares the feeder of eagles,
Wound-serpents sleep in the hearts of the slain—

Red blood runs to feed the rivers,
Horses of Hun-lords trample the heroes.
Enslaved, the sons of earls, or scattered,
Wound-serpents sleep in the hearts of the slain—

The lord of peoples alone lay waiting,
Finished with fighting, the proud folk-warden.   10
Airmanareik knew his need was upon him.[2]
Wound-serpents sleep in the hearts of the slain—

Unwished the wyrd for this king woven,
His own life all he now could offer,
Given to the gods to guard his people,
Wound-serpents sleep in the hearts of the slain—

Sigfrid also, the son of Sigmund,
Fáfnir he fought and fearless, felled him,
Won from the Wurm a wondrous hoard,
Wound-serpents sleep in the hearts of the slain—   20

Happy the hero when all men hailed him,
Woeful the wolf by Wyrd ensnared,
The Leaf King's life blood fed the leaves
Wound-serpents sleep in the hearts of the slain—

Upon the Tree the truest traitor,
The spearman speared in sacrifice.
Hagano's heart a holy harvest,
Wound-serpents sleep in the hearts of the slain—

Beneath the ground the Gundwurm guests,
By serpents circled, I sit and sing   30
To win from Wyrd a warrior's mead."
Wound-serpents sleep in the hearts of the slain—

Wodan's will the word-hoard opens—
Brew of bards to banquet brings,
All-father bears me ale from Asgard.
Wound-serpents sleep in the hearts of the slain—

Idisi come, my days are ended,
Fearless, I follow fallen heroes.[3]
Life I will let go with laughter,
A wound-serpent sleeps in the heart of the slain—   40

from BRISINGAMEN (1984)[4]

For the Goddess Freyja[5]

Hail Freyja! All hail to the goddess,
    Highest and holiest, hail!
Brisingamen's bearer, Bride of the Vanir,
    We boldly bespeak thee now.
Whiter thy arms than snow in the winter,
    Shining in the sun;
Brighter thy eyes than the bridge of Bifröst,
    That bears to Valhalla the gods.
Gefn the giver, gold-bright goddess,
    Grant us thy favor now,   10
There where thou sittest in splendid Sessrúmnir;
    Linen-clothed Lady of Love,
Hörn we name thee; Heið the Wise One;
    And Heiðrún, she-goat of the gods.
As Sýr we salute thee, Hildisvíni's rider,
    Boar-Ottar's savior art thou. . . .

Gullveig the golden, fast bound in the flames,
    Re-forged thou thy fate in the fire.
From thy falcon-form a feather, from thy felines a whisker,
    Give thou to keep us from fear.   20
Mardöll of the waters, mighty thy beauty,
    Mistress of gods and men;
Mare of the Vanir, as Göndul dost thou gallop,
    Bearing kings from the battlefield.
Dealer of death, kind is thy embrace,
    But in the earth-womb's darkness,
Lady of Life, light dost thou kindle—
    Goddess, show us thy glory!

from MASTER OF EARTH AND WATER (1993)[6]

Beltane

Beltane, oh Beltane, blossoming beauty!
At new day the blackbirds burst into song!

The strong sturdy cuckoo sings welcome to summer,
calmed are the harsh winds that brought branches down.

Summer shrinks streamlets, swift horses seek water,
Wild hair of the heather and white bog-down lengthens,
Strengthens the sea swell, soothing sleep bearing,
Deer browse the whitethorn, and flowers fold the world.

Golden the burden of blossom that bees bring,
A king's feast the ant finds, kine to the hills fare.   10
Where peace fills the woodland, soft the wind's harp plays,
A haze on the cool lake, colors blaze on each hill.

Swallows soar circling the hillside with sweet sound,
Abounding with fruit the tree: quagmire's mud chatters.
Swamp water like ravens' wings shining, a wonder,
Yonder the speckled fish leaps from the stream.

Warriors wax in their boldness, maidens in majesty,
Trees in their fullness, wheat stalks strive sunward.
Done is wild winter when white was each oak bough.
Now find we fair seasons, and peace and good cheer.   20

Graceful, birds settle, the white streams rush wildly,
Through green fields the hosts march, bold riders are racing;
Tracing the bright shaft shot into the landscape,
And the water flags, sunstruck, explode into gold.

Though fearful, the wren is persistent, proclaiming
The name that the high flying lark can cry clear.
Hear how the stutterer sings the glad tidings,
Abiding in beauty, blest Beltane is here.

—attributed to Fionn mac Cumhal
freely translated

from HRAFNAR KINDRED RITUAL RESOURCES (previously unpublished)

To the Earth[7]

Erce, erce, erce, eorþan mōdor.
Rooted, we reach for ancient wisdom;
Strength we draw from sacred soil.
Nerthus, now our need is near us,
Honor we offer—a holy harvest.
Bring forth in beauty, Bride and Mother—
Goodly gifts for the kin of Ríg,
Mother Earth, we hail thee!

To Idunna[8]

Holy fruit, in Asgard's heart hid,
Grows in Idunna's girded garth:
In leafless trees life is renewed,
Silver blossoms star bare branches,
Golden the apples given to gods,
Sweet the fruit with its secret seeds.

In Midgard's mirk, men wake from madness:
In fields a thousand years left fallow,
Sleeping seeds at last are sprouting—
Idunna, see the new day dawning,   10
Bear to us thy branch of blessings,
a tree of troth to bless the true.

To Heimdallr[9]

Now may the bridge of Bifröst bear us
To blessed heights of Himinbjörg,
Where Ríg reclines in rainbow radiance,
To watch and ward the blessed gods.
Lest cliff-thurs climb to holy haven,
Thy sword-bright brow blazes in heaven.
Offspring of Ægir's white-tressed daughters,
Ram of the Ninth Wave, with awe we regard thee,
Thy beauty and brightness bless the world.
Watch our works, to our words, bear witness,   10
Father of Humankind, help when we hail thee!

To Freyr and Freyja

Lord and Lady, loudly we call you,
Fertile Freyr and Freyja, brother and bride.
Luck-bringers, lustily giving Earth goodness,
Hear us as we hail you, hither to help us!
Grateful, our gifts to the givers we offer—
Wunjo's wonder we exchange.
In man and maid we make you welcome.
Join us in Joy, fair Lord and Lady!

To Thor[10]

Redbeard, firebeard,   bringer of Lightning,
Life-giving stormlord,   lover of feasting,
Father of freedom,   fighter most doughty,
Donar, defender,   dearly we need thee.
Hear us now, hero,   hasten to help us.
Gifts thy great goats   gallop to bring.
Prosper thy people: pour on earth plenty,
Rain as is needed,   right for the season!

To Frigga[11]

Frigga, fair one, fate all-knowing,
Bright is thy beauty as the white birch tree.
Wyrd the Norns spin, wisely weaving,
Queen over Asgard, in thy arms All-father lies.
Twelve mighty maidens circle about thee,
Torches bright around a hearthfire,
Rivers flowing from a well:
Radiant lady, ram-cart riding,
Bless the mother and the maiden,
The new-born babe, the blood of women.   10
Mother of Mysteries, make us wise!

To Odin[12]

Odin, Óski, Wotan, Wunjo!
Of all that lives, the truest lover,
Sender of Önd, thyself once offered,
Greatest of gifts and greatest giver,
Now open Ódhroerir's ecstasy:
Rider of Yggdrasil, Runes releasing,
Bragi's brew on bards bestowing,
To thy delight let us drink deeply—
All-father, to our feast be welcome!

To Odin, for Rain

Wotan, wish-lord, well beloved,
Opener of Ódhroerir's ecstasy,
Rain clouds bring us, Ruler of Weather,

Pouring out thy power from the skies;
Viðrir, Veratýr, for this we venerate you,
Thund, thrice-holy, we thank you for this rain.[13]

Poem for a Heathen Funeral, in Honor of Paul Edwin Zimmer[14]

All-father Odin, Ale-Giving God!
Rage-giver, Rune-winner, Rider of Yggdrasil!
Guard now and guide to glee in Valhalla
The rider who fares on Rainbow Bridge.
For nine nights' knowledge, on Yggdrasil,
You, Odin, the doom of death endured:
Worldtree Warrior, wisdom-winner,
Through spell and shadow lead the lost one—
Lead home to the feast, fastest far-farer,
The swordsman who strides over Rainbow Bridge!   10
This Bragi-blessed warrior whose name we call!
Edwin! Prepared is your place at the feast!
Unveiled Valkyries the veteran greet;
Let beer now flow freely from barrels,
As the Hero's Portion you divide!
From wandering to wonder, from woe to bliss,
From Midgard's madness, hard on heroes,
Enter another on the Einherior's roll!
Welcome the wanderer to Warrior's Hall!

NOTES

1. In the *Wodan's Children* trilogy (1993–1996), Paxson tells of the bloodiest and most tragic tale in Norse legend: the story of the Völsungs. Her second installment, *The Dragon of the Rhine*, recounts how the hero Sigfrid (Sigurd), who has already slain the dragon Fáfnir and taken the cursed gold of the Niflungar (Niflungs), is murdered by two brothers of his wife, Gudrun. One of these brothers is Gundohar, King of the Burgundians and a poet. In Paxson's third novel, *The Lord of Horses*, she recounts the tragic events—many fused with real history—that later turned into Norse legend. The "lord of horses" is Attila, khan of the Western Huns. To him Gundohar marries off his widowed sister Gudrun, who is still grieving Sigfrid's murder, as a means for ensuring peace, but this peace eventually fails. In 435 AD, Gundohar leads the Burgundians westward, hoping for land, but is crushed by the Romans. Two years later, the Huns invade and destroy the Burgundian kingdom. In Paxson's novel, Attila captures Gundohar and his brother Hagano. Although Gudrun slays the latter, her new husband, Attila, due to having sworn brotherhood with Gundohar, cannot kill

the Burgundian king directly, so he throws Gundohar into a pit of adders. Gudrun, sickened with guilt, throws a harp down to her doomed brother, who plays the following death song.

2. Airmanareik (or Ermanaric) was a third-century king of the Goths. After his defeat by the Huns, he commits suicide.

3. The *idisi* (singular *idis*) are female deities occasionally known as the *dísir*. Unlike other Norse female deities like the Valkyries, *idisi* have no firm role, but they are sometimes—as here—associated with the dead.

4. Brisingamen ("necklace of the Brísings") is a wonderous item owned by the goddess Freyja but deeply coveted by Loki, the trickster god. In Paxson's novel, *Brisingamen*, the necklace is recovered by Karen Ingold; it is then stolen by a traumatized Vietnam veteran, an avatar of Loki, who uses it to initiate Ragnarök. In desperation, Karen—herself an avatar for Freyja—performs the following *seid*, a magic reserved for witches, to gain the goddess's aid in unveiling Loki's location and, therefore, in finding Freyja's necklace.

5. Freyja is the Norse goddess most celebrated in modern Neo-Paganism, and Paxson's following text invokes many of the goddess's attributes. Love and sex are her special purviews; indeed, several times throughout *Brisingamen* the goddess utilizes her avatar, Karen Ingold, for such activities. Freyja abides in the hall Sessrúmnir; travels in a chariot drawn by cats; and wears a cloak made from falcon-feathers. She goes by many names. Several are cited here: *Gefn* ("one who gives"), *Hörn* (possibly "flaxen"), *Mardöll* ("brightener of the sea"), and a name associated with a pig cultus, *Sýr* ("sow"). Although the name *Heið* (or *Heid*, "brightness") is often attributed to Gullveig, a shadowy figure in *Völuspá* who instigates a war between Æsir and Vanir, Gullveig is also sometimes—as here—equated with Freyja herself. In addition to cat-drawn chariots, Freyja, through her association with war, rides a boar named Hildisvíni. Alongside Odin, Freyja claims half those slain in battle, and in this context Paxson's verse equates Freyja with *Göndul*, a Valkyrie attested in Snorri's *Heimskringla*.

The name *Heiðrún* (or *Heidrún*) normally refers to a mythical goat who provides the *einherjar* (i.e., those slain in battle) with mead through its udders; the giantess Hyndla uses this term to insult Freyja in the *Hyndluljóð*. This same poem reveals the ancestry of Ottar, one of Freyja's favorites, whom Freyja once disguises as her battle-boar Hildisvíni.

6. *Master of Earth and Water* is the first book in Paxson and Adrienne Martine-Barnes's *Chronicles of Fionn mac Cumhal* trilogy (1993–1995), and it traces the boyhood deeds of Fionn mac Cumhal, a folkloric outlaw hero and poet from Irish mythology. Near the novel's end, Fionn tastes the Salmon of Wisdom, and is soon overwhelmed by the following poem about Beltane—a Gaelic May Day festival celebrating the start of summer.

7. The following ritual invocations all pertain to the *minnisveig*. Paxson describes this ritual in *Odin: Ecstasy, Runes, & Norse Magic* (2017): before drinking from the horn, each person should express gratitude to the gods in an appropriate prayer. When the circle has passed the horn around, any remaining liquid should be poured into an offering bowl. The ritual's opening line recalls the Old English charm *Æcerbot*

("Land Remedy") from the eleventh century. Nerthus is a Germanic fertility goddess, and "kin of Ríg" (i.e., Heimdall) is a kenning for humanity.

8. Idunna ("rejuvenator") is the Norse goddess who tends the apples the Æsir eat to maintain their youth; Loki lures both Idunna and her fruit away, but the Æsir eventually enjoin him to return Idunna to her proper duties.

9. In her book *Odin*, Paxson writes, "Heimdall [or Ríg] may be invoked as Guardian of the Gate who opens the way to the gods, as Defender of Freyja, as Watcher of the Gods who sees and hears all, as son of the nine waves, as the Ram, and especially as the Father of Humankind" (307). His home, Himinbjörg, is near the Bifröst Bridge. Heimdall is frequently associated with rams, and it was said that he was birthed by nine mothers, all of them daughters of Rán and her husband, Ægir, a sea-giant.

10. Thor is also named *Donar* in Old High German; his chariot is drawn by two goats, Tanngrísnir and Tanngnjóst.

11. According to Paxson, Odin's wife, Frigga (or Frigg), is invoked as the All-mother, queen of the gods, source of wisdom and love, guardian of the home, and the sacred center from whom serenity is drawn.

12. Both this invocation and the next two reference different aspects of Odin. According to Paxson in *Odin*, they invoke "Odin as Giver of the Runes, of the Poetic Mead, and of Ecstasy. Call him Oski, Fulfiller of Desire, and Wunsch—Wishlord. Pass the rune cup around after the horn, and let each one draw a rune for the next person in the circle. After the horn has gone completely around, allow a few moments of silent contemplation in which to savor the bliss of the presence of the gods" (309). Ódhroerir (or Ódrerir) is one of the three vessels containing the Mead of Poetry, which Odin stole from the giantess Gunnlöd. The term *önd* can be translated as "spirit," "soul," or "breath"; Odin bestows *önd* upon Ask and Embla in *Völuspá* 18.

13. *Viðrir* ("stormer"), *Veratýr* ("god of men"), and *Thund* ("rumbler") all invoke different aspects of Odin.

14. Paxson writes in *Odin* that this verse expresses "my understanding of Valhalla. Paul, a swordsman, poet, and writer of heroic fiction, knew Odin long before I did and helped me understand him from a male perspective as well as from my own" (204). The Einherior (or *einherjar*) are the slain warriors who prepare for Ragnarök.

Part II

SOCIETY FOR
CREATIVE ANACHRONISM

Anne Etkin

Anne Etkin was a longtime member of several speculative fandoms, including the Tolkien Society, the Society for Creative Anachronism, and the Markland Medieval Mercenary Militia. Known as Anne of Briar Ditch, she published throughout the 1970s several poems in Tolkien-related fan venues such as *Orcrist* and *Mallorn*, but Etkin also made a lasting contribution to Tolkien scholarship (then in its barest infancy) when she published *Eglerio! In Praise of Tolkien* (1978), a collection of essays, letters, photographs, and other content. The following poem, "Merlin's Dreme," appeared in the summer of 1974. An innovative attempt at mixing alliterative patterning with various devices common to accentual-syllabic poetics, this text deftly captures the sense of fun and sheer exuberance that marked the early SCA.

Merlin's Dreme:
(A Vision of the Nineteen-Seventies)

A dream I dreamed, and deemed I stood
In a far-off land, in a far-off time,
Beyond our days, beyond our shores,
With Chivalry in shadow lying.

Ruined the towers, rotting plundered,
Lost the lay and lost the englyn,[1]
Knights no more and knaves as lords,
With castles gone and caitiffs spying.

✼

A bugle blew, and bravely then
A proud parade appeared afar,   10
A winking, glorious, glittering train,
With heraldry now hither hieing.

Hear fair banter: "Hakke hem
To gobbetys, my gude King,"
A huntsman cried; and harpers played
Old lays of lords and ladies sighing.

Sighs were lost in singing, laughter,
Speech of koomis,² sack and mead,
Of crafts, the deeds of cunning hands,
Of knights in combat nobly vying.   20

All around was wretched chaos,
Reeking fumes that fouled the sky;
They sought the woods, with scarlet, vair,³
And blue and golden banners flying.

"Cook and brew!" I cried aloud.
"Sling your shields and swing your swords!
Sing and play and sip and feast!
Whirl and dance, your world defying!"

In hope I woke: no world is lost
To noisy speed and sordid smoke,   30
While one anachronistic crew
Keeps solid splendor still undying!

—Merlin
as told to Anne of Briar Ditch

NOTES

1. An *englyn* is an epigrammatic quatrain in Welsh and Cornish poetry that uses both rhyme and half-rhyme.

2. Koomis is a fermented dairy product using mare's milk.

3. After ermine, vair is the second most common type of fur (specifically squirrel) used in medieval heraldry.

Paul Edwin Zimmer (B)

Unlike his friend Poul Anderson, who was older, Paul Edwin Zimmer (1943–1997) had an early writing career that coincided with the advent of the Society for Creative Anachronism. Known as Master Edwin Bersark, he made his first publication—a non-alliterative translation of "The Battle of Brunan Burg"—in a 1972 issue of *Tournaments Illuminated*; this translation won first prize in its category that year. As Zimmer grew more deeply involved with the SCA, he continued to publish articles in *Tournaments Illuminated*. Many are short nonfiction manuals on fighting technique; one of his students, in fact, was David Friedman. But Zimmer also actively discussed alliterative poetics. In the following selection, "The Son of Harold's Hoarfrost," Zimmer teases the "bee-chasing bard" of Markland, Jere Fleck, whose nickname, "Bassi," means "great bearlike creature" in Old Norse, for the complexity of his skaldic poetry.

The Son of Harold's Hoarfrost

The bee-chasing Bard should   beware of the frost:
Hairy Ursoid Haraldsson   has hoarfrost in his poems!
The runes he writes, with   rime all a-glitter,
Are Icelandic to excess,   and over-ornate:
Poor Kvasir is cold in   such Celtic adornment:
Has wise one-eyed Woden   with whiskey far-fetched
Mingled his Mead, that   the Markland bards, maddened
Freeze verses in frost?   O Furry Bee-hunter!
Early in Ireland   Yggdrasil's Rider
Gave to the Gael-speech   the glittering frost.   10
Beware of this booty from   beautiful Erin:
Freeze not in frost-flakes   Fenris-Foe's Gift![1]

NOTE

1. For the story of Kvasir and the Mead of Poetry, see the footnote to Zimmer's poem "Invocation." The name *Woden* is an alternate form of "Odin," who is also "Yggdrasil's Rider." The name "Erin" (from the Irish *Éirinn*) refers to Ireland. The kenning "Fenris-Foe's Gift" refers to poetry. The enemy of the great wolf Fenrir is Odin, and it was Odin who gifted the Mead of Poetry (after stealing it) to mankind.

Jere Fleck

Jere Fleck (1935–2017) considered himself neither a poet nor a member of contemporary fandom; in fact, he never even read Tolkien. Instead, Fleck entered the Modern Alliterative Revival almost by accident. As a professor of Scandinavian and German Studies at the University of Maryland, College Park, Fleck built a strong scholarly reputation with articles on Odin's self-sacrifice, Germanic shamanism, and sacred kinship. In addition, though, he advised a newly formed UMD student group, the Maryland (later Markland) Medieval Mercenary Militia. As their faculty advisor, Fleck adopted the role of *þulr*, or priest, of Odin; he set the wording for Markland's coronation and wedding oaths, and once the group incorporated as Hall of the True Gods, which semi-playfully dedicated itself to the Norse deities, Fleck even performed weddings. This was one way in which Fleck helped sustain rituals and traditions reflecting the spiritual, intellectual, and artistic aspects of the medieval centuries he studied. Another way was poetry.

After Markland discovered the neighboring East Kingdom in the early 1970s, it found another fruitful catalyst for its medievalism. At several special SCA events and feasts, Fleck would deliver a long commemorative poem or *drápa* as "Geirr Bassi Haraldsson." Despite Fleck's amateur status, these poems rank among the Modern Revival's most ambitious productions, reviving the long-lost aesthetic of lengthy, narratively balanced skaldic poems intended for courtly settings. Yet, like SCA poetry in general, Fleck's verse places many demands on its listeners. Accordingly, when Fleck published his *drápur* in *Tournaments Illuminated*, he included extensive prose commentaries guiding readers through his many allusions, kennings, and specialized language. In the selections that follow, a short descriptor on the right mimics the effect of these commentaries, and I follow Fleck's practice of numbering each stanza.

Ode to the Two Earls[1]
(*Tveggja Jarla Drápa*)

1 Hearken, all who hear me,
    Heimdall's fame-filled children;
    men at mead-þing gathered,
    maids at ale-feast, hail ye!
    Still stand foaming drink-horns,
    stay the tongue's loud word-play!
    Better beer brings Óðinn:[2]
    brew of skillful tale-skálds.

Stanzas 1–2. Bassi calls for a hearing.

2 Hail, twin lords twice welcome,
    two-fold high-seat holders
    gifts' free-handed givers
    gold-rings break full boldly!
    Hail, all Miðgard's mead-lord,
    mighty Húnar-Atli!
    Here amidst his hirðsmen,
    hail, Jarl Ragnarr argr![3]

3 Warrior guests at wassail,
    well the bane of slain men,
    —friends are half to Freyja,
    Frigg's love's host grows bigger—
    mead-thief's gore-feast givers,
    greedy witch-steed feeders,
    shields have split and shattered,
    shed the strife-tooth's red'ner.[4]

Stanzas 3–4. The male guests are praised.

4 Far o'er grim Rán's foam-road
    —flee, all pale Christ's troth-thralls!—
    River Severn's raiders
    ride on wave-steed *Sae Earn*.[5]
    Hail, all Miðgard's mead-lord,
    mighty Húnar-Atli!
    Here amidst his hirðsmen,
    hail, Jarl Ragnarr argr!

5 Miðgard's hearty maidens
    mead at board afforded,
    —braid-trees are beer-bringers,
    blood-axe wielders seldom—
    but our maids in battle
    blades have oft times softened;
    only woe men won then,
    wounds their only boon fee.

Stanzas 5–6. The female guests are honored.

6   This eve sharpened iron has
all but cooks forgotten;
fair breasts and not spear-blades
bear our land's brooch-wearers.
Hail, all Miðgard's mead-lord,
mighty Húnar-Atli!
Here amidst his hirðsmen,
hail, Jarl Ragnarr argr!

7   Then their lords were trothless
laying all their faith in
oak-trees, artless druids,
or the meek one's weakness.
Now they bow to Njǫrðr,
kneel to Freyr and Freyja,
thanks they give to Sif and
Þórr, the Æsir warrior,

Stanzas 7–8. Bassi reflects on the Militia's past conversion to the true Norse gods.

8   begging boons of Frigg and
Baldr, Nanna's husband;
all their troth is Óðinn's,
All-Father's in Valhǫll![6]
Hail, all Miðgard's mead-lord,
mighty Húnar-Atli!
Here amidst his hirðsmen,
hail, Jarl Ragnarr argr!

9   Yester-year I yoked our
Jarl Ragnarr to Qlrún,
bonded both their bodies,
bedded them in wedlock;
Bassi's þulr-blessing
brings them kingly riches:
Óðinn's lore, Þórr's friendship,
love-play's fee from Freyr.

Stanzas 9–10. The poet discusses Ragnarr's past wedding before mentioning Atli's current wedding.

10   Once again a war-lord's
wedding has been readied;
once again the words of
weal now all are spoken.
Hail, all Miðgard's mead-lord,
mighty Húnar-Atli!
Here amidst his hirðsmen,
hail, Jarl Ragnarr argr!

11   Rise now, all our rime-bards,
raise each voice in praises;
word-smiths met in song-meet,

Stanzas 11–12. Bassi calls for other skalds to add their praises to his own.

singers called to skáld-þing;
fare all forth to gold-gains,
forward toward your war-lords
wend your splendid word-swords,
wield the tongue's wild shield-banes!

12   Pass us Gunnlǫg's lust-pay,
pour out Kvasir's life-spoor;[7]
follow Bassi's foot-fall,
fellow rime-rich spell-wrights!
Hail, all Miðgard's mead-lord,
mighty Húnar-Atli!
Here amidst his hirðsmen,
hail, Jarl Ragnarr argr!

Coronation Ode[8]
(*Konungsvígsludrápa*)

1   Welcome all, full welcome
worthy lords of Austmǫrk,
mighty battle-makers,
marshals of war's sword-play
—shield-splitters, gore-spillers,
spear-shakers, skull-breakers—
stay the awesome strife-tooth,
still list Bassi's skald-skill!

2   And ere all else, welcome
Austmǫrk's maids and ladies,
comely hearth-fire kindlers
clad in gladsome clothing
—seam-stitchers, blood-stemmers,
steer-stewers, beer-brewers—
halt your rede and hear me,
hark the skald and mark me!

3   From afar and near ye
fared to share our feasting,
braving gale and billow
bound o'er mount and meadow;
Eastland's earls and jarls have
all been called to witness
Aonghais, Austmǫrk's king, and
Ysabeau crowned in Markland.

Stanzas 1–3 (proem). The
traditional welcome; Bassi
requests his audience's attention
and discloses the occasion for
this drápa.

4 Woe, that far too short was
ward of lordly Ásbjǫrn!
But few months abode fair
Brekke, Eastland's lady;
sad this skald to see so
soon that kingship ended:
both Ásbjǫrn and Bassi
bears are of the Æsir.[9]

Stanzas 4–7. Recent background in the East Kingdom, and the peaceful transfer of power (and religions).

5 Oft in war were weighed the
worth of Celt and Northman,
—winner once was Óðin,
once the Southland's pale one—
Thus this day Jarl Ásbjǫrn
Austmǫrk's crown laid down and
Eastland's king became the
Creachainn's clansman Aonghais.

6 Castle Craigburn's master
carried off to marry
Lochiel's blue-eyed lady;[10]
long on lonely Treshnesh
held her close confined and
kept her kinsfolk captive
—Donal and Dyannae—
dealt them heartfelt courtesy.

7 Now blood-feud forgiving,
fulsome wrath forswearing,
bound by bonds of friendship,
barred from further warring,
shed all anger's shadow,
share one throne between them:
*Aonghais, Austmǫrk's king, and
Ysabeau crowned in Markland.*

8 Well this hall was chosen
—weal it lends your dealings—
could in all wide Austmǫrk
other stead be better?
Oft its rafters rang with
roaring horns to Óðin,
proud lords loudly proffered
prayers to Þór and Freyr.

Stanzas 8–9. Bassi reflects on their current location, which housed the wedding described in "Ode to the Two Earls."

9 Oft this hall was hallowed,
holy oaths here trothed,

many a heady mead-moot
Markland's jarls here hosted;
wedded here were Ragnar
—warlord he—and Atli,
Bassi bade to wassail,
blessed the festive bridesfolk.

10   Bare the feast where barred is
beer and ale for wassail,
ill-made is the meal where
meat and bread not ready,
sad the throng where singers'
songs do not belong and
barren is that board where
bards' art not afforded.

11   Kings give golden rings to
Carolingia's singers,
oft is speech-craft's ale to
Østgarð's bards awarded,
Bragi's art is bragged by
Bhakail's proud song-makers,
muckle spells are milled by
Myrkwood's word-ore workers.[11]

12   Poet's ale stole Óðin,
eagle-winged, hence bringing
Gunnlǫð's mead to Markland
—mighty drink of singers—
beer-rain fell—a few have
found the rhymester's bounty—
Markland's skalds drink deep of
draughts brought us by Bǫlverk.

13   Rede-smith's skill bought Bragi
berth midst Ásgarð's worthies;
mankind's first skald's thirst for
mead ne'er goes unheeded.
Hár spake: "Tongue is head's bane";
head-geld once paid Egil's,
freed from Eirík's fury,
for fair words rewarded.[12]

14   Thus Þórbjǫrn hornklofi,
Þjóðolf sang, and Þormóð,
Einar, aye and Eyvind,
Arnór Þórðarson and
Gísli, aye and Grettir,

*Stanzas 10–12. Bassi begins his
central theme: the praise of the
skaldic art. He suggests that the
Mead of Poetry belongs to East
Kingdom poets since they alone
practice the skaldic art.*

*Stanzas 13–15. Bassi discourses
upon the greatest Norse skalds.*

Gunnlaug ormstunga and
Harald king hárfagri,
Harald king harðráði.[13]

15   Wealth of skaldic wisdom,
     word-craft's lore knew Snorri,
     how each hight with *heiti*
     —high, on earth, in Hel's realm—
     how to ken the cunning
     kenning's hidden meaning;
     word and deed he wills us
     well with Edda-telling.

16   Behold here skalddom's houses: *Stanza 16. An extended*
     halls within each fourfold,   *metaphor describing the*
     every hall is even   *complex* dróttkvætt *form.*
     —each twice six feet reaches—
     yet each hall shall harbor
     high-seats three to seat ye,
     but in each hall benches,
     beds aye two stand ready.

17   "Wealth will wane and kin will   *Stanzas 17–18. Bassi observes*
     wither in death as you shall;   *that only the skaldic art can*
     nought but man's good name may   *preserve the immortal fame*
     ne'er die," quoth the High One.[14]   *of royalty.*
     Who shall speak that name-spell,
     spread, though dead, good tiding?
     Hail the skald whose craft can
     hold man's soul through word-skill!

18   As long as lords still yearn to
     live in song forever,
     as long as mind of man still
     marks what bards have spoken,
     folk shall not forget this
     feast, nor least, its purpose:
     Aonghais, Austmǫrk's king, and
     Ysabeau crowned in Markland!

Dream Ode in Long Lines[15]
(*Draumdrápa hrynhend*)

1   Heed, my deed-proud Jarl, and hearken,   *Stanzas 1–2. The proem lasts*
     hear this weird, Laird of the Steer's Head! *four lines before turning quickly*
     Fund of wonder will I ponder,   *to Bassi's dream vision.*
     word-spell well worth skald-skill's telling:

stark and dark this lore-rich story,
stern, returned from fearsome journey,
forth from hearth in Miðgarðr faring,
far this bard in dreamworld wandered.

2   Not, I wot, by strong-beamed longship,
nor on four-hoofed steed's back speeding,
not by sled nor yet by roadway,
nearing neither strand nor landing;
deathlike, breathless, darkly dreaming,
deep in chilling stillness sinking,
saw my eye a solemn sign, a
sight of frightful dread foreboding.

3   Fanfares flared, I saw before me,
fashioned fair, with lofty roof-tree,
mead-hall, built of mighty measure,
manned by band of worthy hirðsmen;
boldly hung with brilliant banners,
brightly lit with torches' lightning,
filled rim-full the festive ale-horns,
feast-board's hoard with fare o'erflowing.

Stanzas 3–4. Though not naming him, the poet is describing King Óláfr Haraldsson (St. Olaf) in his mead-hall, two centuries into Bassi's "future."

4   In the din-filled mead-hall's middle,
'mongst his throng of vow-bound vassals,
robed in seemly royal raiment,
regal fur-trimmed gold-rimmed purple,
kingly round on crowned brow carried,
kept in hand the monarch's scepter,
seated haughty on his high-seat,
hallowed lord of snow-clad Northland.

*Answer, Aonghais, Earl of Austmǫrk,
and respond to Bassi's asking:
Do you truly delve the depth of
dream-scene's stream of deepest meaning?*

5   "Hail, you mail-clad broadsword-holder;
health and wealth may aye attend you!"
Bowing low this bard trod toward him,
bade him lend his ear to hear me:
"Worthy weapon-bearing warrior,
wise in lore and worldly learning,
give me, Lord, your leave to query,
list and answer Bassi's questions!"

Stanzas 5–6. Bassi asks leave to question Óláfr, which the king grants despite their different religions.

6   Back spake straight the stark ring-breaker,
bidding me to feel full welcome:

"Ask us all thou wilt, and ample
answers surely shall we grant thee.
Open-doored our royal court is
aye to Iceland's wide-famed rhymers
—Hár and Þórr we scorn—the skillful
skald we meet with regal greeting.

7   "Brightly hued, my Lord, and beauteous   *Stanzas 7–9. The seventh stanza*
banners hang on high around you,   *contains Bassi's first question*
flags with strangely figured forms your   *about heraldry, which Óláfr*
feast-hall's costly walls becover,   *answers in the next two stanzas.*
shield-like store of shining colors
surely bears some weighty moment;
lead me, Lord, to learn their content,
let me understand their wonder!"

8   "By its choice of hues and boss each
banner names its famous owner;
arms of lords and ardent ladies,
limned with heraldry's grave symbols:
seals of state for all our cities,
signs for barony, march, and shire,
every house its family emblem,
every land its several standard.

9   "Here our colors hang in courtly
hall that all shall come and clearly
learn our fatherland's full worth—its
length and breadth, its strength and wealth—for
under every bright-hued banner,
if our sword in righteous war is
drawn, our dauntless hosts will hasten,
hordes of swordsmen, untold hundreds."

Answer, Aonghais, Earl of Austmǫrk,
and respond to Bassi's asking:
Do you truly delve the depth of
dream-scene's stream of deepest meaning?

10 "Glowing wealth of glowing splendor   *Stanzas 10–15. Bassi asks*
glistens fair upon your person: *about the royal regalia, and*
scepter, orb, the crown, broadsword, and   *Óláfr explains the symbolism*
seal-ring on your kingly finger.   *of crown, sword, scepter, orb,*
Signs of well-wrought gold and silver   *and signet-ring.*
serve some high and sacred purpose;
tell me, Jarl, the tale of royal
treasure-trove's unrivalled measure!"

11   "Nobly bears our oil-anointed
       brow the badge of regal power;
       —royal never-ending round—the
       ring that binds this deathless kingship.
       Ruler follows well-born ruler,
       reigns his fated day and passes;
       only earldom's crown lives ever,
       ever radiant, fading never!

12   "At our side we wear the sword, the
       sacred sign of high-born warrior;
       with its battle-bloodied blade we
       won by might both crown and kingdom.
       Round about our throne is ranged the
       realm's proud band of helmed defenders:
       'neath our sword's cold steel each knight has
       knelt amain for belt and chaining.

13   "Harbored in our strong right hand we
       hold the Northland's golden scepter.
       In this staff of lofty state-craft
       stands embodied land-wide law-code:
       justice—kindness joined with mercy—
       judgement—firm and fast and lasting—
       straight and swift our sacred staff shall
       strike him down, the grim law-breaker!

14   "In our left we bear the orb in
       all its regal jewel-set beauty,
       sign of shining worldly wealth and
       wondrous store of boundless fortune.
       From the orb's sphere flows our largesse,
       flood of minted ruddy metal,
       gifts of glowing gold and silver
       grants our hand with gracious gesture.

15   "Silver round of regal grandeur,
       ring gleams on our kingly finger,
       seal of all our realm's sole ruler,
       signet-right to mighty power;
       send we forth as lordly sign of
       sovereign will its well-wrought silver,
       heed all men the crown's command, the
       king is where our signet-ring is!"

       *Answer, Aonghais, Earl of Austmọrk,
       and respond to Bassi's asking:*

Do you truly delve the depth of
dream-scene's stream of deepest meaning?

16 "Give me leave, my sovereign Lord, and
let me query even further;
would fain list to still more wisdom,
welcome would I yet more learning.
There beside your sacred high-seat
sits your corps of favored courtiers;
make me mark their special merits,
marvel at their several service!"

Stanzas 16–24. Bassi's third
question concerns Óláfr's court.
The king explains the roles of
his marshal, seneschal, heralds,
stewards, and his queen, a
patroness of the arts.

17 "Facing us o'er festive board is
found our land's renowned Earl Marshal,
lordly master of the lists and
leader of the jousting steedsmen,
issuer of arms and armor,
able stalwart of our stables;
all our realm depends upon his
peerless force of fearless horsemen.

18 "At our Marshal's side there sits the
Seneschal of Northland's venue,
Lord Protector of the Purse and
pledgor of the kingdom's ledgers;
well he fills with tithe and toll our
treasury with ringing measure,
his the fount that lets us fund our
feoffs and grants, estates and castles.

19 "Here at our right hand our learned
heralds sit in patient waiting;
well they ken our far-flung kingdom's
courtly rite and formal order,
well they know our knights' and ladies'
names and blazoned arms and titles:
syne their blaring horns they sound, then
still stand all, both liege- and bondsman.

20 "Let no man think light the mighty
load our learned heralds carry:
must the land's law fully master,
mark each line's, each word's full import.
Rousing-voiced and ringing-tongued they
read aloud our royal edicts;
as our eyes and ears they serve us,
aid the crown in weighty council.

21   "Here on our left hand we honor
every feast's most fervent servants:
meats they roast and sot to sate us,
subtile sauces, spiced with costly
cinnamon and pungent sandal,
saffron, hyssop, sage, and sesam;
handing out the bakers' bounty,
bread-loaves standing ever ready.

22   "Beer in brimming horns their porters
bring to cheer our kingly table,
heavy mugs of heady mead and
hearty ale they pour unfailing;
fruits and nuts and sweets affording,
festive fare both rare and regal:
lords of cellar, stove, and storehouse,
stewards true and brewers knowing.

23   "At our very side is seated
source of all the courtly graces:
first in courtesy and fairest
from among our kingdom's women;
queen above our Viking kinsmen,
—crown-wearer, Northland's throne-sharer—
consort to the monarch's person,
closer to the throne is no one.

24   "Court she holds for artful bards that
come from far to pay her homage;
minstrels sing their mirthful songs and
mimers play to gain her favor;
flageolets and viols frolic,
flutes and lutes address their mistress:
all the arts are in her service,
all the crafts come at her calling."

*Answer, Aonghais, Earl of Austmǫrk,
and respond to Bassi's asking:
Do you truly delve the depth of
dream-scene's stream of deepest meaning?*

25   "Bear," spake Bassi, "Sire, to answer
but one last remaining question:
still one stool close to your high-seat
stays unfilled spite press of guest-folk.
Say for whom this seat stands empty
—sorry gap 'midst happy-hearted—

*Stanza 25. Bassi's fourth and
final question.*

wherefor bidden lord or lady
lacking from the chosen number?"

26 "Bassi, Iceland's skalds are skillful
—scarcely others dare comparing—
three have served us, three advised us,
three our name in rhyme made famous.
Faithful to the death, we favor
foremost Þormóðr Bersason, who
stood steadfast at Stiklarstaðir,
stalwart coal-browed skald, beside us.[16]

Stanzas 26–28. Óláfr responds by naming three great skalds who have served his court.

27 "Second, Hjalti Skeggjason, who
served with word and deed in Sweden
—waged with willful other Óláfr
war of words—while working for us.[17]
Lastly, he who serves us longest,
living on beyond our reign to
aid our son regain our throne as
at the font he once did hold him.

28 "Glad he sped to Gautland's earl to
give Jarl Rǫgnvaldr Northland's orders;
from the Eastland queenly Ástríðr
Óláfsdóttir brought our bride-bed;
is his chair across from ours, he's
off on distant royal business:
Sighvatr Þórðarson, our courtly
singer, sent on kingly mission."[18]

29 Not one of the names he uttered
knew I from among my landsmen;
whose the festive hall about me,
who the sovereign lord before me
—in my heart the urge to query,
on my lips the words were forming—
thunder groaned and ground resounded,
gone the sight in nightly darkness.

Stanza 29. The dream ends suddenly before Bassi can ask the king's identity.

30 Long I lay and pondered lonely,
lost in thought and restless tossing:
what the reason? Where the purpose?
Why was I to be the seer?
Can—as yet unborn—this king be
come to let us view the future?
Can this dream foresee some coming
carp or weal for Eastland's people?

Stanza 30. Bassi ponders the meaning of this dream for the East Kingdom.

Answer, Aonghais, Earl of Austmǫrk,
and respond to Bassi's asking:
Do you truly delve the depth of
dream-scene's stream of deepest meaning?[19]

Comparison of Kings[20]
(*Konungajafnaðr*)

<table>
<tr><td>6</td><td>Hail, Northland's first holder,
Haraldr King hárfagri![21]
Gyða's offer gave him
goal to rule the whole of
Norway—of all Norsemen
none is claimed more famous—
fiercely Eiríkr's father
fought on Hafrfjǫrðr's waters.</td><td>*Stanzas 6–8. Bassi praises*
King Harald Fairhair, the
unifier of Norway.</td></tr>
<tr><td>7</td><td>Mœr and Þelamǫrk he
mated with his state, then
Raumaríki, Vík with
Rogaland and Sogn, then
Haðaland, Hringaríki,
Hǫrðaland and Agðir,
the Fjords, the Dales, the Forests;
fond his heart for Þrándheimr.</td><td></td></tr>
<tr><td>8</td><td>Haraldr with war's hammer
handcrafted the Northland,
knit into one nation
North and South together;
fellow folk to fellow
fit to form one border;
on the Kjǫlr's stone anvil
union forged for Norway.[22]</td><td></td></tr>
</table>

<table>
<tr><td>11</td><td>Gylfi gave to Gefjon
grant of land in Sweden,
twice two troll-sired sons she
turned to beasts of burden.[23]
Pair to pair she yoked them,
plowed Lake Lǫgrinn proudly
—foam sprayed far, spume flying—
fjord-wide furrow turning.</td><td>*Stanzas 11–13. Bassi relates the*
story of Gefjon and mother of
the Skjǫldungs, a new line of
legendary Danish kings.</td></tr>
</table>

12 O'er the Øresund toward
Óðinsey she drove them,
dragging land to Denmark
—dredging done 'tween sunsets—
firm and fast she moored it
—flow-bound island lowland—
steer-drawn plow-born sea-field:
Selundr, Skjǫldr's wife called it.

13 Kingly hall she held there
—Hleiðra—lofty raftered,
þing of Denmark's þegndom,
throne of Danmǫrk's land-lords,
heart of Selundr's herdland,
home of all the Skjǫldungs,
—town of trade and handcraft—
towered wall-girt power.

16 From this day your fame shall
fare afar from Austmǫrk,
grand your glorious splendor,
great the weight of kingship;
hard weighs on your heads the
heavy crown of power:
short the length of lordship,
long this hall's recalling.

*Stanzas 16–20. Bassi reminds
the king and queen of their
immediate predecessors, and
that only largess ("bounty")
will increase their royal fame.*

17 Mighty men have reigned as
monarchs to East's honor,
long the kingly list of
lords that Austmǫrk warded:
Alaric and Aonghais,
Asbjǫrn—crowned before you—
courtly Cariadoc and
Kings Jehan and Finnvarr.[24]

18 No less noble are the
names of Eastland's ladies:
Yseult and Queen Ysabeau
owned your crown of yore and
Brekke shared its burden,
bore Diana Alene,
Eloise and Alyson,
artful Caellyn wore it.[25]

19 Artist's work can win him
      wealth and famous name, a
      bard is well rewarded
      by his lines remembered,
      knights may build in battle
      brilliant store of glory,
      known are dames and damsels
      due to faith and beauty.

20 Only kings and queens are
      counted by their bounty:
      silver gifts and gold they
      give like flowing rivers;
      lasting law and justice,
      loyalty rich and royal:
      such bond seal yourselves with
      sovereign lords before you!

Ravens' Rede[26]
(*Hrafnatal*)

1 Hail, thou high-built hall, thou   *Stanza 1 (proem). Bassi*
     home of foaming ale-horns!   *purposefully addresses the*
     Ring, ye lofty rafters   *hall—not the royal pair directly.*
     rimmed with smoke-blacked timbers!
     Hear me, mighty high-seat
     hewn with well-honed rune-spells!
     Hearken, fiery hearth and
     heed my skald-brewed word-mead!

2 Rolling surges rage on   *Stanza 2. Bassi describes his*
     Reykjanes—the breakers   *home in Iceland.*
     storm on stone-clad shores with
     strident tireless tides—the
     winds howl wailing down from
     wasteland's ice-bound glaciers—
     lava-floes loom grim 'neath
     leaden-clouded heavens.[27]

3 Overhead they hover;   *Stanza 3. Odin's two ravens*
     high above, nigh-flying,   *appear to Bassi.*
     reel two coal-black ravens
     —restless knowledge-questers—
     land on lofty rooftree
     —loud crow Óðinn's house-thralls—

"Hail, Yggr's helper, Huginn,
Hár's far-searcher, Muninn!"[28]

List, Queen Nicorlynn and
Lord of Austmǫrk, Frederick;
hear the word of Hár and
heed his ravens' rede ye!

    the ravens spake:

4 "Hail thee, skald! The High One
   hight us wend our flight to
   Bassi, bear of Markland,
   bringing wing-borne greeting;
   Austmǫrk crowns a queen and
   king—the mead-hall rings with
   song—why bides the singer
   silent on his island?"

    the skald spake:

5 "Austmǫrk's first will feast in
   farthest southern marches;
   long the rider's road and
   rife with strife and hardship;
   harsh the heat which wears the
   hardest for the Norseman—
   here my heart is easy,
   home in frozen snow-land."

    the ravens spake:

6 "Oft before has fared a-
   far the bard of Markland,
   bore the brunt of hardship,
   burning summer spurning;
   other cause than this thy
   idle biding warrants:
   off from Iceland, Bassi,
   Eastland's feast awaits thee!"

    the skald spake:

7 "Little will her lords feel
   loss or grieve my leaving;
   thrice this skald has thought to
   thaw their haughty grandeur.
   Only one of all of
   Eastland's high and mighty

Stanzas 4–9. The ravens enjoin
Bassi to travel to Eastland's
coronation; the skald offers
three excuses.

sweetly slaked my thirst, he,
sang the bard for Aonghais."

    the ravens spake:

8 "Fared afar the black jarl
forth from thankless Austmǫrk;
widely Aonghais wandered,
welcome guest to Westrealm.[29]
Wouldst thou wait here witless,
wilt thou still stay songless?
Off from Iceland, Bassi,
Eastland's feast awaits thee!"

    the skald spake:

9 "Erstwhile Austmǫrk's king swore
oaths of trust in justice.
Not one single night that
knave kept word he gave then.
Bassi's poem of praise he
paid with spiteful liar's
scowl—this skald shall ever
scorn his court with silence!"[30]

*List, Queen Nicorlynn and
Lord of Austmǫrk, Frederick;
hear the word of Hár and
heed his ravens' rede ye!*

    the ravens spake:

10 "Egill fell in eager
Eiríkr's snare at York—he
sang a song of praise to
save his head—instead of
honor Eiríkr garnered
ill alone; his lonely
doom was shame and downfall:
death, banned forth from Northland.[31]

*Stanzas 10–13. The ravens
remind Bassi that skalds have
always suffered from unworthy
princes; the skald's true lord is
always Odin.*

11 "Hákon jarl hanged Þorleifr's
hull-mates, stole his hold-goods,
burned his billow-charger—
brash wave-steed—to ashes.
Wrought the rime-wright Þorleifr
wrath-rede rich in witchcraft;
hapless Hlaðajarl reaped
harm from skald-formed charm-tale.

12   "Think not on the thanks of
       thegn or reigning king but
       only on thy lord: on
       Óðinn, king of singers!
       Sing thou for thy song's own
       sake—thus praise its maker!
       Off from Iceland, Bassi,
       Eastland's feast awaits thee!"

       the skald spake:

13   "Tell me, friends of Fjǫlnir,[32]
       fleet-winged tiding-bringers,
       why you warn and worry,
       wend me on this sending;
       who shall sit on high-seat,
       whose fair brows the crowns bear,
       hailed by earls and hirðsmen,
       hoards of courtly lordship?"

       *List, Queen Nicorlynn and
       Lord of Austmǫrk, Frederick;
       hear the word of Hár and
       heed his ravens' rede ye!*

       the ravens spake:

14   "Ever shall all think well   *Stanzas 14–25. The ravens*
       on that day in May when   *describe the long SCA careers*
       first guests fought in Westmǫrk,   *of Frederick and Nicorlynn.*
       forged the core of empire;[33]
       skillful weapon-wielders
       warred in tourney on the
       field of honor—fray-thegn
       Frederick fed our kinfolk.

15   "Yet a year afar he
       yearned for Southland's learning;
       once returned to Westrealm
       weapon-art imparted
       Caradoc ap Cador,
       courtliest of warriors,
       and the berserkr, Edwin,
       arms-master of Westmǫrk.

16   "Maiden in Three Mountains
       met and wed Lord Frederick:
       Nicorlynn, the lake-fey,
       lady of Caer Wydyr.

Mere three months he wooed her
—mate-lust hates long waiting—
willing well-bred bride to
wedding-bed led Frederick.

17   "Side by side they toiled to
swell the realm's renown—as
Westmǫrk's tourney-master,
mistress of the lists, she—
hosted helm-clad joust and
hastened reeling mêlée,
bade knights ride to battle,
bare their swords for warfare.

18   "For their work rewarded,
wearing proudly merit's
leaf as liege-lord's gift, they
left the Mists of Westmǫrk,
fared to found new crown-lands
forth to verdant Kornmǫrk;[34]
Midrealm's grain-rich meadows
meet with heart-felt greetings.

19   "Two short years they tarried
twin awards to win—the
stalwart one-horned stallion,
steed, the maiden-heeder—
parting Miðmǫrk's plains their
path they wandered onward;
Eastland's province Austgarðr
offered them new homeland.

20   "Aonghais's uncle raided
Austgarðr, burned and murdered;[35]
ere he reached his sea-ernes
at the bridge they battled.
Holland's son caught Selkirk,
sent him tumbling groundward,
kept brave Jamie captive,
kinsman of King Aonghais.

*Stanzas 20–21. Frederick's
exploits during the fourth
Pennsic War.*

21   "Baring Eastland's banner
boldly, flag unfolding,
fearless fighter in your
fourth war with Miðmǫrk's horde,
—fattening Freki's packmates,

feeding Geri's breed-kin—
foremost into fray, Lord
Frederick sped to spear-þing.

22   "Lady Nicorlynn un-
locked first Gold Key's stock, she
packed as peerless first the
Portable Feast in Eastland;
Austgarðr's Sea-Horse Order's
honor they both won and
ardent service earned him
Eastrealm's Silver Crescent.[36]

23   "Thronging Eastland's throne-þing
thegns of war sought lordship.
Holland felled Jehan and
hewed down Gyrðr and Vísvaldr;
Ælfwine danadómr held
dread blade-trade with Frederick;
rightful rule of Austmǫrk's
realm won lone-horn's helmed son.[37]

*Stanza 23. Frederick's victory
at the Crown Tournament.*

24   "Pour this prince bard's mead, this
princess praise unstinting;
amply fill with skald's ale
every ear that hears thee;
beer them, bear of rime-wrights,
bring them brew of singers!
Off from Iceland, Bassi,
Eastland's feast awaits thee!"

*Stanza 24. The ravens exhort
Bassi one last time to write a
drápa for the royal pair.*

the skald spake:

25   "Hear me, Herjann's Huginn,
Hárbarðr's charm-ern, Muninn:[38]
fairly earned has Frederick
fame as has his dame—yet
will they ward the skald from
worthy seat midst hirðsmen,
will they sneer through smiles new
slight for Markland's rime-wright?"

*Stanza 25. Although partially
convinced, Bassi still fears a
royal slight.*

*List, Queen Nicorlynn and
Lord of Austmǫrk, Frederick;
hear the word of Hár and
heed his ravens' rede ye!*

the ravens spake:

26   "Proud the skald who's paid his
     praise to kings and princes;
     in bards' laud each lord lives
     long as songs remembered.
     Sing thou for thy song's sake!
     Seek not fame nor payment:
     soon is silver spent and
     sworn reward forgotten.

27   "Praise not as lords are but
     as they would or should be;
     if unearned, then scorn shall
     always shame their halls—the
     blame shall bear the lord—the
     bard sings sooth; the truth is
     song—the lord has lied, who
     less is than his praise is."[39]

28   Off the two soared eastward
     o'er the foam-rimmed fjord toward
     geyser's flood and ice-field's
     frozen floes, o'er mountains
     spewing molten spouts of
     spume and fire skyward,
     down to storm-drawn coasts, o'er
     dark blue sea to Norway.

29   Forth we fared then southward
     from the shores of Northland
     to fair Durham town to
     tender Markland's sending:
     greetings from our great ones,
     gifts to blend our friendship,
     hoard of holy word-skill:
     hark skald's art from Markland!

30   Even as Yggr's ravens
     ordered to their glory,
     hearken, hirð, the praise of
     Nicorlynn and Frederick,
     King and Queen of Eastland
     crowned this day—we pay you
     homage: fame and honor
     e'ermore share your lordships![40]

Stanzas 26–28. The ravens dispense some final advice to Bassi and all skalds who must navigate their subservient positions to princes.

Stanzas 29–30. The ambassadorial party from Markland embarks; Bassi at last addresses the royal pair.

Markland's Coronation Oath[41]

I speak the bond,   I bind the spell,
    blessing to bear or ban.
For the hirð to heed,   for the horde to hear,
    holding the oak-stave's haft.

Field and fire,   wind and wave,
    witness well our words:
stern as steel,   stark as stone,
    strong as this oaken staff.

If ever my oath   I overlook
    or alter aught at all:
hurt on my heart,   harm on my head,
    Hel be henceforth my home,

burst my byrnie,   break my bow,
    blunt my brand's broad blade;
wound and wort,   wolf and worm,
    wither my weal to woe!

10

Markland's Wedding Oath[42]

Is it thy wish,   is it thy will,
    here where the hirð may hear,
frank and free   from force or fear
    to offer thy oath for aye:

to share one board,   to share one bed,
    bonded in heart and hand,
in wealth and want,   in weal and woe,
    as long as ye both shall live?

NOTES

1. On April 26th, 1974 (A.S. VIII), Fleck performed "Ode to the Two Earls" to celebrate the wedding of a past Markland warlord, Bruce Blackistone, whose Marklandic name *Attila* is here adapted by Fleck into "Húnar-Atli" (Attila the Hun). The ceremony was performed by Fleck himself. Since Markland's current warlord, James Cooper (Ragnarr the Badde), was also in attendance, this kenning-rich *drápa* celebrates both figures.

2. A *þing* ("thing") is an official gathering; *Óðinn* is the Norse spelling for "Odin." Although letters such as *thorn* (þ) and *eth* (ð) are now obsolete, Fleck prefers to preserve

as many authentic or variant Norse spellings and diacritical marks as possible; accordingly, I have not sought to standardize his Norse names with the rest of this anthology.

3. These last four lines constitute the poem's refrain; all *drápur* require one. *Midgard* is the world of men (from which Tolkien, incidentally, derives "Middle-earth"). A *hirð* is a prince's following; Fleck uses this term in multiple kennings. In Old Norse, *argr* means "bad" (for Ragnarr the Badde).

4. This third stanza requires significant mythological knowledge. Lines 3 and 4 depend specifically on knowing that Freyja and Odin (Frigg's husband) each take half the warriors slain in battle. For the fifth line, the assembled warriors have given "gore-feasts" (carrion) to ravens; technically, Odin stole the Mead of Poetry in eagle's form, but Fleck here expands his kenning to include any large carrion-eating bird. "Witch-steeds" are wolves, an animal that witches are said to ride. The final line includes a complex kenning for *blood*, a substance that "reddens" swords.

5. In this case, the kenning "Rán's foam-road" refers to a river—specifically, the Severn River in Maryland. The *Sae Earn*, whose name in Old English means "sea eagle," is a converted twenty-six-foot Navy motor whaleboat, *Mk II*, from the Korean War. Blackistone drew inspiration from a Kirk Douglas film, *The Vikings* (1958), and founded the Longship Company, an organization affiliated with the Markland Confederation.

6. This last passage cites several principal Norse deities. Þórr (or Thor) is god of thunder, and his wife, Sif, has golden hair. Njörðr (or Njörd) is linked to fertility. So are Njörðr's children, Freyr and Freyja, who each have significant cultic importance. For a list of Freyja's attributes, see the footnote to Paxson's "For the Goddess Freyja." Frigg is wife of Odin and mother to Baldur the Beautiful, whose death is famous in Norse myth. To preserve her son's life, Frigg compels a promise from all things, inanimate and animate, never to harm her son. When the trickster god, Loki, discovers that Frigg failed to extract a promise from the mistletoe, however, he has Baldur killed with one.

7. "Gunnlǫg's lust-pay" and "Kvasir's life-spoor" are two separate kennings for the Mead of Poetry. For more on this myth, see the footnote to Zimmer's poem "Invocation." Likewise, stanzas 12 and 13 of Fleck's poem "Coronation Ode" describe some of the mead's backstory. There, *Bǫlverk* (or *Bölverk*) and *Hár* are two more names for Odin; respectively, they mean "evildoer" and "high one." The first skald to whom Odin gifted the Mead of Poetry was Bragi—hence, "Bragi's Art."

8. On October 11th, 1975 (A.S. X), Fleck performed "Coronation Ode" to celebrate the SCA's coronation of Aonghais Dubh MacTarbh and Ysabeau Cameron of Lochiel. As a gesture of goodwill, the Markland Confederation sent an ambassadorial deputation, including Fleck, to "Austmǫrk," the Marklandic name for the SCA's East Kingdom.

9. The East Kingdom's outgoing monarchs are Ásbjǫrn and Brekke. Their departure saddens Fleck, he claims, because their heathen (Germanic) faith is more to his liking than Aonghais's Christianity. Fleck reinforces their mutual connection by punning on *Ásbjǫrn* and *Bassi*; each name denotes a bear or bearlike creature in Old Norse.

10. The backstory to this sixth stanza is complicated. As a Christian Celt of the clan Creachainn, Aonghais was formally "Castle Craigburn's master." During a dis-

pute, he "kidnapped" Ysabeau of Lochiel and her two relatives, Donal and Dyannae, but, although Ysabeau still refused to marry Aonghais, they resolved their feud amicably by agreeing to share the East Kingdom's throne.

11. The four SCA baronies mentioned in this eleventh stanza have their centers at Boston (Carolingia), New York (Østgarð), Philadelphia (Bhakail), and the Baltimore/Washington region (Myrkwood).

12. Besides the various poetic synonyms ("Bǫlverk," "Hár") and kennings ("Redesmith") for Odin, Fleck is referencing Egil Skallagrímsson's famous "Head-Ransom" poem. Greatest of the Norse skalds, Egil was captured one night by his enemy, King Eirík Bloodaxe, but he composed a poem overnight praising Eirík, who admired it so much he spared Egil's life. Fleck presents this incident to contravene the prior statement by Odin ("Hár") about tongues, which Fleck takes from verse 73 of *Hávamál*. For more on Egil's life, the fantasist E. R. Eddison translated *Egil's Saga* in 1930, and Poul Anderson's historical novel *Mother of Kings* (2001) includes major portions of the skald's life.

13. Having already named Bragi Boddason and Egil Skallagrímsson, Fleck now names other famous Norse skalds: Torbjörn hornklofi and Thjódólf of Hvinir (ninth century); Tormod Bersason kolbrúnarskáld (eleventh century); Einarr Helgason skálaglamm (tenth century); Eyvindr Finnsson (tenth century); Arnórr Thordarson (eleventh century); the outlaw poets Gísli Súrsson from *Gísli saga* and Grettir Ásmundarson from *Grettis saga*; and Gunnlaugr ormstunga (or "serpent-tongue," tenth century). In the last two lines, Fleck cites Harald Fairhair (tenth century) and Harald Hardrada (eleventh century), two Norse kings known for composing verse. Fleck devotes stanza 15 to Snorri Sturluson, author of the early thirteenth-century *Prose Edda* and our primary source of information on skaldic poetics, *heiti* (poetic synonyms), and the mythological references necessary to kennings.

14. These lines from Odin derive from verse 75 of *Hávamál*. They originally appear in an eddic meter, *ljoðaháttr*.

15. On January 5th, 1976 (A.S. X), Fleck performed "Dream Ode in Long Lines" before the East Kingdom's King Aonghais and Queen Ysabeau. Unlike his earlier "Coronation Ode," Fleck addresses this *drápa* directly to Aonghais Dubh MacTarbh, the "Laird of the Steer's Head," whose emblem is the severed head of a steer. Notably, Aonghais is a Christian monarch whose faith, in real history, came to replace Bassi's own Norse paganism. In Fleck's prose commentary, he calls this dream ode an example of *speculum regale*, the "poetic image of the ruler."

16. Tormod Bersason kolbrúnarskáld (or "coal-browed skald") fought side-by-side with King Óláfr Haraldsson at the battle of Stiklestad (Stiklarstaðir) on July 29th, 1030. In this battle, both died. Fleck also cites Tormod in the fourteenth stanza of "Coronation Ode," but he here pretends to not recognize Tormod or the other skalds because each lives long after the time period of Fleck's Bassi persona.

17. Hjalti Skeggjason is best remembered as an emissary to the court of the King of Sweden, Olof Skötkonung (c. 980–1022). By naming this "other Óláfr," Óláfr Haraldsson indirectly reveals his true identity.

18. Sigvat Tordarson is one of the most famous skalds and diplomats in Norse literature. After Óláfr died at Stiklestad, Sigvat served his son, Magnus the Good, for whom Sigvat stood as godfather and also had baptized.

19. After reciting this ode, Bassi reports that Aonghais and Ysabeau accepted it as graciously as they had "Coronation Ode"; Duke Cariadoc (David Friedman) then spoke a half-stanza *dróttkvætt* in praise, but this has not survived.

20. On October 9th, 1976 (A.S. XI), Fleck performed "Comparison of Kings" for the coronation of King Laeghaire O Laverty and Queen Ysabeau Cameron. He later alleged that Laeghaire, as king, had broken his "sworn oath to uphold law and justice." According to Frederick Hollander, their dispute centered on certain promised offices in the SCA branches that shared territory (and populace) with Markland.

21. Fleck here refers to Haraldr Hálfdanarson hárfagri, or Harald Fairhair, father to Eirík Bloodaxe, and the king who unified Norway after winning at Hafrsfjord (Hafrfjǫrðr) near the Stavanger Peninsula in 872 AD. According to Snorri's *Heimskringla*, Harald began these conquests to gain Gyda's hand in marriage after she made her acceptance contingent upon a unified country. In Fleck's seventh stanza, he names the fourteen petty kingdoms united under Harald's sway.

22. The Kjǫlr (or "keel") is the north-south mountain range running Norway's length.

23. This set of stanzas alludes heavily to a famous story about Gylfi (or Gangleri), Sweden's earliest recorded monarch. According to legend, Gylfi promised the goddess Gefjon all the land she could plow in a single day. She, therefore, transforms her four sons into oxen and carves out Lake Lǫgrinn (now Lake Mälaren) in Sweden. Next, Gefjon transports this excavated dirt to the city of Óðinsey (Odense) in Denmark, and then she forms an island that she names *Selundr* ("sea-meadow," now modern-day Zealand). *Øresund* is the strait separating Selundr/Zealand from Sweden. Afterwards, Gefjon marries Skjǫldr ("Scyld Scefing" from *Beowulf*) and, together, they found the Skjǫldungs, an ancient line of Danish kings. Their town Hleiðra is now the modern-day city of Lejre.

24. This SCA kings list covers the previous four years; Fleck leaves out only Akbar, crowned for the third time in January 1973. Cariadoc, Aonghais, and Asbjǫrn all served as monarch twice.

25. Because only Queen Ysabeau served a second term, Fleck's queens list covers only the previous three years.

26. On October 8th, 1977 (A.S. XII), Fleck performed "Ravens' Rede" to celebrate the coronation of Frederick of Holland and Nicorlynn of Caer Wydyr.

27. Reykjanes is the peninsula in southwestern Iceland where "Bassi" makes his home. Descriptions of nature are quite rare in skaldic poetry; this second stanza is balanced by stanza 28.

28. Huginn ("thought") and Muninn ("mind") are two ravens who bring Odin (i.e., "Yggr" and "Hár") information from all over the world.

29. After Aonghais's reign ended the previous year, he moved out west to the Kingdom of Caid (southern California and Nevada). He would later be expelled from the SCA.

30. The "knave" in question is King Laeghaire O Laverty, to whom Fleck had dedicated "Comparison of Kings." Bassi believes the slight even more grievous considering how his poem had urged the royal couple to "bounty."

31. The ravens are reminding Bassi that Eirík Bloodaxe's shameful end brought no disgrace upon Egil Skallagrímsson despite him praising Eirík in an earlier poem, "Head-Ransom." Even more to the point, as the ravens observe, the skald Thorleif Asgeirsson suffered grieviously when the jarl of Hladir, Hákon Sigurdarson, stole his goods, burned his ship, and hung his shipmates. However, when Thorleif next encountered the jarl, the skald exacted appropriate revenge by reciting a magical poem that caused Hákon permanent harm.

32. *Fjǫlnir* is another name for Odin; it means "wise one" or "concealer."

33. This reference to "Westmǫrk"—the Marklandic name for the SCA's West Kingdom—indicates that Fleck is speaking about the SCA's famous inaugural tournament on May 1st, 1966; Frederick Hollander ("Frederick of Holland") participated in that event. Afterward, Frederick studied for a year in the south before returning to California, where he and Lady Nicorlynn married after dating for only three months. In addition, the ravens mention two other SCA members by name: Caradoc ap Cador (Gabriel Carrillo) and Master Edwin Bersark (Paul Edwin Zimmer). Although Diana L. Paxson is known as Lady Diana Listmaker due to her propensity for making checklists, the West Kingdom's "mistress of the lists" was the person who tracked the results of fighting in tournaments. Lady Nicorlynn acted in that capacity while in Dumnonia.

34. While living in the Mists, a SCA principality in the Bay Area, Frederick and Nicorlynn earned the Leaf of Merit, an award for service. They then moved to Iowa City (then within Midrealm) and founded the now-defunct Barony of Dumnonia ("Kornmǫrk"); they soon won a second award for service, the Order of the Uni-Corn (a name punning on how "Dumnonia" is also an old Brythonic kingdom located in modern-day Cornwall). As the next stanza indicates, the couple then moved to Austgarðr (or "Østgard") in New York.

35. According to Fleck's commentary, his twentieth stanza recounts the fourth Pennsic War in 1975 (often called "Pennsic Pour" due to heavy rains), but Frederick Hollander notes that the capture of Jamie Selkirk happened somewhat earlier at a preparatory event *for* the upcoming Pennsic. Selkirk, the "uncle" of then-prince Aonghais (technically, "Selkirk" is an alternate SCA persona for the same person who played Aonghais), raided the event's participants, but he was captured by Duke Frederick at a final bridge battle; several months later, Selkirk was "beheaded." The periphrasis *sea-ernes* (literally "sea eagles" but meaning boats) uses a Middle English variant of the Old English word *earn*. Geri and Freki are the names for two wolves who accompany Odin.

36. Nicorlynn established Østgard's Gold Key "office," which is a collection of spare clothing available to help newcomers dress in period-appropriate garb, as well as the kingdom-wide "Order of the Portable Feast," which encourages gracefulness and elegance in dining. The Order of the Sea-horse and the Silver Crescent are additional awards.

37. Because Frederick uses a unicorn as his emblem, the ravens call him "lonehorn's helmed son."

38. *Herjann* ("leader of hosts") and *Hárbarðr* ("gray beard") are two further names for Odin.

39. Cruelly, this final advice from the ravens to Bassi would prove unexpectedly—and horrifically—relevant in real life. About eight years after Fleck celebrated Aonghais Dubh MacTarbh in "Coronation Ode," this former king, whose real name is Paul Michael Serio, was hired along with another man by real-estate developer Paul Hamwi to murder Hamwi's ex-wife. Initially, a neighbor with schizophrenia was convicted of the crime, spending nearly nine years in prison, but in 1992 the filming of an episode of the tv series *Unsolved Mysteries* encouraged local police to reopen the case; the neighbor was released, and Serio and Hamwi then spent their final years in prison. In an earlier article, I misidentified Aonghais as Hamwi, not Serio. For a longer discussion of the situation, see Wise, "Antiquarianism Underground," in *Studies in the Fantastic* (Summer 2021), pp. 40–41.

40. As Fleck reports, this skaldic poem was met with great applause. King Frederick bestowed praises, arm-rings, and a formal financial contribution to a scholarly series being launched by Fleck, *Studia Marklandica*. Fleck eventually produced one volume, a thirty-six-page booklet called *The Old Norse Name*. After hearing this poem, David Friedman recited "Praising Geirr Bassi" in this volume.

41. As the spiritual leader or *þulr* of Markland, Fleck wrote the following two oaths using the *ljóðaháttr* meter.

42. In the circa 1976 issue of *Sword in the Sludge*, the Militia's official newsletter, Fleck provides an extended description of a Marklandic wedding as it had developed to that time; see *Sword in the Sludge*, c. 1976, pp. 13–14, www.markland.org/file-share.

Barchan the Kipchak

Barchan the Kipchak (b. 1950), who prefers to go by his Markland name, is a founding member of the Maryland Medieval Mercenary Militia; he began as the organization's Vice Warlord (i.e., second officer). Although he never took any courses in medieval literature or Old Norse, Barchan participated enthusiastically in Markland's historical reenactments. In the early 1980s, he helped introduce "cavalry"—initially, only a few horses—into battles. In due time, specifically from 1987 through 2015, Barchan began jousting in full armor, and, after 1993, he began competing in full-scale "knock-off" jousting tournaments. He eventually took second place in the 2006 World Jousting Championship, later serving as a tournament judge from 2012 to 2016. In literary terms, Barchan writes verse only as an occasional whim. The following text, "Mark Well, Men of Markland," appeared in the 1979 "Special Orc Issue" of *Sword in the Sludge*, where it earned second place in a small internal poetry prize. The narrated fight is imaginary and has no basis in any real Markland event.

Mark Well, Men of Markland

Mark well, men of Markland,
mind this tale of glory.
Hear how Harald Horn-helm
hacked and hewed Sir Crangon.
Cringe as Crangon crumbles
crippled from the head down,
freely flails while falling

finding groin of Harald;
fairness triumphs finally
for both forfeit fiefdoms.   10

Fierce with flags and firebrands
far-famed Harald Horn-helm
leading loathsome armies
loaded down with booty
came upon the castle
cared for by Earl Crangon.
Daring death he loudly
did demand his Danegeld.
Five stout feudal bowmen
failed to pierce his mail shirt.   20
Keen and cunning Crangon
could but issue challenge;
each would engage singly,
else there'd be mass mayhem.

At the appointed hour,
armored to the utmost,
armies all assembled
arrayed to watch the fray.
"Craven coward, Crangon.
"Crawl back home," hailed Harald.   30
"Horny Harald hugs hogs,"
harangued haughty Crangon.
When these words were uttered,
warlike cries resulted.
Still, things might have stayed staid
save that chance stepped in.
Saxon slipped in sheep shit,
stabbing Dane in stomach.

Harald's harness held firm.
He was harmed but little.   40
Wrathful rage enwrapped him.
Raised he then his war axe;
doomed to death seemed Crangon
down slipped Dane on cow crap.
Both jumped up and boldly
battled with great fierceness
whereupon at once they
well knew who fought better.
Harald hit the Saxon's head

so hard his heels hurt. 50
Kicked and cudgeled Crangon,
casting him in dung heaps.
Thrice he threw Earl Crangon
through some thorny thickets.
Still the Saxon staggered
stunned but still not dead yet.
Swatted by a swipe, he
swung his flail while swooning
crushing Harald's crotch-plate
crunching Harald's gonads. 60
Ergo, each fell earthward
even as the cows came
startled and stampeding
straight for Dane and Saxon.

When the worst was over
where there once were foemen
little left was living,
least of all two fighters.
Awed were all Dane archers,
axemen, pikemen, horsemen. 70
Sad were Saxon swordsmen,
serfs and humble peasants.

And the armies parted;
all went to their homelands.
Some sang songs of heroes.
Sick were some with sadness.

Peter N. Schweitzer

As a geologist, Peter N. Schweitzer (b. 1957) has been employed by the U.S. Geological Survey since 1991, having earned his doctorate in oceanography two years earlier from the WHOI/MIT Joint Program in Oceanography. Schweitzer, though, spent his undergraduate years at the University of Maryland, College Park, where he encountered the Markland Medieval Mercenary Militia. One of several geology majors in the group, he took his Marklandic name—Talus the Blue, or TþB—from the word describing a slope composed of broken rock: "talus." While a member, Schweitzer wrote several short literary pieces. One was a rendition of the group's constitution and bylaws in iambic meter, although at Jere Fleck's urging he revised this into imitation Old English alliterative meter, something Schweitzer had learned while taking coursework. In the following poem, "The Witan of Markland," originally published without a title in *Sword in the Sludge*, Schweitzer numbers Markland's leadership positions, which he calls a "witan"—technically, a council of advisors to early English kings prior to the Norman Conquest. Today, Schweitzer's artistic interests center mainly on music, particularly flute and piano.

The Witan of Markland

Hear now, hirðsmen,   herald and skald:
Maryland Militia,   Markland's birthplace,[1]
laws now lays   for all to learn
forged in friendship   foes to fetter.
Hear the hard rules   high in thought held
mull in memory,   meanings ponder.

Lo, then, listen;   learn these rules now—
let this list   be said aloud:
fyrd the folk be,   free to vote, they.
Greatly this group's   gatherings must be   10
filled with folk;   of half the fyrd.
Twice in every   twenty-eight days
all of ours we   find attending
fyrd will now be   for the next month.
Warlord, wisest   of the Witan,
maker of moots,   mans our helm.
Foreign friends and   foes alike must
to our lord, our   leader, listen.
Warlord of Vice is   one of the Witan;
Sword in Sludge he   sees to print.[2]   20
Hirð's history   and its heraldry
he should help to   have preserved.
First Wench, foremost   female member
finds of fyrd the   frailer ones,
rends from roster   —not retaining—
ones whose interest   wanes too much.
Spoils Keeper   sense must have—
stuff to care for,   clean and count.
Marshall minds our   meeting manner;
makes the rules be   read and known.   30
Armorer always   war attending,
mailed fist and   helm makes fast.
All these earls and   every member
must to see these   tasks here set
filled full well,   no falsehood failing
fyrd betraying;   forceful folk.

NOTES

1. The Maryland Medieval Mercenary Militia began as an University of Maryland, College Park, student organization in 1969. In 1974, the group incorporated as the *Markland* Medieval Mercenary Militia to allow graduated members and non-students to participate.

2. *Sword in the Sludge* was the newsletter for Markland. An incomplete archive of issues from 1972 through 1990 can still be accessed through Markland's website.

David Friedman

David Friedman (b. 1945) is an economist and legal scholar best known for books like *Law's Order* (2000) and *The Machinery of Freedom* (1973), a libertarian theory of anarcho-capitalism. As Duke Cariadoc of the Bow, however, he has gained near-legendary status within the SCA. One oft-told folktale involves how Friedman once became the only monarch to declare war on his own kingdom—and lose. Yet Friedman has always had a guiding interest in poetry. Most appears in his online compendium, *Cariadoc's Miscellany*, and he performed the following *dróttkvætt* in spring 1978 following Jere Fleck's recitation of "Ravens' Rede." The king in question, Frederick of Holland, had just publicly thanked "Bassi" for his poem by letting him drink from the royal goblet; Frederick also provided several gifts. The previous year, Eastland's king had inadequately appreciated Bassi's poem "Comparison of Kings."

In contrast, Friedman explicitly composed "Hildebrandslied" as an SCA performance piece. He translated this poem from Old High German with the help of another English translation. Although scholars acknowledge the clear corruption of the original text, its main focus seems to have been on the tragic situation of two champions from opposing armies, likely the Huns and Goths, being related by blood: a father (Hiltibrant) and a son (Hadubrant). The poem contains no detailed descriptions of persons, backgrounds, weapons, armor, or achievements—just this central encounter. Since the original ending does not survive, Friedman invents his own.

Praising Geirr Bassi

Austmǫrk's king looks eager
ire of bard to pardon,
gifts Geirr Bassi, reft by
greedy lord from Eastland.[1]
Skalds for gold are greedy,
give their praise in payment.
Payment get in plenty,
prince! Break rings for Bassi!

Hildebrandslied

I have   heard it told
how between two   hosts the heroes
Hiltibrant and   Hadubrant
son and father   fought together,
fought apart.[2]   The heroes fasten
well-tried war-coats.   Over ring-shirts
belt their brands on,   ride to battle.
Hiltibrant the   ancient hero
asked the other   his ancestry
who among the   hosts his father   10
what his family.   "Noble folk
ken I all with   in the kingdom
so your sire's   name suffices."
Hadubrant spoke,   Hiltibrantson:
"Ancients of the   tribe have told me
Hiltibrant   hight my father.
I hight   Hadubrant.
He fled east   from Odoacer's
royal wrath fled   Hiltibrant
with his warriors   to Theotrih,[3]   20
left behind him   wife in bower
babe and young wife   both behind him.
Theotrih   that was so friendless
first of all his men   my father
loved who   loathing Odoacer,
joyed in battle,   brave at forefront,
brave men knew him well.   He died
I doubt not   long ago."
Hiltibrant spoke,   Heribrantson:

"God hold witness   from the heavens   30
never be thou   battle met
with so close to   thee a kinsman."
Drew the arm-rings,   king-gifts golden,
from his arm, the   Hun king's presents:
"These I give thee   glad in friendship."
Hadubrant spoke,   Hiltibrantson:
"Such things seek I   with my spear point,
point to point in   open battle.
You are old in craft,   most cunning,
when your words make   me unwary   40
then your spear-throw   quick will kill me;
you grew old by   such deception.
Word comes over   western waters;
sailors bring it,   say in battle
dead is Hiltibrant   Heribrantson."
"From your brand and   bright ring-jerkin
I can see your   lord is kindly.
From his hand thou   never had
exile and cruelty,   God me pity, Comes my fate.
Thirty summers, thirty winters,   I have wandered,   50
held the front   in each fierce battle,
stormed before the walls,   still no man
brought me death in   any battle.
Now my son's brand   batters me down,
else I slay him   with my sword.
If thou hast courage   come with death,
winning war-coat   from warrior old,
an easy task to him who for such things   has any right.
Not the most fearful   of Eastern folk
could fight deny, thou art so eager   come; see of us who   60
gives up his battle-coat,   who brings home two."
The heavy ashen spears   they hurl like rain
to cluster in the shields.   They close on foot
breaking the battle-boards   with heavy blows,
splitting them till   the fragments fall apart,
broken by blows . . .⁴
                    . . . Now blade is loud on blade,
twice Hiltibrant bleeds,   but not heart's blood.
A third time Hadubrant   brings down his sword
full on   his father's helm.   70
The blade falls,   fountains fire, the helm
groans like a gong,   glances the blow.

Then Hadubrant cries aloud, "Curse on the crippled blade.
The old Hun's head   is hard as fire rock,
his helm defends him   though his blade is dumb.
His craft is in this treasure   and his tongue;
I'll split them both."   Throws down his broken shield,
with both hands wheels   his sword up to the height.
Hadubrant lets fall the blow.   Hiltibrant flings high his shield.
The broken oak   binds fast the falling blade.   80
Then Hiltibrant,   hot with rage,
strikes with a heavy hand.   The blow goes home,
bursting the rings   beneath the helmet rim,
through golden collar   and through collar bone,
broken,   battering a way.
Hadubrant falls.   With both hands
Hiltibrant tugs out the blade.   Blood follows.
Hadubrant,   Hiltibrantson,
dies in his blood   while weeps above
Hiltibrant,   Heribrantson.   90

NOTES

1. At this time, the king of the SCA's East Kingdom ("Austmǫrk") was Frederick of Holland (Frederick Hollander). For more backstory on this incident, see the ninth stanza of Fleck's "Ravens' Rede" and the accompanying footnote.

2. It is unlikely that Hiltibrant (or Hildebrand) is a real historical figure. Germanic folklore usually makes him companion to Deitrich von Bern, a legendary version of Theodoric the Great, king of the Ostrogoths, who invaded the Italian Visigoths in 489 and defeated Odoacer, their chieftain, four years later; King Theodoric then ruled both Gothic kingdoms from 493 to 526. To mitigate personal blame, however, "Deitrich" often appears in oral tradition as Italy's rightful king, not as an invader. In time he became as famous in southern Germany as Siegfried became in the Rhineland. As Deitrich's faithful servant, Hiltibrant follows his lord into exile before finally returning home for this fateful encounter against Odoacer's forces.

3. In Friedman's translation, "Theotrih" refers to Dietrich/Theodoric, the lord whom Hiltibrant follows into exile.

4. This is where the original manuscript ends.

Ron Snow

Ron Snow (1946–1997) was a highly popular and deeply respected poet within the SCA kingdom of Ansteorra, and his efforts earned him one of that realm's highest honors: the title "Lion of Ansteorra, Defender of the Dream." In his mundane life, after a four-year stint in the U.S. Navy, Snow worked as an artist, copywriter, and graphic artist for various companies in the San Antonio region. Snow's literary inspiration, though, blossomed within the special context provided by the SCA. Stirred early by the Kirk Douglas film *The Vikings* (1958), Snow made a Norse persona a key part of his SCA identity. Among his peers he was known as Ragnar Ulfgarsson, and he customarily wrote on topics tied to SCA events. For instance, in the poem he considered his masterpiece, *Blardrengir Saga*, Snow recounts in passionate detail the Battle for the Lost Lands, a "war" that occurred in Ansteorra in 1988. Snow was also a fan of Tolkien and an avid D&D master.

Blardrengir Saga[1]
(The Saga of the Blue Warriors)

PROLOGUE

Fast the glory-road is ridden
and rise will the wise man early,
for high deeds are done by day,
and the rough day is short enough.

I. HOW BARON OLAF'S PLAN TO RAID THE LOST LANDS
WENT AWRY[2]

Olaf of Kharkov called helm-trees
to come ride the wide foam-road
for the Lost Lands where booty
for bold men lay gleaming gold.
A hundred raised sworn swords
and steely made the raiders' song,   10
for who is loathe to leave
lofty halls when glory calls?

A hundred men set sail
to explore the lore-sung land,
and bring the bright legend-
hoard aboard brilliant decks.
But ill luck wrought the Raven God
to bring cold Rán her watered gold.
Wide the trestle feast she spread
for soggy bread brings bright rings.   20

Few of the sea-steed herd
safe sailed that whale-road.[3]
Still beckoned the Lost Lands,
from ill luck to pluck riches.
Bold spear-friends they found
when fair to land the band came;
for Olaf's call was clear
to southern kin and shield-men.

But spied they chieftains come
to check with might their right.[4]   30
Embers from camp flames flew,
fierce gleamed and seemed like stars.
Like yellow grain sprang greed
with grim men to win the harvest.
By morning would gray geese fly
down to lakes of bloody ground.

Iron-hammered steel struck
the startled flight of night birds
as straight warriors wrought
the wound-blades soon to work.   40
The men Olaf called came
to pick camp in thick woods,
the better to watch the way
and when weary sleep deep.

II. THE GATHERING OF THE RAIDERS

The camps the scouts skirted
and said when spied they wide:
"Seamus of the Cats called
his carls to camp to hamper
Dinar the grim Graf and
great dreams of Olaf's plunder.   50
A hundred shields show
bold the gold of Seamus.[5]

"Another hundred purple hang,
the hand of Dinar's men to show.
Few we are, but mighty men—
and mighty men may win the day.
Let our count number now
the names who seek the hero's fame
that stands where shields clash cold
when light marks the killing fight."   60

Forth strode staunch CAMERINUS;
his spear-wood stood beside
his shield-man, sturdy STEPHEN.
Then up stalked hard RISHARD
and weapon-girt GAIUS
with minds to gain great fame.
Bold CORRBIN fierce in firelight
followed blame-ridden ROLLO.

Battle-maid bright, BRIGITTA,
and CONNALL bred for red slaughter,   70
with SEAN LINDSEY laughed
loud till dawn through battle songs.
DUNCAN MACLEOID's lifted
blade open laid the ale cask,
then FURY BAN MCMORN filled
full the cup he lifted up.

ALREK and broken-toed TARL
together downed brown ale.
Dagger-eyed DAFYDD dared
the morrow's doom with brave AVERY.   80
The giant KARL smiled sly
as stone honed his broad axe,
and DANIEL told of dark days
and dire ones soon to bloom.

Then to Olaf's camp came
a few to crew the hold;
and found the fighters'
pack fair victual lacked.
For the warriors' weal
welcome drew Anastacia.   90
From far Bjornsborg, Blanche
brought the fat battle feast.[6]

Red-tressed Bonnie's timely
tread brought the heroes' bread.
From the south sought Moonbear,
shining battle-gold to hold;
with Ragnar to take the tale
and tell well the bold saga.
Thus had the number named
now to swim the grim blood-sea.   100

III. THE CHOOSING OF THE CHIEFTAN

Though his doom drove Olaf
down to Njörd's tall hall,
his bold banner will wave
for his wyrd steered the course.[7]
But must a chief be chosen,
the champion's fame to aim
and point the straight spear
down storm-roads red to tread.

Since Olaf's ships lost land,
only luck and skill plucks   110
fruit from the battle trees
the field grows on the morrow.
Must be cunning and craft
the rede that leads this crew.
So what fierce chief fares
to make the wake they follow?

Gave the Roman this rede:[8]
"On the red field they'll wield
not the sharper sword, but many
stand ten to one against us.   120
So the woods our plan must make,
most to strike like a hound
at the heel of the host
and him drag down to ground."

FURY BAN MCMORN followed:
"The forest boar cuts deep
as did my Pictish people;
so do we pursue them.
We shall be the wild wind
that wreaks blood streaks.   130
Of these briar lands, Lords,
our lofty claim names us."

This Pict the raiders raised
upon the red shield and said,
"You shall steer our quick course
to carry us to victory.
Of our band the banner
and bane of foemen slain,
blue as woad will it be,
to wave the brave men on."   *140

IV. THE BRIAR LORDS DEAL WITH DINAR TO BATTLE SEAMUS

The Pict in dark night did
dare fare to Dinar's fire.
The white shield he bore bade
behind their line safe pass.
Received Graf Dinar his gifts
and gave an ear to hear
spoke the battle bargain
bold, the lost gold to claim.

At light's dawn the Gold Duke
down the battle-track did sound   150
his array of bright byrnies.
Barred there his pass Dinar's
men held grim their halberds,
a host to reap the gold wheat.
Formed Seamus his shield-wall
to spite the wound grouse flight.

The shield-line bright spears stung.
Swords pranced the silver dance.
Purple halberds hacked gold,
as howling spears shed red.   160
Kicked and shivered shield-walls,
biting like fighting stallions.
Then from the flanking forest
flew the blue warriors.

Like a *thurs's* back broke
by Mjöllnir's bite, the bright
shield-wall shuddered and fell.[9]
With spears-fear raised,
men from the rent gap ran;
bright red blades made them swift.   170
Scorn words Seamus shouted:
his shield-men to group again.

The blood struck fierce and fast
the fold of golden sheep
until the Lion roared his wrath
and raised up their dazed shields.[10]
Back to the forest ferns
fell the dire Briar Lords—
men, at the lure leaping,
left red dew on blue spears.   180

Tight held the shields of Seamus,
shone they though less brightly.
The far way back they fought;
forest dread sped them home.
Silver ransom well rode
raiders heavy laden;
bright rings bought noble heads
and stealth brought golden wealth.

V. THE WRATH OF THE GOLD DUKE

Vengeance the Gold Cat called
on the camp the raiders made.   190
Malice, his mind, steeped strong
for storms thundered under
gold helms badly battered.
Black venom from men's hearts.
His greatest heroes gave
grave oaths sworn with brave words.

At dawn rode ready men
when raider tracks hounds found.
The forest broad they braved,
the bright teeth of wolves to pull.   200
Wary they traveled the trail,
a tread soft led the host.
But a trail covered cannot
long conceal the ale song.

From raider beards fell foam
from fearless horns of beer.
Loudly mead-soaked heroes howled
in the hall of the tall forest.
Then fell hard upon heads
the great hammer of Seamus.   210
The victory ale's cold keg
must not be cracked too soon.

Men with foggy brains brawled
to break away from slayers.
Quick were scattered weapons snatched
to scar the cold gold shields.
But the fight the mead marked,
and men swayed in the fray.
Brave FURY BAN MCMORN fell
sore before the Duke's fist.   220

The shield of strong STEPHEN
staunch guarded his liege lord.
"Retreat!" called CAMERINUS,
but came to this aim none.
Then hard the battle-band
of men beat STEPHEN down.
Enraged, the Roman swore
vengeance red on gold heads.

The safe haven few found
of forest wide for hiding.   230
Wet chains wrapped the raiders.
Red the bands bound round them.
In thralldom lay the lofty
crew the call of Olaf drew.
The net of wrath Seamus wrought
tight wrung the blue fighters.

VI. HOW CAMERINUS CAME TO STAND BEFORE THE
STRONGHOLD OF SEAMUS

But one escaped to claim
the cloak of forest oak.
Speedy were his long legs
and light as nightfall's dew.   240
CAMERINUS slew some
sly loud hounds that found him.
In a leafy loft he
lay to plan man-slaughter.

The Roman found no friends
where foes had made their raid.
The shattered shield of STEPHEN
showed where the bowyer fell.
The trampled grass dark grew;
grim from the rain of bloodstains.   250
He tight gripped his great spear
and grimly stalked the open road.

Bloody raiders railed at
rusty chains and wound-pain.
Sour wine and bark bread
was broke to choke the heroes.
"Slim the ransom from landless
lords," did muse Duke Seamus.
"Where is your cunning craft?
Can luck pluck no ransom?"   260

A warning the gate guards
gave of a tall man standing
with a staunch and fearless stance,
and a stare that dared much.
Loud called CAMERINUS
so careful ears could hear.
"This road I ride is gray
but red should be instead.

"Bring your thanes to thrust
my thirsty spear clear through.   270
All at once or one by
one come feel my steely blade."
Arthur of the Fen faced
fierce the tall bold Roman;
six armed men followed fast,
full wary of the dare.

"Do yet the hounds hang back?"
howled the warrior's words.
Arthur called, "Come to us
brave CAMERINUS must,   280
for his fellow curs crawl
in our cage, and wagers
say he is wont to work
well sore the galley's oar."

Camerinus speaks:
"Your knights knelt before us
and not so long ago.
Our best beer and meat eased
their bonds with fair repast.
If won this contest could
by callous customs foul,   290
you are far more famous
folk than we hope to be."

Sir Arthur speaks:
"Your long legs outstep our
line, so stand if man you are."
Straight the Roman raced them
to rush around their ground.

Camerinus speaks:
"Do you follow then through
thorny ways, or scorn glory?"

Sir Arthur speaks:
"You shall not draw us down
to sore divide our force."   300

Two men marched silent soft,
and so around they found
the warrior's broad back.
Braver deeds need daring.
Sprung thus the timely trap
that about the hero closed.
So fared the Roman's fate
that oft' follows heroes.

VII. THE COMING OF BATTLE BLANCHE

Left in the wake of waste
where Seamus won the fray   310
gathered there were those who
thought were lost the caught men.
To flee and find safety
from the foe showed good sense,
the camp's followers felt,
before more doom came down.

"With one mission we met
and made to raid these lands,"

cried the feast-bringer Blanche.
"Bargained we to share fair
the hoard of glittering gold.
For good support would we
well earn our red gold rings:
ripe spoils for loyal friends.

"Now the bloody chain chafes
our champions brave, gravely.
I will not leave our lords
lacking freedom while we
flee to warm soft safety.
Steady and true our blue
banner should wave to wake
wild the deep sleep of heroes."

The banner of her band
she bound tight round her hair.
The kettle's wood cover
became the shield she'd wield.
For her sword the stout ladle
swung, in slight grip, mighty.
Armed thus with just jutted
jaw she strode the red road.

Dust swirled at her sharp step
and shadows fled her tread.
Wolves ran low with tails tucked
from the track of black storms.
High above the red road
ravens dark barked hungry.
Come then did Battle Blanche
to break the gates of fate.

In her eyes the fire flamed
fierce to pierce the guardsmen.
Spears drew bewildered back
and barred they not her way.
Up then paced Pendaren,
proud and mighty fighter.
The path he dared hold hard
and hinder swift her tread.

Him, lightning swift, she smote
her stroke and broke a shard

320

330

340

350

from out the ladle large,
to lodge deep in seat-meat.[11]   360
Up then Seamus shouldered
to shout above the thane's pain.
"Do hold your great spoon still
and swat no more men sore.

"Do you bring ready ransom
for rogues the hounds found?"
"No ransom I bring," barked
Blanche, "but a challenge shall
I make to set lords loose.
Let them free, or fight with me."   370
She raised the buckler brave
and brandished ladled hand.

Seamus up raised his hands
to hold away the blow.
"Strike me not with stir sticks,
for stout heart gains you fame.
If for ransom courage counts,
complete the debt you met.
Take all your heroes home
to heal and eat your meal."   380

And so were shackles struck,
and stalwart heroes followed
out from camp Battle Blanche:
bright savior of the fighters,
fair keeper of the cauldron,
cruel beater of the hip meat,
breaker of the blood brawl,
bride of war and valor.

VIII. THE COUNCIL OF THE BLUE WARRIORS

Bloody sore and great were wounds
wrapped fair with careful herbs.   390
Loaded were trestle trays
with tasty meats and sweet
wine for vigor's stout strength.
Strong were warriors' hearts.
To them was brought the beer
to boast with mighty toasts.

After wounds sore were soothed
they sat for council round
the brands that brightly burned.

Brooded then the men of blue. 400
Their Pictish chieftain[12] charged,
"Change we now sword for plow?
Beaten men here sit sad
who scorned once the Norns' thread.

"Shall we pack gathered goods
and grovel to the tall ships,
afraid to cringe or crawl
or chance a backward glance?
Hard we fought and hard fell,
For that's what heroes do. 410
Shall now blades dance at dawn
to drive Valkyries nigh?"

Men jumped and held high
their heads and cried with pride:
"Our stand, the morrow marks,
may make us fall to death,
but none we face will force
the field to see us yield.
All-Father, may you mark
where mighty fights the few." 420

IX. THE WAR WAIN

The light of day burned bright
and brought the horde of swords
to gleam upon the pale plain.
Perish there would good men,
to drown beneath the broad
and bloody flood of battle.
Red muzzles of wild wolves
woke and spoke the rune.

Graf Dinar, ahead his host,
hailed loud the proud Seamus. 430
Ended he trusted truce
with tribute thrown salute
to the warrior's brave blue
band standing at the wood's rim.
Then thunder rolled roaring
and rumbled from the forest.

Mead-heavy, shield-sided,
spear-bristled, beer-laden:
the Briar Lords' War Wain

was watched by wary eyes.   440
Battlemaids draped their deck
to dare a boarding horde.
From kegs, beer flowed foaming
to fall in amber splendor.

  The Blue Warriors said:
"We mean to share the spoils
sought by all who brawl here.
Come sware your war-weapons
to well defend this end,
and see well how we host
with heavy keg this levy.   450
Well-honored truce we'd toast;
you thirsty men to win."

But no man fared forward
to fast seal the booty deal.
Fear of chieftain's gruff glare
or greed was worse than thirst.

  The Blue Warriors said:
"Know then your horns will hold
hostage drink from chain links.
We will baffle and bind
your best men once again."   460

X. THE FINAL BATTLE FOR THE LOST LANDS

Then were champions chosen
by chiefs to contest best.
DAFYDD of the blue banner
bore the war challenge.
Shields clashed in mounting might
and made the blades bite deep.
DAFYDD swung dripping death
and drew he life from strife.

A severing blow broke
bone to lay his foeman low.   470
Loud then did fierce horns howl
to hail the battle gale.
Then broke the storm of slaying
swords upon the field of shields.
Savage halberds harshly
hacked to rend attackers.

The great shield-walls washed
with bloody gore and scored
with axe-bites cruel and crafty,
crawled like brawling serpents. 480
The wound-blades fiercely fell.
Few fled that day of slaying.
Rich the raven's fat feast.
Full the gorge of gaunt wolves.

Seamus won the Lost Lands;
his legion shared fair gold.
The Lords of Briars bore
the brunt of war's glory.
Long their death-song sang.
The safe way they shunned. 490
On that last daring day
drew the Valhalla's maids.

EPILOGUE

Warriors of the banner blue—
bold, lost gold, sea raiders.
The eyes of Ulfgar's son saw
the spear-rain on Belmead plain;
well-filled was my high horn
with Gunnlöd's heady mead.
So ends this skald's saga
of that shining battle time. 500

NOTES

1. In Snow's unpublished text, he uses punctuation with some inconsistency. When the intent is clear, I clarify syntax as needed. When Snow's meaning is less than clear or even obscure, as sometimes happens, the original text stands. SCA names and Norse names have been corrected and standardized when applicable.

2. Unfortunately, I could not find any SCA member who still remembers what the Lost Lands were. Snow has a short introductory note to *Blardrengir Saga* but says of the Lost Lands only that they were rumored to contain "much wealth and many [buried] artifacts." This note does say more about the battle itself, however. According to Snow, "Baron Olaf and his army met with many mishaps on the way to the battle. Only seventeen men arrived to fight under his blue banner. I had pledged my support to Baron Olaf and arrived to find his seventeen warriors already swaggering like saga-heroes. They were vastly outnumbered but were determined to ride the glory road. What occurred was the stuff of sagas and so it was written."

3. "Sea-steed herd" is a kenning for ships, "whale-road" for the sea. It seems likely that, given Snow's Viking persona, he took some poetic license in describing how the Blue Warriors traveled to the battle site. The Raven-god is obviously Odin, and the Norse sea-goddess Rán is often associated with drownings.

4. These chieftains discovered in the Lost Lands are Duke Seamus of the Cats and Graf Dinar (Dinaris the Wanderer); *graf* is a historical title of German nobility meaning "count."

5. Seamus's color is gold—hence, "Gold Duke"—and Dinar's color is purple. Although Ragnar claims their armies numbered a hundred men each, Snow's introductory note observes that they really had "only thirty to forty men each." At the end of Section III, Ragnar reveals that Olaf's color is blue; hence, the "blue warriors." It is unclear whether these are heraldric colors or simply team colors chosen for the event.

6. Bjornsborg is a Ansteorran barony that services the San Antonio region in Bexar County.

7. Njörd is associated with voyages, fishing, and the sea, and he dwells within Nóatún, a seaside home filled with ships. Because Njörd's mythology indicates fertility and growth, not death, Snow's specific meaning is unclear. Still, he seems to suggest that, despite issuing the initial call, Olaf himself was one of those who couldn't ultimately attend the battle; certainly, Olaf does not figure in any further action.

8. The Roman is Camerinus, whose full Society name is Valerius Fidelis Camerinus, although the warrior Gaius, judging from his name, had a Roman persona as well.

9. Mjöllnir is Thor's hammer, and *thursar* are giants.

10. The epithet "Lion" could be Snow's pun on the sudden ferocity evinced by Duke Seamus of the Cats; however, the Duke also earned the formal designation "Lion of Ansteorra, Defender of the Dream" a few years earlier in 1986.

11. The story of Blanche breaking her ladle—a huge wooden spoon—is still remembered by Ansteorrans today. Originally, she borrowed this spoon (plus a large iron cauldron and tripod for cooking) from Melissa Snow, who reports that it took her a long time to find a replacement of similar size.

12. This passage seems to refer to Fury Ban McMorn despite him "falling" to Duke Seamus in Section V.

Sandra B. Straubhaar

Sandra B. Straubhaar (b. 1951) has taught at the University of Texas at Austin since 1998, where she's a distinguished senior lecturer for the Department of Germanic Studies. Academically, she is perhaps best known for her monograph on Old Norse poetry, *Old Norse Women's Poetry: The Voices of Female Skalds* (2011), but Straubhaar is an active Tolkien scholar as well. In addition to articles, she has contributed several entries to *The J. R. R. Tolkien Encyclopedia* edited by Michael D. C. Drout. Within the SCA, however, Straubhaar—aka Brynhildr Kormáksdóttir—is one of the group's most active alliterative poets. Focusing on Norse forms, Straubhaar's compositions typically commemorate friends or events, and she excels at mentoring young poets. Perhaps the most notable instance among many involves teaching a course that led to a committee-created skaldic poem, "Vestrríkis Drápa," which *Tournaments Illuminated* published in its Winter 1976 issue.

Straubhaar's *Háttatal*[1]

I. *Rétthent*

If bored ye be of Snorri,
if Bragi soundeth foggy,
If your lust for musty lay-craft
laggeth back and draggeth,
take up your sword and slake its
salt cravings in new ravings.
Be a berserk! That works
best when one is restless.

II. *Áttmælt*

Ate we all the oatmeal,
also drank the rank ale,   10
swallowed swill by buckets,
sweet rolls inhaled neatly;
we flooded gills and gullets,
got quaking belly-ache then;
we barfed it, thick, in buckets.
Best it was to rest then.

III. *Sextánmælt*

Swords swish, saxes clash,
serpents rage, mages chant,
balefires burn, blackbirds soar,
bards conspire, hardships reign;   20
creatures crawl, all men quail,
thunder cracks, crazed wolves snack,
witches wail, wights stand watch,
the world ends, with banners furled.

IV. *Dunhent*

Lacking fish in the lake,
Leif bakes an herbal cake;
noshing—squish!—on seeds
(such feeds not his needs!),
Leif vows he'll take his life.
Leif's wife wants no such strife,   30
shoots tender, toothsome meat.
"My treat," says she: "Leif, eat."

V. *Runhent*

Warriors are wont
to wax rather gaunt
while hurriedly harrying
hard, meantime burying
appetites awesome,
not opening their maws some.
But when battle's passed by,
bladesmen home fly   40
for a snort and a snack,
not sad to be back.

Baltimore Harbor: Rower's Chant[2]

Break our backs, crack our bones!
Bottoms hurt, thud on thwarts.
Sweet our hard-earned sweating
on swan-road heavy-laden.
Blisters, bowed backs, stiff necks,
brave our longship's striving.
Kingly keel-bird winging,
coxswain never stopping.

Swift and deep, O sweepsmen!
Swan-road gleams but wanly.   10
Ribs pop, sweat beribbons
backs of bare-sark oarsmen.
Kingly keel-bird winging.
"Captain, are we stopping?
Oars wet, eyes wet, sky's wet. . . ."
Atli answers: "Hold oars!"

Skaldic Lament[3]

Whither went the warriors,
wild-eyed and smiling,
hawk-eyed and haughty
heroes, naught afearing,
bold and battle-ready
bladesmen, made for striving,
all who lived aforetime,
each one, whether went they?

Whither went the war-maids,
wise in more than war-craft,   10
seeresses and skald-maids,
shape-shifters, sly ones?
Fared they all to Freyja,
foremost of the Vanir,
to sup and practice swordcraft
sundered from us always?[4]

Worshipped we the Wanderer,
one-eyed wily Odin,
thief; and Thor the Redbeard,
thewed like the ice-bear;   20
gave honor to the elf-folk,

awe to the *dísir*;[5]
were chary of the changeling,
ill-born, ill-spoken Loki.

Strove we on strong ships,
sinews strained at oarlocks
(spirits rose when sails rose),
spent starlit nights on thwart-beds;
rode we with rash kings,
hard-rulers, reckless,   30
our steeds, manes stormtossed,
stamping on the sea-cliffs.

Once we won the new lands:
Wild Eire, Iceland,
godforsaken Greenland,
goodly isles of Orkney.
Once we sailed on new seas,
swanroads undiscovered,
tried our luck with Leifr,
dared to fare with Eirik.[6]   40

Gone our ancient glory:
gone the songs of gleemen,
sundered are the shieldmaids,
swordsmen, doughty warriors.
I the skald am grief-struck,
doomed to stand deserted,
raven-hoarse and rasping,
wretched, fey, bereft.

Björn's *Drápa*[7]

The tale of Tom
(told boldly,
tallied truthfully)
tell I now.

Trustworthy Tom,
trim and tactful,
toiled tedious,
true engineer.

Served unceasing
(seasons endless)   10

General Motors,
motley masters.

Tom got tired
toting briefcase,
tallying, tinkering,
toying, tabulating.

Tom took trunk,
traveled on trips:
sought he Sweden,
explored Down Under.   20

Maze-filled mists
met, and parted:
Tom's tenure faded:
Björn was born.

No more toils Tom
for motley masters:
Tom's retired,
retreats before Björn.

Björn the bear,
burly Viking;   30
cunning, crafty
keen-eyed thane.

Björn the bold,
battle-ready;
Björn blade-maker,
box-crafter brave.

At Björn's side Ailikn,
all-skilled, indomitable,
valiant Valkyrie,
versatile, bold.   40

Björn builds boxes,
chips at carvings,
shops and vacuums,
whilst a-viking goes Ailikn.

Dutiful daughter
departs her studies,
heads home,
hears the news.

"Father's flipped,"
frets Björn's daughter.   50
Prankful parents
perturb and perplex.

But Björn and Ailikn
become yet Norser,
seek more vivid
Viking adventures.

Hail Björn!
Hail Ailikn!
Hawkland Moor's halls
hail you welcome![8]   60

A Birthday Poem for Gunnvǫr Silfrahárr, the Viking Answer Lady

Gunnvarar afmæli[9]

Hear me hail the heroine,
the hardy Finn, with bardcraft:
steadfast-striding shieldmaid,
skillful silvertressed one.
A goddess glad is Gunnvǫr,
glorious midst mere mortals;
learned multi-Laurel,
likewise prized in friendship.

Only idiots blithering
say: burdensome are birthdays.   10
(Never! says dame Damaris,
Deftly basting feast-meat.)
Glasses raise for Gunnvǫr,
gold-goddess known for boldness;
honor this hour, and hail her,
Answer-Lady, Swordmaid!

Rimsholt's Winter Revel (January 1991)[10]

Thorri, thin month,
thrust upon us:
its yearly onset
says Yule is over.

Feet and fingers
feel frost:
winds wail,
wolves know hunger.
Happy the human
who hearth possesses;   10
wanderers well know
woes of winter.
Rimsholt renders
rescue to us,
bards and outlaws,
bladesmen, ladies,
skalds and scoundrels,
scum and nobles;
opens to all
its august halls.   20
Fire, fellowship,
food is here.
Praise the people
who pay us welcome!

Praise I also
prince and lord,
our crowned king,
clan chieftain.
Bold is Blackwolf
in battle and bearing;   30
dauntless is Dag,
daring of deed.[11]
Hardy, hawk-eyed,
high his kinship;
black-haired, black-browed,
brave his glance.

Laud have I also
for land's lady,
Ilsa the only,
unequalled in glory: 40
southern cousin
to Saxon clans,
tribal treasure,
Tyrkir's kin.[12]
Finned and foamy
friends has she:
diving daughters
of darksome wave-gods.

Hail our hosts
and laud our lieges!   50
—Bard backs off now,
begs for bounty.

Ode to Calum Creachadora, A. S. XXIX[13]

Finn the forceful
and fair Garlanda
Midrealm monarchs
make now wreathing—
crown here Calum
with crest of Laurel—
Skillful skald
this son of Eire—
battles bold
this bard retelleth—   10
sings he sagas
smooth-tongued, swift—
Wealth of wordcraft
wells from Calum—
lilts he lark-like—
loud his mouth-cave—
Bodacious bard
brash in sword-play—
loyal liegeman—
Laurel now—   20
Glory give him—
Grant him honor—

NOTES

1. This sequence was inspired by Snorri Sturluson's *Háttatal*, a string of stanzas demonstrating different poetic forms. Since Straubhaar's original text uses underlining, boldface, and italics to indicate metrical features such as alliteration, rhyme, and slant rhyme, she probably used this poem as a teaching tool.

2. In a note to "Baltimore Harbor: Rower's Chant," Straubhaar explains that she once heard "Prof. Björn Sigfússon of the University of Iceland suggest that *dróttkvætt* stanzas were originally utilized to pace rowing. This suggestion, coupled with my own (at the time) recent experience rowing the Maryland Longship Company's *Fyrdraca* (Firedrake) around Baltimore Harbor, inspired the poem above." The rowing event occurred on Labor Day weekend, 1983. Bruce Blackistone, the "Atli" (or Attila)

named in Straubhaar's last line, notes that the Longship Company took the name for its vessel *Fyrdraca*, the successor to *Sae Earn*, straight from *Beowulf*.

3. This lament by Straubhaar, a species of the *ubi sunt* genre, won Midrealm's Poetry Laureate contest in A.S. XIX (May 1984–May 1985). She uses a variation on Norse prosody that she describes as somewhere between "very loose *dróttkvætt*" ('Court Meter') and very strict *fornyrðislag* ('Old Lore Meter')."

4. For more on Freyja's many attributes, see the note to Paxson's poem "For the Goddess Freyja."

5. The *dísir* are protective female spirits whose functions within Norse myth vary.

6. Norse settlers founded successful colonies in Ireland, Iceland, Greenland, and the Orkney Islands just north of Scotland. Erik Thorvaldsson (Erik the Red) founded the Greenland settlement, and his son Leif Erikson made an important voyage to North America. For a longer account of their deeds, see James Dorr's "The Westfarer" in this volume.

7. "Björn's *Drápa*" is a rare example of SCA poetry that breaks its fourth wall by celebrating the retirement of Tom Yasin (Björn) from General Motors. Although called a *drápa*, which is a skaldic poem with a refrain, this text uses the *fornyrðislag* meter.

8. "Hawkland Moor" is the SCA's name for Pontiac, Michigan, a northwestern suburb of Detroit, which, among other things, explains General Motors.

9. The word *afmæli* is Icelandic for "birthday"; Gunnvǫr's epithet *silfrahárr* means "silver-haired."

10. "Rimsholt's Winter Revel" is among the dozens of commemorative poems Straubhaar has composed for special SCA occasions. Rimsholt is a canton in the Middle Kingdom's Barony of Andelcrag—specifically, Grand Rapids, Michigan. Thorri (or Þorrablót) is a midwinter Icelandic festival named for the month *Þorri* in Iceland's historical calendar, which lasts from mid-January through mid-February. Andelcrag has been holding its Winter Revel annually since the mid-1980s.

11. Dag Thorgrimsson (Jeff Skevington), the Blackwolf, is Midrealm's most prolific king, having won his kingdom's crown an outstanding eight times. His heraldry is marked by a black wolf's head. This Winter Revel occurred during Dag's first reign; Ilsa von Westfal served as his queen.

12. Historically, Tyrkir was a servant to Leif Erickson during his voyages to Greenland around 1000 AD. Since the equivalent to his name is commonly thought to be Dietrich, he might have been German—hence, "kin" to Ilsa von Westfal. Furthermore, Ilsa has a mermaid on her heraldry, which explains Straubhaar's following reference to "diving daughters / of darksome wave-gods."

13. Calum Creachadora (Eric Panek) served as Midrealm's bard in 1994–1995, and Straubhaar composed this ode to honor his laurel-crowning ceremony in 1994. His works include a one-hundred-line narrative poem in Old English meter about the Battle of Clontarf in 1014, which was fought between a Norse-Irish alliance led by King Sigtrygg Silkbeard and others against Brian Boru, High King of Ireland. The latter won decisively. Over Calum's crowning presided Midrealm's two monarchs, King Finn Herjolfsson (Kevin Griggs) and Queen Garlanda de Stanas (Kellene M. Stets).

Christie L. Ward

Christie L. Ward (b. 1962) is a lifelong Texas native and an independent scholar focused on the history of Viking Age Scandinavia. Since the 1990s, she has been running an award-winning website, *The Viking Answer Lady*, dedicated to all things related to Norse life, history, and culture. Under the name Gunnvǫr silfrahárr, Ward is also an active member of the SCA. She wrote the following poem to celebrate another member, and it first appeared on Paul Douglas Deane's website *Forgotten Ground Regained*. Sandra B. Straubhaar dedicates a poem in this anthology, "Gunnvarar Afmaeli," to Ward.

Lady of Cats

Greater than goodness, those granted glory
of beauty beyond mere fairness of form.
So shall I speak of she like the moonlight—
as pale as the ash, as pale as the moon.
Ship-giver is she, a deep minded seeress,
the Lady of Cats, her hair gold as corn.
The poppy is placed by her feet, pure flowers,
But bested by far its beauty by hers.
On fist the falcon, fair as the frost is,
Ice by a diamond, its beauty is dimmed.   10
Hers is the herb-craft, knows her hands healing.
Swift fly her fingers on bronze strings' bright songs:
High over harpstrings sounds out her singing.
Fair are all these, still she is more fair.

Frida Westford

Since joining the SCA in 1975, Frida Westford (b. 1944) has been a prolific poetic presence within the organization. She especially prefers Germanic and Old Norse alliterative meters. It was when studying medieval French literature as a graduate student, however, that Westford discovered her passion for Old English and Old Norse. In particular, she came to admire *Beowulf* and a Middle English poem, *Sir Gawain and the Green Knight*, quite highly. As an SCA poet, Westford—who goes by Jófríðr Þorbjarnardóttir—benefited greatly from early mentorship by Sandra B. Straubhaar. Subsequent encounters with other SCA members and the Indiana University Icelandic Club, to which she belongs, have helped Westford further hone her craft. To date, her most ambitious poem is a twenty-stanza poem, the "Oak and Olive *Drápa*," commissioned as a wedding gift for Midrealm's crowned rulers, Finn Herjolfsson and Tamara di Firenze, who reigned from September 1999 to April 2000. In 1996, Westford was elevated to the Order of the Laurel, the arts and sciences peerage, for her literary contributions to the SCA.

Skaldic Stress *Lausavísa*

Strict this count of stress in
staves of skalds, nor wavers
lest sought praise be lost and
laughter rise to rafters.
Tight the measures taught and
test all, many besting.
Dreadless meet hard *dróttkvætt*—
dare to make nor fake it.

Lausavísa for Starfarers

Starry depths we'll steer now;
sternward leave Earth turning.
New worlds wait, and knowledge—
let none dread the unknown.
Fare we out now fearless:
from our homes go roaming;
over star roads, ever
eager, plying skyways.

Poul Anderson's Lay[1]

A shapely ship shall bear him forth,
Stem to the stars standing, not loth,
Viking-hearted voyager bold,
Who wended once to Wonderstrands.[2]

"Mary O'Meara": made he that lay,
Few will forget faring after;
The tales he told, both true and tall,
With goodly glee gladdened hearers.[3]

In heroes' high hall they wait
Great ones to greet him with golden mead—   10
Holger Dane hails, and Hrolf Kraki:[4]
"Skald most skilled, *skål*, welcome be!"

Oak and Olive *Drápa*[5]

Skilled one asked for skaldship,
scribe from east, that feasting
fairest maid and fearless
foe of rings have singing.
Son of Abdul sends me
sweet to make this meeting,
happy wish these hopeful:
health be theirs and wealth too.

To Hár's theft give hearing;
heed and show your breeding![6]   10
Warden now of word-fame
wends here seeking friendship.

Bragi's brew for swigging,
best of gifts uplift I;
lend your ears, ye land-wards,
lofty ode's bestowed here.

Jarl from Fenix faring
foremost among warriors,
rough-coat feeds and reddens
ravens' beaks that seek him.   20
Few withstand him, foemen,
fields and goods they yield, our
dear lord often daring
din of storm of linden.[7]

Wolf all white did welcome
winsome Sif of linen;
deeds of worth there did she,
deemed they were as seemly.
Kenned her maid of Connor,
kindred mind there finding   30
—e'er she chose the useful—
owns her kith Fiona.[8]

Best of book-leaves, wist all
baroness wrought fair for
mighty ones in mead-hall;
made a name unfading.
Stood I by when steadfast
steered Finn home, was cheered, to
Tirnẏwẏdd returning;
Tarquin Laurel marked him.[9]   40

Swordsman fared on swan-way,
sailed to northward mail-clad.
        Oak in arms to's liking
        olive holds enfolded.

Hild of gems beheld he,
hair rich, fine eyes shining
candles; love was kindled,
king amazed with gazing.
Dark brow-moons then dirk-bright
darted beams that gleamed as   50
Gefn of gold bands laughing
greeted Dane-lord meetly.[10]

Rose from Waters Rising
raiment-bright girl lightly,

speech most welcome, spoke to
spear-play crafty hero.[11]
Bonds they soon were binding,
both did seek betrothal;
rich the match was reckoned,
rede was soon agreed to.   60

Wide lands hail the wedding,
well seems news in telling.
      Oak in arms to's liking
      olive holds enfolded.

Mighty king called meeting,
Midrík's war-oaks bidding;
far-flung kingdom fain was
Finn for's love to win there.
Hard that shield-þing heard I,
held in May, Gunn's playing;   70
rime-cold gore in Rimsholt
ran as Wyrd felled hirðs-men.

One's left scatheless only;
heirship son of Herjolf's
taken; royal token,
true crowns brought forth duly.
Blissful Florence's blossom's
brought to man who sought her;[12]
merry, soon Tamara
mead-full horn has borne him.   80

Lore of elders learn they
long to rule and strongly;
      boldly broad land wielding,
      both shall hold to oath-words.

Reign should lords as Ragnvaldr,
raise for such high praises.
Wine-Frigg hail, the winsome,
well-sung Arabella.[13]
Goodly gifts they left us,
game they seek now, blameless.   90
Have kings burdens heavy,
hold they shall laws olden.

Lod's kinsman's green lady,
leafy, has new chieftain;[14]
fell troop, young queen, follow,
freely throng to keel-lord.

Good kings strong folk guiding
get their trust with justice;
so, like blown glass blooming,
breaks not law of Drake's land.[15]   100

Kingdom keep they happy,
corn-rich fields be thornless;
      boldly broad land wielding,
      both shall hold to oath-words.

Hallowed thrice with help of
hammer, cups raised upward,
Thor's and Odin's, therewith
thirdly may hailed Freyja.
Gods them give long lives and
goodly meads and woodlands;   110
each pledged troth to other,
all who saw recall it.

Hills now smile and hollows,
holt and lea seem gleeful;
Æsir, Elves, have blessed us,
ills are far and sorrows.
Stock in steads not lacking,
—stilled are feuds and killings—
want may none this winter,
warless tide greet bridal.[16]   120

Now the twain are twined as
turn the leaves to burning;
war-leader's full worthy,
wise the bride beside him.
Cares new-crowned they'll own and
kind shall be, high-minded;
land to kings is loaned, but
lass is given glass-smith.

Gave I, mead all-golden,
Grímnir's flood o'er-brimming;[17]   130
bold folk ranked on benches,
beer you've drunk most cheerful.
Fell song-stream ears filling,
friends stilled tongues and young ones;
stern ones here in Sternfeld,
store is spent of lore-speech.

Skald has sung, not scolding,
skein of verse unfeigned here;

hoard of words made holy,
hall with staves said gravely.   140
Filled Tarik's wish fully,
finished work for kinsman;
heard ye well my hard ode,
high and less have blessing.

The Year Runs Away in Yesterdays

"And so the year runs away in yesterdays many."[18]

Lovely-hued lilacs of delicate scent,
Then blood-red rose in bloom rules the summer.
Poppies soon show proud heads through the barley—
Maples next, a marvel, mantled in scarlet.
Grey then grow skies that were glorious blue,
White winter walks in, and all waits in silence.
Easy to say that we see also seasons,
That lives of creatures last so little time.
Cities and states also stand not forever.
Do good dauntlessly, then, for your dear ones,   10
Since to hold fast your heart's desires is hopeless.
Yet sorrow not sooner than sorrow you must,
                    But joy
          In fair times spent with friends.
          Let worry not annoy
          Even though all else ends—
          Nothing can love destroy.

NOTES

1. Westford wrote "Poul Anderson's Lay" shortly after learning of his death in 2001.

2. In Anderson's most frequently reprinted poem, "Ballade of an Artificial Satellite" (1958), Anderson draws a parallel between Sputnik, an artificial satellite launched the previous year, and Thorfinn Karlsefni's eleventh-century discovery of a coastline in Vinland, which he names "Wonderstrands."

3. "Mary O'Meara" is a ballad Anderson includes in his novel *World Without Stars* (1967); it became quite popular within genre fandom and became a frequent folksong.

4. In Norse mythology, heroes gather in Valhalla after they die. Here, Anderson meets two heroes from his own fiction: Holger Carlsen from *Three Hearts and Three Lions* (1961) and Hrolf Kraki from *Hrolf Kraki's Saga* (1973).

5. Westford originally intended "Oak and Olive *Drápa*" as a *flokkr*, a long skaldic poem without a refrain. It was commissioned early in 1999 by the "scribe from the east," Master Sayf al-Qamar Tarik ibn Abdul, a skilled calligrapher and bead-maker, as a wedding gift for Finn Herjolfsson (the oak) and Tamara Di Firenze (the olive). After Finn won his third Crown Tournament in 1999, however, Westford expanded her intended *flokkr* into a *drápa*. This new poem was included with a letter of conveyance dated October 29, 1999 and presented to their majesties at a Crown Tournament held in Sternfeld (in Indianapolis and surrounding counties) to choose Finn and Tamara's successors. Westford then performed "Oak and Olive *Drápa*" publicly.

6. "Hár's theft" refers to Odin stealing the Mead of Poetry and giving it to Bragi Boddason. For more on this particular myth, see the footnote to Zimmer's poem "Invocation."

7. In order to win his first kingship, Finn left the Barony of Fenix (southwest Ohio and northern Kentucky) on May 24, 1992, to fight in Midrealm's Crown Tournament held in the Barony of Nordskogen (the Twin Cities region). Finn is here called a feeder of *wolves*, "rough-coats." The kenning "storm of linden" (i.e., wooden shields) refers to *battle*.

8. Having discussed Finn, Westford now turns to his bride, Tamara, the "Sif of linen"; the goddess Sif was married to Thor. The heraldic symbol for Ealdormere, an SCA kingdom in Ontario, is the White Wolf; hence, "wolf all white." Tamara served as protégé to Fiona Averylle O'Connor, a member of the Order of the Pelican, the peerage for service, and produced elaborate scribal scrolls for the court.

9. In November 1995, King Tarquin raised Finn to the Order of the Laurel on the strength of his skills in glassblowing. Finn's elevation occurred in the Shire of Tirnýwýdd (in Columbus, Ohio).

10. Both "Hild of gems" and "Gefn of Gold Bands" are kennings for *woman*. In Norse mythology, Hild was the beautiful daughter of King Högni, and *Gefn* is another name for Freyja, goddess of fertility and love.

11. Rising Waters is a barony in Ealdormere, Tamara's home kingdom.

12. Given that Tamara Di Firenze's persona is Italian, Westford here invokes the city of Florence, where the olive is also a typical tree.

13. Westford here praises the outgoing monarchs, Ragnvaldr Jonsson and Arabella Silvermane, and hopes for a peaceful transition of power.

14. The "green lady" is Earth, who belongs to the kinsman of Lod (or Lodur): Odin.

15. Westford enjoins the newly crowned King Finn, the glass blower, to keep the laws of Midrealm, which was known as the "dragon kingdom" for its heraldry and its *Draco Invictus* motto.

16. The new royal pair will rule during a peaceful winter. This is a safe prediction, however, because SCA wars occur only in summer, not winter.

17. Grímnir ("masked one") is another name for Odin, so "Grímnir's flood" is another kenning for the Mead of Poetry. The end of this stanza refers to Westford's public performance of this *drápa* at the 1999 Crown Tournament in Sternfeld.

18. Westford's epigraph comes from Tolkien's translation of *Sir Gawain and the Green Knight* (1975), stanza 23, line 14. The original Middle English line reads: "And thus yirnes the yere in yisterdayes mony."

John Ruble

John Ruble (b. 1965) is a nonpracticing astrophysicist who, as he says, administers an "international array of computers to earn his daily lefse." Among members of the SCA, he is known as Ulf Gunnarsson, and his comic poem "Lutefisk and Yams," though never officially published, has become an underground internet classic. According to Sandra B. Straubhaar, Gunnarsson's poem has been posted on Lutheran humor websites, the Sons of Norway homepage, and even Internet Finland. Live performances of the poem can be found on YouTube. Although part of the poem clearly owes something to Dr. Seuss's *Green Eggs and Ham*, most of "Lutefisk and Yams" appears in excellent *dróttkvætt* meter, including the form's highly difficult internal rhymes.

Lutefisk and Yams

(with apologies to Theodore Geisel)

Hark and 'ware, oh warrior!
Wyrd of Sven now hear you.
How good Lars he harried,
Pestered him with questions.

Late at mead-hall light burned.
Lars did strive to largen
Belly with a bowl of
Boiled fish his mission . . .

And some chunks of chicken . . .
And cheese, and ham, and pea soup . . .   10
Finally pounds of pancakes
Paired with lingen berries.

Smallish snack he snuck while
Woozy wife lay snoozing,
When inside there wandered
Forth a fellow northman.

Lars did greet him greatly
For he knew the gruesome
Tales of hosts who hasten
Traveller forth from doorstep.   20

"I am Sven," he stated.
"Sven I am," he said.
"Do you like Lutefisk and Yams?"

"Nay," said Lars, "though largely
Like I food most goodly . . .
I do not like Lutefisk and Yams.
I do not like them, Sven I Am."

"Ah," said Sven, "my friend.
Would you eat them on a trip?
Would you eat them on your ship?"   30

"Nay," said Lars, "though largely
Like I food most goodly . . .
I do not like Lutefisk and Yams.
I do not like them, Sven I Am."

"Ah," said Sven, "but wait.
Would you eat them on a raid?
Would you eat them with a maid?"

"Nay," said Lars most strongly,
"Like I food most goodly, but
I do not like Lutefisk and Yams.   40
I do not like them, Sven I Am."

"Well," said Sven, "good fellow.
Would you eat them on the field?
Would you eat them off your shield?"

"Nay," said Lars most wrothly,
"Like I food most goodly, but
I do not like Lutefisk and Yams.
I do not like them, Sven I Am."

Sven then looked most crafty.
He then slyly stated: 50
"Would you eat them served up cold?
Would you eat them if I paid you gold?"

"Well . . ." said Lars, "since largely
Like I food most goodly . . .
I might like Lutefisk and Yams.
I might like them, Sven I Am."

Sven produced the Swedish
Yam and Lutefisk sample.
Lars did test this tasty
Treat then longly pondered.   60

"I . . . despise Lutefisk and Yams.
I despise them, Sven I am."

And he slew Sven.

Mary K. Savelli

Mary K. Savelli (b. 1958), who goes by the persona Isolde de la Ramée, is a recipient of the SCA's Order of the Laurel for her research into Old English. She came to the language through unusual channels. Despite holding a BA in history from Wright State University, Savelli learned the language entirely on her own. Having read a bad translation of *Beowulf* in high school, she made the decision—after turning forty—to teach herself Old English so she might read the text in the original. Although this decision had little to do with Tolkien's work, Savelli specifically credits *The Lord of the Rings* for convincing her that, despite her dyslexia, reading could be enjoyable. Her first major Old English project was to write a grammar that she later self-published on Amazon in 2011. Afterward, Savelli translated all Midrealm's ceremonies and award texts into Old English; she later provided this service to the kingdoms of Calontir and Ealdomere. She has also self-published an Old English phrase book, a book on the Germanic lyre, and (from publisher Anglo-Saxon Books) a cookbook with Old English recipes. Overall, Savelli's excursions into verse have been few, but the following in memoriam poem remembers a close friend killed in a car crash; he had a Norse persona, and Savelli often called him Týr in disguise.

All Asgard Mourns
(*Eall Osgeardes Murnþ*)

for Craig Cox (Thorbjorn Osis)

Sorgaþ Freo fæger   and fela teara
hire hordcofa   heapaþ oferfull;
eac Wodnes werod   wepeþ tosomne
swa murnþ eall Osgeardes   þone æfwyrdlan.

Helle healfbroþor,   heardsefan Garm,
treowþe toteah   and Tiw forswealg.
Sarlice seofaþ   swær norþanwind
þær æne heah hleahtor   hlynede bliðe.
Na ma magon mægeþ   magorinc seon,
sculdras strange,   scienende ansien;   10
na ma dælaþ drengas   dryncehorn mid him
ne sprecaþ beotword   on beorscipe.
Þone wæpenwigan,   wer bealdostne,
slitere besyrwede   on siðe hamweard.
Nu ane we on swefnum   geseoþ heaðurinc,
beorna beaggiefan,   beaduwisan.
Ac frofor lytel fint   fæcnum æt swefnum
æðelicu ides   þære ealdorlic freond
mid wulfe wæs   gewegen of hire.
Weccende wuduwe   werigferhþ æthwierfþ;   20
wepeþ eall cyðð   for cwene sorge.

Grieves fair Freyja; with tears falling
her gold-chest heaps glit'ring overfull.
Too, Woden's hosts weep together
just as all Asgard mourns absent friend.
Hel's half-brother, hardhearted Garm,
broke he the truce and Týr devoured.[1]
Sorrowful north wind sighs sadly now
where once deep laughter echoed loudly.
No more may ladies look on warrior,
strongest shoulders, shining count'nance;   10
no more may spearmen share his strong beer
nor make in mead-hall daring promises.
That bravest knight, bold champion,
destroyer tricked him on trip homeward.
Only in sleep will we see him now,
gift-giver of men, gallant leader.
But noble queen finds no comfort,
solace in sleep, whose sweetest love
was carried off by crafty wolf.
For waking widow, wretchedness returns;   20
weep all kinsmen for queen of sorrow.

NOTE

1. During Ragnarök, Týr is fated to die by Garm, a wolf or hound associated with Hel. Some mythologists link Garm (Garmr) to the wolf Fenrir whom Tyr had bound with an unbreakable chain at the cost of his hand.

Ana Keveney

An American born of Cuban parents, Ana Keveney (b. 1961, née Areces) enjoys challenging verse forms. Mostly she prefers sonnets, particularly ones using the more difficult Petrarchan rhyme scheme, but she also delights in northern medieval poetry. She reports, for instance, rereading Tolkien's *The Return of the King* with even greater joy after realizing the battle between Éowyn and the Witch King was, as she says, "practically alliterative verse masquerading as prose." Her poetic work for the SCA generally focuses on praise, on mild satire, and—increasingly—on acts of mourning. The following text, whose opening deliberately evokes a famous tenth-century elegy, "The Ruin," was originally written as a moral chronicle about human works destroyed by natural disaster. The next year, however, a real natural disaster—Hurricane Katrina—devasted New Orleans, so Keveney revised her text into a praise poem for Tonessa West Crowe (Duchess Isabella of York, the "Lady Night-Pearl"), a high-ranking fellow anachronist in the SCA's East Kingdom who organized an aid drive sending fabric and sewing machines to the hurricane's victims.

An Old English Chronicle Praise Poem

Once were great halls, wondrous honey springs,
where many made merry, mingling their laughter.
Hunters and warriors held horns brimming.
Song-weavers' hands drew sweetness from sound-looms,
as Mary's son's speakers soughed against vanity.[1]

Wild was the night of wailing wind-song.
Sky-rivers burst, sowing sorrow.
Whale-bearing walls went widely spreading,
sundered households, cities swept far,
splintered long-ships, sacked granaries.   10

Wide is the swath where the swan-road has swallowed.
Gather the mourners, for gone are the great-halls.
What hunters remain harvest the dead,
build now the barrows, bury and burn.

What weregild repays these waves' wages?
What hands will rebuild high halls fallen?
Son's speakers will sigh, sounding the Father-bells.

Lady Night-Pearl, of noble name,
Dame of Dawnland, dealer of linens,
calls countrymen, casting nets wide   20
to mantle the naked, to mind Mary's son.
Nornir's daughters' deft fingers dance,
the warp and weft worthier than gold,
many gifts gleaning, Gleann Abhann bound.[2]

NOTES

1. *Song-weavers* and *Mary's son's speakers* are kennings for harpers and Christian priests, respectively. In the next stanza, "whale-bearing walls" refers to waves.

2. *Nornir's daughters* (i.e., daughters of the Norns) is a kenning for spinners and weavers; Gleann Abhann is the SCA's nineteenth kingdom, and it includes the area of New Orleans.

Leigh Ann Hussey

Leigh Ann Hussey (1961–2006) was a lifelong Californian with deep ties to the state's Neo-Pagan communities. During her years at UC Berkeley—she graduated in 1984 with a music major and a Celtic Studies minor—Hussey discovered the New Reformed Orthodox Order of the Golden Dawn (NROOGD); one personal legacy lay in composing a highly popular pamphlet, later translated into several languages, that explained Neo-Pagan practices to outsiders. Blessed with a copious memory and a ferocious desire to learn, Hussey's interests were wide and varied, especially when it came to languages. She could comfortably speak French, Welsh, and Gaelic; knew a smattering of another half-dozen tongues; and had mastered Swedish sufficiently that Lucas Arts once hired her to play-test a Swedish language *Star Wars* video game. Hussey's talent for languages also found an outlet within the SCA. The following dual-language poem commemorates the knighting of her friend Jay Hoffman ("Alfred of Carlyle") in June 1993. In addition, Hussey was an avid musician, playing fiddle in a local Celtic rock band; she also studied mythology, crafts, and published several fantasy stories. She passed away in 2006 from a motorcycle accident.

An Anglo-Saxon Praise Poem

Hwæt! Hieraþ oð ic herge,   heorðwerod Westerne,
Ælfred awelere,   æðele and cræftig—
Middrices man,   macode hlisan,
begen handa bæron   bana to fahne,
he dal ut deaþ,   se dracan þegn.
Bealdum Beowulfe gelic   gebletsode wyrdes,

hwa folgian feohtetir   to fame teah.
westweardes wendend   to gewinnan blæd,
on fene under forstmiste   ferde þæt Ælfred,
secgrof and sangglæd,   striuende cunnian   10
in cene gecampe   his cræft and heortan.
Ellendædas geearnodon   æþeles worðmynde—
ðeah sum him forsægon,   stod he swa bysene,
heahicgende hæleþ,   gehealde his grund.
Lociaþ hu he lifaþ   to landes welan:
ricra is rice   for ðæm hringum he gifð,
scopas songcræft haniaþ   secende his freogan—
god is se ræd gold   þe gegongaþ fram his handa.
Seo bares byrst   and se blæc wælæsc
and wisdaroð wealdeþ   þe se wundaþ hyda.   20
Strang is his sawol,   stedefæst his geþanc,
riht ræd hafaþ,   raðe he gifð hit.
Hieraþ him nu hatte,   hærlicost ordsecg.
Ælfred ealugyfa,   ecgwer and cræftega,
treowig tacnsteorra   and triewe hererinc.
Cyþþ and ceorlas,   cuppan nimaþ in handa—
sæliaþ him stiðlice,   min spell is gedon.

Hear as I hail him,   hosts of the West,
Alfred awl-wielder,   artful and princely—
man of the Midrealm,   made him renown,
both hands bearing   bane to his foes,
he dealt out death,   the dragon's thane.[1]
Like bold Beowulf,   blessed of fortune,
who to follow fame   to the foam took him,
westward wending   to win a name
on fen under fog   fared that Alfred—
sword-edged and song-glad,   striving to prove   10
in keen conflict   his craft and heart.[2]
Able acts earned him   honor as a prince—
though some scorned him,   he stood as example;[3]
high-minded hero,   he held his ground.
Look ye, how he lives   to the land's welfare:
richer the realm is   for the rings he gives,
scops hone their skills,   seeking his favor—
good is the red gold   they get from his hand.
The boar's bristle   and the black war-ash
and the wise dart he wields,   that wounds the hide.[4]   20
Strong is his spirit,   steadfast his purpose,
right rede he has,   ready to give it.

Hear him now hight,   hero most noble,
Alfred ale-giver,   armsman and craftsman,
trusty token-star   and true knight.
Kinsfolk and carls,   take cups in hand
skoal him now stoutly,   for my speech is done.

NOTES

1. Hussey dubs Alfred of Carlyle (Jay Hoffman) an awl-wielder because, in addition to combat, he excels at leatherwork and shoemaking. During tournaments, he fought with two swords rather than the usual sword-and-shield combination.

2. A few years earlier, Alfred had moved to California (the West Kingdom) from Illinois (in Midrealm). Since Midrealm's mascot is a dragon, Alfred is the "dragon's thane." The phrase "fen under fog" refers specifically to the San Francisco Bay Area.

3. Alfred served as "Prince of the Mists" from May 1992 through November 1992, during which time his general youth and enthusiasm, it seems, rubbed some older SCA members the wrong way.

4. According to an interview with Hoffman, medieval leatherworkers used boar bristles to stitch shoes together, and the "wise dart" might mean a leather awl. However, Hussey might also be cleverly linking Hoffman's craftsmanship with his martial endeavors. Spears, a weapon used by Hoffman in non-tournament combats, were historically made with ash wood, a fact attested to by *Beowulf* (line 330), and "boar's bristle" is a potential kenning for *sword*. Because boars were associated with the Norse God Frey (or Freyr), boar imagery often adorned pagan arms and armor.

Beth Morris Tanner

Like many other poets in this section, Beth Morris Tanner (b. 1967) is a voracious reader of Tolkien, and she's most drawn to those aspects of his work reminiscent of Old Norse or Old English verse—for instance, Théoden's call to the Rohirrim. Other contemporary medievalist authors whom she has studied include Poul Anderson, C. S. Lewis, and E. R. Eddison. As an undergraduate at the University of Maryland, College Park, Tanner's interests led her to take classes in Norse literature and history from Jere Fleck, whom, in "Olaf Kunungr's *Drápa*," she lists among the great skalds. The SCA has also greatly inspired Tanner. Known as Mistress Keilyn FitzWarin, she considers the alliterative meter an especially appropriate vehicle for recounting tournaments and battles. In 1993, Tanner co-edited a short volume under her maiden name called *Ars Poetica Societatis* in the Compleat Anachronist booklet series. Here, Tanner conveys her philosophy of writing poetry in SCA contexts. This volume, besides analyzing the SCA's unique social constraints and opportunities, also presents multiple examples of period-appropriate verse forms. For these efforts, Tanner and co-editor Terry Sheehan were elevated to the coveted Order of the Laurel, the SCA peerage for contributions in the arts and sciences.

Lausavísa for **Rowan Dróttning**[1]

Bright swords in the battle
Bring death to the ring-giver.
Rowan strikes with redden'd
Ruthless hard-won strife-tooth—
Swings with silver killer,
Slays the one she lays with.

Now the nobles, awe-struck,
Know they see Queen Rowan.

Sea Wars, A.S. XXIII[2]

Departing the dreary, dark-shrouded Northland
South to the sea-land, sailing away:
Battle-bound brothers—boldly faring—
Follow the floodwater's fickle sea-road.
Swiftly sailing, seeking battle
Northmen nightfaring, never fearing,
Famed fighters, full of might,
Merry in mead-hall, now march southward:

Mail-clad man, marauding giant—
Dark-maned demon, descended from Danes—   10
Bearing bright sword and blue-painted war-shield:
Beer-drinking bridge-leader, brave son of Ingolf;
Cross-bearing comrade, clever in speech,
Golden-haired Gaul-man, great in strength—
Willing with women, warlike in bearing,
Eager for eagle-feast, angry in battle.[3]

Kings command, comrades are summoned
answering aid-call; armies assemble.
Behold the war band, boldly goes forth:
Braid-trees bravely, brilliant among them.   20
Helms and hauberks are hot and heavy—
Tales are told, travelling southward
Knowing that not all North will return.
Many will mourn missing comrades.

Bright battle-maiden, boon companion,
Stands and stares into starry darkness,
Waiting weary for word from warland.
News, nightborne, of narrow escapes—
Tales of trouble, tearfully heard,
Dreading the death of dear hearth-companions,   30
Promises prayers for prompt return
of gold-giving lords, gore-smeared but whole.

Ready to rend, ravens are circling:
Witch-steeds will feed on war's remains.
Lines are laid out, luck is wished.
Few are fighting many foes

But might is better and best of champions
Than thrice one hundred weakling thralls.
Sea-bound spearmen smite the shield-walls;
War-wall is riven, southmen are weeping.[4]   40

Weary with wains, laden with war-prize,
Bloody banners are homeward borne.
Some will stay to lie with sea-folk;
Others with ale, oaths will take
To return reaving, rings to gain
Gold and glory gotten by battle,
But now at night, from noble skalds,
We hear of heroes, homeward faring.

Olaf Kunungr's *Drápa*[5]

I.

Welcome all to word-play!
Well-met for the telling!
Hearken well and hear me
How the sea-land crown was won.
Brew of poets for brave men,
Bright words heard in firelight—
Ale is drunk and all attend
Eager for words of eagle-feast.

Hasten best of hirðsmen,
Heed you now the rede-craft.   10
Call the huscarls all for
Kennings from the singer.
Wordsmiths tell of warriors' might,
Winning gold with spinning steel!
Hail the heir, hail Olaf
High-seat-holder, Askold's son!

II.

Heimdall's children: handsome lords,
Hearth builders, ring weavers,
Mighty warriors, men of valor,
Malt-brew drinkers, strong-thewed   20
Swift-ship builders, sword bearers,
Swearing oaths and making boasts.
Proud and powerful warlike men,
Princes and freemen side by side.

Bravest of warriors, best of poets,
Brawny men of the sea-land.
Come and hear how kings are made,
Crowns are won, and fame as well!
Wordsmiths tell of warriors' might,
Winning gold with spinning steel!   30
Hail the heir, hail Olaf
High-seat-holder, Askold's son!

III.

Brooch wearers, bright ladies:
Braid-trees come and heed me.
Hearth-fire keepers, home-makers,
Help-meet to death-greeters;
Battle-maidens bearing swords
Beside the men their homes defend—
Wise in witchlore, clever in craft,
Women dancing in the mead-hall.   40

Fairest ladies, finest queens,
Fiercest she-wolves of the sea-land:
Come and hear how Queens are made,
Crowned and cloaked in majesty.
Wordsmiths tell of warriors' might,
Winning gold with spinning steel!
Hail the heir, hail Olaf
High-seat-holder, Askold's son!

IV.

Come and hear the king-tale
Of combat for the crown-right.   50
Hear the tale of how the
Hero won the thrones.
Fabled king of old he
fights against the sword-knights
To once more win the
War-right, showing his might.[6]

The speaker speaks the laws,
Spells out the words of warfare;[7]
Calls forward the combatants
Crown-law and sword-law to hear.   60
Wordsmiths tell of warriors' might,
Winning gold with spinning steel!
Hail the heir, hail Olaf
High-seat-holder, Askold's son!

V.

Challenge is the choice of
Checky-bearing kingseeker.[8]
Travelling far, warlike Tremayne
Trembles not before the foe.
Helm-splitter and hewer of men,
He chooses to fight the hero.   70
Bravely he battles with sword,
Blows like the snow they fall—

Shield-maid and squires all
Shirk not the final sword-work,
Carrying the conquered man,
Crownless but not for long.
Wordsmiths tell of warriors' might,
Winning gold with spinning steel!
Hail the heir, hail Olaf
High-seat-holder, Askold's son!   80

VI.

Long-armed lord from Welsh-land,
Loth to yield the war-field;
Heir to Kings and archer,
Again he seeks the high-seat.[9]
Grimly he gives combat.
Gold he would have, and holdings,
But even best of craftsmen,
Beaten, Odin greets them.

Shivered is his war-shield,
Shaken with the breaking;   90
Fuel feeds the yellow flames
Fanning the Welshman's pyre.
Wordsmiths tell of warriors' might,
Winning gold with spinning steel!
Hail the heir, hail Olaf
High-seat-holder, Askold's son!

VII.

Fearsome knight from Frankland
Fights to win the King-right,
Wandering from West-home.[10]
Warfare he seeks and heir-ship.   100
Bright swords have now bitten—
Blood spilt makes him ruddy;
Like the wounded lion
Loudly he roars, uncowed.

Gold he shall be given,
Great fare for his burial.
Weapon-won coronet is
Worthless to the lifeless.
Wordsmiths tell of warriors' might,
Winning gold with spinning steel!   110
Hail the heir, hail Olaf
High-seat-holder, Askold's son!

VIII.

Next a Northland hirðsman,
Noble son of Gundaar,
Swift of foot and swinging
Sword from dragon's holding:
Countrymen in combat.
Cold tomb is one man's doom.
Bitter is the battle;
Bright steel in the sunlight.[11]   120

Red blood flows in rivers
Rushing from the dying.
Countrymen and kin will
Carry him home for burying.
Wordsmiths tell of warriors' might,
Winning gold with spinning steel!
Hail the heir, hail Olaf
High-seat-holder, Askold's son!

IX.

Fairly having thus far
Fought, so none have caught him: 130
Daring is the dancer,
Drunk on ale from tale-skalds.[12]
Two swords try to trounce him;
Two he wields, unyielding.
Light of foot and limber,
Lucky blow has struck him.

Great the grief and wailing
Groans, and bitter moaning:
Blades fly, bright blood flows
Bearing away life and heir-ship.   140
Wordsmiths tell of warriors' might,
Winning gold with spinning steel!
Hail the heir, hail Olaf
High-seat-holder, Askold's son!

X.

Final one to fall was
Fearsome son of Saxons,
Thegn's son in thrall-land.[13]
Through all the host he slew,
Seeking the sea-land's kingship—
Silver crown and power   150
Southman's might is great but
Mastery is past him.

Weary of the war-strife,
Weak with life-blood leaking,
Thrice worthy to be thegn,
Thus the new heir spares him.
Wordsmiths tell of warriors' might,
Winning gold with spinning steel!
Hail the heir, hail Olaf
High-seat-holder, Askold's son!   160

XI.

Few now dare to face him,
Fearsome golden Northman.
See what his sword wins him:
Sweetest flower of the East—
Slim and slow to anger,
Sleek daughter of sheiks—
Now is Queen in Northland,
Noble in Eastern robes.[14]

Bitter were the blows that
Brought him to the Kingship.   170
Many were the mighty
Men who now have fallen.
Wordsmiths tell of warriors' might,
Winning gold with spinning steel!
Hail the heir, hail Olaf
High-seat-holder, Askold's son!

XII.

Hero's seat in mead-hall
Holds the golden Northman.
Grants this gracious prince,
Giving it to the living   180
Southern man who sought to
Slay him in the mayhem,
Honoring him with oaths and
ale, words from tale-skalds.

Honor from the heir and
Odin's gift to winners;
Golden rings are given;
Glory to the gore-stained.
Wordsmiths tell of warriors' might,
Winning gold with spinning steel!   190
Hail the heir, hail Olaf
High-seat-holder, Askold's son!

XIII.
Malt-brew maker's rival,
Man who rules the sea-land;
Goth's friend, Gallows-lord,
Gives victory to the living.[15]
Kingship, silver crown are
Kept now in the Southland—
Drums do tell of death and
Dancing in the King's hall.   200

Noise of victory, night-borne.
New-made verses chanted.
Some would speak the words of
Sagas from their homelands.
Wordsmiths tell of warriors' might,
Winning gold with spinning steel!
Hail the heir, hail Olaf
High-seat-holder, Askold's son!

XIV.
Gunnlǫg's lust-pay grants to
Givers of tales the ale-right.   210
Immortality is Odin's gift,
Only given through verses.
Web of words from poets
Weaves a cloak for heroes;
Kings do well to keep such
Cup-companions by them.

Wise is the war-maker
With poets as his hirðsmen.
Fame is spread and fortune
Finds those who honor skalds.   220
Wordsmiths tell of warriors' might,
Winning gold with spinning steel!
Hail the heir, hail Olaf
High-seat-holder, Askold's son!

XV.
Doing the duty of poets,
Deeds and kings remembered:
Brave was Bragi of old,
Best of Odin's wordsmiths;
Heir to Odin is Snorri,
Ablest of the tale-skalds;   230
Bassi too is blessed with
Bounty of countless words.[16]

Few there are with fierceness to
Fight the night-long word-war.
New poets now must master the
Knotty words of a hirðsman's duty.
Wordsmiths tell of warriors' might,
Winning gold with spinning steel!
Hail the heir, hail Olaf
High-seat-holder, Askold's son!   240

An Alliterative Acrostic Poem[17]

Gold is gained by gore-clad Northmen
At awful slaughter of the English;
Loud laughter is heard in lofty mead-halls.
Men at meat call comrades to mind—
Rings and respect are rewards of the warrior.

NOTES

1. This poem commemorates the first woman in SCA history to win a Crown Tournament and attain the rank of queen in her own right, Rowan Beatrice von Kampfer. She reigned in Ansteorra from January through July 1991. During the finals, she defeated her soon-to-be consort (and real-life partner) Hector Philip Martel, dubbed "ring-giver" by Tanner because he had reigned twice before as king. *Dróttning* translates as "queen" in Old Norse.

2. Written by Tanner in 1990, "Sea Wars" appeared in *Ars Poetica Societatis* as an example of Old English meter; it describes her housemates departing for an SCA war in Georgia (near the kingdom of Trimaris in Florida) that Tanner herself, living in Maryland (Atlantia), could not attend. In SCA reckoning, these events occurred in *Anno Societatis XXIII*, which, in the Gregorian calendar, runs May 1988 through May 1989.

3. This second stanza describes Tanner's two housemates: in the first four lines, Galmr Ingolfsson (Wayne Precht), who stands six foot, four inches tall; and in the last four lines, Christian Darmody (Clint Darby), whose heraldry has crosses on it.

4. Since the kingdoms of Atlantia and Trimaris both have sea themes, "sea-bound spearmen" deftly refers to warriors on both sides, but the more "southern" army belongs to Trimaris. "Witch-steeds" are wolves, an animal said to be ridden by witches in Norse mythology.

5. This *drápa* celebrates Olaf Askoldssonn (Michael Curtis), four times king of Atlantia, for winning his fourth Crown Tournament in 1990 and, thus, his sea-themed kingdom's "sea-land crown." He is legendary within the SCA for fighting with two swords, and in 2018 he self-published a booklet on technique called *Real Men Don't Use Shields: The Two Sword Fighting Style*. In Old Norse, *kunungr* means "king." Eight of Tanner's thirty stanzas originally appeared in *Ars Poetica Societatis* in order to exemplify the skaldic *dróttkvætt*.

6. Considering that Olaf won his first throne in 1983, or seven years earlier, he earns the description "fabled king of old."

7. Before a tournament begins, an official reads out the rules of combat.

8. This section details Anton Tremayne (Doug Stevens), whose heraldry bears black-and-white checks like a checkerboard; the adjective "checky" is the anglicized version of *chequy*. As Tanner relates in the next stanza, although Tremayne lost against Olaf this time, the following year he would win the Crown Tournament.

9. Dafydd ap Gwystl (David Kuijt), a noted craftsman, had participated in several tournaments.

10. Cai de Lyon (Richard Auklandus) hailed from the SCA's Kingdom of the West. The next reference to a roaring lion will play on his persona's surname.

11. This eighth section refers to Thorvald Gundaarsson (Matthew Severns), who, like Olaf, has a Norse persona.

12. The dancer is Robyyan Torr d'Elandris (Dennis Sherman), who is also a musician. Like Olaf, he fights with two swords, and he had gone undefeated in the tournament ("none have caught him") prior to meeting Olaf.

13. Olaf's last opponent is Cedric of Thanet (James Eason) from southern Atlantia. After he falls, Cedric will be spared by Olaf, who then honors his opponent in Tanner's twelfth section.

14. Olaf's lady, Aislinn Shattenwald (Suzy Curtis), was a belly-dancer with an adopted Middle-Eastern persona.

15. Olaf is "rival" to his fellow sea-king, Ægir, a jötun often associated with brewing ale, and Olaf achieves his victory with Odin's aid. Since Olaf lives geographically below traditional Norse climes, he keeps his crown in "Southland"—technically, the southern portion of Atlantia.

16. In this stanza, Tanner names three great skalds of the past: Bragi Boddason, Snorri Sturluson, and Geirr Bassi Haraldsson (Jere Fleck).

17. Tanner dedicates this alliterative acrostic poem to Galmr Ingolfsson (Wayne Precht), one of the main combatants in "Sea Wars." He is now a duke and recently elevated to the Order of the Laurel for woodworking.

Daniel Marsh

Like many fellow anachronists, Daniel Marsh (b. 1970) learned his poetic craft through the SCA. After joining in late 2001, he adopted a Viking-era Scandinavian persona and soon found the *fornyrðislag* meter particularly to his liking. Under his kingdom's apprentice system, he learned the basics of alliterative metrics from M. Wendy Hennequin and Michael Dixon ("Toki Redbeard"); he also studied Lee Hollander's and Henry Adams Bellows's scholarly introductions to *The Poetic Edda*. However, Marsh's closest study of alliterative metrics stems from his own analysis of medieval poetry. Though unable to read Old Norse itself, he tracked the alliteration in various Norse poems when learning those meters; after turning to Middle English, Marsh, who goes as Grim the Skald, created extensive spreadsheets for following the metrical patterns he perceived. His poetry reflects these studies. Most is alliterative: Norse meters, mainly, but also Old and Middle English, the latter of which he performs as Matthew Grymm. Of the following selections, his first is a *flokkr*, a short work without a refrain in the *dróttkvætt* meter. The second poem, *Snowberg at the Bridge*, is a battle poem celebrating the thirty-seventh Pennsic War, which Marsh wrote while studying and translating lines 3745–3889 of the *Alliterative Mort Arthure*. He was raised to the Order of the Laurel in 2008.

The Poem of Lutr
(*Lutrsflokkr*)

A gift from Konrad von Ulm, king of the East Kingdom, to Midrealm's King Lutr Ulfskjald
and Queen Tessa of Wight at the Thirty-Seventh Pennsic War (A.S. XLIII).

Odin's mead I offer
East-King's gift to Midrealm:
poem for peerless Lutr,
proud Tessa his lady.
Struck he true at tourney!
Test of Dragon's Ruler
as scion—then sovereign—
served the Middle Kingdom.[1]

Folk-king's thread of fate was
fraught with ill and troubles   10
cruel—his Queen had suffered
crushing hurt to ring-home.[2]
For his lady Lutr
looked for aid and respite;
meanwhile, needful message
missed its destination.

City of small grain fields
—seat of Kings' law-keepers—
ne'er received the notice
naming Lutr sovereign.[3]   20
Stark and strict the law reads,
states a king must always
cut for court at Law Rock
current runes of joining.

No law-breaker, Lutr
lapse he well acknowledged,
honored royal oath and
yielded crown of Midrealm.
Kingless stood the country.
Close their neighbors threatened.   30
Knights were now conflicted
no liege-lord to follow.

Realm of Dragon's Regent,
regal Palymar, raised.
The law-keeping council
came upon an answer:
at the test of arms where
heirs would soon be chosen,

second sword-debate must
serve to name the ruler.[4]   40

Palymar took pains to
point out that brave Lutr
could come to this Tourney;
combat was his blood right.
Came then crownless ruler
—caring not for glory—
to win for wife only:
woe to all who faced him.

Two great knights then tested
Tessa's lord with dagger,   50
sword, and small-shield striving—
saw well they his mettle.
Ne'er lacking was Lutr
like in strength to dragons;
if foes yielded field, on
fair duels he insisted.

Battle-brights he crossed with
brother in war Theodric—
Lutr's leg he wounded,
lent he point of honor.   60
"Quarter I'll not curry—
come again," said Lutr.
Then in second sally
sword-oak Lutr triumphed.

Lutr faced in final
fight a Duke of Midrealm—
dauntless Dag Thorgrimsson:
drakkar he'd been granted.[5]
First two swords they flurried;
fell the Midrealm pillar.   70
Then their shields they shouldered,
shining swords they readied.

Tall stood Dag, intent, and
took off shield and helmet.
Handed both to Heralds,
harkened all to listen.
Lutr, oak of Odin,
eager for shield-tussle,
foe-cuts fierce would take, but
from the Duke words tumbled.   80

"I speak of the spurred ones;
split are we in thinking.
We are sworn to one king;
where now is our ruler?
Lord of men is Lutr,
laws of realm he heeded.
True king we must call him;
clash I not with liege-lord."[6]

Fierce Lutr came forward,
friendship's hand extended—
noble Dag did naught but
kneel before his Sovereign.
Roaring crowd erupted,
raucously cried, "Hoobah!"
Kingless time concluded—
crown had journeyed homeward.

Hear this lay of Lutr
loyal man and faithful,
feared on fields of battle,
feeder of his people.
Crowned twice king of Midrealm
kept the laws with honor—
hewn from head his crown, but
heart was kingly always.

90

100

Snowberg at the Bridge

*This is a tale of the Thirty-Seventh Pennsic War held on July 25–August 10, 2008 (A.S.
XLIII). Written in the alliterative long line of the fourteenth century, the poem ends with
a rhyming couplet. The East Kingdom's Snowberg Army combines two separate forces:
the Baronies of Bergental (western Massachusetts) and Concordia of the Snows (New
York State Capital District).*

This tale I tell—listen—   of Tygers at war,
undaunted by the Dragon   though dreadful the odds.[7]
Golden-crowned Konrad   was King of the East,
a defiant foe he faced—   the fierce King Lutr.
In forests and in fields   they fought with vigor.
All of the Eastern Army   earned glory there,
but about the Battle of Five Bridges   I bid you now hear
and of the bearers of blades   from Bergental and Concordia—
how the soldiers of Snowberg   seized victory then.

At the second bridge bided   the Barony's two warriors;   10
at the left of the line's fore   was their leader strong:
the baron clad in black,   bold Angus Kerr.
He bade his brave band   to forbear a moment;
to hold their place behind   hardy Lochleven
and wait 'till their weapons   would be most needed.[8]

Lead by lightning-fast Collin,   Lochleven sallied forth
and met the Midrealm warriors   with a mighty rush,
but the foe blocked their battle-charge,   standing like a bulwark.
Then the dragons drove back   with a dire assault—
but the fierce Scottish fighters   stood fast their ground;   20
and so these steel-hearted sides   struggled with each other
neither yielding an inch   to their dread enemy.

The swords of Snowberg   stood ready to charge,
but Duke Lucan, white-clad warlord,   went to the fighters,
ordered he Angus   elsewhere to battle:
"Our Loyal Atlantean allies   lay into the fifth bridge,
but came crashing against   Calontir shields;[9]
those brave men nearly   made their way through
but are spent and spread thin: speed to them now!

While to the Falcons fell   those few allies left,   30
the soldiers of Snowberg   sallied to the fifth bridge.
Like a lance their line   lunged at the enemy;
with dread-armed Deacon at its head   they drove through the foe;[10]
the hero hewed a gaping   hole in the shields.
The remainder of the men   moved through the gap.
Battered first by bright Atlantia,   then broken by the East,
the fierce carls of Calontir   crumbled before Snowberg.

From off the breached bridge   bravely Snowberg charged
and fought up the flank   of the fearsome Dragon;
at the back of the next bridge   they bore upon the enemy,   40
and to their embattled brothers   they brought much aid
by fighting the foe they had faced   on another front.
Swiftly the Midrealm soldiers   were sundered by this strife,
and the men of the mighty Tyger   moved to the next bridge.
Soon the Snowberg warriors   saw just before them
brave Lochleven breaking through   a barrier of Dragons,
and roared then a rousing greeting,   rushing to their aid!
All foes on the field   fell to these heroes.
Great was the glory   garnered by Snowberg—
                              Thereby   50
            this fashion Baron Angus found
            to breach the bridge the long way 'round.

NOTES

1. Since Midrealm's heraldry shows a dragon on a red-and-white field and the motto *Draco Invictus*, Marsh refers to Midrealm as a "dragon" kingdom.

2. Here, "ring-home" is a kenning for Tessa's arm rather than her hand.

3. SCA Corporate is based in the Californian city of Milpitas, which is Spanish for "little corn field." The line about "law-keepers" refers to the SCA Board of Directors. Specifically, Lutr allowed his membership within the SCA to lapse, which disbarred him from kingship.

4. On May 17th, 2008, when Lutr's kingship ended, the previously reigning king, Duke Palymar of the Two Baronies, became regent. Luckily, this situation occurred right before Midrealm's next Crown Tournament on May 25th, and it was decided to hold two tourneys that day: one would determine the current kingship, and the other would (as normal) determine the heirs.

5. A *drakkar* is a Viking war-ship, which Dag Thorgrimsson (Jeff Skevington) bore on his arms.

6. The "spurred ones" are knights. This stanza represents Marsh's rendition in verse of Dag's post-combat speech. As duke, he held the ducal prerogative of standing aside after winning his first bout in the morning tournament's finals.

7. Marsh refers to the East Kingdom and the Middle Kingdom by their most common symbols. Midrealm's heraldry shows a dragon and the motto *Draco Invictus*. Although the East Kingdom's heraldry contains a yellow crown on a purple field, their populace badge bears a blue tyger commonly given the name "Sparky."

8. Angus Kerr was Concordia's baron at the time, and Lochleven is a martial, Scotland-themed Household based in eastern Massachusetts. Together, they often fight alongside Snowberg, comprising the 2nd Division of the Northern Army.

9. Eight times king of the East Kingdom, Duke Lucan von Drakenklaue commanded the Eastern forces. Since Atlantia lay within the East Kingdom's southern states, it thus fell under Duke Lucan's command. In contrast, Calontir belongs to Midrealm and encompasses Kansas, Nebraska, Iowa, and Missouri. Since a falcon graces Calontir's populace badge, Marsh refers to its warriors as "Falcons."

10. This Snowberg charge was spearheaded by Deacon de Chatillon, who now goes by the SCA name of Dmitri.

Robert Cuthbert

Since beginning to study Old Norse poetry in 2014, Robert Cuthbert (b. 1975) has composed a minor wealth of alliterative verse. It can be found on his website, http://ronanfionn.com/, and it includes explanatory documents and audio recordings for some texts, including *Finnsvísur* (2017). This poem is Cuthbert's introduction to a much longer planned work. In this introduction, the speaker tells how Rónán Fionn ÓDubáin's Irish father, Fáolán, meets his Norwegian mother, Ellisif, in battle at Dublin, which, during the ninth century, was a Viking settlement. Future sections will feature their son as a skald and as the poem's hero. The second selection, "Quest for Valhalla," chronicles a one-day SCA event in 2015. The event was partly held as a memorial for the Lion Skald, Ragnar Ulfgarsson (Ron Snow), but it also included a pageant of Norse gods, a youth's combat event using foam weapons, and other activities.

Finnsvísur

Hearken close and hear of
Heroes' stories soaring.
Ellisif finds Fáolán,
Forming bonds by *orm's* bites.[1]

Fenrir's stalking sons pad
Slyly by in Rán's hall.[2]
Westward bore the beasts and
Brought the dawning autumn.

For Sif's hair and hoarfrost
Have the havoc-reavers   10

—Strong and brave bringing
Blood-eels for the shield-flood—

Set sail o'er the seal-plains;
Sword-song and word-fame craved.
Felling Ægir's ale head,
Elli's courage swelled much.[3]

Fat the crow then flew with
Feathers o'er the heather,
While the windswept whale-road
Whisked away the fray-sweat.   20

Dreadful warning words did
Wind southward by mouthfuls,
Filling *conriocht* Fáolán's
Fiery eyes with ire dark.[4]

Cearbhall's wind-fish whirling
Wildly styled the Boiling
Serpents near Blackstairs, and
Summoned Fáolán's steel fangs.[5]

The crow-feeders cawed and
Clamored, damning north men!   30
Ranging for An Ruirtech
Rovers covered much earth.[6]

Finally meeting fighters
From the eastern sea, the
Ire-fueled men of Eirinn,
Eager for spear-tears of

Band of White and Boneless,
Bellowed vows, beat bodhráns,[7]
Hefted shields and shafts so
Sharp, were sharks in frenzy.   40

The cold storm of swords was
Savage. Fáolán's steel had
Hewn many foes. Howling
He fed the war-corbies.

Ell the steel-eyed all but
Equaled—for the corbies—
His fare and best feasting.
Fearless the spear-maiden!

Raised swords, face to face they
Fought blow for blow tireless   50

'Till ring-givers granted
Gore marked the war-shearing.

Ellisif found Fáolán
Fully matched her passion
In blade dance, and bed rolls;
Blessed him with handfasting.

Weeper of Gold welcomed
Wedding with a bed-seed,
Sprouting white-crowned son in
Summer warm and stormy.[8]   60

Father kenned him Fionn but
Flame-eye kenned his fame. With
Honeyed waves the Wanderer
Wet his lips with sip-fulls.[9]

Quest for Valhalla

Dawn broke in the Bear Lands
Bringing the gods themselves[10]
Groups in the grass there
Gathered to heed the call

Freya's resplendent form
Fueled courage in the men
The brave took up their blades
The blood-song to be sung

Frey himself took the field
Fighting amongst the mortals   10
Storm-god looked on in splendor
Staking claim to heroes

Odin was elusive
Instead his ravens sent
From their noble Fort they
Flew to join us this day[11]

The Jotnär came yelling
Yielded to the younglings
Glory over giants
Gained great fame for the cubs[12]   20

The skulls of the slain were
Spangled by great artists

The finest of them filled
The full length of Hel's Hall[13]

Then did Loki's luck find
Latch upon both my eyes
By hex or curse laid low
Left afternoon untold

By Madylyne's magic
My eyes gained sight again[14]   30
In time to see the scene
Stephen Crowley revered

Remembering Ragnar
And raising Crowley's fame
Gifts of the great skald were
Given to him this day[15]

Vast the feast that came forth
Feeding all abundant
Vanquished hunger and voice
Victory in silence   40

Baron and Baroness
Brought honors to their folk
We joined in the wonder
With words both new and old

The Great Horn then hefted
Horns and cups all now filled
Stories of the Lion Skald
Spun through the starry night

All claimed by drink or day
Destined to fade away   50
We slept and when we woke
We were still left dreaming

NOTES

1. *Orm* means "snake" in Old Norse, and, since swords were often compared to snakes, the phrase "*orm's* bites" means sword-strikes; Fionn's parents will meet on the battlefield.

2. Rán is the goddess of the sea, and longships are the "wolves" who pad through her watery halls.

3. The last three stanzas describe Norse raiders descending upon Dublin. "Sif's hair" is a standard skaldic kenning for gold; "blood-eels" are swords, and "havoc-

reavers" are the Norse warriors who bear them. The phrase "Ægir's ale head" requires some mythological knowledge. The jötun Ægir is god of the sea and also Rán's husband; he's associated with brewing ale as well. Cuthbert's kenning therefore refers to sea foam.

4. A *conriocht* is a mythical Irish werewolf who protects the weak and helps lost travelers.

5. "Cearbhall's wind-fish" is a kenning for flags—in this case, the Boiling Serpents emblem of King Cearbhall of Osraige—flapping in the wind. Cearbhall was a ninth-century Irish king who fought the Vikings, and his emblem derives from Irish legend: a healer named Diancécht once threw three snakes discovered in the heart of the Morrígan's son into the River Barrow, where they boiled to death. All this occurred near the Blackstairs, a mountain range in Ireland bordering Wexford and Carlow counties.

6. The River Liffey (*An Ruirtech*) runs through Dublin.

7. Bodhráns are a type of Irish frame drum. Cuthbert's reference to the "Band of White and Boneless" indicates the Vikings Olaf the White and Ivar the Boneless, who both made Dublin into a thriving ninth-century trading port.

8. The Weeper of Gold is Freyja, who weeps tears of red gold when her husband, Óðr, is away; Freyja is also goddess of fertility and love.

9. "Flame-eye" is Odin the Wanderer, whose "honeyed waves" are the Mead of Poetry.

10. The Bears Lands refer to the Barony of Bjornsborg (from the Norse word *björn*, "bear") in Texas's Bexar County; notably, Texans pronounce "Bexar" as *bear*. "Quest for Valhalla" is an event that begins with a pageant involving the Norse gods.

11. That is to say, Odin sent his "ravens" from the Barony of Raven's Fort, which is based out of Huntsville and contributed quite a few people to the event.

12. The youth's fighting event featured the use of foam-boffer weapons. The giants whom the youths "slew" are the SCA's largest adult armored combatants.

13. Since *Día de Muertos* is widely celebrated in the San Antonio region, SCA members held a small skull-bedazzling competition to celebrate.

14. Due to a migraine, Cuthbert missed a few hours of the event, at least until a fellow member lent him some Excedrin.

15. Stephen Crowley is the SCA persona for the fighter who won that day's combat tournament. Ragnar Ulfgarsson (Ron Snow) was known as the Lion Skald for having been awarded the title "Lion of Ansteorra, Defender of the Dream," one of his kingdom's highest honors. Much later that evening, Cuthbert recited an original alliterative *dróttkvætt* in Snow's honor, "Ragnarsvísur," which is available on Cuthbert's website.

M. Wendy Hennequin

M. Wendy Hennequin (b. 1967) is a medievalist and literature professor at Tennessee State University, and she has been active in genre fandom all her life. After cutting her teeth on *Star Trek* and *Star Wars* fan fiction as a young writer, Hennequin advanced during college to the Dargon Project, a shared-universe creative-writing project inspired by the Thieves' World anthology series. More recently, Hennequin has written for an interactive site of Harry Potter fan fiction (now defunct) called *Witherwings*; her current project involves a series of fantasy short stories set in contemporary America. Yet, for Hennequin, research and literary passion are two sides of the same coin, and studying medieval literature, including alliterative poetry, helps her better understand how and why medieval poets have made their particular literary choices.

In the following two selections, fandom and scholarship show their twin influences on Hennequin. In "Guðrinc's Lament," Hennequin echoes the style, epithets, and misunderstandings that might have characterized a genuine Old English poet. The poem is an elegy spoken by Andromache, wife of Hector, whose name in Greek means "battle of men"; the poet therefore mistakenly assumes she must have been an Amazon and names her *guthrinc*, "Man-Battle." In the second selection, "Deor's Flyting," Hennequin marvelously parodies modern scholarship as well as Deor's famous medieval lament poem. This parody follows a mini-tradition within the SCA: tales from the fictional Boreal Master, an Icelandic poet who produced a substantial amount of medieval poetry, all of it terrible. Framed as a translation from an alliterative original, each stanza anachronistically refers to a different contemporary fandom.

Guðrinc's Lament

Once were these walls   —well I remember—
Carved with serpents,   covered with gold,
Shining and splendid.   Steadfast and strong,
They bravely stood,   when the sea-riders,
Ship-warriors,   the shore invaded,
And conquered the sand.   Shining, they stood,
Bright guardians,   gated in glory,
Bearing warriors   in bright helmets,
Battle-brothers   brave among men,
Who first charged forth,   famous in war,   10
To fight with the foemen.   Fallen and broken,
Wounded in limbs,   they lie on the earth,
Proud guardians,   plundered for stone,
Carried away,   like carrion for beasts,
As high houses   and holy dwellings
For the out-landers,   old lie-crafters.
Where are you now,   walls of splendor,
Brilliant as dawn,   bravely shining,
When I came riding,   ready-hearted,
Eager for war,   and you welcomed me   20
With open gates?   Glory in battle
I came seeking,   sent by the queen,
Skilled in fighting.[1]   Fleeting it was,
Ten winters long   of war-battle,
Before the walls   —weary of the fight—
Fell to the earth   after the fierce struggle,
And lay, resting,   after the long battle.
There, the gold-giver   greeted me kindly
Beneath the wall-gate,   woven with gold,
While the sea-riders,   ship-warriors,   30
Mocked my coming.[2]   Keenly they paid!
There, did I stand   beside the shining wall,
Spear in my hand   for hard fighting,
Shoulder against shoulder   with the sword-warrior,
The man-killer,   mightiest prince,
And Man-Battle   my mother called me.[3]
Well did they learn it!   The line-warriors
Fled before us,   fast to their ships,
Before the might   of the man-killer,
Mighty warrior,   and Man-Battle.   40
That noble warrior,   wisest of princes,
Praised me for skill—   the ship-raiders
Plundered his bed-rest   for beaten gold.

Shield against shield,   they shattered the walls,
And I stood at the house   of the high maiden,
Holy dwelling,   and hefted my spear,
Shoulder against shoulder   with my small sister,
Seer of truth;   she a sword wielded.[4]
She fought nobly!   Fallen that house,
But no foemen's hands,   foul defilers,   50
Sullied the maiden.   Smiling, she stood,
When the noble prince,   proud warrior,
Gave me a ring   of ruddy gold,
Ring-giver's gift   for glory in battle.
Against the ancient custom   of my kinswomen,
I, glad, received it.   Gone is that house,
The good dwelling.   Gone is the prince,
The man-killer,   mighty in war.
Gone is the mead-hall,   gleaming with gold,
Where the high-lord sat,   longing for war,   60
The noble youths   yearning for battle.
The young fighters,   famous in war,
Fell by the wall-gates.   Folded in earth
Those kinsmen lie,   kinswomen too,
Noble war-women   in white armor,
Slain beside the walls.   I watched, weary,
From high towers,   as the heathen foe,
Dreaded shipmen,   shield against shield,
Fought on the shore,   shared their sword-blades.
Eager for battle,   babe in my arms,   70
I longed for my spear.   My sword-brother,
The man-killer,   mighty in war,
Famous in battle,   fated to die,
Circled me in arms,   spoke comfort to me.
I found joy in that—   fierce sorrow too.
And the child knew not   his noble father,
Nor noble mother;   many the tears.
Where is the warrior   who walked beside me,
Strong on the field,   fierce in battle,
The brave hero,   brilliant in helm?   80
Where the ring-giver,   ruler of the town?
Where are the princes,   the proud fighters?
The city-dwellers,   seeing no harm,
Opened the gates.   Gone the ring-giver,
The kinswomen,   and the warrior-queen!
Gone is the city,   shining as dawn!
Gone are the walls,   where I watched, maddened,
When fell the might   of the man-killer,
Skilled on the field,   and the ship-warriors,

Foreign foemen,   defiled his flesh-home.[5]   90
The walls shattered   before the sea-riders' might,
And they plundered the hall,   heavy with silver,
And plundered the tombs,   treasure-laden,
And raided the house   of the high maiden,
And slew all the warriors   and wise women,
Maidens and wives,   and many children,
And flames engulfed   the gold-city.
They freed me later,   fools that they are,
Spared me my son   and the seer of truth.[6]
The ship-warriors   sent from the city   100
My kinswomen,   keen in the fight.
We walk, exiles,   who once were rulers,
Queen and kinswomen,   keen warriors,
Long for the days   of dear-worthy joys,
Shield and sword-fame,   songs of the fight,
Feastings in hall,   and heart-friendships.
Oh, the man-killer,   mightiest prince!
Oh, the ring-giver,   ruler in hall!
Oh, worthy queen,   keen warriors,
Battle-companions,   brave in the fight,   110
Brothers and cousins,   keen kinswomen!
Oh, the bright city,   shining and splendid!
We wait by the walls.   Well I remember.

Hear you, Steel-Heart?[7]   The song you began
And thought finished   when fell the walls
Of the radiant city   I, ready-hearted,
Sing new verses,   noble in deeds,
Weaving with words   a warrior's ending.
I shall end easily   what you, eager, began:
A battle song.   120

Deor's Flyting[8]

Editor's note: All footnotes for "Deor's Flyting" belong to Hennequin as an original part of her text and appear at the end of this chapter (notes 8–16). This poem also included a pseudo-scholarly introduction—cut here due to space—presented originally to the tongue-in-cheek "Pseudo Society" at the International Congress on Medieval Studies, the major conference for medievalists held annually in Kalamazoo, Michigan.

Harold Secende was born on the sword's edge:
Deaðflyma murdered his mother and father.
His godfather perished in the feud,
And his foster-sister Godlufe was borne away.[9]
At last the old king fell,

And giants smashed the mead-hall to splinters.
Yet he triumphed, so too did I.
So, Deor, bite me!

Luca Rodorfarende had a terrible choice:
To avenge his father's death   10
He had to kill his father.
His sister's husband was turned to ice,
And their kin-home was destroyed by fire.[10]
Yet they triumphed, so too did I.
So, Deor, bite me!

Eomer Eadmund's son was exiled unjustly
Along with all his shoulder-companions,
Because his uncle, the ancient King,
Was poisoned by a serpent's tongue.[11]
He rode, miserable, far from the hall,   20
While orcs[12] attacked the folkland
And an unworthy one courted his sister.
Yet he triumphed, so too did I.
So, Deor, bite me!

Haelethu was slandered by her husband
On the very day of their wedding.
Her father reviled her,
And she walked alone into exile.[13]
Her kinswoman wept at the hall's door
And plotted vengeance with Eadig.[14]   30
Yet she triumphed, so too did I.
So, Deor, bite me!

Inda the Scholar[15] was wise in lorecraft,
But his foemen surprised him at night.
They stole the golden treasure-coffer,
And buried him, living, in a host-king's barrow
With a serpent-troop.
Yet he triumphed, so too did I.
So, Deor, bite me!

I am an expert poet,   40
A man wise in all of songcraft,
And Heorrenda is my name.[16]
But no one noticed my harp's power.
I had no place in the hall,
And my songs languished for want of hearers.
And yet I triumphed, though Deor whines—
So, Deor, bite me!

NOTES

1. Specifically, Andromache was sent to Troy by the Queen of the Amazons.

2. In other words, Andromache is greeted by the "gold-giver" Priam, king of Troy. His other epithets here include "ring-giver" and "high-lord."

3. The "man-killer" is Hector, whom Homer in the *Iliad* calls "killer of men," and we also receive our first indication of the speaker's identity. "Man-Battle" is a rough translation for both *Andromache* and *Guðrinc*.

4. Andromache's "sister" was Cassandra, a seer cursed with true visions of the future that no one would believe. In this version, she is a warrior as well.

5. After Achilles kills Hector, he mutilates the Trojan's body by dragging it behind his chariot.

6. Although it's unclear whether Old English writers had direct access to *The Iliad*, they did have Dares Phrygius's retelling of that story in late antiquity. Unlike other chroniclers, Dares has Astyanax survive the Trojan War, and Andromache, Cassandra, Helen, and Queen Hecuba are all freed.

7. "Steel-Heart" refers to Agamemnon, king of Mycenae and commander of the Greek forces.

8. Strangely, the title morphed from the erroneous "An Invitation to Deor" to "Deor's Flyting" although Deor is the flytee in this poem, not the flyter. A more appropriate title would be "Heorrenda's Flyting," but as usual in academia, tradition and error often trump correction, advances, and common sense.

9. Critics predictably argue over the allusions made in this verse. Harold Secende, his foster sister Godlufe, and their adversary Deaðflyma are unattested elsewhere in Old Norse or Old English. Angus MacSoennicle contends that the names Deaðflyma ("Death-fugitive") and Secende ("Seeker") are symbolic of any and all participants in feuds and therefore the verse makes no specific allusion whatsoever (McSoennicle, "Reading Too Much: Shipping and Slashing in Boreal Scholarship," in *Splinter in My Scholarship*). John H. Watson, on the other hand, reminds us that many criminals were fugitives from death under Anglo-Saxon law; he suggests that Harold Secende was some sort of bounty hunter, and that his tale, if found, would constitute an early example of detective fiction ("The Science of Detection: Early Examples in Medieval Literature, Which Unfortunately Includes the Boreal Master," *Strand* 36 [1895]). No one has yet ventured a symbolic explanation for the name of Harold's foster sister, Godlufe ("God-love" or "Good-love"). Nor has any scholar yet taken the sensible yet obvious stance that perhaps the names were actual names of historical figures who received their names before their apparently famous feud started.

10. Until recently, this verse, with its unidentified allusions, sparked wild debate and wilder theories and at least three brawls at the dance at the Forty-Third International Congress on Medieval Studies in Kalamazoo, Michigan. Theories tended to fall into two camps. The first, originating with Hugh G. Sigar, asserts that the story of Luca Rodorfarende was a Germanic version of the Oedipal myth ("Sometimes a Phallus Is a Phallus: Oedipal Riddles in the Boreal Master," *Rank Speculations* 46 [1994]). The second, proposed by Ghiek, believes that Luca's surname, Rodorfarende

("Sky-farer"), refers to some story of an early Germanic sun god ("A Last Minute Conference Paper on the Names in Old English Translations of the Boreal Master"). However, Jackson Crawford's startling discovery of the *Tattúínárdœla Saga* (*The Saga of the People of the Tatooine River Valley*) sheds new light on this verse. One of the main heroes of this saga, Lukr Himingangari, is called upon to avenge his father's death, only to discover that the murderer was, indeed, his father, Anakinn (who is alluded to in "Deor" as Anacen Heofongangende) (*Tattúínárdœla Saga*, 10 Mar. 2010, www.tattuinardoelasaga.wordpress.com; accessed 7 July 2011). Lukr of the saga has a brother-in-law, Hann or Hani, who is turned to ice, and the surnames Himingangari and Heofongangende (Heaven-goer) correspond to the Old English translator's alternative but equivalent Rodorfarende (Sky-farer).

11. Since Eomer Eadmund's son is unattested elsewhere in Old English, Old Norse, or any other early Germanic literatures, it is impossible to know Eomer's story. As usual, this lack of evidence has not hindered Boreal scholarship. Badcock and Weiner propose that the "serpent's tongue" refers to a homosexual relationship between the "ancient king" and a thane or advisor, with which the corrupt advisor is able to blackmail the king into exiling his nephew ("Queering the Boreal Master: It Wasn't Hard," *Rank Speculations* 61 [2009]).

12. Krapp and Dobbie argue that this word, *orcneas* (*orcs*), is stolen from J. R. R. Tolkien's *Lord of the Rings* series and thus postdates any genuine Old English poem by at least eight hundred years. On the basis of this argument, Krapp and Dobbie conclude that "Deor's Flyting"—and all the other poems of the Dodd Manuscript—are poorly executed forgeries constructed by a science-fiction/fantasy geek with too much education and too much time on her hands (*The Anglo-Saxon Minor Poems*, 6 vols., Columbia UP, 1942). They may be correct, but the word *orcneas* is hardly conclusive evidence, as Tolkien stole the word *orcneas* from *Beowulf* in the first place (*Beowulf* 112), a charge that Christopher Tolkien vehemently denies in his foreword to his father's "The Boreal Master: The Horror and the Crisis" (*More Works Tolkien Never Wanted Published*, edited by Christopher Tolkien, Cambridge UP, 1996, p. 272). Litigation is still pending.

13. Sr. Mary Martyr believes this verse refers to a virgin saint in the *miles christi* (soldier of Christ) tradition, as her name seems to be a feminization of the Old English *hæleð*, hero (Martyr, *The Boreal Master and Other Penance Manuals*, op. cit.).

14. Omen and Harbinger postulate this is a reference an early Germanic death god thought to be the origin of Iron Maiden's mascot. This god's name is never mentioned in manuscripts or runic inscriptions—Omen and Harbinger believe it is forbidden to speak it—and Eadig, or "Blessed One," is a euphemistic reference ("War, Famine, Boreal Riddles, and Death," *Miskatonic Apocalyptic Quarterly* 13 [2001]). Norton Myron Ghiek argues that Haelethu is a code name for Edith Godwine's daughter, queen of Edward the Confessor, who was rejected and nearly divorced by her husband (*A Last Minute Conference Paper on the Names in Old English Translations of the Boreal Master*). However, none of Edith's brothers were called Eadig, and it is unlikely (as Ghiek proposes) that Eadig is a pet name for Eadweard, her husband's name, as he's the one who rejected her in the first place. Mookerji cites this as a reference to Sita, the wife of Rama, who was kidnapped by Ravana and later rescued by

Rama and his monkey army ("I Publish More Than You Do: Sanskrit Origins in the Names in the Kashmiri Sutra," *Journal of the Southern Arizona Icelandic Literature and Sailing Association* 23 [2008]).

15. Yotelehi Mookerji, with predictable tenacity, claims that Inda is a scribal misrendering of Indra, the ancient Hindu god, and this verse refers to Indra's battle with the dragon Vritra ("Vedic Hymns of the Kashmiri Master," *New Hindu Review* 51 [2009]). The evidence is unconvincing. According to ancient Sanskrit tradition, Indra ruled sky and storm and was also a patron of warfare; he was not, in fact, a scholar, nor does his battle with Vritra the dragon involve an entire serpent-troop. In a startling turn of events, however, Mookerji's theory seems to be the frontrunner for wont of other suggestions. The only serious challenges comes from postcolonial critic Latifa Sulu-Uhuru; she theorizes that Inda the Scholar's premature burial mirrors an ancient Voodoo ritual imported from Africa and practiced in medieval Iceland (Latifa Sulu-Uhuru, "Viking in Africa: Voodoo Magic and Other Weirdness in the Boreal Master," *Unsettling Postcolonial Quarterly* 15 [2007]), and Henry Jones Sr., who believes Inda's experiences constitute an ancient Germanic religious ritual (*The Boreal Canon and Other Medieval Literary Disasters*, Obscure Midwestern UP, 1949).

16. Strange as it may seem given the usual rabid tenacity and wild theories in Boreal scholarship, no scholar has yet discussed the identification of Heorrenda as the speaker/poet here. The Dodd Manuscript does not present "Deor's Flyting" within a story or tale; the poem seems independent of context and clearly names Heorrenda as its author. If Heorrenda is the author of "Deor's Flyting," a poem clearly included within the Boreal canon, then we may finally have a real identity of the Boreal Master: Heorrenda. Among other things, the equation of the Boreal Master and Heorrenda completely explains why Deor is so upset he lost his job—and finally gives scholars at Miskatonic a precise name to include in their ritual curses.

Part III

LATER REVIVALISTS

Marcie Lynn Tentchoff

Horror and dark fantasy are two specialties for Canadian poet and short story writer Marcie Lynn Tentchoff (b. 1968), whose most common themes include bitterness, the making of difficult choices, and the darker aspects of human character. She grew up reading writers such as J. R. R. Tolkien, C. S. Lewis, Poul Anderson, and Paul Edwin Zimmer, but the poetry of Tolkien and John Myers Myers carried a special impact. Her interest in the medieval alliterative meter, though, stems from her time at Simon Fraser University. There, she devoured Arthurian literature—later composing a long Arthurian poem, "Surrendering the Blade," which won an Aurora Award in 2001— and took classes in Middle English, Old English, and Old Norse literature. *Beowulf*'s metrics, for instance, clearly influence "The Deed of Snigli," and Tentchoff's poems in Old Norse meters are guided by the notes and prologues from her old textbooks, particularly George Johnston's edition of *The Saga of Gisli the Outlaw*. One of the few true SF poems in the Modern Revival, in fact, is "The Song of the Dragon-Prowed Ships," a text in a skaldic meter about aliens who've crash-landed on Earth. To date, Tentchoff has published three collections of verse: *Sometimes While Dreaming* (2007), *Through the Window: A Journey to the Borderlands of Faerie* (2008), and *Midnight Comes Early* (2021).

The Song of the Dragon-Prowed Ships

Raiders, we, the red-grimed
reavers of doom's grieving,
battle-scarred wave beaters,
blade dipping, oar laden,

we mastered lands mist-filled,
mined towns for rich findings,
then heaved our ships homewards,
heeding our bold leaders.

Seasons flew like seedpods,
sending us, backs bending,   10
wavewards, sword-blades weaving,
weeping red with reaping.
Lands to raid grew leaner,
lightless grew our fighting,
dull became such duelling,
drab as mindless stabbing.

Scalds who'd praised our sailing
(savoring all our braveness),
burdened now by boredom,
bade us seek new raiding,   20
foes with distant faces,
forests on far shorelines,
glory in fresh gorefields,
gold from virgin holdings.

Dark-eyed, we sat drinking,
daunted by scalds' taunting,
songs not worth the singing,
sighing for dreams dying,
when, with bleakness winning,
wailing filled our sailyard,   30
rousing us to rising,
raging for fight waging.

Then, amidst strange thunders,
thirst-dry skies came bursting,
shuddering as they shed a
ship through gale-foam whipping,
down where we were droning
dim, our battle hymning,
waiting for fate's weaving,
wary, yes, but daring.   40

Fought we there too fleeting;
few were strange-made hewers
left among the living,
low down in the glowing
belly of the bowl-ship,
bright as harnessed lightning.

They who showed some thistle,
those as thralls were chosen.

Forced by us to fashion
fittings for star-flitting,   50
vowed with us to voyage,
varied lands and rare ones.
Seek we now the skypaths,
sailing till blades fail us,
raiders, star-ship riders,
red-drenched moonbeam treaders.

The Deed of Snigli

I hight Snagtooth   Lord of Posies
wondrous wordsmith   story-weaver.
Here I weave the   Tale of Snigli,
hungry hero   wave-drawn warrior.
Dragon maidens   weeping, wander,
search in sorrow   for their Snigli.
He shall never   rise a'rutting,
lusting, thrusting   at the ladies.
Sleeps he soundly   in the clam beds,
never hearing   mourning moanings.   10
Hear then now the   Tale of Snigli,
how he came to   meet his maker.

Snigli had a   love of herrings.
Snigli had a   midnight craving.
Snigli rose for   sneakfull snackings
as the moon was   softly shining.
Down the cart track   to the harbour,
stumbling, fumbling   fogged and weary,
deafened by his   tummy's grumblings,
down the wharf and   past the fish boats,   20
hound-honed nostrils   flaring, leading,
past the humans   safely sleeping,
to the hoards of   brine-born treasure:
heaps of herrings   primed for selling,
nestled glimmering   in the fish sheds.

Mighty Snigli   broke the padlocks,
found and gathered   savory silver,
turned and started   towards his sleep place,
streams of eager   drool a' dribbling.

Fair bewitched by   tempting odours   30
from the spoils   he had garnered,
hero Snigli   had no warning
of the swooping   wind-blown vermin:
pesky seagulls   swift as houseflies,
brooding bandits   of the airways.
Cruel their weapons   beak and talon.
Scales were falling   blood was flowing.

Snigli faced his   fowl tormentors
for one moment,   then he scooted,
dropping prizes   loot stealth-gotten,   40
leapt, and flying   sought the moth-roads.
Little thought he   of the odours
sweetly wafting   from his plating.
Little dreamt he   his tormentors
would not pause to   scarf their winnings.
Swiftly flew he   foes behind him,
o'er the darkly   rippling ocean,
twisting neck to   face his foe fowls,
breathing out a   gout of fire,
sending two to   blazing glory: 50
well roast seagull   tasty eatings.

Then did Snigli   hear his death knell
in the ringing   of his eardrums,
as his body   winging backwards,
hit the cliff face   near the harbour,
plunging downwards   towards the water.
Thus did Snigli   take the squid-roads,
sinking swiftly   no more Snigli.
Never fought there   fiercer foe-beast,
fearsome Snigli   bane to seagulls.   60
So says Snagtooth   Lord of Posies,
wondrous wordsmith   kin to Snigli.

The Changeling's *Fornyrðislag*

Foster mother   you found me trembling,
crying soft   in cradle wrappings,
brought me here   where hearts are kinder
and lonely tears   are left behind.

My days are spent   in dancing airborne,
laughing, drifting   on dragons' backs

in fogs of myth   and fairy wonder,
loved and wanted   at least for now.

But age brings changes   we children grow
too fast for dim   undying folk   10
and many friends   I've made and played with
are cast aside   or servants now.

I will not ask   for wondrous giftings,
for love beyond   your lease of time,
but can you please   if caring lingers
not send me back   to soul-bound lands?

James Dorr

James Dorr (b. 1941) is an Indiana-based short story writer and poet specializing in horror and dark fantasy, with forays into mystery and science fiction. He has published numerous collections, including *The Tears of Isis*, a 2013 Bram Stoker Award finalist for Superior Achievement in a Fiction Collection, and *Vamps (A Retrospective)*, a collection of vampire-related poetry. While earning his M.A. in English from Indiana University, Dorr specialized in medieval literature, and the two long narrative poems that follow show touches of alliterative prosody. In "The Westfarer," an ominous tale about werewolves attacking the failed Viking settlements in Vinland, Dorr clearly uses Old English caesuras. Similarly, "The Worm in the Wood," which reimagines the Arthur legend from the perspective of Britain's aborigine people, contains metrical echoes from *Sir Gawain and the Green Knight* as well as Dorr's more immediate source inspiration, Rudyard Kipling's "A Pict Song."

The Westfarer

Know this: The world   is wide and bowl-like,
Its extremities up-curved   at every corner,
To north, ice-locked Thule,   night-bound Nifelheim,
Home of Hel, goddess,   of death's hungered gnawing;
To south, fiery Muspel,   hall of bright Surtr,
Birthplace of sun and stars,   flame's heat and searing;[1]
To east, dawn, beginnings,   destiny's first day,
The morning of men's lives,   of mead and brave sailings;
To west, only endings.
      I sing now of west-faring,   10

I, Signy, Helmsdottir, bondsmaid and seeress,
Dark haired, dark fortuned, sailmaid and dire traveler,
Sing I of wanderings, of three men, and one more.
The first I sing, Bjarni, the son of glum Herjolf,[2]
Made sail south to Ireland, then Iceland and Greenland,
Was caught first by north wind, then calmed in a white fog
His ships drifting westward, saw at last woodlands
And hills unfamiliar; north then he set helm,
Disdaining to beach there, until, dim in cloudbanks,
His tired eye saw ice fields, and, so turning east again,   20
Entered at last the fjord of Eirik Redbeard.
This, then, was Greenland, Bjarni's last landfall,
From whence sailed the second, Leif, Eirik's eldest son,
Blown, too, by winds west, backward on Bjarni's course
To a land of black stone, high and ice-summited,
Which named he Helluland hailing cliffs' flatness;
Next founded he Markland, fairer and forested,
Willow-wrapped and with spruce meet for ships' siding;
Yet went he on south and west, seeking new wonders,
Till he found a grass valley, frostless in winter,   30
Its streams filled with salmon, its dew sweet as honey,
Its hills vine-encumbered and heavy with wine fruit.[3]
Here Eiriksson wintered, then, weighty with new lore,
Returned he to Brattahlid, byre of his father,
From whence, third, came Thorvald, thane and Leif's brother,
To west to the new land, and north for exploring
Found inlets and rivers, ice-laden Kjalarness,
Named for his keel's scraping on hard sand bottom,
And found he there *Skraelings* or, as we say, "Screamers,"
The men of this new place who, making no welcome,   40
Set on him with arrows until, slain, his crew made sail
Heavy with grief, home.[4]
       Thus weave the Nornir
The fates of men, earthbound, unvisioning futures,
Save that I, Helmsdottir, am cursed with seeing!

Listen as I sing: The fourth man *I* sailed with,
Thorfinn Karlsefni, from Iceland to Eiriksfjord,
Greenland's south settlement; I, Signy, first of three
Women I tell you now, and, later, one again.[5]
Second was fair Gudrid, gaunt Thorvald's widow   50
Who, at Eiriksfjord, betrothed Thorfinn our captain.
Filled she that winter his ears with wonder,

With tales of the travelings   of the first three I sang
Until, with spring's budding,   three ships he fitted,
Broad *knarrs* meet for blue water,   deep and strong-bottomed
And high, with their oaken strakes   near overflowing
As goods he had brought aboard,   cattle and brood-sows,
Corn-seed and women—   yes, wives we took with us too—
Seeking to settle   these new strands of plenty.
Oars straining, we pushed to sea,   then, with the wind   60
Raised sails of dyed wool-cloth   as red as sun's setting,
Our masts tall as ice clouds   kept pole star to rightward,
As, wave-thunder tossing,   we followed the whales' track
Until the black, flat stone   of Helluland sighting.
Thence bore we to larboard,   as had Leif before us turned,
Sails tacked to carry us   south with the current,
Until we passed Markland   and came to a place of streams,
Fast racing waters,   and there, winter near us—
So long had we journeyed!—   spent we our first snow time.
Huddled we now in huts   cursing the harsh wind   70
That blew ice and coldness,   beyond expectation,
As some called aloud to Thor,   others to Odin,
Others the White-Iesus   worshiped of Christers,
While I, alone, friendless,   away from the hearth fire,
Banished with bond-slaves   to sleep in far corners,
Dreamed, shivering, of shadows.
                                   This was the first sharing:
This, my first Norn-vision,   gifted by Verdandi,
She of the Always-Now—   later would I, weeping,
Come to Skuld's blessing,   the skald-sense of Will-Be—[6]   80
This showed me ice creeping   from west and north crevices,
Steadily southward,   until, the world shifting
Once more back to sunlight,   again at last came spring.
And so again did come spring,   so sailed we further,
Surprised by the land's cold   that not Leif nor Thorvald
Had claimed to encounter;   yet climbed we the wave crests,
Our ships' timbers groaning,   as groped we again to south,
Finding both fruit-vines   and honeyed meadows,
Until came we to a bay,   arm-like, encircling,
Protected from currents   and storms' harsh keenings,   90
And here we entered,   made fast our anchors,
Built byres and longhouses,   pens for our meat-beasts,
Sowed rye and barley   thus for our abiding.
And dreamed I this place at night   not yet of coldness,
But shadows, of shapes melting,   shifting in moonlight.

⁂

Autumn brought Screamers,   our first meet with Skraelings,
Ugly-haired, squat men,   with broad cheeks and huge eyes
Who crept, their feet soundless,   in sandals of furred skin,
Until, nearly at our gates   whooped they their greeting
In shrill ululation,   in shrieks and mad soundings.   100
Their tongue we knew not,   yet gestures made Thorfinn
To show we desired trade,   their furs for our dyed cloth,
Red as the sun's rays,   and also sweet milk we gave
Fresh from our grazed beasts,   frothing and well-fatted,
But one thing we would not   offer despite their wish,
That being weapons,   our steel swords and spear points.
Alas, it turned not well,   our metal they lusted for;
One took to stealing   and quickly we slew him,
Then others screamed foully   and fled to the forest,
Leaving us for that night,   but the next morning   110
Returned they in numbers   near overwhelming.
Screeching, they shot at us,   sharp arrows coursing,
Then with clubs fell on us   forcing us backward,
Driving us to rock cliffs   where clung we in despair
To our lives' last hour.
                            My tale would be over
Save, as I sang before,   just as three men there were,
Three who began it all,   braving, first, western seas,
So, too, were three women: I, Signy, song-teller;
Gudrid the second,   fair bride of Karlsefni;   120
And third now bold Freydis   Eiriksdottir,
Who, in heat of battle,   tore loose her byrnie
And, baring her breasts to all,   took in hand sword's blade,
Stung it against her teats   terrifying,
Through magic of womenkind,   milk and blood mixing,
Birth and death drawing   in dire steel together,
Our enemy Skraelings   who, screaming the louder,
Fled once again forestward,   leaving to us the field.
So passed the second year   of Thorfinn's settling
Of grape bedecked Vine-Land.   130
                            The winter grew on us,
But milder now, easy   for us to endure the cold,
Save it seemed fiercer   the closer to spring it came.
Then the next growth season   came back the Screamers,
But cautious now, canny,   content with harassment,
Unwilling to brave the walls   we built in winter,
Protecting our village—   but came back, too, visions:

⁂

This time I attended   a band of armed hunters,
A servant to skin the deer,   scrape from meat, entrails,
To clean and to carry,   as my masters cared me to.   140
Thus marched I through the wood,   marveled at autumn,
Its early arrival,   trees orange with brightness,
And how left the Skraelings   with passage of summer.
At night cooked I meat for men,   shared in their mead, too,
Until in a stone place   surrounded by boulders
Our fur skins we wrapped us in,   fitfully slept then,
And dreamed I of shadows.
                              In shade form my vision
Took me to a stone land,   much like that I slept in,
But north, by a great lake,   choked full with ice mountains,   150
And there saw I men as wolves—   men clothed in wolf-skins,
But shifting, arising,   grown huge now, slavering—
Men who as wolves themselves,   howled forth in anger.
Listened I to their words,   heard I their hatred
Of ship-borne men such as I   lately had sailed with,
Of eastern men, artisans,   builders and hunters,
Despoilers of virgin earth,   bane of their Vinland.
Showed me the future then,   of farms and homesteads,
Of axe-leveled forests,   fields cut from wood they felt
Earth-Mother owed them,   they, Her erst protectors,   160
And, thus to prevent such wyrd,   this their revenge was:
The cold, they commanded;   men's crops would they wither
Through ever-harsh ice seasons,   increasing winter-blight,
Hamper thus sea-lanes,   snow sending southward
Not just in these western lands,   but the world over.
Then saw they me in my dream,   huddled in sleep-dress,
But feared they the magic   of Freydis—*all* women—
Just as did the Screamers   that first meeting's season
And so left me, waking,   warm, curled in fur blankets,
Once more with my own kind.   170
                              But woke I now, shrieking,
Beholding the slaughter   of men slain around me,
Of dark entrails steaming   in sunlight of morning,
Of throats ripped and tooth-chewed,   limbs torn from bodies,
All heaped in a fell hill—   thus arose I, alone!
Snatched I up sword and shield   lest I find Skraelings,
Or wolf-manlings—Fenrir's folk—   lurking in forest;
I knew not, my breasts I bared,   prayed their protection,
As trod I not bravely,   but trembling through wood-trails,

Until at last, fainting,   came I from the forest   180
To homestead and Freydis,   to Gudrid and Thorfinn.
Told I then of slaughter,   of gore stained on stone ground,
And warriors took oath   to rush into woodland,
To search out the Skraelings,   to lay at rest slain men,
But when at last night fell,   returned, finding nothing.

Thus came our third winter: Behind walls we waited,
Feared frost, the snow's howling,   the wolf cubs of Fenrir,
And when spring's days lengthened   took ship and departed.
We sailed north to Greenland,   anchored at Eiriksfjord,
Glad of the ice-glint   of that far land's glaciers;   190
Told we our tale there,   then, fearful to tarry,
Sailed eastward to Iceland,   from there to the sun's rise.
And yet I had visions—   no more would they leave me!—
Of winters grown worse,   of ice-sheets increasing,
Of blight ever following,   haunting our footsteps,
Of Skraelings across the sea,   sailing in skin boats,
In Greenland itself fared south,   *Inuit* seal-catchers,
Following cold to come   soon to the farmsteads:
There saw I too,   as I say, a fourth woman,
A fourth after we, the three,   left for the east-lands,   200
A Skraeling, Navaranak,   whispering to Norsemen,
And then, again, to her own,   sowing forth enmity.
Then saw I *umiaks*,   skin boats of Skraelings,
Disguised well as ice floes,   sneaking through fjord-mouths,
Approaching the homesteads   as men, inside, sleeping,
See not flame and arrows   until they lie, dying;
And thus, too, passed Greenland,   last of west thane-holds,
And nearly as well, Iceland,   as cold increases,
As winters grow bitter,   the blight of the wolf-men,
That ever spreads south.   210

But sing I one more tale,
One last before ending,   of earth and its future:
Of one final seeing   that comforts my night-sleep.
Know you that the world   is vast in its bowl shape,
Its northern side rising,   but south, too, up-curving;
That where Hel and Nifelheim,   home of Wolf-Fenrir,
Hold sway in their highness,   so too, south, opposing,
The mountains of Muspel   grow men wise as foxes.
In dream-vision saw I this,   one man among them

Prostrating before a queen,   begging this bounty,   220
That from her pawned jewel-hoard   be hired ships and seamen,
A sailing to west be planned,   with ships' holds groaning
With byrnied and armed men,   with barrels that shoot fire,
And—see I this also,   ye wolf-folk and wolflings,
This wyrd I foretell *you*—
                          These foxes spread northward.

The Worm in the Wood

> *"But, forasmuch as it was on this wise that they possessed them of the country, it hath been only by an injustice that they have taken tribute thereof. For nought that is taken by force and violence can be justly possessed by him that did the violence."*

> —Geoffrey of Monmouth, *History of the Kings of Britain*, IX.16

> *"And so as he yede, he saw and hearkened by the moonlight, how the pillers and robbers were come into the field, to pill and to rob many a full noble knight of brooches, and beads, of many a good ring, and of many a rich jewel; and who that were not dead all out, there they slew them for their harness and their riches."*

> —Sir Thomas Malory, *Le Morte D'Arthur*, XXI.4

As so it lies, spoilage for ravens and robbers,
the *Alpha* and *Omega*, I, who speak to ravens,
ken of them tales both of future and past, know
to this it comes, always.
          I, who now through ravens' eyes
see Lucan bending, lips whisper to Arthur
that, wounded, he must be moved;[7]
Bedivere, butler to him in more noble times,
bowing as well, lifting in his arms that king,
Lucan from this labor also expiring. I,   10
through ravens' ears hearing also the king's request
see, too, how greed's grasp even now causes
loyal Sir Bedivere's hand to hesitate,
holding the sword too long, seeing its hilt sparkle
bejeweled beneath the moon, twice instead hiding it
before returning it to the lake whence it came—
even here, at Death's side, loyalties divided:
just as Sir Gawain's must for his lost brother
supplant the kinship he owes noble Launcelot;[8]

Launcelot in his turn trysting with king's wife, 20
love for lust trading; King Arthur for his part thus
tearing his kingdom—
     Oh, it was not Mordred's fault—
I, who through ravens' eyes foresee the future
know, yes, that some will blame *him*—but
this playing out Fate's game was no whit more his
than the doing of Morrigan-named king's half-sister,
the Lady le Fay, for all that blood may join us,
she through her dead father, her learning of death-lore;[9]
I through ravens'-speaking, carrion-formed kinship to 30
Fea and Macha, she of "Macha's acorn crop,"
enemies' heads piled in empty-eyed windrows, to
venomous Nemon, to Badb of the battle-cry
crow-formed and banshee-voiced—all of these *bean-sidhe*,
the women of fairy-mounds, even Queen Morgan herself
at the end of it—so taking Arthur, too,
to appled-island vales; but not *their* blame
either.[10]

⁂

Nor was it even mine, instrument though that
I willingly was, I who have seen the past as well, 40
that of my people, who lived here before Celts came,
those of the mainland who called themselves "Soldiers' Sons"
they in turn conquered by ravening Romans,
they themselves also by Saxons and Angles—
even the *name* of the island thus stolen—
then Arthur, at last, in blood the land reconquering:
land that was never *his*.
     I and the others
so biding in shadows as blood upon blood soaked
an earth once green, peace-formed, of 50
dappled sunlight on leaves, fair winds on flowered-
fields, meadows grass-mounded for cattle to feast on—
this field that I and my carrion-fed sisters
now pick through as robbers, and not *rightful* owners—
thus we, the worm in the wood ever waiting
to sting where chance offers, watched as Arthur's city rose.[11]
Dwelt we in forest then, blue-woaded, tattoo-disguised
so as to blend with dark, watching the blood well up
even in *games*—the "tournaments" as these new
conquerors called their sport—more so in war-making, 60
blood upon blood always to earth returning,
blood upon blood to *pay*.

And so we waited.
Some of us now, too, to seek work as scullion-maids
within the kitchens and larders of Camelot,
to be set there by Sir Kay to scrub pots clean
as he, as seneschal, so doled out duties
for us the most menial; others to dress the hair
of noble ladies, enduring their pinches
their pique-filled, spiteful slaps; others, the men of us,   70
to work in stables—thus, always, our time staying—
thus learning where chinks lay, where lay their weaknesses,
scryed we their secrets.
        Learned we of ladies, too,
not content to let the men alone spill life, so
attired they themselves all in single colors—
rather had *us* dress them, we who worked as their maids
otherwise fading to invisibility, we the unnoticed
save when we were *needed*; which suited our purpose—
thus decked out, they made delight that they as lovers   80
would take none but he who in battle-clash killed *three*,
so claiming by this ruse to save their chastity.
So causing more blood to soak the gore-laden ground;
the ground that was not *theirs*.

⁂

        This ravens told me,
or this, perhaps, I had seen, I who toiled also
in Camelot's pantries, poisoning not the food
but rather minds of men, filling their thoughts with fame,
far-ranging quests to try: Gawain perhaps the most
noble, once, of them all, now to test axe-strokes   90
against a lord, forest green—one of *our* kind,
you see—there to be found wanting, even if so slightly
as to be scarcely (as *we* were scarcely, oh we made sure
of *that*!) if at all noticed[12]; others to crave a cup
that sinners could not seek (and who of them were not
sinners, at least, in blood?); others for women's love.
Thus for idleness depleted the court of its most doughty,
itself its enemy, scattering loyalties,
sending its life-blood forth, serving no purpose
though no doubt most well-meant, most nobly intentioned,   100
save spilling more blood *en route*—on way to *no*where;
while elsewhere the land's peasants labored just as we,
who within Camelot's marbled walls took the tasks
nobody else desired; we did the drudge work,
yet careful to bide our time; I in the kitchen

who found me a cow's horn, who whittled it, tapering,
into a bow—a tiny arc, barely two hands' spans
from point to point, yet powerful—who strung it
with my own hair.
 And hid it in my cloak's hem. 110
While outside others toiled, waiting as we did,
who gained no gifts as a king's noble knights might,
those who were of the court, or, through noble birth—
stealers of their own lands, just as *this* king was,
in that way, perhaps, kindred—came to seek entry
and, so, shared in his largess: others, as I say,
those left without, of the land, we who were here *before*,
we gained no favor but rather in forests skulked,
fields labored, kitchens toiled, bedchambers laid out
and swept indiscretions out with other secrets, 120
on our selves, you understand, thus *supported*
the glory of Camelot, yet gained nought from it.
We, the little folk, the *aborigines*—whose land it was
they *took*—bided us, so, our time;
whispered we with ravens, Morrigan, Nimue—she
of the Moon's brightness—Vivien, Ana, Badb,
Nemon and Macha. . . .

We the worm in the wood.

And nought that is taken by force and violence
can be justly owned by the one who conquered it— 130
Mordred was just a tool.
 While on that last morning,
Mordred himself facing, fourteen knights with him,
Arthur with *his* fourteen, both hosts arrayed behind,
every man watchful as king and knight parley, each
waiting the other's first hostile wavering,
swords sheathed by agreement—
 I, I in the grass waiting
now took my little bow. Now took I also
a needle I borrowed from some lady's bedroom, 140
fixed into an arrow, and creeping, unseen,
I shot—
 stinging one's ankle, of which side I do not know,
one of the knights alone, but he, confusing
that prick for an adder, a poisoned snake at his feet,
so *drew* his sword out. . . .

So started the battle.
And so now, by nightfall, a hundred thousand laid dead
upon the down, Mordred and Arthur at it with each other,
one slain as well, one wounded, soon to die also—   150
thus Camelot ended.
     And after, I who see with ravens' eyes wandering,
thus later I visited Glastonbury in guise of a servant
and saw with my *own* eyes the stone with its carving, of
Hic jacet Arthurus Rex, quondam Rex que futurus,[13]
and, later still, still disguised, visited Almesbury,
to which the queen had come to pray there as a nun,
and whence came Launcelot seeing her there but once,
taking the robe himself; and in these both resorts
where those within might have reason to wish me harm,   160
everyone saw me—
     Yet not a one noticed.

NOTES

1. According to ancient geographers, Thule is the world's northernmost land; here, it seems to overlap with Niflheim ("dark world"), a misty realm of primordial ice and cold where the goddess Hel and those who die of sickness and old age reside. Muspel is a primordial realm of fire to the far south. It is guarded by the fire-giant Surt, who will kill the god Frey during Ragnarök.

2. Bjarni Herjólfsson was a Norse explorer who, in 986, probably became the first European to sight the Americas. Original accounts of the Vinland expeditions are told in *Grœnlendinga saga* ("Saga of the Greenlanders") and *Eiríks saga rauða* ("Saga of Eirik the Red"). The four men whom Signy mentions are Bjarni; Leif Erikson and his brother Thorvald Eiriksson, who became the first European to die in North America; and Thorfinn Karsefni, who followed Leif's route to Vinland in circa 1010.

3. When Leif Erikson retraced Bjarni's route, he made landfall at three locations: Helluland, Markland, and an allegedly grape-filled headland he named Vinland. Scholars continue to debate the locations of these places.

4. Brattahlid (or Brattahlíð) on Eiriksfjord in southern Greenland is where stands the estate of Erik Thorvaldsson, Lief and Thorvald's father. When Thorvald later sailed west himself, his ship ran aground and lost its keel at Kjalarnes ("Keel Point"); thereafter he fell victim to the "Skraelings," the Norse name for the indigenous Inuit peoples of Canada and Greenland.

5. The first three women in "The Westfarer" are our fictional narrator, Signy Helmsdottir; Thorvald's widow Gudrid, who later marries Thorfinn Karsefni; and Freydís Eiríksdóttir, the half- (or full-) sister of Leif Erikson. The fourth woman appears much later in the poem: the Skraeling woman Navaranak.

6. Here Signy names two of the Norns: Verdandi ("present") and Skuld ("future"). One reason commonly offered for the disappearance of Viking settlements from

Greenland is their failure to adapt to changing climate conditions related to the Little Ice Age.

7. The narrator is viewing the aftermath of the Battle of Camlann between Mordred and Arthur. Sir Lucan and his half-brother Sir Bedivere, who survived the battle, had both been loyal companions to King Arthur.

8. In many versions from the Arthurian romance tradition, Launcelot is directly responsible for the death of Agravain, one of Gawain's brothers.

9. As her name implies, Morgan le Fay has semi-divine fairy powers. Her first name derives specifically from the Morrígan, a threefold entity in Irish mythology who, in some accounts, is comprised of Ana, Babd, and Macha (or sometimes Nemon or Fea). This trinity is strongly associated with war and fate, and, in the Morrígan's role as foreteller of doom, she often appears as a crow. Both Morgan le Fay and the narrator share kinship with the Morrígan. Morgan le Fay herself descends from Duke Gorlois of Cornwall and his wife, Igraine, with whom Uther Pendragon—disguised as her husband through Merlin's magic—conceives Arthur. Gorlois is killed that same night and so becomes Morgan's "dead father."

10. "Macha's acorn crop" refers to a battlefield littered with corpses (or sometimes just severed heads). The *bean-sidhe* are female spirits in Irish folklore whose cries herald imminent death. The "appled-island vale" is Avalon, so named for being an isle rife with apple (or fruit) trees.

11. The phrase "worm in the wood" comes directly from "A Pict Song" by Rudyard Kipling; both texts call them "the Little Folk" as well. In Kipling, his Picts oppose the Romans, but Dorr transfers their opposition to Arthurian Britain. "Arthur's city" is specifically Camelot.

12. These lines refer directly to the ending of *Sir Gawain and the Green Knight*. The Green Knight is created directly through the agency of Morgan's magic.

13. Latin for "Here lies Arthur, the Once and Future King." According to legend, Arthur was buried at Glastonbury in Somerset, England.

Jo Walton

Jo Walton (b. 1964) is a highly lauded Canadian writer of fantasy and science fiction with deep ties to fandom and her Welsh roots; her grandmother was a well-known Welsh scholar and translator, and Walton herself speaks the language nearly fluently. Among Walton's accolades, she has won a World Fantasy Award for *Tooth and Claw* (2003), two Mythopoeic Society Awards, plus the Hugo and Nebula Awards. Her debut novel, *The King's Peace* (2000), won the John W. Campbell Award for best new writer, and it covers the conflict between the Saxons and the Celts in a fictionalized fantasyland Arthurian setting. Each chapter begins with an epigraph or verse fragment. One example is "Lew Rosson's Hall," a variation on a famous Irish legend retold in the alliterative manner. Walton also writes independent poems; most appear on her website. Her long poem "In Death Dark Halls, A Dog Howls" recounts in a quasi-alliterative style the Greek myth of Proserpina. Additionally, Walton is an adept literary critic. In 2008, she began for the website Tor.com a series of highly readable reviews, mostly retrospectives on older SFF classics; these were eventually collected into *What Makes This Book So Great* (2014).

Lew Rosson's Hall

—a Jarnish retelling of an Isarnagan story[1]

At meat they sat, uneasy peace
forced by their feasting in the king's hall.
Talk fell to fighting, hard-fought war
between the borders long disputed.

Emer was boasting, keeping count
seized heads slaughtered, slain of Oriel.
Provoked past endurance, Conal Cernach
replied in kind, corpses of Connat.[2]

Beaten in bragging, Emer sat sneering.   10
"Bold the boasts you gave against me.
If you should meet my mother, Maga,
that would make the counting different."

Conal standing flung a fresh head
rolling the rushes, crashing by her feet;
"So you say, but see, I know her,
met we have, and here is Maga!"

In Death's Dark Halls, a Dog Howls

I: THE POMEGRANATE SEEDS

Proserpina, torn between
love and how she wants to live,
weighs the pomegranate seeds
in her warm and living hands:[3]
waiting, wanting, choice withheld,
sees that still and silent hall
deathly hush and pillared dark,
deeper darkness stretching out,
echoed eaves where shadows hang
curl and linger, throng and mass,   10
purposes that haunt the hall,
shades who flit the columned aisles
bereft of names.

            She's weeping.
The seeds are chill; counting them
on her pale palm, clad in white,
she paces through hollow halls,
uncertainty echoing
each footfall on marble.

Can she live in this half place,   20
between the worlds, life and death,
she who is life, up above
whose steps are flowers in life's realm,
up on the green living Earth?
In spacious fields, orchard groves

vines and fruits swelled by the sun,
she loves the work, done in joy,
tending planted terraces,
choosing to tame fertile earth
with hedge and plough, next year's hope,   30
plant and gather, pluck and grow
sunlight on skin, cool air, rain,
the twining green, songs of birds,
her mother's hearth, bright and clear.
She yearns for it.
   But loves him.
This is his realm, his domain
these chill-veined floors, pillared halls,
dark river's tides, shores of death,
this dark his dark, these shades his,   40
his charge, his work, what he chose
(though drawn by lot long ago)
his world, his cares, these drear dank
and shadowed halls, these walled ways,
this underworld, death below.
Between these streams all folk pass
across the Styx, life to death
through Hades's realm, then plunge in
through Lethe, to a new life,
forgetting self, to choose chance.   50
The lingerers must learn here
not to cling on, to let go
and start again naked once more.

He cannot leave—she asked him,
telling the names of earth's joys,
beads on a string, her best hopes.
He wept salt tears, shook his head.
Sunlight hurts him, but his face
is light to her, touched by love.
Still on his throne his face set   60
he will not speak will be fair
her own free choice but his eyes
plead loneliness and matched love.

Seeing him there her heart moves
to stay and build life with him;
life in death's halls, together.
Slowly with use come to care
for shades of grey for his sake,
not best of all, but worth it.

Her heart pounds at time to choose   70
the green world or her heart's lord.
She eats three seeds, starts to choke,
her mouth filled with death and dust
his warm dark eyes, concerned now
his kind hand held out to her
to take the throne by his side
she tries to smile, swallows.

II: THE CORNSHEAF

Then from afar, drawing near
a new sound, plashing of oars,
Charon is come, out of time   80
the dark boat crosses Styx stream
no freight of souls, not this trip
a goddess, sure of herself.
Under the throne, Cerberus
growls very low, hackles rise.

Ceres's shoes snap on marble
angry and proud, her daughter
belongs to earth, must not stay
in this dark hole, no matter what.
She marches in, ready for war   90
glowing with light, life and health
no weapons shown, save being here.
No glance she gives the throne room
she walks straight in swift and sure
stands to defy the dark king
and his pale bride on one throne.
Presents demands: "The girl back,
my daughter, please, returned now."
Straight on to threats without pause,
"Or the world dies, nothing grows,"   100
in jealous pride, "All laid waste
withers and falls, if she stays,
end to all life, and all hope."

Proserpina pales, her choice
to leave the world, not slay it.
Vainly she pleads. Ceres smiles
a tight lipped smile, taps a sheaf
of gold corn on marble floor.
"Fool of a girl—shall all starve
and the world die for your sake?   110
In the sunshine I missed you.

I know your heart, what you wish
you are my kin, must come back
who could choose gloom and half-death
when poppies bloom in gold corn?"

Cerberus growls; three heads raise;
lips peal from three sets of teeth.
Hades stirs on his dark throne.
"By all the laws of all worlds,
she is my wife by free choice   120
she has eaten of death's food
and so must stay, relent now
you have your world and we ours,
she is my queen, no prisoner;
you may see her in sunlight
as she chooses to go forth."

A pale gold stream, her hair falls
as her head turns, her lips part.
He grins at her, and she laughs.
Laughter's echoes light the hall.   130
Shades draw closer, sensing hope.
The air seems warm, their hands touch.
Ceres just sneers. "How touching,
you offer her a few crumbs
of my hard work, as your gift.
Not good enough, dead man's god.
I want her back."

          "But Mother,"
she says at last, "I ate them,
my lord's right, I want to stay   140
by my own choice, and live here.
Let the world be, I love him."

"What do you know of love's taste
the honeyed wine of true joy,
you're a child still, I know best.
You ate three seeds, spit them out,
and we leave now, the boat waits."
She reaches out one swift hand
to snatch the girl off the throne
and a dog's jaws snap and close   150
on Ceres's arm, red blood flows,
but falls not far, the shades rush
shroud her in dark, lap the blood,
take solid shapes, memory

stirs in their eyes as eyes form.
Ceres recoils, has fed them,
now they are there and will speak
in thin bat-voices, longing.

"Chrysothemis was my name.[4]
I saw such death, such blood fell,
my father slew my sister
then my mother struck him down
my brother and my sister
killed her and both fell then.
Revenge? For what? We're all dead,
and I as well, it's no good,
hear me Great Queen, walk your path
as she walks hers; let her go."

"I was a queen; my lord fell,
my son slain, city burned;
and then a slave, bore more sons.
Sorrow and pain, they died too.
Now I am here, my name lost.[5]
What will you then, to cause harm?
Children are grief; let her go."

"A warrior I, in North lands,
lived past my time, saw all die.
He vanquished me, let me live
to bear his son, whom he killed.
I give up grief, even my name:
let her be free, let her go."

"Lady, I died a king's death,
wed to the plough, my folk thrive,
a noble end, on I go,
passing through here heard your words.
Consider us suffering
up on the Earth, we weak men
a sacrifice you might make:
put by this grief, let her go."

"Ah life is sweet, blood is life,
now I am dead, blood is sweet.
I think I was a mariner
sailed far away many seas.
Take up your joy where it falls
and do not bind what goes by:
she made her choice, let her go."

160

170

180

190

The chorus rises: "Let her go!"
Cerberus's snarls scarcely heard
above the clamor, the dead,
the whirling shades reaching out   200
for life, for blood, for memory
for breath to speak one last word
swirl, and are gone to darkness,
off to Lethe, off to life.
Ceres steps back, blood all dried.
Hades sets a gentle hand
upon his dog's far right head.
Cerberus slumps by the throne.
Proserpina, in the calm,
holds her mother's gaze and says,   210
"I have eaten, I will stay."

"Then nothing grows. I don't care
to sacrifice my one child,
if you are here, they'll join you—
all folk be shades whirling through
born just to die with no food."
"Mother, you're mad."
          "I mean it.
          My grief is great without you."

Hades's slow voice. "A compromise.   220
Half her time here, half above."
"Then half the time crops will grow."
"Is that enough?" he asks straight.
Proserpina shakes her head,
slow tears fall, then draws breath.
Ceres, smiling to herself,
is startled when the girl speaks.

"My father[6] taught, long ago
that with our power comes a trust
to use it for people's need,   230
the good of folk and not harm,
and, though they don't understand,
to harm them not by our whim.
They are our kin, and our charge,
and we, as they, are bound by fate.
This is your whim: let me go."

Uncertain now the first time
she bites her lip, not all mad;
on that dark throne the two shapes

slip hand in hand and wait words.   240
At last she speaks: "One third, then!
One third down here, this dark hell,
condemned to this, my poor child;
the rest with me, the green world
stops still and waits without you."

Hades then bows, and his queen
stands tall and straight and steps down
setting the day she comes back
a cool exchange, they touch not.
Their eyes speak what words can't say.   250
The boatman rows, looking back,
Ceres serene with a smug smile;
she knows her own and hoards it,
and the set-faced queen of hell
the world she loves turned to pain.

III: The Road to Hell

The growing world green and fair
until summer when she leaves
and all scorches without her.
She picks sad flowers in green fields.
Her mother asks now and then   260
in plaintive tones without thought
why she works now so very quiet
when before songs were joyful
dismisses all her answers.

Proserpina counts the days
till she can leave the tilled earth;
beauty she loves—trees and streams—
sunshine that falls on branches
borne down by weight of red fruit,
to walk among dark dread halls   270
where her heart lies with her lord.
And when she comes, time is short,
for Ceres's spite never stops.
The growing things bake and droop,
and hunger comes up above
their days of joy far too brief
all measured time, a high price,
time ticks by the pillared halls.
They meet and part, meet and part
in joy and love, together.   280

And while she walks, sorrowing
flowers at her feet, through fair fields
she sighs and stops, her face falls;
this is not home, no longer,
her mother's spite poisoned all,
the flow of life, and love's flow.

Far down below in dark halls
a dog howls from three throats,
his master's lap weighed with heads;
the king of death strokes six ears—   290
waits like stone for her return.

Still Odin

Speech is a kingly gift,
Shared open-handed, unlocking our word-hoard.
Under bare trees, broken sky,
The wind greets at year's back end:
An old beginning, a held breath,
And crows answer, black rune against frosted field,
Written word, spoken sign.

A worn-down god, time-scarred, wyrd-scarred,
One eye bright beneath his hood,
Lord of Heroes, Ale-Sharer, Giver of Rings,   10
Questing for his son, his brother, his assurance,
Wending his way through worlds
Until the low moon is a worn gold coin,
Dragons have eaten all the words.

Here he stands, bare-backed without currency,
Shouldering blame in a world grown stranger,
While the wolf waits and the witch is dead,
With nothing ahead but the long end
Time to come, wordless darkness, lit by doom
As lightning strikes a lone tree,   20
On high moorland, where farm is folly.

But, drawing the next breath, taking the next step,
He goes on, aslant across the furrow,
As the year ends, begins, swallowing its tail,
Stacking up riddles, as the crows answer the wind,
Taking thought against tomorrow,
Wanderer, Maze-Minded, All-Father,
Alone, holding his own.

NOTES

1. "Lew Rosson's Hall" retells the story of Bricriu's Feast appearing in the Ulster Cycle. Bricriu is a trickster figure who strongarms several Ulster heroes into attending a lavish feast where challenges were held; one challenge was a beheading game, which some scholars suggest influenced *Sir Gawain and the Green Knight*. The Jarns are Walton's fictional analogue to the Saxons; the Isarnagans are the Irish.

2. Connaught ("Connat") and Airgíalla (or, as here, "Oriel") are two provinces in Ireland.

3. The pomegranate, considered the fruit of the dead in Greek myth, plays an important role in several versions of the Proserpina myth. The number of seeds Proserpina eats will define how many months per year she must live in Hades.

4. Chrysothemis was daughter to Agamemnon and Clytemnestra. Because her father sacrificed her sister Iphigenia in order to speed the Greek invasion to Troy, Clytemnestra had him assassinated upon his return home. Chrysothemis's other siblings, Orestes and Electra, murdered their mother in revenge, but Chrysothemis does not participate.

5. Here, either Andromache (Hector's wife) or Hecuba (Priam's wife) reveals that, unlike Chrysothemis, she has been in Hades long enough that she has forgotten her name. After this, the memories of the shades become even more indistinct.

6. In some versions of the myth, Zeus is Proserpina's father by Ceres.

Michael R. Collings

A professor emeritus from Pepperdine University, Michael R. Collings (b. 1947) has found success as a prolific poet, author, bibliographer, and literary critic. His specialties are horror and SF. Altogether, Collings has written over a hundred books on writers as diverse as Dean Koontz, Peter Straub, Piers Anthony, Orson Scott Card, and Brian W. Aldiss; he has written almost a dozen books on Stephen King alone. His interests extend even to John Milton—indeed, Collings earned his doctorate from UC Riverside with a focus on Renaissance literature and a minor in medievalism. One of Collings's first novels, *Singer of Lies* (2009), reimagines *Beowulf* as set on a distant and isolated colonial planet; he later penned an allusion-filled Miltonic epic in twelve books, *The Nephiad* (1996). The following three speculative poems, which combine traditional Old English subjects with elements from horror and the fantastic, come from Collings's collection *Dark Designs* (2016). In 2016, the World Horror Convention awarded Collings their Grand Master Award for lifetime achievement.

Riddle

Though formally foes   as friends we'll be waiting,
Arms outstretched   to hail your coming.

We care not for color   creed or belief;
You all are equal   longed for alike.

We lack liveliness;   our limbs will not vault,
So refrain from running   remember to walk.

We need to know everything   never more keenly;
We've sensed your center   surely you won't mind.

We understand agony   yet ache to share ours.
It gnaws at us now   a nibble won't hurt.   10

Who are We?

Grendel's Mother

This man is the monster   menacing, merciless,
He wanders the wayside   weaponed and unflinching,
Seeking in green secrecies,   slyly approaching,
Bringing deft battle   to bright skies above.
He comes cautiously   clever but fear-filled,
Though none but I note   the knocking of his heart.
He approaches my pool.   The potent predator,
Knowing the need   of noiselessness now;
Wearing his war-sword   well-worn with bloodletting—
The blood of foes blisters   his battered life-protector,   10
Marred with the red mark,   the mating of evil,
Desolate death-tree   of his dying god—
Little help it will hold for him   as he hastens to his doom.
I shall greet him, grasp his hand,   gash open his blood-casket,
Spill his gore on the ground,   grieving for my son
With every effort.   Then I shall march
On the mead-hall, menace   the man crouching there,
Hrothgar the Hoar,   helpless without his hero.
He reins his ride.   I ready my claws.
Songs will be sung,   surely, of our sanguine tryst.   20
Songs will be sung.

DCCXCIII—A Fragment

Here were dreadful forewarnings come over the land of Northumbria, and
woefully terrified the people: these were amazing sheets of lightning and
whirlwinds and fiery dragons were seen flying in the sky.

—*Anglo-Saxon Chronicle*[1]

In that hour the horrors come, harvesters of souls,
With wailing winds, with whirl-winds
That tear stout timbers from thatchéd rooftops.

Livid lightning lays waste
To corn, crackling shoots, casting them aside.
Starvation will stalk at summer's end,
Hunger will hollow houses with the snows.

But worse, within the winds ride wyrms a-wing,
Flinging flames upon fractured ruins,
Wringing wrath from the willing air.   10
Venomous vermin, vast and angry,
Avenging others' acrid blood,
Slain by southron slaughterers
Who feared the force of fangéd foes,
Demon-drakes and their dominion in the air.

And worst, in the wake of wingéd beasts,
Flying on the foam, furrowing the whales'-road,
Come captors, conquerors from the north-lands,
Ice-hearted invaders intent on evil,
Bounden to burn, to bury warriors   20
Still left alive from lightning and from dragons.
Not yet here, yet their heralds haunt our lands,
Slay our servants, spoil our lands;
No better can we bargain for, when the beast-men arrive.

NOTE

1. [*Author's footnote.*] This entry in the *Chronicle* speaks of events preceding the arrival of Norse invaders in the eighth century [793 A.D.] and indicates that, at the time at least, dragons were not considered mythical beasts at all, but serious omens and threats.

Frank Coffman

Frank Coffman (b. 1948) has spent decades working in speculative poetry and fiction, especially horror, fantasy, and the weird. Now a retired professor from Rock Valley College in Illinois, he first began to love things legendary, folkloric, mythic, ancient, and medieval thanks to reading Tolkien at an early age; Tolkien also inspired Coffman's fascination with runes, which can be seen in "Freolaf at the Bridge." Later enthusiasms for C. S. Lewis, G. K. Chesterton, and W. H. Auden only augmented these early loves. As a poet, Coffman strongly endorses formal poetry. His major collection to date is *The Coven's Hornbook & Other Poems* (2019), but Coffman has produced many scholarly and literary writings. He is a former editor of *The Dark Man*, a journal devoted to Robert E. Howard, and he has written several essays and poems on Howard's work. In addition, folklore and medievalism have especially captured Coffman's attention. In "Grettir's Battle with Glám," Coffman offers his take on one of Norse literature's classic examples of folkloric horror, and his two poems on the fictitious Freolaf, whose name he glosses (with some license) as "Lover of Freedom," further reflect his undertakings in alliterative poetics. Coffman is a member of the American Scandinavian Society; during the 1970s, he briefly participated in the SCA.

Grettir's Battle with Glám

from *Grettir's Saga*
(a poem in *fornyrðislag*)

All Thorhall's farmstead feared each night.
An undead wight worked horrid havoc.
A grim ghost was Glám, great in evil.

Surly shepherd he'd been, but slain by a demon.[1]
His body found: blue, bloated, big as an ox—
Returned as revenant roaming the darkness.
Thorhall was most glad: great Grettir agreed
To sleep some nights 'neath the great roof.
Two nights nothing, but the next morn,
Grettir's horse found broken—all bones in its body!   10
"Leave! Save your Life! Leave!" Thorhall urged him.
       "No! it shall pay a price for my steed!"
A trap he set—shaggy fur covered Grettir;
Sight-hole pulled small, he saw the main door.
A ruckus on rooftop was raised by the thrall.
Then it burst boards, the broad door of the hall.
The fur on the floor the foul fiend pondered,
First poked, then pulled—but the cloak pulled back?
Grettir sprang forth, found a grip 'round its waist,
But the foul beast, brawny, broke free.   20
They fought such a fight, all furnishings shattered,
Then outside to earth full under the moon.
Glám deemed he was doomed, that Death awaited.
To Grettir he spoke, speaking a curse:
"Your strength is great, but greater it mote be
Had you not stayed to slay me this night.
No more will it grow, though great it is now.
An outlaw alone, you will wander the Earth."
At this Grettir cried out and cut off Glám's head
With one stroke of his sword, steady of hand.   30
The head, big and beastly, on buttocks was placed—
On arse of the evil enemy of men.
Thus, Thorhallstead was freed from fiendish ghost.
Grettir was given a great handsome horse.
His temper was tried many times after that.
But "Grettir the Strong!" sing all skalds today.

The Birth of Freolaf

A fragment from the Freolafsmol *in* fornyrðislag

When Freolaf came forth into this fierce world,
As Rædwyn wrote in his Red Book,[2]
The sky-candle shone in welkin so high,
A raven riding that realm's winds.
That Sage saw then with sorcerer's sight,
Pondering these portents, a pattern

The life that the lad was fated to lead:
Great wight of war, far wandering.
With brave, blue eyes that boy would see
Wonders of this wide world.   10
He would grow great in guile and cunning,
Strong of limb, stern and stalwart.
The Wizard would weave words of protection;
Those blessings would prove a boon
As the boy braved the broad lands and blasts
Of the Sea's assaults in seasons to come.
Forsooth! It was fine this coming forth,
This awakening to the world's awe.
Freolaf would fare as the "Far-Treader,"
Ranging 'neath Sun and the Raven's Road.   20

Freolaf at the Bridge

A fragment from the Freolafskviða *in* málaháttr[3]

ᚹ   Freolaf was fell in battle's face;
ᚾ   Under strong spells he stood his ground.
ᚦ   This[4] worthy thane threw fear aside,
ᚠ   Smote with strength the savage foe.
ᚱ   Rædwyn the Red Mage runes had wrought:
ᚲ   Keen the courageous should conquer foes,
ᚷ   Giving great help a magical gift,
ᚹ   When that great warrior went to the fray.
ᚺ   He alone held with hero's might;
ᛏ   Not a single knight who neared the youth—   10
ᛁ   Intent on inflicting injury or death—
ᛋ   Joyed as he joined the jolts of war.
ᛃ   Æsir would aid this ætheling bold;
ᚳ   Planning his peril would prove short-lived.
ᚤ   Zeal and able axe they also aided:
ᚻ   Stood this young slayer single on that bridge.
ᛏ   Terrible trials he knew. But true to his king,
ᛒ   Blow after blow he battered the foe.
ᛗ   Even his enemies, eager to conquer,
ᛗ   Marveled at his might—so many he slew.   20
ᚱ   Long will his lay last with the people,
ᚦ   Singing[5] his song. Strong did he stand,
ᛟ   Daring grim Death, doing his duty,
ᛉ   Only obeying the old king's command.

NOTES

1. In Icelandic folklore, Glám (or Glámr) is technically a *draugr*, not a demon. The most common translation is "ghost," but *draugar* are nonetheless corporeal undead creatures. Accordingly, some translators prefer "barrow-wight," and folklorist Andrew Lang even picked the term "vampire" for *The Book of Dreams and Ghosts* (1897). Originally, Glám was a human shepherd, a thrall, set to guard sheep in a haunted valley, but his transformation occurs after being killed by the valley's resident evil spirit. When the hero of the saga, Grettir Ásmundarson, arrives to protect Thorhall's homestead, he defeats the *draugr* but, in the process, is cursed by the monster's magic. He spends the final nineteen years of his life living as an outlaw in permanent exile.

2. According to Coffman, Rædwyn's name means "Friend of Wisdom (or Counsel)." Coffman's reference to a Red Book evokes the historical *Red Book of Hergest*, a large vellum manuscript written shortly after 1382. This book influenced Tolkien's conceit of a Red Book of Westmarch for *The Lord of the Rings*.

3. This poem follows the abecedarian form—that is, a poem whose first lines begin with every letter of the alphabet in sequence—but Coffman uses the runic letters of the Elder German Futhark, thus making it a "Futharkian."

4. The rune *thurs* (Þ) represents the obsolete letter *thorn* (þ), which is most often transliterated by the consonantal diphthong "th" in Modern English. Technically, *thorn* has a voiceless pronunciation, meaning that one's vocal cords don't vibrate when uttering words like *thing* or *thought*. In contrast, the letter *eth* (ð) is voiced, such as in *this*, *that*, and *the*.

5. The rune *ingwaz* (◇) represents the obsolete letter *eng* (ŋ), which is most often transliterated by the letters "ng" in Modern English, as in *singing*. Since no words in Modern English begin with this exact sound, Coffman improvises.

Paul Douglas Deane

Paul Douglas Deane (b. 1959) holds a doctorate in linguistics from the University of Chicago, and he currently focuses on writing assessment for the Educational Testing Service (ETS). His long-standing interest in poetry, however, was rekindled by his involvement with Elendor MUSH, a text-based fantasy roleplaying game set in Tolkien's Arda. Deane played an elven bard living in Rivendell, and as part of his involvement he wrote several epic-length "fanfic" poems in alliterative meter. One such poem was "The Redemption of Daeron," about the Sindarin Elf in *The Silmarillion* (1977) who was jealous that Lúthien loved a mortal instead of him. In addition, Deane runs an important website called *Forgotten Ground Regained*, which collects alliterative and accentual poetry—both older and contemporary—in modern English; several poems in this anthology first appeared there. The following poem comes from the not-yet-published fantasy novel that Deane coauthored with his late friend Kimbra Wilder Gish, whom he met through Elendor MUSH. Deane frames this heroic poem, which tells of a legendary princess within Deane and Gish's storyworld, as a fragment from a much longer tale.

Aislin's Ride: A Fragment

Plague and pestilence are perils that fall
like mist in the morning. As mourners dream,
dawn creeps uncalled-for over clammy cheeks,
over faces and foreheads freckled with sweat.
Neither courage nor cowardice count against foes
that batter at bone and blistering flesh.

Whether young or year-worn they yield
and are buried deep. In Redholt, prayers.
                    The women weep.
                    The king despairs.   10
                    Dark fever keeps
                    his son and heir.

Where the king has called his council together,
gray heads and grim eyes gaze back unspeaking.
Where the red earth rises raw over graves,
the dirge is undying. For dreams of tomorrow
have melted like mist or morning dew.
But with purposeful strides the princess enters
the court. She is Aislin of the flashing eyes—
                    both fair and tall,   20
                    and near man-size,
                    whom many call
                    both good and wise.

"Wait longer," she warned, "and this woe consumes us!
Blessed and bountiful, the Bright Folk will aid us:
Let us look to their learning, for their lore is deep."
"It is far to the Firthlands," her father replied.
"Winter walls us about, whiteness unbroken,
and night gnaws at day. When noon lies in shadow,
dark shapes awaken, shadows unnamed,   30
breaking the bonds that bind them in stone.
Who will dare such dark roads where doom lies waiting?
Whom shall I send into certain death?"
                    "I dare,"
                    the girl replied.
                    "The blood I bear
                    turns night aside
                    and binds despair."

The ruler's eyes rest on his rod-straight daughter,
frowning and thoughtful. Faint-heard around them   40
breath catches in throats claw-gripped to silence,
for high birth's a heritage harnessed to duty
by the blood of heroes. She bent her head. At last,
                    he sighed.
                    "Now hope and dread
                    must coincide.
                    I'd see you wed—
                    but now you'll ride."

A Cry to Heaven (after Psalm 6)[1]

At least a wall might crack, crumble, weaken, fall,
Tumble, overturned by roots, rain, wind, and weather.
At least the hail that blasts fields bare might falter, fail,
Till roar rattles, patters, pitters, melts midair.
But ah! Your anger, Lord, lasts longer than my bones can bear!

How long? Relent! In mercy mend me, for my spirit, spent,
Faints as a fire's embers glowing go to ash.
How long? Return! Restore me, stir me, blow me bright
With love released! Come brand hope's blessing as a brilliant coal
Whose mark remains forever, whose burning makes me whole.   10

Is death my destination? Plummet, pell-mell expiration?
The grave may be good for headstone silence, but I never knew
Its plots to sing your praises, God! What glory does it bring
That my bed's an abyss, that my sheets like shrouds tossed in storm-tumult
Are slick with sweat? Must I weep forever? Will you hear me yet?

And yet He hears echoes crying heaven's tears
Like rain running free down face of gaunt granite
Which it softens into soil. Just so God's grace like an aromatic oil
Confounds its fragrance with the sorrows that it soothes. Begone! You lie
Who mock and scoff at God, for Heaven hears my cry   20
And answers every echo that proceeds against the sky.

Freeway Dawn

Stop-and-go traffic staggers along,
bumper-to-bumper past the brink of dawn
till the raw gaze of the ragged sun
            glances off fenders
            and glares on the hills.

The news-anchor's voice keeps nattering on,
like the humming motor or the hissing fan,
and with rapid pulse an arresting tone
            pierces right through
            each portable cell—   10

There's a public listing for this private hell.

But under the brush on bright-edged hills
where pattering feet turn poised by holes,

and high up in haze where hawk-shadows wheel,
    and cloudbanks mirror
    the colors of dawn,

and even where traffic inches and crawls,
another pulse measures patterns revealed
in balance of limb, in breath held still,
    when a moment freezes,   20
    moves, and is gone

like a sudden deer in the slanting sun.

NOTE

1. Psalm 6 is one of the seven "penitential psalms" expressing sorrow for sin. Usually attributed to King David, it laments that if David were to die, he would no longer be able to sing God's praises. When God relents, David shames all the enemies who had rejoiced in his suffering. Deane uses six-beat alliterative lines with internal and end rhyme.

Adam Bolivar

Adam Bolivar (b. 1970) is a poet of dark fantasy, a writer of weird fiction, and a marionette-maker who is particularly interested in "Jack" tales—that is, a folkloric tradition centered on the trickster-hero Jack dating to medieval times and that is still preserved today in isolated reaches of the Appalachian Mountains. Bolivar specializes in the ballad form, which he considers a successor to long-form narrative verse in an alliterative meter. His collection of spectral balladry, *The Lay of Old Hex*, was published in 2017 by Hippocampus Press, and he has two more books of verse, *Ballads for the Witching Hour* (2022) and *A Wheel of Ravens* (2023). A collection of occult detective stories, *The Ettinfell of Beacon Hill*, appeared in 2021. In the following adaptation of "Jack the Giant-Killer," Bolivar attempts to lay down a reconstructed pre-ballad version of the folktale in Old English meter. Although many ambiguities from the modern folktale remain, Bolivar revives the links to Norse mythology that have allegedly disappeared from modern fairy-tale versions; he also frames "The Lay of Gēac Ettinfell" as a comic tale—originally told by a fireside, translated now by himself—written long ago by a "mischievous Saxon monk," someone trained imperfectly in *scopcræft*.

The Lay of Gēac Ettinfell[1]

I

Now to my lyre, listen,   and learn the tale
Of artful Gēac,   the Ettinfell
A Hel-harrower,   a hero like Thunor
And wise as Wōden,   his wit quick-fire.[2]
In a wild woodland   his war began:

299

A fearful fox   fleeing Gēac,
His lantern's light   leaping harelike.
His heart leapt too   as he hurried to the cave
To set a snare   with a serpent's craft.
Delving deeply,   he dug a pit,   10
Careful to cover it   with a carpet of sticks,
And, hefting his horn,   he heartily blew.
An ettin awoke,   angered by the bedlam,
With staggering steps   to stumble out
And fast falling   into the fateful trap.
Gēac jeered then   at the giant's plight,
And pointed a pickax   to pelt his head
With bloody blows   that broke his skull.
Joyful was Gēac!   The giant was dead,
His efforts earning him   ageless renown.   20

II

On a journey to find   more giants to kill,
His heart happy,   with hands on his belt,
By a fountain Gēac   fell into slumbers,
Then, snatched suddenly   by a snarling ettin,
Was carried to a castle   of crumbling stone,
Bones on the bulwarks,   boding evil.
Locking Gēac there,   the loathly ent
Fetched a kinsman   for a foul supper.
Mournful moaning   emerged from the darkness:
Women wailing   warnings to Gēac   30
To flee as far   and fast as he could.
But, daring and doughty,   dauntless was Gēac:
Eager to end   his enemies' lives.
Tying two nooses   tightly together,
He ringed the ropes   around their necks,
The other ends   over a rafter,
And throttled the ettins,   a thrill in his blood.
In a dark dungeon   the damsels he'd heard
Were thin from starving,   three in number,
From hooks hanging   by their hair and wretched.   40
Gēac loosed them,   and, lulling their fears,
Led them to liberty,   his luck boundless.

III

Wandering to Wales next,   the wayfarer tired
And looked for lodging   at a lonesome manor.
A towering, terrible,   two-headed ettin
Ushered him in   and offered a room,

Muttering of the morsel   he'd make of Gēac,
Clubbing him crudely   and killing him in bed.
Gēac smirked at that   and swore otherwise.
In the bed's blanket   a billet he laid,   50
And crouched quietly   in a corner in the dark.
The ettin entered   at early morning,
Battering the billet   with blows from his club,
And, with a lively laugh,   left for breakfast.
Jolly was Gēac   when he joined his host,
Saying how soundly   he'd slept that night
But for the tickling tail   of a tiny rat.
The ettin then offered   an oversized bowl
Of poorly prepared   porridge to eat.
First placing a pouch   for the pitiful mush   60
In his shirt shrewdly   to shovel it therein,
Gēac slit next   the sack he'd hidden
And the porridge poured   pattering downwards.
The jealous giant   jeered at the mischief,
And crowing that he, too,   could cut his belly,
He stupidly stabbed   his own stomach and died,
Earning Gēac   an added triumph:
In nurseries his name   would never be forgot.

IV

An ætheling came   one autumn to Wales,
For at home he'd heard   the horrible news   70
Of a lovely lady   lowered by demons,
And vehemently vowed   to vanquish them all.
Midday at market   he met with a rabble
Hindering the headway   to hallowed ground
Of a dead debtor,   bedeviling his rest.
Pity this prince took   and paid the merchants,
Which left his leather   lacking silver.
Gēac noticed   this noble deed
And offered aid   to the innocent prince.

They came to a castle,   the keep of a giant   80
Who was three-headed,   his hair like flame.
"The King is close-by!"   called Gēac to him,
"A thousand men,   thirsting for blood!"
"Then hurry! Hide me!"   howled the giant.
"Lay me and lock me   in this lightless vault."
Gēac chuckled,   cheerfully obeying,
And made merry   with his master that night
In the ettin's hall,   emptying the larder,

Raising a rumpus   and raiding the coffers.
Later the giant   lavished gratitude,   90
And furnished Gēac   with four armaments:
A singing sword   which sundered all matter,
A cloak of concealment,   conjuring obscurity,
Boots which bore one   in the blink of an eye,
And a cognizant cap,   counsel unerring.
So equipped, Gēac   escorted the prince
To the haunted hall   of the haughty lady.
Welcoming the wayfarers   to her wintry keep,
The lady served lamb   and laughed wickedly,
Ordering the ætheling   to unearth her handkerchief   100
By daybreak or die—   a dastardly errand.
Gēac's cap soon   uncovered the secret,
And, shoes speeding him,   enshrouded by the cloak,
To Hel he hastened   where the handkerchief lay.
A new labor   the lady decreed:
The prince must expose   who planted a kiss on her
Over the night,   or else he would die.
Well, the lady's lips   had with Lūca's met,
And Gēac's sword   severed the head
Of the Lord of Lies,   loosing his hold   110
And ending his evil   influence on her wishes.[3]

V

Earning the epithet   of Ettinfell
Gēac tasted   triumphs aplenty:
The twofold throats   of Thunderdell no hurdle,
Nor Nimrod's nose;   never failing,
He slew giants   with a jaunty air,
Their heads carted   to the King as gifts.
His final foes were   a foul enchanter
And an ugly ettin,   acolytes together,
Roosting repugnantly   in a ruined tower   120
Guarded by griffins   growling in fetters.
His cloak covering him   to keep unseen,
Gēac evaded   the eyes of the beasts,
And happened on a horn   which hung from a chain,
Like Hāmdæl's horn,[4]   heavy with portent.
Etched underneath   were ominous words:
Be bold, be bold,   and blow this horn,
To banish the night   and bring the dawn.
Sounding the signal   and smiting the ettin
Gēac satiated   his sword with blood.   130
The alchemist abdicated,   his art undone,

And a distressed damsel,   the daughter of a thane,
Was freed from the form   of a four-legged hind.
Gēac was elevated   to earl by the King,
And merrily married   the maiden he'd freed.[5]
His songs are sung   unceasingly now,
Raucously roared   and rousing gladness.

NOTES

1. *[Translator's note—A.B.]:* As this poem was written by an unknown monk of the eighth century, it does not formally count as a traditional lay; nonetheless, it seems to preserve a native pre-Conquest folkloric tradition. Although "Jack" as a name does not appear anywhere in Old English, *Gēac* (which means "cuckoo" or "simpleton") is found in several places. Since the standard OE pronunciation of *Gēac* would be something like "yay-ack," this particular manuscript proves the existence of a certain regional variation. In later copies, the same name is spelled *Iac*. The distinction between the *i*-sound and the *j*-sound was often blurred.

2. *Thunor* (or *Þunor*) and *Wōden* are the Old English equivalents to the Norse gods Thor and Odin.

3. "Lūca" is a reconstructed Old English spelling for Loki, who shares with Jack a trickster status.

4. "Hāmdæl's horn" is called Gjallarhorn. When Heimdall sounds this instrument, it will herald the onset of Ragnarök.

5. In the modern fairy tale "Jack the Giant-Killer," its hero is a subject of King Arthur. Here, the king goes unnamed because Arthurian literature was unknown to the early English people.

Michael McAfee

Michael McAfee (b. 1969) is a software quality assurance engineer who has been active in speculative poetry circles and the SCA for most of his adult life. He discovered the SCA during his senior year at Boston University, and, as Christian Lansinger von Jaueregk, he soon found an important outlet for his interests in form-based poetry. Classes offered at SCA events then introduced McAfee to verse composed in an alliterative style. The following example is in *ljóðaháttr*, an eddic Norse form, and it hails from McAfee's 2016 collection *Tarot Poems*. Since he views the Norse sagas as about "tough people getting through tough times," he thought it natural to associate a Norse meter with the Nine of Swords, a card that depicts a woman filled with doubts and fears as she sits up in bed, covering her face with her hands. Currently, McAfee is writing a Shakespearean verse drama in iambic pentameter, and in the last two years McAfee has begun using his theatrical training when performing poetry to gather a fan base at filk concerts and conventions.

The Nine of Swords

Across the sod, that solid sea,
    Women, weavers of peace,
In their beds, where balance is berthed,
    Up and cover their eyes.

Though sundered, all have sensed the same.
    They know the news is noxious.
They bore the weight, bit the bullet—
    Alas, what that led to.

The wondrous nurse, wound worker,
    Saw past the pain; 10
The marine, military mortal,
    Furnished to forgive her foes.

The assassin, soul slayer,
    Wondered, was it worth the woe?
The werewolf, warden-warrior,
    Pondered her purpose in life.

The mercenary, money-minded,
    Re-valued her role;
The officer, overseer of oaths,
    Censured poor policies. 20

The goblin, pest and peril to people,
    Proved her worth in war;
The maenad, mistress of maliced mind,
    Traveled into a trance.

The writer, mythic moon-maiden,
    Acted as she ought;
Women of worth, working for good,
    Now feel the fear.

All took a tough turn—
    Some committed sin; 30
Each knows that evil, eagerly,
    Walks back this way.

They thought that they were done with this
    But hidden in their hearts
They knew it couldn't cut so clean—
    The ending curls the cord.

Joshua Gage

Joshua Gage (b. 1980) is a Cleveland-based poet with an MFA in Creative Writing from the Jack Kerouac School of Disembodied Poetics at Naropa University. His work generally privileges shorter forms such as tanka, ghazals, and haiku (scifaiku, horrorku, etc.). As he says, these forms have a "lot of speculative potential that remains untapped." Published chapbooks include *Inhuman: Haiku from the Zombie Apocalypse* (2013), *Origami Lilies* (2018), and others. Steampunk and weird westerns, however, have influenced Gage as well. He originally intended the following poem, "Demetrius Yardley, Fire Nurse," for a planned sequence of twenty or so steampunk poems in various meters; unfortunately, he wrote only a handful before losing his notes and character sheets. In story terms, though, Potetopolis is a magnificent floating city ruled by brandy-drinking robber barons who exploit a toiling underclass. As for Gage's alliterative metrics, he took his primary models from *The Practice of Poetry* (1992; rpt. 2001), an anthology edited by Robin Behn and Chase Twichell.

Demetrius Yardley, Fire Nurse

Unnoticed, Fire
                Nurses are nomads
between the tubes
                that tunnel beneath
the city and the sanctuaries
                    of sleep. We dwell
in lands caliginous,
                looking after

gas hoses, altimeters,
                    and the holocaust that holds   10
this city aloft
                    and its boulevards illuminated.
Goggles, blackened,
                    blind our eyes to the blaze
that singes our beards
                    and stinks our suits;
leather gauntlets
                    guard against
the sparks that scatter
                    to scorch our skin.   20
We are covered against
                         combustion, but the fire calls
to us, invites us
                    into the inferno.
I've seen men stare,
                    then simply slip
through the furnace doors
                         and drop into the devouring
pyre that pulls
                    us all. Parson   30
sips brandy at the Archer
                         with Bagley, blustering
smoke that smolders
                    through the salon, smothering
the floor like fog.
                    They finance their empires
with mines and men,
                    but cannot imagine
the real fire, the faces
                    we feed in the furnace   40
that grow with gas
                    and coal, ghosts
who lost San
          Leonardo's lottery[1]
and succumbed to the gloom,
                         now summoned to steam
and push the propellers
                    of Potetopolis,
stokers who just stopped
                    their shovels and stepped   50
away, these are the convalescents
                         we cure, who call

to us, urging us
>
> to unite with them,

and no sleep or ale
>
> will ease these echoes

that travel the tunnels,
>
> terminal as breath.

NOTE

1. In the coalmines of Potetopolis, "San Leonardo's lottery" refers to the one day per month when miners can keep what they discover in the mines. If they win, they're rich; if they lose, they keep working or die. One of the superstitions of the Fire Nurses is that, in the fires they tend, they can see the faces of the people who lost the lottery. Another poem in Gage's steampunk sequence is entitled "La Lotería de San Leonardo."

Patrick Rothfuss

In 2007, Patrick Rothfuss (b. 1973) became an epic fantasy sensation with *The Name of the Wind*, his first novel in a projected—though still incomplete—trilogy, *The Kingkiller Chronicles*. Besides earning high praise for strong writing and sharp dialogue, Rothfuss excels at reimagining standard fantasy tropes in startling and unprecedented ways; his world-building often includes surprising adaptations from primary-world social and cultural history. Rothfuss continues these practices in *The Wise Man's Fear* (2011), his second novel. Although the novel has only two poems, each attempts to echo the classic alliterative meter—they're written in "Eld Vintic," a clear linguistic analogue to Old English. Both poems, furthermore, depend highly on context for meaning. In the novel, Kvothe and his friends are seeking a book of protective spells written by a long-dead artificer named Surthur, the *Facci-Moen ve Scrivani*. Luckily, the character Simmon has taken classes in Eld Vintic. He describes its poetry as "thunderous," and his first impromptu composition describes their friend Fela finding the desired spell-book. Simmon's second composition recounts Fela's playacted confrontation with Ambrose, the novel's main antagonist. By distracting him with her voluptuousness, she gives her friends time to destroy a clay mommet Ambrose had been using to torment Kvothe.

Sought We the Scrivani

Sought we the Scrivani   word-work of Surthur
Long-lost in ledger   all hope forgotten.
Yet fast-found for friendship   fair the book-bringer

Hot comes the huntress   Fela, flushed with finding
Breathless her breast   her high blood rising
To ripen the red-cheek   rouge-bloom of beauty.

Fast Came Our Fela

Fast came our Fela   fiery eyes flashing,
Crossing the cobbles   strength in her stride.
Came she to Ambrose   all ashes around him
Grim was his gazing   fearsome his frown.
Still Fela feared not   brave was her bos—[1]

NOTE

1. The poem cuts off here as Simmon, who's composing this poem off the cuff, grows embarrassed at an unplanned reference to his friend's bosom.

Rahul Gupta

Rahul Gupta (b. 1976) is a poet and medievalist born in England and committed to the revival of Old English alliterative metrics in modern epic poetry. In 2014 he completed a dissertation called *"The Tale of the Tribe": The Twentieth-Century Alliterative Revival*, which argues that a modern alliterative revival has only been possible since philologists in the late nineteenth century began reconstructing the ancient Germanic meter; for Gupta, this newly revived meter promotes an archaizing, epic, and mythopoeic construction of "archetypal" Englishness. As a poet, Gupta is currently composing a mythopoeic epic centered on King Arthur. Although our first selection, "Tropos," is a poem in mixed alliterative traditions, the next two selections hail from Part II of this *Arthuriad*, a "seasonal interlude" that describes the Wheel of the Year as it slowly turns and grows darker: a symbolic journey as the Sun King approaches Midwinter. A prose description for Gupta's ambitious project can be found in the 2018 issue of *Temenos Academy Review*.

In terms of style, Gupta employs a dense yet atmospheric descriptiveness, an exhaustive mythological erudition, and a diction that seemingly harnesses the entire history of the English language. Because of the highly mythopoeic character of Gupta's work, his Arthurian excerpts are best considered dark fantasy. The first excerpt, "An Army of Hallowe'en Toadstools," which is slightly abridged, creates an oppressively Lovecraftian atmosphere as Gupta follows his imaginary Albion from sky to earth (and even beneath) as decay germinates throughout Arthur's kingdom. In addition, the underworld revealed by "Hallowe'en Toadstools" partially indicates the planned site for Part III of Gupta's *Arthuriad*: a subterranean arena for two dueling fays—Merlin and Morgen—as they struggle for supremacy over one other.

Tropos: A Norse *Étude*

Now it is but hours after inaugurals[1]
—rough-voiced ravens—of rich pickings:
heavens dusking (while hosts muster
the edge-banesmen for Odin's choosing)
with harsh harbingers of the hazelled ground,
those heralds hungering for haft's-talk-with-shield,
feathers beating;
                              fierce-taloned their claws
awake for work,
                              and from the wold prowling   10
grisly Greyhame,[2]
                              the greedy one
with hoar hackles,
                              and horny-nebbed
the hooded crow,
                              hoarsely crying:

                                    Flanged arrows as flinder-
                                    fledges leapt from edges
                                    over shields, bows shrilling,
                                    when shank-deep was dankness   20
                                    of gore.
                                              Then steel-geared they
                                    girded murder-hungry
                                    blades amid the bloody
                                    blend of that foe-spending.

Now on fallen fighters may fowl and beast
of battles bloat. Birds choose the slain
with whirl of wings. Wheeling, stooping,
swarthy shadows beswarm the field,
corbies carping. At the corpse-banquet,   30
with flirt of feathers, they flit hopping,
to feed their fill in feast's parody
—with men for meat.
                              Mayhem ended,
from points'-parley, the poets' wages:
wend smiths-of-war, by wordsmiths' craft,
from hammers'-leavings to harp-music:
so as on Eagles' Acre, in the aftermath,
the head-harvest of the Hawk-Of-Wounds,
the scaldcrows scoff amid skulls and throes   40

—with bloody blessing of blue faces
they mouth the dead (their dainty morsels)
and prize their preys— praise-singing bards
—while scavengers scream—skalds, turn verses,
poems ply-forging, pattern-welding
the twining strands; in the twisted steel,
etched out with venom, adder-markings.
—Thus they fashioned: these staves I shape
are as words woven from that web of swords.

from THE ARTHURIAD (2021)

An Army of Hallowe'en Toadstools

A charge changes. Through the chafing airs
tension tingles, like the tightening wire
of a harpstring humming. [. . .]
                With roar and wuther
the flashpoint flares. Floodgates unsluice
slashing downpours of slanting rain
on galeforce gusts. Guns, drums, and bombs
—an astounding crash—and storm explodes   *A late summer storm*
as atmospheres, in avalanches,
collapse like landslides. In the loud tumult
—blunderbuss boom, bang of ordnance,
hubbub and rumpus and hammer-battering:
the thudding thump of thundercracks—
lightning bolts launch from louring billows.
The illumined landscape, with its leaping skyline
—a fleeting glimpse like the face of the Moon—
brands bright its image in the backs of the eyes.
Zigzagging tines, zed-shaped lightning's
pronged weapon probes the primy soil:
and we[3] follow the flash, foining groundward
in his points' pathway, to pierce the turf.
Let the earth open. We enter within.
Here levels below living daylights   *Follow the lightning into the earth*
an under-earthen, otherworldly
landscape layered below the surface
nests beneath us.
              This unknown domain,
her roofs writhing with roots of trees,
is the nameless netherdepth, benighted regions
of an occult kingdom:[4]

necropolis   *Katabasis: the Underworld*
of catacombs;
sarcophagi
decayed in crypts,
caves inhuming
putrid matter;
sepulturings
enwombed in warrens,
winding myriad   *Tombs*
charnel-chambers,
chimneys linking
fœtid fogous,
foul souterrains,
deep-delved dungeons:
dusky vaultage
—heaped-up deathsheads—
—hoards of longbones—
of grave-galleries;
      groping steeply,
tombpassages twist
through turnagains
to undercrofts,
while oubliettes
fold fathoms downwards,
to Filth's Mansion.
Pell-mell we plunge:
in panoramas
horizons range
as we reach deeper:
like tumbledown,
topsy-turvy
sunken citadels,
a sewerscape
of terraced wards,
tiers and platforms,   *Sewerage*
doors downfallen,
to dark culverts
with grille-gratings,
green slime-curtained;
canted causeways
on the chasms' brink:
skewed screwthreading
escaliers
leaning, looming;
the labyrinthine

abyss beckons,
                          the bowels of the Earth. [. . .]
From the maze of tombs, the morgue-ullage
bleeds to these bilges; their black vomits
emulge and merge, commingled blend
of what seeps from cellars, with sordors leaching
to earthy entrails. For from all the jakes—
from every addlepool and each latrine,
siegehouse, cesspit—of our sunlit world,
helter-skelter, the whole system's
sickly surfeit of sewage-waste,
in a swilling swelchie, is swallowed down
from the upper echelons to the enclaves beneath:
engulfed by gulches. The gurge of sludge
empties ordures to the uttermost sump:
a prodigious dungheap.
                          Dirts steam. Dritt of foxes,   *Excrements*
                          deer-turds. Merd and fewmet,
                          scat, spraint; fiants, scumbered
                          skite of otter-crottels;
                          brock-muck. Brown waggyings
                          brew, mix: sharn of vixen,
                          critters' crap, hare-buttons,
                          crudded spoor, boars' lesses
in a cradling crucible.[5]

⁂

The realm of rottenness is rich with life.
From clouds to clods, cleaving lightning
wracks with raptures rainsodden loam,
and by split seconds the span between
the high Heavens and humble Earth
is bridged in brightness: embracing partners
space sprung apart espouse again.
Once twins entwined, that twain sundered:
the husband halved from the whole forebear;[6]
now sibling-father, and sister-wife   *Autumn Equinox*
marry for a moment: to mate powers
high, dry and hot—with the humid deep.
Attraction triggers the trident-bolt,
the warm wedding to wet and cold,
the air to fire; earth to water:
as when Burn-the-Wind,[7] at his blade-forging,
that the redshort rod be wrought to temper
steeps it in wetness—the steel is slaked

in quenching oils, to quell its ardour
(and the venoms unveil viper-chevroned,
woven-welded, worm's-tongue markings)
—so the glowing glaive, in glutting thrusts
shooting downward, ensheathes his length.
Ground engulfs him. In her gravid belly
the charge is channelled; for change kindles
where his liquid lightnings enliven dust.   *Lightning fecundates the earth*
Behold the happenings of the hidden places;
witness wonders—from the worms' vantage.
Shocks shaking her, he sheds darting,
fork-formed currents, forces spending
their virile virtue.
                            Pervading the clays
are pores pooling with pregnant fluids.
Through dropsied ducts, drenched syrinx-glands
in coral clusters, course her issues,
unctions oozing, by ebbs and swells:
what subtle liquors seep and filter,
yeast-yielding brines, yolky syrups
and saps surging, sifted lispings
in fistule-fissures? Fecund venters
congest with juices, like the jellied slutch
that showers downward from shooting stars
estranged to earth; sticky chrisms
spill through spiracles; from sponge-bladders,
limbeck-tinctures, elixirs stilling—
moist motherlode, milch with nectars.
                The stagnant gulfs stretch out for leagues
under fen-fastness, fog-bound marshes,
mould-mildewed tarns and misty fells:
like troves of ore, treasure-laden
rills running through the rankling dung,
mine-wealthy malm. The Moon shines down,
her beams bathing foreboding depths,
the lodes ripening in lunar rays,
and the mire is rife: minims thriving
at their feast of filth feed and batten;
its sweats swelter. The swamp-mosses
hum with humours; heats are brooding
in queachy quags, bequickening
eggs underground. An urgent drive,
for a spell, spurs them. Spores are stirring
awake to sprout in their weird springtide;
pollen pullulates, to the pulse of the Moon:

cells in seedbeds. These seminal motes,
cocooned kernels, like chrysalids
shog in their swaddlings: shoot spicules forth,
chaffhusks chinking as chits are hatching
from bulging pods, with bat-squeakings,
in throbbing throes. Threadlets burgeon
and barbs burrow from the umbilical stalk;
spikes spawn outwards, spidery talons
sneaking snakewise.
                                    Snail-horn probings
now creep, recoil; then crawl anew,
reaching runners, with ramifying
twig-antennæ, that tillow again:
look how the likeness of the lightning-flash
imprints and repeats in the pattern figured
as izzard emblems by the angled forking
of vein-branches against the varves' blackness,
like marbling maggots: the murky clods
riddled with roothairs. Wriggling vivers
flex flossing wide, in flower-whorling
topdownward trees, their tufted plumes
of glairy gauzes, like gossamer skeins
of squirming thongs.
                                    Squirreltail, thistledown,
filigree fibres frond their tassels,
twisting, twining; the twirling bines'
chenille nervures. Thus the node-weaving
germs engender a giant ganglion,
mercurial cobweb, catscradlewise;
node knits to lobe, as a loom shuttles
a weft-texture, the wiry members
tendril-tissued: a teeming polyp,
quarl of quicksilver. By quetch and spasm
the molten mass is mapped in darkness,
leviathan-vast.
                                    It is vivifying,
inhales and heaves: a heart panting
or brain beating, or as breathing lungs
work in entrails; and wavering sobs
retch restlessly. With rippling surges
the sprawling globe spreads yet farther
by ceaseless seethings, circulating
lymphs and ichors; till in labour-pangs
its ballooning shape dilates warping.
The morphing mesh transmogrifies,

and with thrilling shudders it thrusts aloft,
climbs in corkscrews up to the crust overhead:
fat fruitbodies, forcing through turves.
          From shadowed taths, shapes come pricking,
grope above the grass. Growths are stirring,
bald and gibbous; bulbs are swollen,
puffball-like orbs, whose pimpled membranes
are groined with gills, glabrous-wattled
blanched blubberflesh, bloated organs,
limbs lazarlike. Leprous-hided,
sepulchral-pale, they poke upward
from cadaverous depths—dead men's fingers;
bearded bellyache;
                              bugs' agarick,
webbedpate, skullcap;
                              witches' button,
the lewd stinkhorn
                              and livid earthshank;
skewbald hoodwink,
                              scurfy funnel;
dwarvish dwalecup,
                              dwimmer-goblet,
clubfoot-candle;
                              carl-on-horseback,
charnel-bonnet;
                              chilly waxglove,
sallowbracket,
                              sickly milkgall.
Squame-warted squabs squeeze in sending
stems striking out. Staves like truncheons
unsheathe their shafts, to show helmets,
raise round targes with rimmed umbos:
espy these spears—a spectral levy
of midnight-mustering homunculi,
wan weaponed-men, in worm-eaten
carrion-coloured accoutrements
of clammy coifs and clinging veils,
by rank on rank, or in rancid circles,
lifts its lances, locks the shield-wall:
earthen armies. From under the ground
—the reek of decay—rotting scarecrows—
they advance in onslaught, an invading horde,
wraiths risen again, arrayed for battle
in dark dreamings dawn breaks shivering
their feinted front; falter, melt blurring

to stipes like straw . . . the stuff of shadows
that dwindle to dust. The day broadens
till wilting culms, and caps withering,   *The autumn toadstools*
return as toadstools.[8]
     It is the time of Samhain.

from THE ARTHURIAD (2021)

The Winter Solstice Mumming Play

  [. . .] Teams of rhymers
mooch in moonbeams to their Mumming Rites.
They surround the halls, rhyme out the squire,
and by the light of torches, they lay their scene
amid staring eyes, and steaming breath:
parade the ring, harangue the watchers
with loud palaver, and lilt doggerels,
sing-song patter, they recite by heart.
Masks muffle the words, as they mouth their speeches
in stiff poses, with stilted mimes
—well-worn business. Their wonted roles
the familiar cast of the mummer's comedy:
the feuding Knights; the fair Damsel;
a juridical King who renders sentence;
a surgeon enters, for the scene at the end,
and is quizzed by the Chorus: the Quacksalver,
who performs his cure as the fifth business;
a logic-chopping, yet leech-crafty
medicine-man, whose mumbo-jumbo
restores the dead.
     The stage is set.
Dumbshow and dance the traditional mode
for the play's action, the plot is a fable
forever the same every yeartide,
never-changing: as known to all
by the sword-dances on Summer's threshold
that portrayed his triumph, and the tryst of Robin
with the Maid of the May, so the moons of Winter
are The Fool's regime. His phase ascendant
since Autumn Equinox, he ousts The Hero
as the eternal tanist returns to reign
the waning year, Winter's moiety
when the Holly King is at the height of power:
Midwinter-month; a mock-sovereign

for his allotted term, the Lord of Misrule
whose hour of glory is the eve of his downfall.[9]
        Old archetype of an annual strife
in the lore of the land, this love-triangle
is retold as legend: how the Two Brothers
were sibling suitors of the sacred Maiden
whose beauty embodies the budding life
in crops and cradles, that crowned Goddess
whose kiss is kingship, and of their combat to win
The Bride's embrace; but the brothers are fated
to be twin champions who twice a year
must fight and fall in a feud of the ages,
for the yearly cycle is the youths' wooing,
of Oak for his May, the Ivy by Holly,
in the ceaseless tourney of the seasons' wheel,
or as Robin and Wren, or as rival heroes
the bright Belinus and Brân the raven,
sue for sovereignty by civil war:[10]
growth springing green then grimly withering
to Winter's waste. As in the womb of Britain,
at the island's centre, angry monsters,
scales scathed by talons, escape thwarted,
writhe restlessly, their ravening fangs
gnaw at the navel—the nest of worms
broods embroiled there: with braiding necks
those twin dragons twist and rankle,[11]
chafe in the chamber, till they chew their own
lizardly limbs and the loops of their coils
fold to fasten figure-of-eight
entangled turns as the tail-biters
clasp close-grappled, and cleave twining
—so these ancient enemies, in their endless battle.
Stalled stalemated, still-vying duel's
strange stranglehold, the struggling powers
are locked in a loop.
                    Release denied,
champion and challenger exchange their roles
and counterchange, contrariwise:
each kills the other, his own likeness,
turn by turn about. Thus they taste the oneness
—yet the nuptial night is never tasted—
of woman wooed and wedded bride,
of victor and victim, and reverse again
the face of defeat (as they perform their roles

as mirror-selves) in the mask of triumph
time and time again, to-and-froing
from yester-ever till the yarn of Time
spins out her span. As in the spiral dances,
Mayday Morris, the maze-stepper
of the town in the turf, the turning castle,
moves motionless, so the Mummers' plays:
of bout worsted and won battle
and winner losing till world's ending.
Ruddock fallen, the Wren of Yule
kills Cock-Robin.[12] Yet the conquering hero,
the hedge-kinglet, the Holly Lord,
is but mock-monarch. Midwinter Night;
who waxed is waning. Winter ages.
It seemed they saw Summer vanquished;
enter the Doctor.

NOTES

1. Gupta intends "inaugurate" in its literal Latin sense of *in-augur-ate*, the taking of omens or an augury, furthermore with a suggested etymology of *avis* ("bird") and *garrire* ("to talk").

2. "Greyhame" is a kenning for *wolf.* The name derives from Old English *grǣghama*, meaning "grey skin, clad in grey," and it is attested by the *Finnesburg Fragment.*

3. This first-person pronoun is a narratorial royal we. It does not denote any specific person.

4. In one sense, this passage continues Gupta's extended metaphor between the Wheel of the Year and Arthur's Albion. In a more literal sense, the upper layers of these "nameless netherdepths" are man-made sewers.

5. The specialized diction in this catalog of excrements—a partial parody of epic poetry's catalogs—derives from medieval texts on hunting, specifically the different terms for animal droppings.

6. Here, Gupta's lines refer to the ancient mytheme of Sky and Earth as forming (though now separate) a single androgynous primordial entity. More metaphorically, they intimate the sundering of the World of Mortal Men from the Otherworld, which forms a major aspect of Gupta's epic world-building.

7. "Burn-the-Wind" is a periphrastic epithet in Scots dialect, a kenning for the word *smith.*

8. The rise of these toadstools, feeding on rottenness, suggest the "rise" of Mordred in Arthur's kingdom. It also suggests the trickster Gwydion, who, in the *Mabinogion,* conjures illusory and soon-withering hounds and horses from toadstools in order to deceive Pryderi into trading his pigs. More faintly, this passage finally suggests the rise of an army of undead warriors from the cauldron (or "grail") of Arawn/Bran in

Welsh mythology. Many specific names in the preceding catalog of toadstools, though designed to sound folkloric, are inventions by Gupta.

9. The Holly King and the Oak King personify winter and summer, respectively. Whereas the Oak King regains power at the spring equinox, the Holly King regains power at the autumn equinox. This Holly King reaches the height of his strength at midwinter, whereupon his power begins declining as winter starts fading into spring.

10. English oral tradition often links the robin with the wren, which leads to the saying, "The robin and the wren are God's cock and hen." Brân the Blessed was a giant and king of Britain in Welsh mythology; the name "Brân" means *crow* or *raven*. Elements of Brân's life might have influenced the tale of Belinus and Brennius, two warring brothers, as told in Geoffrey of Monmouth.

11. In the *Mabinogion*, the twin dragons refer to the red dragon who fends off a white dragon's invasion. Although this Welsh tale may be the original source, the first manuscript attestation actually occurs in Nennius's *Historia Brittonum*. Here, in Gupta's mummers' play, the twin dragons are another incarnation of the seasonal archetype represented by the Holly King and the Oak King.

12. In Ireland, one tradition holds that a wren should be chased, captured, and killed on St. Stephen's Day (December 26th) to commemorate Saint Stephen, who was stoned to death. In the reconstruction of pagan religion suggested here by Gupta, the blood-vivid Robin represents the King (the Sun), who is then ritually killed at Winter Solstice by his *tanist* (the Wren) before being "resurrected" at the Mumming Play.

Mary Alexandra Agner

Mary Alexandra Agner is a freelance writer and American author of speculative short fiction and poetry. She has written several books, including one—*The Doors of the Body* (2009)—that contains fairy-tale and mythological retellings, and a SF novelette in verse, *O Susannah*. She discovered the alliterative meter during her MFA after seeing an excerpt by W. H. Auden in *The Shapes of Our Singing: A Comprehensive Guide to Verse Forms and Metres from Around the World* (2002), an anthology edited by Robin Skelton. In the following text, Agner uses the meter to describe a single year lived under the modern Pagan calendar year, which follows the major solar events of the solstice, the equinoxes, and their midpoints.

The Eightfold Year

YULE
I yearn this year for yams yanked
straight from the sod, their yellow skins seared
in the heat of the hearth, home and healing
baking into my bread, the crust bursting
with rosemary. Rushing, their faces red
my family leaves the frost, comes to the fire,
welcomed, warming their hands, waiting
for the smell of soup simmering over flames.
The melting wax makes us merry, mellow,
playful. Our pagan practices plait   10
our good, our grudges, our groans and gaffes
to a single strand of sweetness.

IMBOLC

We sweep the stoop, shake the sheets
into frozen February, their flannel fabric
like waves of warmth to wash away winter.
We light the candlewicks, the white wavering
in the Chinook's call.[1] Our house clean
we paint the ceremonial plough pastel,
plant it, and water it well with whiskey.
We watch for the marks of the Maiden   20
sifting through seeds, sowing spring,
unrippling the roots of radish and rose.
Our yard soon unfolds yawns of yellow:
dim young daffodils to dwarf the darkness.

OSTARA

I scuffle through thin snow, separating stalks
of grass, grinning at their green.
I stoop at the pine tree, pushing the wet pile
back from the weathered bark at its base.
My woodruffs, wilted, weighted by winter:
one final fleece of frozen water.   30
I remove my mittens, mixing the meltwater
I touch on the tips of the leaves, tracing
the lines lengthwise. I long to lift
the petals, pick them. My ears prick up: your pencil
scrapes your sketchbook. You shift the sheet so I see
the batch of blooms burst from the book.

BELTANE[2]

The bonfire begins with the band of blue
sky burgeoning purple, prolonging the display
of light. Leaning against a limb, I look on
as you dance in the darkness, leaping and dipping.   40
May wine in one hand, I whisk you away
to the mossy mound I've marked with marigolds.
The sweat on the skin of your palm is sweet
when I taste it, my tongue teasing the tips
of your fingers, then your forearm, the flush on your face.
I submerge in your smell, your smile, the softness
as you nuzzle your nose from my throat to my navel
and we laugh between kisses, like the Lady and Her Lover.

LITHA

We depart in the dimness before dawn,
our picnic basket packed with asparagus, peaches,   50

bread, and cheese, bound for the beach,
the sunshine, golden as a strawberry seed,
reaching over the horizon. Our ritual
for the longest light of the year: listening
to the surf sound the seconds until sunset,
digging deep into the sand and there discarding
our fears, the year's failures. With firewood,
we obstruct the opening, then douse all with oil.
The fire twists the tints of twilight.
Our mistakes move from ash to mist to moonlight.   60

LAMMAS
I bleed between the briars of the blackberry
bush, sweat sliding over my skin, slipping
around my wrist like the sun waning in the west:
a handful of the new harvest to carry home.
In the kitchen: one cup of flour for the Crone,
the Mother, and Maiden.³ More for me.
My palms push into the dough, pull it, prod
invisible sheets of gluten, sticky with summer.
I press the fruit firmly into the final shape
of the bread and bake the loaf brown,   70
hollow, hot, like the humid hours
of August that autumn's arrival will ease away.

MABON
Against the west wind, we wander
under autumn arches: oak, ash,
a giant maple, gathering leaves for garlands.
We scuffle our shoes in the sloughed-off sun,
searching for a conjunction of colors that casts
lights like dawn deepening to day. The dark
breath of winter blows, benign, without bite.
We lean on the wall to watch the weather.   80
Nature mimics the Mother: in mourning, misting,
drowsy, her head drooping, her drizzle
falling as varnished veins. The verdure vanishes
lost in leaves aloft, released, unleashed.

SAMHAIN
Grey gloom connects sky to ground. Groping
branches, bare without leaves, beat about
windows. The wind whistles, then whispers
when the sun sets. The year's shadows stand up.
I pick up a pile of pictures: people

I love, now dead. The darkness and dimness   90
blur their beginnings, their bodies, my breath
condensing in candle and moonlight, as I call
up my memories. I murmur how much I've missed them,
share the excitement and sadness of seasons since.
Outside my garden: children giggling, ghosts
laughing to be liquid among the living.

NOTES

1. *Chinook*: a strong wind in the interior of western North America.

2. For another account of Beltane, which names both the festival and the month, see Paxson's poem "Beltane" in this volume. Beltane is associated with fertility and various rituals, including maypole dancing. In this stanza's last line, the Lady and Her Lover represent the May Lady (the Triple Goddess) and the May Lord (the Horned God).

3. In Wicca, the maiden, the mother, and the crone all aspects of the Triple Goddess (the May Lady), to whom the speaker here gives a portion of flour. Given that Lammas is the calendar's first harvest festival, it is common to mark the holiday with a bread ceremony that bakes dough into the figure Lug from Irish mythology. The festival's name, "Lammas," comes from *Lughnasadh*, or "Lug's Assembly."

Mike Bierschenk

An educational technologist by trade, Mike Bierschenk (b. 1982) has always been fascinated by language, poetic language in particular—a love he discovered initially through epic fantasy and such poems as Tolkien's "A Elbereth Gilthoniel." Other inspirations include several American poets—Walt Whitman, Robert Frost, Elizabeth Bishop—as well as folk musics from the English, Scottish, and American traditions. Nonetheless, Bierschenk's studies in Old Occitan and the troubadours—he holds two graduate degrees, an MA in French from Louisiana State University and an MFA in poetry from the Ohio State University—have proven especially fertile in shaping how he approaches modern bardry. A member of Three Cranes Grove, a congregation of the international neopagan/druid church Ár nDraíocht Féin, Bierschenk wrote the following invocation in 2015 as part of the liturgy for his grove's anniversary rite on the autumn equinox. This poem calls upon the Gaulish god of eloquence, Ogmios, a deity whose rare iconography often depicts a smiling face with chains of amber and gold leading from his pierced tongue to the ears of his followers. Bierschenk takes his poetic form—a modified variant on the Old Irish *rosc*, an accentual-alliterative meter with different rhythms in each stanza—from *How to Kill a Dragon: Aspects of Indo-European Poetics* (2001) by Calvert Watkins. Now grove bard for his congregation, Bierschenk remains a prolific hymnodist, songwriter, and liturgist.

Invocation to Ogmios

Hail, honey-tongue, hearer of heartfelt overtures, Ogmios, orator!
Open our ears to ancient echoes of sweetness and singing. O speaker
of spirit and skill, send us resounding in the ways of the wise and well-spoken.

May our words waft on feathers of flame;
may our singing sweeten the gifts of the gods;
may eloquence enter the prayers of the people —

Ogmios, inspirer, accept our offering!

Michaela Macha

Michaela Macha (b. 1973) is a German poet and an adherent of Asatru, a Neo-Pagan religion rooted in the beliefs and mythology of pre-Christian Scandinavian peoples and the continental German tribes. Besides her regional community, the Asatru Ring Frankfurt and Midgard, Macha shares close ties with The Troth; both organizations firmly emphasize inclusiveness, diversity, and tolerance. Overall, Macha uses poetry as a devotional practice that puts ancient myth into relation with modern life. Her songs and verse in German and English have been used for ritual and liturgy in Asatru gatherings both local and international. Although Macha prefers rhymed syllabic meters, she composes a fair amount of alliterative verse on Norse subjects. A poem like "Hadding," for instance, recounts the life of the same legendary king as featured in Poul Anderson's *The War of the Gods* (1997); "Under the Cloak" details a conflict between paganism and Christianity at the turn of the first millennium; and "Angrboða" invokes a lesser-known mythological figure in a meter reminiscent of *fornyrðislag*. Just as importantly, Macha is webmaster for *Odin's Gift*, a vast collection of Norse-themed verse, song, and myth, much of it Asatru. This site includes alliterative poetry from nearly a dozen different poets.

Hadding: A Sea-King's Death[1]

A dear friend's death   in distant lands
offered the omen   to face my own;
words rise half-drowned   from drowsy oblivion:
No hand but my own   would bring my end.

329

No arm of woman   lay ever as lightly
around my neck   as now the noose,
nor did my kinfolk   greet me as keenly
as high now the ravens'   call overhead.

The boughs above me   bend in the breeze;
set are my sails   but not for the swan's path.   10
A branch of ash   will be my oar,
parting soon   the wine-red sea.

The vessel is rushing,   taut is the rope;
my life-boat held   by Hangatýr's hands.

Under the Cloak[2]

All courts have come   hard counsel to hold,
People are gathered   on Parliament Plain.
Growing dissent,   a gap divides us:
Two creeds compete   our customs to rule.

Some oaths are sworn   by Öku-Thor,
some by the White Christ;   which ones are valid?
Rites bind agreements,   religion keeps law;
peace will fail   if we pursue both faiths.

Charged was I   to choose for us all:
The cross or the hammer,   the High Ones or Christ.   10
A heavy burden   they bid me bear;
alone I seek counsel   under my cloak.

How can I turn   to betray my Gods,
not honor the Æsir   my ancestors' way?
Thorgeir they named me,   Thunderer's Spear;
Thorgeir the traitor   they may yet call me.

The Gods took blots   and gave us blessings;
will barren become   the fruitful fields?
Bitter it is   to break our troth
to follow the One   from foreign lands.   20

Norway urges   the new way on us,
holding as hostage   our helpless children.
War they would wage,   and weak we are
Torn in this quarrel,   torn as am I.

The old faith I offer   on unity's altar
As sacrifice   for sake of our folk.

No public worship;   in private, perhaps,
and sagas survives   a seed for the future.

Chill before sunrise   settles the fog;
Dawning of Christ's age,   dusk for the Gods.   30
I cast away   my cloak and my hope;
Fare thee well, Thunderer,   here at Thingvellir.

I must go, they are waiting.   With weary words
I will tell my folk   which faith we shall follow.
Some will go gladdened   and some will go grieving,
But one we become   in custom and creed.

Angrboða[3]

In Iron-Wood's wasteland,
Wild wolves she whelps;
Her brood is bringing
Both balance and bale.

Hati is harrying
Máni to move,
Sköll in the sky
Is pursuing the sun;[4]

For night and day,
They never may dally;   10
Time cannot tarry,
Flees ever so fast.

To Býleist's brother,
Breaker of bonds,
Three boundaries she bore,
Three barriers birthed:

Limit of Life,
Hel holds what she has;
Only what ends
Has value and worth.   20

Edge of the Earth,
Serpent encircles us;
Borders and bounds
Define who we are.

End of Everything,
Fenris will fall,

A new age from ashes
Beginning again.

Both grief and gain
Are the gifts she begets,   30
The Járnvidja jötun,
The Womb of the Wood.

NOTES

1. According to Saxo Grammaticus, Hadding (or Haddingus) is a legendary Danish king raised by giants and, with Odin's aid, the winner of many remarkable battles. At some point, false rumors of his death reach King Hunding of the Swedes, who holds a remembrance ceremony for his beloved lord; however, he drowns by accident in a vat of ale. When Hadding hears this tragic news, he hangs himself before all his subjects, dedicating his death to "Hangatýr"—that is, to Odin, the Gallows-God.

2. At the end of the first millennium, Iceland converted to Christianity by a parliamentary decision at Thingvellir. A major factor in this decision was Thorgeir Thorkelsson, a pagan priest who decided in favor of Christianity after meditating for a day and night under a fur blanket. As a compromise to the pagans, he advises them to practice their faith in private.

3. According to Snorri's *Prose Edda*, the giantess Angrboda gave birth to three monsters: Fenrir, the Midgard-serpent, and Hel. Their father was Býleist's brother Loki. The *Elder Edda* also mentions an Iron-Wood Forest in which a female jötun lives, a Járnvidja ("iron-wood dweller"), possibly Angrboda, who is mother to all wolves.

4. According to Snorri, the wolf Hati endlessly pursues Máni (the moon), and the wolf Sköll endlessly pursues Sól (the sun). They will catch their prey at Ragnarök, thereby darkening the world.

Math Jones

Math Jones (b. 1964) is a London-born Pagan poet who, like Michaela Macha and others, writes poetry inspired by—and celebrating—the pre-Christian religions of northern Europe. Much like another Pagan poet, Paul Edwin Zimmer, Jones is self-taught. In his youth, Jones forewent college and pursued an acting career, followed by years as a bookseller; he eventually enrolled in drama school, graduating in the late 2000s. Jones encountered Heathenism after reading the "Old English Rune Poem" in the mid-1990s. Alongside Tolkien's writings on Old English meter, this discovery helped launch Jones into his literary conversion from mainstream poetry to alliterative verse. The Norse poems of W. H. Auden are another powerful influence—the poetically "truest" translations of Norse literature, Jones says, currently available in English. He also feels a special kinship with Orcadian poet George Mackay Brown. To date, Jones has published two short books, *Sabrina Bridge* (2018), a general poetry collection, and *The Knotsman* (2019), which tells the life and times of a seventeenth-century cunning-man. Much of Jones's Heathen poetry can be heard on *eaglespit*, a spoken-word digital album available on the streaming service Bandcamp (https://mathjones.bandcamp.com/releases).

Housepost

Second nature, now, this load,
that once was weight of wealthy canopy,
full in the forest. Felled and brought
to sit on stone, straightened edges,
honed to a heartwood, a house set upon me,
I, the bearer, beams upon my shoulders,

with god-nails hammered in my gathered brow,
Thunor my mentor.[1] Though thunder rounds
its crash about me, catches at the walls,
presses on my roof, push and shove,   10
and rainfall flings, fierce arrowheads
of hail and water, how can I be anything
but steadfast, true, the trust of those below me
steadied in the storm, in my staunchness founded.
The walls have bent, awake through the night.
Doors have shuddered, shook to their hinges,
beating on their bolts. The beams on my shoulders
have ground in their sockets, groaned with the heft
of the sheltering tiles, shielding timbers.
But I am standing, strained maybe   20
by the weight of the weather, warding like the thunder-god
the holiness of space, the hearth and benches,
the loom and the weaving, the life new awoken
kept in the warm. Quiet I stay,
with this weight upon me, winsome and glad
that this might engrained with grace remains.

Lenctenlong[2]

In Hordaland, the harvest long
as hay was gathered in the wain,
Thjódólf honed his thanks
to Thorleif; he raised that lord,
a bridge of words. Bragi!
bright Valhalla's skald,
bestow your mead on Math
to make his verse no worse.

For has Thorskegga Thorn,
like Thorleif, a battle-board   10
given as gift: a shield
with gold and stories told
of deed-famous *dísir*
and daring way-farers.
Striven have I for staves
to stand as worthy thanks.

                    I
Early comes the harvest home
to the hall of Thor, falling
sheafs of shim'ring strands

(Shears in the hands of Fenrir's 20
father—snik and snak!)
as the Snotra of Bilskírnir gloats—[3]
troubles need bring treasures:
trade for a crop of braids.

Lofty reaper's lacking
the lady's store of foresight:
thinks he to thoroughly vex
Thunderer's sense of fun!
But his health shall stand as hostage
for hair, with gold repaired, 30
and boons for the Gods, and bounty,
else bones unknit, and groans.

Down among the Dark-álfs,
Donar to flee, has gone
the loose-tongued long-one;[4]
laughing at dwarven craft,
a gadfly galling their pride,
(Gild may yet a shield
provide!) till forge and fire
flare for hammer and hair. 40

The Saga of Thrúdheim speaks
summons the gods to come
and weigh the worth of treasures
won by Fárbauti's son.
Loki's wagered head is lost,
his lips are tightly stitched,
for the mighty hammer, Mjöllnir,
and a mane of golden grain.[5]

                    II
See I too a goddess gain,
glad in necklace (reckless 50
ploy, to pledge her troth),
plights her body one night
to each of four earthworms
Arms a-gleaming, her charms
shall buy Brísingamen in
beds of stunted runts!

Broad in their needs and bruising,
unbridled in a rutting wild,
Dark-álfs delve the Vanadís.
She draws from each a glory 60

never known in Dwarfhome,
till Nordri's kin begin
a long and loving *galdr*
to lay on tears of Freyja:[6]

"This *dís* shall dazzle the eye,
desire in all arising;
her heart shall harden armies,
her hall shall guest the fallen;
her hands shall proffer healing,
hale from battle and bale;   70
her steps shall foster flowers,
fields rich harvest yield."

III

Out upon the ocean's rim,
Earth's son is also one
to walk this wheel of Hild:[7]
in western seas he tests
his fishing line: his feet
firm braced against the wyrm,
his hook baited with bull,
the boast given his host,   80

Hymir, hard-rock dweller,
to hurt the World-girdler!
Churns the bloody channel
the child of Loki, wildly
seeking the sea-way's depths,
sore in tooth and maw.
The hard-biting hook and line is
hauled by swan-road's trawler!

Timbers of the boat are burst,
breached by Thunder's feet!   90
Hymir's heart is in his pants,
hues the rope in two!
World-wyrm flounders in the flood,
flies Mjöllnir 'tween the eyes
of sore-headed serpent
splits that thought-house to bits!

Hymir is food for fishes,
falling to Ægir's hall
at Atli's urging. Now,
the heirs of Heimdall fare   100
o'er leagues with lifting steeds

to lands beyond Jörmungandr,
have e'en moored in the meres
of Mundilfari's son.[8]

IV

Last on this lid to tell:
a lord, the boast of Njörd,
brought by Golden-bristles.
(Brokk and Eitri put flight
into jogging hog's hooves!)
Heartsore Ingi-Frey sings   110
a mournful *galdr*, to guide
the ghosts of a giant's spite.[9]

With Dáin's wand as weapon,
Wain-god has the jötun slain.
His flesh now feeds the earth
of farmers he worked to harm;
cattle and grain are given,
gear to keep them the year,
but none may numb the grieving,
naught can mend the slaughter.   120

Such scenes have been painted
on circle finely worked.
Thorskegga Thorn has made it—
Thunder's *dís*, a wonder![10]
These staves must stand as thanks,
strophes of worth-ship and troth
praising the girl and her gods,
for goodly leather and wood.

Mothers' Song

A thread stretches, strong and unbroken,
through the web of Wyrd. A winding length,
drawn by the Sisters through darkness of night,[11]
spun from its spool, spilling a rune
from the wombs of women, washed in blood,
linking our lives to long-dead kin.

From mother to mother, through Máni's faring,
through Amma and Edda, Embla's kin,[12]
through layers and lives, the line still carried
from daughter to daughter. Dear are the *idisi*,[13]   10

held in our being, as they held in their bellies
the children of their children and their children beside.

Mothers of ancient-days, mighty in wisdom,
cunning in council, come to your son:
as ever the bairn, unwise to his heritage,
bursts from your body, broadens his lung-house
to greet the mother: he grows into knowledge
of his folk and fathers, their fame and riches;
so might Math, make greeting to you,
with *wód* and worth-ship, your worth to sing.[14]   20

Too long dishonoured, the daughters of Embla,
in Christendom's fires, feared by their priests;
we of the kindred kindle our torches,
wives of wisdom, women of power,
friends of the goddess, to greet your return.

You have been shield-maidens, unshy of battle,
alongside your loved ones, locked in the spear-play,
blade smacking breast, bare and unfettered
in the face of the fiend. Ferocious women,
sending your fetches, *seidh*-borne furies[15]   30
with flame-shooting fingers, fending your men
from wyrd-driven wounds. Wives of heroes,
no less in mood than the menfolk you shielded.

You have been wives wed to end slaughter,
peace-weavers sent to the place of your foemen
to hold out the horn to hewers of kin;
bringers of *frith*,[16] where feud has been master
and death has been queen. Dauntless to face,
in the husband's house, hurt and mistrust
from woe-meaning women, and wound-nursing men.   40

Wardens of worth, you work the life-store,
soul-woven knots, by the Nornir bestowed,
into son's sinews, into souls of your daughters.
You harden the *haminja*,[17] honing the mood,
chiding the children, when challenged by strife,
to face their fear and find the prize,
the healing and help to be had from need.

You have travelled, treading new lands
as far-reaching wanderers. Freydís in Vinland:
she braved the Skraelings, her brother to shelter,   50

her baby to ward. You have built towns,
and girded good bridges: Gunnvor Thydrik's daughter
marked it with runes, in memory of Astrid;
and Waterloo women, in war-shattered London,
crossed the Thames with a concrete arch.[18]

In factory and field, full is your toil
to help in the harvest. At home you are fee-makers,
spinning and weaving the wool into gold,
dresses and shirts for your daughters and sons.
Good is your craft. Grain is your metal   60
kneaded to bread, or brewed into ale.
Wealth you weave through winter's nights.

Words you have worked, *wód*-bearers of craft,
skilled skald-konas: scathing the metres
of *wód*-mighty Steinunn: the White-Christ's strength
was shown to be short, when the ship of his servant
was shattered on shingle, shaken by thunder.
Thor made Thangbrand thoroughly wet![19]

You were the sisters, suffragette warriors
under Týr's banner, battling for right,   70
who showed off their shackles, no shame in the chains
that held them to railings: ready to die
by the horse's hoof, to be heard at the Thing.[20]

Hear you the song of this son of mothers,
ash from the elm. Alvig the Wise
to Halfdan the Old, gave eighteen sons,
nine in one night, nurtured them all.
She had the might of a mother in need.
Idisi bright, in the birthing time,
come to your kinder with kindly heart,   80
bring her the might of mothers in need:
a woman awaits, wife and mother,
with horn of milk and honeyed bread,
gyfu-engraved, to gain your friendship.[21]
Bring, for this bairn, birth-runes ruddy.
Loosen all knots, and lend to your daughter
the might beyond measure of mothers in need.

Here settle, idisi, *settle here and there:*
Some to help the fettered, some to harry the foe.

Fall upon the fear-bands, fetters of might. . . .   90
Unbind the birthing, bring forth the child!

Blessed and bright are the bearers of children,
the givers of life. Great in the belly,
the callow one turns, kicks into ribs,
pounds on the gut like a pup of the thunderer,
a weight to his mother, a wyrm under earth.
The ninth-moon waning, womb in her hands,
she groans and grimaces, grabs at the birth-runes
burning in her belly, braces the womb-web,
thews of Thrúd, to thrust the kinder—[22]   100
a brand to the flame. Her brow is hot,
wet the linen—the lake of the belly
has burst its bank. With bands of might,
gripping tightly, she goads the young one,
earthwife's cargo, out of the darkness,
from womb to the world. Wailing and bloody,
the babe is brought to breast and milk.
The cord is cut. Cradling her womb-song,
defiant, she dares any deny her her prize.

Hoar-headed Holda, hostess of the unborn,   110
has kept well the kinder.[23] Her cavern is daunting,
in glacier guarded; gaunt is her welcome.
Hard are the mile-paths, murky and fog-bound,
the *fylgjur* must fetch the frolicsome babe
to lich and to life. And loose is the *ørlög*
till ninth night passed and name bestowed.[24]
She has kept the stillborn, the stunted and wyrdless:
born into better times, these bairns now will thrive.

More blood is shed in the birthing-hall,
than is spilt in spear-play. Spared from the tumult,   120
the mothers of men are marked for wounds,
bloody and grim, from grave-threat'ning strife.
None can foresee the foe that awaits
the woman in labour, life-bearing danger,
as wyrd is woven, a wight to bring forth
or a *dís* to destroy. Deadly the peril
that waxed unseen to seize on Hnossa,

treasure of the Vanadís: tight was her womb,
her waters broke—the babe, she held,
ready to fly, free from her body.[25]   130
Bold life-bearer, her blood was shed:
born by the blade, brought forth was the child.
His mother sang, marked with a verse
the bloody fray, bludgeoned the face
of the fierce-gripped fiend that fettered her womb,
threatening the birth of her boy-child.
His pelting cry and pasty grimace,
sig-bearing song, was a sign of triumph![26]
I was her *fro*, father to the boy,
stood at her side, saw her mood: 140
I hold her in honour, hold her in love,
witnessed the worth of my wife most dear:
proud-hearted woman, priceless jewel.

NOTES

1. "Thunor" (or Þunor) is the Old English name for Thor, Norse god of thunder.

2. A tenth-century Norwegian skald, Thjódólf of Hvinir, named his poem "Haustlöng" (meaning "autumn-long") for the length of time it took him to complete this work. Since Jones wrote his own poem over the spring, he calls it "Lenctenlong." Jones's poem takes its form because Thjódólf had offered "Haustlöng" in praise of a shield given him by his lord, Thorlief, in Hordaland (located in modern-day Norway). Accordingly, Jones wrote "Lenctenlong" after his friend, Thorskegga Thorn, gave him a decorated shield for Yuletide. Her shield depicts four separate scenes: Loki cutting off Sif's hair; the creation of Freyja's necklace, Brísingamen, by dwarves; Thor fishing for Jörmungand, the Midgard Serpent; and the god Frey riding in a boar-drawn chariot. After Jones's initial prologue, each section will narrate these episodes in order. Following Thorskegga's pictorial retellings of these tales, though, Jones will deviate slightly from the canonical Norse stories.

3. Thor resides in the hall Bilskírnir, and his wif, Sif, is therefore the "Snotra of Bilskírnir"; Snotra is a goddess whose name means *clever*. The god Loki, father of Fenrir, once maliciously decided to cut Sif's golden-colored hair, an act that may have represented the harvesting of wheat in the autumn.

4. "Donar" is the Old High German version of Thor's name. "Dark-álfs" (or dark elves) are dwarves.

5. The "Saga of Thrúdheim" is another kenning for Sif; "Thrúdheim" is another name for Bilskírnir. The son of Fárbauti is Loki. Unfortunately for Loki, he bets two dwarves, Brokk and Eitri, that they couldn't forge anything so wonderful as the items in his possession, but he loses at the price of his head. Since neither dwarf, however, can take Loki's head without also taking his neck, they instead sew up his mouth.

6. The dwarf Nordri ("north") represents a cardinal direction; Nordri's kindred are dwarves in general. A *galdr* is a spell. One source attests that four dwarves made Brísingamen for Freyja, goddess of love and fertility, after she slept with each on four successive nights.

7. Hild is a Valkyrie. While the phrase "wheel of Hild" is traditionally a kenning for *shield*—in this case, Thorskegga's shield—it also suggests the rim of the ocean (or world) being walked by Thor, the "Earth's son." When Thor goes fishing for Jörmungand, he lets the jötun Hymir accompany him.

8. Ægir is god of the sea. "Atli" is another name for Thor. Mundilfari is father to Máni (the Moon).

9. Loki loses his bet with the dwarves Brokk and Eitri after they'd created a wonderful boar named Gullinbursti ("Golden-bristles"). On Thorskegga's shield, her boar is pulling the chariot of Njörd's son Frey, and this chariot is surrounded by the ghosts of the people slain by Beli, a jötun. According to myth, Frey wishes to slay Beli for those evil deeds, but, unfortunately, the god had already given away his sword in order to win his wife Gerd. As a result, Frey must wield a stag's antler—"Dáin's wand"—instead. Dáin was a stag who famously ate among the branches of Yggdrasil.

10. Since Thorskegga is a devotee of Thor, she is called "Thunder's *dís*."

11. The three Norns governing fate—sometimes described as sisters—are a trio of maiden giantesses: Urd ("past"), Verdandi ("present"), and Skuld ("future").

12. As attested by *Völuspá*, Embla is the first woman created by the gods. In Old Norse, *amma* means "grandmother," and *edda* arguably means "great-grandmother." Each name appears as a person in *Rígsthula*, an incomplete poem describing how humanity derived from Ríg the wanderer (i.e., Heimdall). Máni is the male personification of the moon.

13. The term *idisi* hails from the first Meresburg charm, one of two medieval magical spells in Old High German. The *idisi* themselves are female spirits now often linked with the *dísir*. Later in the poem, Jones will include an adaptation of this first Meresburg charm, originally a spell freeing captured warriors from their fetters, but now a charm to "unbind" (i.e., deliver) a child from its mother during birth.

14. Here, *wód* is a form of poetic frenzy; it constitutes the first element of *Woden*. "Worth-ship," meaning worthiness, stems from the Old English word *weorþscipe*.

15. *Seidh* (or *seid*) is a type of Norse magic, often associated with witches, whose use is restricted to women.

16. *Frith* (or *frið*) is an Old English word that means "peace," "tranquility," "security," or "refuge."

17. The *haminja* ("luck") is a familial spirit who, somewhat akin to the Greek *daimon* or Roman *genius*, conveys an individual's or family's good fortune.

18. In the saga, Freydís Eiríksdóttir, sister to Leif Erikson, protected her family in Vinland against incursions by the Skraelings. Likewise, a Norse woman named Gunnvor—at least according to a famous runestone just north of Oslo in Norway—once erected a bridge in memory of her daughter, Astrid. Finally, during the 1940s, London's Waterloo Bridge was rebuilt using a largely female workforce. It's often colloquially known as "Ladies' Bridge."

19. Steinunn Refsdóttir, a tenth-century female Icelandic skald, once wrote a poem mocking the Christian missionary Thangbrand by saying that Thor caused his recent shipwreck because Thangbrand's god, Christ, was too afraid to accept a duel offered by Thor.

20. In the early twentieth century, banners used by British suffragettes often employed an arrowhead symbol that resembled the *tiwaz*-rune (↑) associated with Týr—hence, "Týr's banner." In 1913, suffragette Emily Wilding Davison was killed on Derby Day after deliberately running in front of a racehorse owned by King George V.

21. In the runic alphabet, the rune *gyfu* (X) means "gift" or "generosity."

22. Thrúd is Thor and Sif's daughter. This name also belongs to a Valkyrie in *Grímnismál*.

23. Holda is a shadowy Germanic goddess often associated with childcare. Sometimes she appears as a protector—sometimes as a thief—of children's souls. In the pre-Christian era, Norse people named their children on their ninth day, but if a child died before the ninth day, their spirit was given over to Holda's care.

24. The *fylgjur* ("fetches") are protective spirits born alongside a child and who accompany them throughout life; some have suggested a connection with the afterbirth. An *ørlög* is another representation of someone's luck or fate.

25. In Norse mythology, Hnossa ("jewel," "treasure") is the daughter of Freyja ("the Vanadís") and Odin. It is also the by-name adopted by Jones's wife at the time, who required a caesarian for delivery. The *dísir* are female spirits; Freyja's title "Vanadís" literally means "*dís* of the Vanir."

26. Although the rune *sig* (ᛉ) is usually associated with the sun, in one version of the Futhark alphabet it is associated with victory.

Part IV

SPECULATIVE ADJACENT POEMS

James Blish

James Blish (1921–1975) first got involved with SF fandom as a teenager, joining the Futurians—a New York-based fan group—where he became close friends with such luminaries as Damon Knight and Cyril Kornbluth. An impressive career followed. His "Okie" stories were collected eventually into *Cities in Flight* (1970), and he produced a classic novel, *A Case of Conscience* (1958), plus two books of intelligent SF criticism. In later years, Blish wrote or collaborated on several *Star Trek* novels. Yet Blish also had a deep and abiding passion for literary modernism, especially James Joyce and Ezra Pound. The latter impacted Blish on several levels. The pseudonym under which Blish wrote criticism, "William Atheling Jr.," is a clear homage to Pound, who wrote music criticism as "William Atheling"; the surname roughly means "prince" in Old English. Likewise, although Blish seems to have had no direct experience with medieval literature itself, his style in "The Coming Forth" is heavily indebted to Pound's alliterative poetics in Modern English texts such as "Canto I" and *The Seafarer*. Tellingly, as a modernist poem, "The Coming Forth" (1957) was originally published in the prestigious *Beloit Poetry Journal*, far outside the venues normally reserved for speculative verse.

The Coming Forth[1]

The glare on the godly sledge crawled between crags;
Redder the rays than before, the road bleaker;
Dust that year dimmed the river, dry at the due time,
Wooden gears ground in the gorge, wound by the buffalo,
Sakiyeh squeaked, buckets of shaduf baled sludge[2]
Thick up the terraces; men of dun color

Still harrowed and seeded sand as the hornéd lamp passed,
Leaving the unleavened dead droning among the potsherds,

> We have done no sin, we have not sinned,
> Our hearts have not been hasty,   10
> We have not broken the corn, we have not been covetous,
> We have not robbed, nor reduced the size of the measure,
> We have not slain men, nor spoken overmuch.

Slower the god, light lowered, all day gone to this hour.
Poised white in the hide trembled the pendulous slow-wheeling tears
Of stars in the shaduf, rived from the trickling river,
Straws without bricks, skulls ticking in blackness,

> Our crimes are not, we have done no evil,
> Our voices have not been high, nor have we lied,
> We have not slaughtered divine bulls, not blasphemed a god,   20
> Not taken god's property. We stand not impure before god.

Into the great double house the dim disc, hollow the groans of his going
In the mouths of the Memnons,[3] ringed with his rubbish,
> We have not burned dung in god's presence
And the duned gold clean drifted over the forepaws of time.[4]

NOTES

1. Blish's title could doubly refer to the Egyptian *Book of the Dead*, whose name originally means "book of coming forth by day," as well as to Psalm 121:8, which in the King James Version reads: "The LORD shall preserve thy going out and thy coming in from this time forth, and even for evermore." Whereas the indented lines evoke the Psalms in style, the non-indented lines echo Pound's experiments in Old English alliterative prosody.

2. A *sakiyeh* is a type of waterwheel used for raising water along the banks of the Nile; a *shaduf* is a handheld device that uses a pole to lift buckets of water.

3. The Colossi of Memnon are two massive stone statues, just west of the modern city of Luxor, that date from the reign of Pharaoh Amenhotep III, who died circa 1350 B.C.E.

4. This line was selected by editor Keith Allen Daniels as the epigraph for his introduction to Blish's posthumously published collection, *With All of Love: Selected Poems* (1995).

P. K. Page

A Fellow of the Royal Society of Canada, P. K. Page (1913–2010) is one of Canada's most lauded twentieth-century poets, earning during her lifetime numerous accolades, awards, and honorary degrees. Throughout the 1950s, she spent time in Australia, Brazil, Mexico, and Guatemala as part of her husband's various diplomatic postings, until returning to Canada permanently in the mid-1960s. Known for the abundance and vividness of her poetic imagery, Page had an ongoing engagement with alliterative metrics as well; her book-length verse memoir *Hand Luggage* (2006), for example, deploys a four-beat accentual meter. The following two selections each appeared in a 1987 special issue of *The Malahat Review* on poet George Johnston, a close friend of Page and an internationally respected translator of Old Norse and Icelandic sagas. The first poem, "Crow's Nest," is a *dróttkvætt* adapted into 10-line stanzas. Its subject implies a startling analogy between crows' nests and skaldic poetry, and, as such, it bears comparison with stanza 16 of Jere Fleck's "Coronation Ode." The second poem, although not alliterative itself, brilliantly describes the experience of reading skaldic poetry; the text comes from volume two of *The Hidden Room*, published in 1997 by the Porcupine's Quill Press.

Crow's Nest

In hard hats with hoses
and halyards to haul it
from tree-bough, with tridents
and truncheons tight-clenched in
clad fists, we are fastened

by friendship, dependent
each upon each; arching
arms, torsos and ordered
preparations (prayers
too?) now to be proven.   10

We pry at crow's palace
to poke it from oak-bough.
We teeter near tree-top.
From tall ladders call down
on crow imprecations
and curses. Lodged firm, it
is fused to branch. Fashioned
fast, that nest. A lasting
tribute, a fine triumph
of technique and crowdom.   20

Hose, wet it with water!
Down-wash it with flash floods!
This strictly built structure
sits, settled for better
or worse. Wears forever.
No waters dislodge what
stands steady through sudden
fierce savaging havoc—
staunch galleon, gallant
through gale and great hailstorm.   30

Crows homing start cries of
"Caveat!" and "Have mercy!"
"Duck, oh my dear ducky,
lest divers survive us."
Cry peace lest a posse
of partisans hurtles
with black wings to break us
with black beaks to crack us.
Cáw cáw caw caw cáw caw.
Caw cáw cáw caw cáw caw.   40

George Johnston Reading

A slow January, grey, the weather rainy.
Day after day after day the ceiling zero.
Then you arrive, comb honey from your hives[1] pulled from
your suitcase, head full of metrics, syllable count,

rhyme—half-hidden, half rhyme and alliteration—
the poem's skeleton and ornamentation—
to give a reading as untheatrical as
it is subtle, elegant and unexpected.

I had not anticipated your translations
from Old Norse, your saga of heroic Gisli—[2]   10
good man, strong man, man who could split an enemy
as butchers split a chicken, clean through the breastbone—
driven to running bloody, head drenched in redness,
dreamer of dark dreams prophetic of his downfall.
Writer of skaldic verses. Gisli, crow-feeder.
Great Gisli, dead of great wounds, son of whey-Thorbjorn.

Nor had I been prepared for those skaldic verse forms
(three-stressed lines in four pairs, final foot trochaic)
that made my head hum—their intricate small magic
working away like yeast till eight lines of court metre   20
are glittering and airy, furnished with pianos,
each short line, inexplicably a pianist
recreating for me the music of Scarlatti—
crossing hands on the keyboard, crossing and crossing.[3]

Or—working away like bees in blossoms, shaking
a pollen of consonants on the audience
which sat, bundled and bunched in mufflers and greatcoats
in the bare unwelcoming hall where poets read
in Victoria, city of rainy winters.[4]
And thinking about it now, I remember sun   30
and how honey sweetened the verses, made them gold
and tasting, that mid-January, of field-flowers.

NOTES

1. After Johnston retired from academia in 1979, he spent time raising bees.

2. Johnston published his translation of *Gísli saga* under the title *The Saga of Gisli the Outlaw* (1963). Gísli Súrsson was a tenth-century outlaw whose father, Thorbjörn Thorkelsson, earned his nickname *súr* (meaning "whey") after using this milk-derived product to douse a fire burning down the family home.

3. Doménico Scarlatti (1685–1757) was an Italian composer known for his numerous keyboard sonatas.

4. Victoria is the capital city of British Columbia, a Canadian province.

George Johnston

George Johnston (1913–2004) was a Canadian poet and renowned translator of Icelandic sagas. For nearly three decades, he taught in the English department at Carleton College (now Carleton University), retiring in 1979 to write and raise bees. His original work often celebrates friends, family, and suburban life, and it frequently shows the metrical influence of Norse poetic forms. By dint of his highly regarded scholarly translations, however, Johnston joins William Morris, E. R. Eddison, and Lee Hollander as an influential force in conveying Norse style to a wider audience. In one of his best-known translations, *The Saga of Gisli the Outlaw* (1963), Johnston presents the story of an outlaw forced to avenge his brother-in-law by killing another brother-in-law, and it was this work that inspired "George Johnston Reading" by P. K. Page. The following deft *dróttkvætt* is a pure praise poem in celebration of Page.

Crows' Nests in Court Metres

for PK, in admiration for her "Crows' Nests"

Gisli's tale beguiles you:
gold-breaker, bold smiter,
hard-pressed poet outlaw,
prince of artificers;
rhymed he in wrought metres
ruefully, his broodings
dreams of deep-browed women,
dark and bright harbingers.

Clear are your uncluttered
cadences, that radiate
brave wit and bright, ringing
bell notes; now they welcome
norse metric; new-turned it
knows you for its poet,
skilful in your scaldic
version, Page excursion.

Crows' nests in court metres
Call forth your resources:
outlandish, extravagant
images, one simply
marvels at your merry
music; your abusive
sharpwitted, showering
showdown with black crowdom.

10

20

Earle Birney

Earle Birney (1904–1995) is a major modern poet; a two-time winner of Canada's top literary honor, the Governor General's Award; and a prolific novelist, playwright, and nonfiction writer as well. During the 1930s, ardent Trotskyism moved Birney into political activity; yet, eventually, he left the Socialist Workers League he helped found because his colleagues refused to support the Second World War. Birney trained as a medievalist, too, and he often utilized medieval poetics in his poetry. Although his dissertation focused on irony in Chaucer, the greatest of narrative poets in Birney's view, little of this admiration manifests directly within Birney's own work; according to M. J. Toswell, Old English prosody had a much greater impact. The two selections below, for instance, both follow a loosened form of Old English meter. The first, "Oil Refinery," is a sensuously mythopoeic poem that connects the ancient dragon from *Beowulf* to the pollution-heavy outgrowths of modern industrialization. The second poem, "Anglosaxon Street," critically explores the connections between medievalism, class, and English racial identity—a theme rarely, if ever, taken up by other revivalists.

Oil Refinery

Under the fume   of the first dragons
those spellbinders who guard   goldhoards under barrows
whole fields of warriors   wilted: even Beowulf
fell in balebreath   from firedrake fangs

Yet this hugest of Worms   though he outburst heaving
from deepest of meres   under farthest moor

is led leaping and leaping   at last to these shores
and hour by hour   overhewn and whelmed

Not without fury resists   flames in the night
blasts the world air   wans all blue day   10
Ho! a handful of thanes   in helmets threaten him
in silver keeps stab him   the old swartshiner
with gauges bedevil   with dials with cyclonesnuffers
endless they slaughter   that slimiest of Nadders

Hwaet! he is quick again   thousand-toothed Queller
whirls his ghost in our wheels   unleashes or locks them
Yea he twins twentyfold   twines in our graveloot
breath of that sly snake   stifles and clings
slides from our long ships   coils round our steadings
Eala! we are lost   in the spell of his loopings.   20

Anglosaxon Street

Dawndrizzle ended   dampness steams from
blotching brick and   blank plasterwaste
Faded housepatterns   hoary and finicky
unfold stuttering   stick like a phonograph

Here is a ghetto   gotten for goyim
O with care denuded   of nigger and kike
No coonsmell rankles   reeks only cellarrot
attar of carexhaust   catcorpse and cookinggrease
Imperial hearts   heave in this haven
Cracks across windows   are welded with slogans   10
There'll Always Be An England   enhances geraniums
and V's for Victory   vanquish the housefly[1]

Ho! with climbing sun   march the bleached beldames
festooned with shopping bags   farded flatarched
bigthewed Saxonwives   stepping over buttrivers
waddling back wienerladen   to suckle smallfry

Hoy! with sunslope   shrieking over hydrants
flood from learninghall   the lean fingerlings
Nordic nobblecheeked   not all clean of nose
leaping Commandowise   into leprous lanes   20

What! after whistleblow!   spewed from wheelboat
after daylong doughtiness   dire handplay
in sewertrench or sandpit   come Saxonthegns
Junebrown Jutekings   jawslack for meat

356 Speculative Poetry and the Modern Alliterative Revival

Sit after supper   on smeared doorsteps
not humbly swearing   hatedeeds on Huns
profiteers politicians   pacifists Jews

Then by twobit magic   to muse in movie
unlock picturehoard   or lope to alehall
soaking bleakly   in beer skittleless   30

Home again to hotbox   and humid husbandhood
in slumbertrough adding   sleepily to Anglekin
Alongside in lanenooks   carling and leman
caterwaul and clip   careless of Saxonry
with moonglow and haste   and a higher heartbeat

Slumbers now slumtrack   unstinks cooling
waiting brief for milkmaid   mornstar and worldrise

NOTE

1. Both "There'll Always Be an England" (a patriotic British song from 1939) and the "V for Victory" campaign were important messaging slogans for Great Britain during the Second World War. During his tenure as prime minister, Winston Churchill made the "V for Victory" sign highly popular.

W. H. Auden

W. H. Auden (1907–1973) was the foremost poetic voice of his generation, so much so that literary critics often dub the "political 1930s" as the Auden Generation. While attending Oxford in the late 1920s, he befriended C. Day-Lewis, Stephen Spender, and Louis MacNeice. Together, they produced a powerful kind of political poetry that, imbued with leftist sentiments and Freudian psychology, sternly rejected the apolitical modernism of the decade prior. In time, Auden came to repudiate some of this earlier work, including famous texts such as "Spain" (1937) and "September 1st, 1939" (1939), as, during his later career, he turned toward a more personal poetry that explored his newly rediscovered Christian faith. Yet it was also at Oxford that Auden first heard Tolkien recite *Beowulf*. This event inaugurated for Auden a lifelong love affair with alliterative poetics, which can be felt in his last long poem, *The Age of Anxiety* (1947). In this text, Auden examines a group of strangers who have met randomly in a New York City bar. Each represents one of Carl Jung's four psychological functions of consciousness—intuition, thought, sensation, and feeling. Rosetta, a Jewish woman from England, is "feeling." She idealizes her childhood and prewar English country home, and, in the first excerpt, which occurs during Part Three, she participates in a dream quest where they journey through a "landscape bearing symbolic resemblance to the human body." At one point Rosetta enters a house and, looking out a window, witnesses a scene from her childhood, seen now through adult eyes. The second excerpt closes out Rosetta's powerful final speech at poem's end: her great moment of epiphany and full self-realization.

Rosetta's Vision
(from "Part Three" in *The Age of Anxiety*)

ROSETTA answers:
> Opera glasses on the ormolu table
> Frock-coated father framed on the wall
> In a bath-chair facing a big bow-window,
> With valley and village invitingly spread,
> > I got what is going on.

> At the bend of the Bourne[1] where the brambles grow thickest
> Major Mott joins Millicent Rusk;
> Discreetly the kingfisher keeps his distance
> But an old cob swan looks on as they
> > Commit the sanguine sin.

> Heavy the orchards; there's Alison pinching
> Her baby brother, Bobby and Dick
> Frying a frog with their father's reading-glass,
> Conrad and Kay in the carpentry shed
> > Where they've no business to be.

> Cold are the clays of Kibroth-Hattavah,[2]
> Babel's urbanities buried in sand,
> Red the geraniums in the rectory garden
> Where the present incumbent reads Plato in French
> > And has lost his belief in Hell.

> From the gravel-pits in Groaning Hollow
> To the monkey-puzzle on Murderer's Hill.
> From the Wellington Arms to the white steam laundry,
> The significant note is nature's cry
> > Of long-divided love.

> I have watched through a window a World that is fallen,
> The mating and malice of men and beasts,
> The corporate greed of quiet vegetation,
> And the homesick little obstinate sobs
> > Of things thrown into being.

> > I would gladly forget; let us go quickly.

Excerpt from Rosetta's Final Soliloquy
(from "Part Five" in *The Age of Anxiety*)

> My poor fat father. How appalling was
> Your taste in ties. How you tried to have fun,
> You so longed to be liked. You lied so,
> Didn't you, dad? When the doll never came,[3]
> When mother was sick and the maid laughed.
> —Yes, I heard you in the attic. At her grave you
> Wept and wilted. Was that why you chose
> So blatant a voice, such button eyes
> To play house with you then? Did you ever love
> Stepmother Stupid? You'd a strange look,
> Sad as the sea, when she searched your clothes.
> Don't be cruel and cry. I couldn't stay to
> Be your baby. We both were asking
> For a warmth there wasn't, and then wouldn't write.
> We mustn't, must we? Moses will scold if
> We're not all there for the next meeting
> At some brackish well or broken arch,
> Tired as we are. We must try to get on
> Though mobs run amok and markets fall,
> Though lights burn late at police stations,
> Though passports expire and ports are watched,
> Though thousands tumble. Must their blue glare
> Outlast the lions? Who'll be left to see it
> Disconcerted? I'll be dumb before
> The barracks burn and boisterous Pharaoh
> Grow ashamed and shy. *Shema' Yisra'el:*
> *'adonai 'elohenu, 'adonai 'echad.*[4]

NOTES

1. The River Bourne flows through Warwickshire in England, near Birmingham.

2. According to the book of Numbers, the *Kibroth Hattaavah*, which in Hebrew means "graves of craving" or "graves of lust," is a location through which the Israelites passed during their exodus. It was the burial place of those stricken dead by Yahweh after complaining about having eaten a more varied diet, including meat, back in Egypt.

3. As established by the "sixth age" in Part Two of *The Age of Anxiety*, Rosetta associates her childhood dolls with an arcadian Primal Age that remains forever youthful and innocent.

4. Observant Jews consider the Shema—a confession of belief in the oneness of God—as the centerpiece of prayer service. The passage recited by Rosetta comes from Deuteronomy 6:4 and, in the New International Version of the Bible, it translates as "Hear, O Israel: the Lord our God, the Lord is one."

C. Day-Lewis

When most people today remember C. Day-Lewis (1904–1972), it is most often as a key member of the Auden Generation: a group of leftist poets who, in the 1930s, took their guiding lights from the restlessness and energy of W. H. Auden. Although Day-Lewis was the only member to join the Communist Party, his poetic sensibilities were essentially Georgian and Romantic; his later poetry gave up political commentary altogether. As an Oxford undergraduate, however, Day-Lewis attended some of the same lectures by Tolkien as his friend Auden, and although Old English metrics never entered as deeply into Day-Lewis's soul, they still exerted a noticeable impact. As with his earlier collection, *Transitional Poem* (1929), the lyric sequence in *From Feathers to Iron* (1931) uses a variety of stanza forms as Day-Lewis ruminates on journeys, explorations, and transitions. In the unnamed twelfth section, he uses a modified alliterative meter. At the time, many critics took *From Feathers to Iron* as political allegory despite its deeply personal nature; indeed, many sections can be read in two ways. The twelfth is no exception— either as Day-Lewis caught in liminality of expectant fatherhood, or as our collective "birth" into modernity, the iron machine age of new workings that stand on the ruins of the old.

As One Who Wanders into Old Workings

As one who wanders into old workings
Dazed by the noonday, desiring coolness,
Has found retreat barred by fall of rockface;
Gropes through galleries where granite bruises
Taut palm and panic patters close at heel;

Must move forward as tide to the moon's nod,
As mouth to breast in blindness is beckoned.
Nightmare nags at his elbow and narrows
Horizon to pinpoint, hope to hand's breadth.
Slow drip the seconds, time is stalactite,   10
For nothing intrudes here to tell the time,
Sun marches not, nor moon with muffled step.
He wants an opening,—only to break out,
To see the dark glass cut by day's diamond,
To relax again in the lap of light.

But we seek a new world through old workings,
Whose hope lies like seed in the loins of earth,
Whose dawn draws gold from the roots of darkness.
Not shy of light nor shrinking from shadow
Like Jesuits in jungle we journey   20
Deliberately bearing to brutish tribes
Christ's assurance, arts of agriculture.
As a train that travels underground track
Feels current flashed from far-off dynamos,
Our wheels whirling with impetus elsewhere
Generated we run, are ruled by rails.
Train shall spring from tunnel to terminus,
Out on to plain shall the pioneer plunge,
Earth reveal what veins fed, what hill covered.
Lovely the leap, explosion into light.   30

John Heath-Stubbs

Awarded a Queen's Gold Medal for Poetry in 1973, John Heath-Stubbs (1918–2006) first came to prominence as an undergraduate during the early years of the Second World War after he contributed to *Eight Oxford Poets* (1941). This short collection, edited by two close friends, advocated for a neo-Romantic sensibility while also rejecting the political and psychological concerns of the Auden Generation. All told, Heath-Stubbs's style is characterized by a cool tone, an erudite classical allusiveness, and an abiding faith in the power of the Romantic image. These qualities all impact his masterpiece, *Artorius* (1973). In this modernist epic, whose complex structural layerings draw inspiration from James Joyce's *Ulysses* (1922), Heath-Stubbs follows the pre-Malloryian aspects of Arthurian legend, Geoffrey of Monmouth in particular, while emphasizing Artorius as a Romano-British war leader entwined with Welsh myth, history, and legend. Hence, many otherwise-familiar names follow an older spelling: "Merddyn" for "Merlin," for instance. In the following excerpt, which occurs at the exact midpoint of Heath-Stubbs's poem, the speaker recapitulates everything that has happened thus far: the Battle of Badon, the synod against heresy at Oxford, Artorius's descent into the underworld. Merddyn then explains that Artorius must now set the laws of his new kingdom. Nonetheless, despite nominally focusing on law as a subject, every element of the fable Merddyn recounts foreshadows the inevitable end of Artorius himself.

Merddyn's Fable
(from "Calliope III" in *Artorius*)

At the autumnal equinox, in even opposition,
The bright and heavenly Balances hold
The softness of summer and the savagery of winter;
As on a field of fighting, the fierce tides
Doubtfully turn, in indecisive tumult.
Yet the doom of Summer is sealed, though the sun
Suffuses the landscape serenely with light.
There is an edge of death in the dank air,
And the fading leaves, as listlessly they fall.
The swallow and the swift, and the sylvan warblers   10
Have moved off on migration; no more is heard
The note of the nightingale, nor the nightjar's churning,
The calling of the cuckoo, nor the dry-voiced corncrake;
Richly the apples ripen in the orchards;
The harvest is garnered and hauled into granges;
Geese are set in the stubble to glean,
With relish, the residue of the reaped grain,
Fattening their flesh for the feast of Michaelmas.[1]
        Such was the season when Merddyn suddenly
Came to the king, Artorius, in his court.   20
The wizard addressed these words to the Ymheradwr:[2]
"Confide no more in my counsel and my comfort;
The time is near; for Nimue the nightmare
Summons me to her secret and subterranean kingdom.[3]
I must abide there in darkness till the Day of Doom;
The sweet sunlight will see me no more
On the upper earth, nor the air embrace me.
        "Listen to my words, the last of my wisdom:
In the sign of the Ram, in the raging slaughter
Of the field of Badon, the four-sided fortress,   30
You prosecuted war for the promotion of peace,
Establishing externally the order of empire;[4]
In the sign of the Bull, the bishops in synod
Determined by dogma the *limes* of doctrine;
In the sign of the Twins, song and sentence,
The lines of communication, by your laureates were cleared;
The conduits of rhetoric were cleansed of rubble:
The frogs of the fens found their vocabulary;
In the sign of the Crab, I sent you to Ceridwen,
From the maddening moonlight to the Mother's cauldron,   40
To face your futurity, and encounter your fears
And your utmost anxieties—an inner order

Was created in that descent to the darkness of her cavern;
In the sign of the Lion, the loud suffrage
And the plea of the people prompted you to your crowning;
In the sign of the Virgin, this was validated by the solemnity
Of wedlock to a bride—the wine and bread
And the common cup, signify the completeness,
The consummation of life: to the crowned couple
The guests do homage, in gladness of that grace: 50
May the screaming birds of scandal be sent
To their Stymphalian marsh, nor mar the merriment.[5]
          "Now is the time for this knowledge to be translated
Into forms of government, to guide those who follow;
That stability of the state may stand the firmer,
And a code of law be left to the land.
Summon then to council your senators and your commons,
To deliberate and determine, in form of debate,
Wisely and lucidly—of weight and learning,
Knowledgeable for this matter: I shall not be of the number."   60
          Artorius, with awe, answered his utterance:
"Legislation lodges in the letter that killeth;
For the hardness of the heart it is held a necessity;
But, as who trusts in the sword by the sword shall be slain,
Who leans on the law shall be judged by the Law.
I call to my memory that merciless king,
Feasting in Babylon; but fingers of flame
Scrawled on the stonework the sentence of his doom:
'You are weighed in the balance, and wanting, Belshazzar!'
In that night he was slain, and the sovereignty was to Cyrus."[6]   70
          Merddyn, the master, answered his misgivings:
"Justice is fixed on no firmer a foundation
Than a fallible construct, for the conservation of freedom;
Apart from her arbitration, in error and anguish,
We wander in the wildness of the primæval wood,[7]
Treacherous and trackless; and terrifying beasts,
Monsters whose dens are in the mind of man,
Perilously couch there—Passion and Pride.
Remember Minos, who mightily and marvellously
Reigned at Knossos, in the realm of Crete:[8]   80
With the sails of his galleons he swayed the seas
And the isles of the Aegean, and even Athens
Was a feudatory fief, in fear of that potentate;
He laid on them his rule, and the laws he received
From the divine Distributor, in the cavern of Dicte.

In the halls of the dead he is held now as doomster,
With righteous Rhadamanthus, rigid and incorruptible,
And Aeacus also, acting as assessors.
Yet lust and covetousness came upon that king:
The bull he had promised as a present for Poseidon,   90
To be slaughtered in sacrifice, he slyly withheld,
Captivated by its beauty, he kept it in his byre.
But his queen, likewise, was caught up by love
Of that horned brute, by a hideous and heinous
Stratagem she sought to solace her desire;
Begotten of her body, was brought forth the Minotaur,
The loathsome man-eater, that was lodged in the labyrinth,
Where Theseus subsequently sought it out and slew it.
But the ravished ruminant, in rabid must,
Went raging and rampaging round about the island,   100
Destroying the cities in seismic disturbance,
Till Heracles butchered the horrible beast:
You have learned the lot of Minos the lawgiver—
How animality injured that island emperor.
          "But supposing the story has a different significance?—
Maybe by the labyrinth is meant the law,
With all its tortuosities, its illogical turns,
Containing the monster of cruelty and malice.
The cunning Dædalus was the craftsman who designed it:
The favoured fosterling of Hephæstus the farrier   110
(The only honest Olympian, who alone
Toiled, though lame, at a trade for his living).
Put in that dungeon for his part in devising
That prurient subterfuge for salacious Pasiphäe,
He escaped, issuing into the upper air
Flying on wide-spread wings of feathers;
Reasonably, he ranged through the middle regions
Of atmosphere, but Icarus, exalted and enjoying
The new sensation, soared to the sphere
Of the blazing sun, but those burning beams   120
Mollified the wax of his wings, and they melted—
Downward he crashed in disaster to death.
Alas for Icarus, alas for all
Young men who fly too fast and too far,
Too superbly soaring, so near the sun!
I leave you to negotiate the labyrinth of law,
And ponder this fable. So, farewell my friend."
"By your departure," said Artorius, "I also am diminished."

NOTES

1. The Christian feast of St. Michael the Archangel, Michaelmas, falls on September 29th. In the northern hemisphere, the autumnal equinox usually falls between September 21st and 24th.

2. "Ymheradwr" is a slight misspelling of the modern Welsh word *ymerawdwr*, a loan from the Latin *imperator*; it means "emperor."

3. In *Artorius*, Nimue is one aspect of the goddess Ceridwen whom Artorius had confronted during his prior descent into Annwyn, the Welsh underworld. In many iterations of Arthurian legend, Nimue is the Lady of the Lake who grants Arthur the sword Caliburn ("Excalibur") and, thus, sovereignty of the realm.

4. The twelve signs of the zodiac constitute a major structuring device for *Artorius*. All twelve sections correspond to a different sign. The Battle of Badon happens in Book 1, which occurs in March under Ares the Ram. Other signs mentioned here are the Bull (Taurus), the Twins (Gemini), the Crab (Cancer), the Lion (Leo), and the Virgin (Virgo). This excerpt belongs to Libra, whose symbol is the scales of justice. Accordingly, Merddyn takes up the subject of law.

5. In the section dedicated to Virgo (the Virgin), Artorius's nephew Modred escorts the Lady Guanhumara, his uncle's betrothed, to Camelot, thus setting the stage for the "scandal" of their later affair. In addition to the zodiac, Heath-Stubbs also structures *Artorius* according to the Twelve Labors of Hercules. The Virgo section corresponds to the labor where Hercules defeats voracious man-eating birds from the Stymphalian swamps.

6. According to the book of Daniel, King Belshazzar sees mysterious handwriting on the wall, which Daniel interprets as a negative judgment from Yahweh; later Jewish tradition imagines Belshazzar as evil and tyrannical. Unfortunately for Artorius, he seems unaware of how this story echoes his own earlier, nightmarish experience in Annwyn, in which a figure had removed his heart and placed it on a set of scales.

7. In some versions of Arthurian legend deriving from the romance tradition, Brocéliande is a legendary enchanted forest. Since Heath-Stubbs avoids this tradition in *Artorius*, however, his "primæval wood" is merely a symbol, not an actual place.

8. In Greek mythology, Minos was a Cretan king who received tribute from Athens and other towns. The laws of Crete allegedly came from Zeus himself, and, after Minos died, Minos became (alongside his brothers Rhadamanthus and Aeacus) one of three judges in Hades who dealt with newly arrived shades. During life, Minos had famously imprisoned the Minotaur in a labyrinth constructed by the architect Dædalus. This monster was birthed by Minos's own wife, Pasiphäe, who had sexual relations with a bull dedicated to the god Poseidon. The consummation of her passion, though, was assisted by a "wooden cow" device built by Dædalus. Enraged, Minos imprisoned Dædalus and his son Icarus in the labyrinth. Although both men eventually escaped on wings built of wax and feathers, Icarus flew too close to the sun, and he plummeted to earth. In due time, the Minotaur was slain by the Athenian hero Theseus, and its rampaging bull father was killed by Hercules.

Carter Revard

Carter Revard (1931–2022), a professional medievalist and poet, grew up on an Osage tribal reservation in Oklahoma. After receiving his bachelor's degree, he won a Rhodes Scholarship to undertake graduate work in medieval studies at Oxford University. There, like Auden and Heath-Stubbs, he encountered the curriculum created by the Inklings; he finished his Ph.D. work at Yale. Most of his academic career was spent at Washington University in St. Louis, teaching medieval literature and linguistics, but, while in his forties, Revard began to write verse. His first collection, *Ponca War Dancers*, appeared in 1980. Although inspired by Osage traditions, Revard has nonetheless cautioned readers against making too much of his Native American background, yet his core hybridity appears in *An Eagle Nation* (1993), perhaps Revard's best-known work. This volume contains several alliterative poems, including "The Birch Canoe." Set within an alliterative meter borrowed from northern medieval Europe, the poem itself embraces subject matter from Revard's Osage heritage. Notably, the birch canoe, from whose perspective this poem is told, recalls the speaking Cross in "The Dream of the Rood."

The Birch Canoe

Red men embraced   my body's whiteness,
cutting into me   carved it free,
sewed it tight   with sinews taken
from lightfoot deer   who leaped this stream—
now in my ghost-skin   they glide over clouds
at home in the fish's   fallen heaven.

Fred Chappell

Fred Chappell (b. 1936) has enjoyed a unique literary career. Now a retired professor of English from the University of North Carolina at Greensboro, Chappell writes comfortably in both poetry and prose, and he has forged a reputation for himself in mainstream literature as well as in horror, fantasy, and science fiction. His earliest success came from a horror novel, *Dagon* (1968), based on Lovecraft's Cthulhu Mythos; the French translation won Chappell the coveted Prix de Meilleur des Livres Éstrangers. His other work has garnered similarly prestigious accolades: the Bollingen Prize in 1985; the T. S. Eliot Award in 1993; and the Thomas Wolfe Prize in 2005. Intimately identified with his home state, Chappell served as North Carolina's poet laureate from 1997 to 2002.

This excerpt comes from *Midquest: A Poem* (1981), where Chappell blends American folk tradition, his communal roots in rural Appalachia, and faints hints of Southern Gothic into a luminous, almost mythopoeic long poem of Dante-esque pilgrimage. Divided into four parts, *Midquest* narrates four times a single day in the speaker's life—Chappell's thirty-fifth birthday, the midpoint of his existence. Each part, which is structured according to the classical elements (water, fire, wind, and earth), contains eleven sections. Across these forty-four sections, blank verse and free verse predominate, but Chappell supplements with a wide variety of poetic forms through which he hopes to "suggest a kind of melting pot American quality." Old English poetics guide "My Grandfather's Church Goes Up," which occurs in the pivotal sixth section—the midpoint—of the poem's "Bloodfire" portion. It combines themes of time, memory, fire, and spiritual rebirth.

My Grandfather's Church Goes Up
(from *Midquest: A Poem*)

(Acts 2:1–47)
God is a fire in the head.

—Nijinsky[1]

Holocaust, pentecost: what heaped heartbreak:

The tendrils of fire   forthrightly tasting
foundation to rooftree   flesh of that edifice . . .
Why was sear sent   to sunder those jointures,
the wheat-hued wood   wasted to heaven?
Both alter and apse   the air ascended
in sullen smoke.
                    (It was surely no sign
of God's salt grievance   but grizzled *Weird* grimly
and widely wandering.)   10
                    The dutiful worshipers
stood afar ghast-struck   as the green cedar shingles
burst outward like birds   disturbed in their birling.
Choir stall crushed inward   flayed planking in curlicues
back on it bending,   broad beams of chestnut
oak poplar and pine   gasht open paint-pockets.
And the organ uttered   an unholy *Omega*
as gilt pipes and pedals   pulsed into rubble.

How it all took tongue!   A total hosannah
this building burgeoned,   the black hymnals whispering   20
leaves lisping in agony   leaping alight,
sopranos' white scapulars   each singly singeing
robes of the baritones   roaring like rivers
the balcony bellowing   and buckling. In the basement
where the M. Y. F.   had mumbled for mercies[2]
the cane-bottomed chairs   chirruped Chinese.
What a glare   of garish glottals
rose from the nave   what knar-mouthed natter!
And the transept tottered   intoned like tympani
as the harsh heat   held hold there.   30
The whole church resounded   reared its rare anthem
crying out Christ-mercy   to the cloud-cloven sky.

Those portents Saint Paul   foretold to us peoples
fresh now appeared: bifurcate fire-tongues,
and as of wild winds   a swart mighty wrestling,
blood fire and vapor   of smoke vastly vaulting,

the sun into darkness   deadened and dimmed,
wonders in heaven   signs wrought in the world:
the Spirit poured out   on souls of us sinners.
In this din as of drunkeness   the old men dreamed dreams,   40
the daughters and sons   supernal sights saw.
God's gaudy grace   grasped them up groaning.
Doubt parched within them   pure power overtaking
their senses. Sobbing   like sweethearts bereft
the brothers and sisters   burst into singing.
Truly the Holy   Ghost here now halted,
held sway in their hearts   healed there the hurt.

Now over the narthex   the neat little steeple
force of the fire   felt furiously.
Bruit of black smoke   borne skyward   50
shadowed its shutters   swam forth in swelter.
It stood as stone   for onstreaming moments
then carefully crumpled   closed inward in char.
The brass bell within it   broke loose, bountifully
pealing, plunged   plangent to the pavement
and a glamour of clangor   gored cloudward gaily.

That was the ringing that wrung   remorse out of us clean,
the elemental echo   the elect would hear always;
in peace or in peril   that peal would pull them.

Seventeen seasons   have since parted   60
the killing by fire   of my grandfather's kirk.
Moving of our Maker   on this middle earth
is not to be mind-gripped   by any men.

Here Susan and I   saw it, come
to this wood, wicker   basket and wool blanket
swung between us,   in sweet June
on picnic. Prattling   like parakeets
we smoothed out for our meal-place   the mild meadow grasses
and spread our sandwiches   in the sunlit greensward.
Then amorously ate.   And afterward   70
lay languorous and   looking lazily.
Green grass and pokeweed   gooseberry bushes
pink rambling rose   and raspberry vine
sassafras and thistle   and serrate sawbriar
clover and columbine   clung to the remnants,
grew in that ground   once granted to God.
Blackbirds and thrushes   built blithely there
the ferret and kingsnake   fed in the footing.

The wilderness rawly   had walked over those walls
and the deep-drinking forest   driven them down.   80

Now silence sang: swoon of wind
ambled the oak trees   and arching aspens.

In happy half-sleep   I heard or half-heard
in the bliss of breeze   breath of my grandfather,
vaunt of his voice   advance us vaward.
No fears fretted me   and a freedom followed
this vision vouchsafed,   victory of spirit.
He in the wind   wept not, but wonderfully
spoke softly   soothing to peace.
What mattered he murmured   I never remembered,   90
words melted in wisps   washed whitely away;
but calm came into me   and cool repose.
Where Fate had fixed   no fervor formed;
he had accepted   wholeness of his handiwork.

Again it was given   to the Grace-grain that grew it,
had gone again   gleaming to Genesis
to the stark beginning   where the first stars burned.
Touchless and tristless   Time took it anew
and changed that church-plot   to an enchanted chrisom
of leaf and flower   of lithe light and shade.   100

Pilgrim, the past   becomes prayer
becomes remembrance rock-real   of Resurrection
when the Willer so willeth   works his wild wonders.

NOTES

1. In the book of Acts, the Holy Spirit arrives as a violent wind during Pentecost and, with "tongues of fire," enables everyone in a crowd to speak God's wonders. Despite speaking different languages, their words are understood by all. The apostle Peter then explains to the onlookers that they must repent and be baptized, for Jesus, both Lord and Messiah, has been resurrected. Notably, in a previous poem from *Midquest*'s water section, the speaker's grandfather comically demands to be baptized by a Baptist minister despite hailing from a long line of Methodists.

Chappell's second epigraph, "God is a fire in the head," is a slight misquotation from the expurgated version of *The Diary of Vaslav Nijinsky*, which reads, "God is *the* fire in the head." Its author, Nijinsky, was a legendary Russian ballet dancer who lived from 1889 to 1950; he was also a diagnosed schizophrenic.

2. "M.Y.F." is a common abbreviation for a Methodist Youth Fellowship.

Matthew Dickerson

A professor at Middlebury College with affiliations in multiple programs, including computer science and environmental studies, Matthew Dickerson (b. 1963) has produced a versatile corpus of writing. His subjects include literary criticism; trout, nature, and fly fishing (he is an avid outdoorsman); folk rock singer Mark Heard; and philosophy of mind. His novels encompass medieval historical fiction and fantasy. While earning his doctorate in computer science from Cornell University, Dickerson satisfied a lifelong passion by taking coursework in medieval studies and Old English, and this work partly resulted in Dickerson's first historical novel, *The Finnsburg Encounter* (1991), wherein he reconstructs the fragmentary yet tragic tale of the Frisian king Finn and his Danish wife Hildeburh. A sequel, *The Rood and the Torc* (2014), takes place six years later. Among Inklings scholars, though, Dickerson is better known for his literary criticism: three books on Tolkien, one on C. S. Lewis, and another on myth and fantasy. His themes include environmentalism, the concept of heroism, Christian spirituality, and free will. Of the following selections, Dickerson wrote "Morning Berries by the McKenzie" in 2016 while serving as writer-in-residence for the Spring Creek Project. The second poem hails from Dickerson's sequel to *The Finnsburg Encounter*.

Morning Berries by the Mckenzie

Blueberries, blackberries,
and half a banana bless
my breakfast bowl.

I did not plan a morning meal
so alliterative. But alas,

fruit will ferment
once picked. Once paid for.

The bananas I think must be
from rainforests far away.
The blueberries,
pre-packaged and plump,
from almost anywhere.

But the blackberries! Ah!
The blackberries found beside
the McKenzie—found mainly
by luck when looking
for rising rainbow trout.
Found free and thick.

And we, unprepared
for such sweet grace
held them in a hat
once soaked and stained
with salt of human sweat,
now blotched dark blue.
Carried them with care
back to the cabin.

These berries picked, not purchased—
grace gladly received though
through thorn-scarred hands—
were sweetest and fairest by far.

10

20

30

from THE ROOD AND THE TORC (2014)[1]

Ulestan's Hope

From Hwitstan he went,   the wise thane Ulestan,
from hearth, from home,   from hall and from king.
A weary wanderer,   but he walks not alone.
He went with God's man,   the good monk Willimond.

No foe drove him forth.   No fear made him leave.
He did not seek   that sorrowful way.
One command he received,   one care from his ruler.
To him was trusted   the highest of tasks:
this boy to keep,   the king's own blood.

Thus Ulestan did take,   traveling so far,
the sad road south   with snow close behind.

10

They promised to protect   the prince between them.
And by God's grace,   by the good One's mercy,
to joy and to peace   their path may still lead.
And hope is held high   the third may come home.

A king to Friesland,   Finn's son Kristinge.

NOTE

1. The premise for *The Rood and the Torc* is that, shortly before the Finnsburg slaughter, which saw the deaths of Hildeburh's husband (Finn), brother (Hnæf), and firstborn son, their family arranged for the safety of Hildeburh and Finn's *second*-born son—a character invented by Dickerson. This infant, Kristinge, is taken from Hwitstan village by a Frisian warrior, Ulestan, and an Irish-Saxon monk, Willimond. The bard Dyflines sings the following song to Kristinge, who, now a young man, is trying to live quietly in Frisia as a monk. As the song implies, however, Dyflines and others know his true heritage, and soon hereafter they urge Kristinge to reclaim his birthright.

Appendix A

Letter to the Editor of Star*Line, *by Steve Rasnic*

LETTERS TO THE EDITOR:

The magazine's name is changed to UMBRAL, a quarterly. There will be an UMBRAL SUPPLEMENT, containing statements, reviews, articles, commentary, etc. First issue will have an article by Sandra McPherson on her poem "Collapsars," and perhaps a poem by her. There will also be material by the experimental writer Carol Berge. Submissions for this are also welcomed.

I'd like very much to see some formal verse, but formal verse which really makes use of the form—for example, Pound's imitation of the Anglo-Saxon in his first, "Greek," canto. In other words, using the formal verse pattern AND diction AND imagery to draw parallels, analogues between different cultures and periods of history. Cramming material into metre and rhyme does not make a poem. The idea of verse parallels between the future and a past culture excites me.

Prose poems and fables also wanted. The first issue will be out the end of July. Price is 75 cents. $3.00 for a year (4 issue) subscription.

Thanks again,
Steve Rasnic
P.O. Box 2042
Ft. Collins, COLO
80522

Steve Rasnic's call for poems in *Star*Line*, May 1978. Image by UC Riverside Library, Special Collections & University Archives, 2022.

Appendix B

Metrical Essay on Three Alliterative Traditions

For readers of poetry in Modern English today, few things about the alliterative meter come naturally. Most of us simply haven't grown up surrounded by structural alliteration, strong-stress meters, or verse with an irregular but systematically constrained rhythm. Say what one will about limericks or nursery rhymes, at least they do a fair job of introducing people to the basics of traditional prosody. Anyone who knows the man from Nantucket, for example, already knows something about rhyme scheme and anapests, and the same goes for anyone familiar with Old Mother Hubbard or the three blind mice. Even if most people can't remember the name for a specific poetic device, we still intuit the underlying principles readily enough on a cultural level. Alliterative poetry, however, is another beast entirely. Since the mid-sixteenth century, such poetry has mostly vanished from the English-language literary tradition, and if contemporary readers know anything about this archaic medieval form, their knowledge probably came later in life, usually from college, and most often from a book. Even tongue-twisters don't really help. However many pickled peppers Peter Piper may have picked, Mr. Piper's exploits only teach us about the ornamental kind of alliteration, not the structural kind.

Accordingly, this metrical appendix has one simple goal: describe in a way accessible to lay readers three different metrical traditions important to the Modern Alliterative Revival. For the most part, I'll follow the common accounts found in textbooks. Although scholars add every year to what we know about alliterative poetics in the Old English, Old Norse, and Middle English traditions, few of these advances have yet touched many practicing poets. Most alliterative poems in an Old English style, for instance, follow a metrical system first devised by Eduard Sievers over 130 years ago. This system was famously reproduced in Henry Sweet's *An Anglo-Saxon Reader in Prose and Verse* (seventh edition, 1894), an influential textbook for decades, and, even more accessibly, J. R. R. Tolkien's essay "On Translating *Beowulf*" (1940, 1983). Of course, more theoretically robust systems have come forward since Sievers, and models such as Geoffrey Russom's word-foot theory or Nicolay Yakovlev's morphological account provide revivalists with exciting new ways of replicating an Old English alliterative style.[1] For anyone intrigued by such possibilities, a selected bibliography appears in Appendix D. Within the Modern Revival, however, older models proliferate, and I'll cite current research only as it highlights problems, nuances, or trouble points in our better-established systems for understanding alliterative poetics.

On a final note, let me caution readers against taking this metrical appendix as strictly normative. My intention is more modest: explaining what alliterative metrics *are*, or at least have been, but not necessarily what they must or ought to be. Normative guides certainly exist, and classic examples include Snorri Sturluson's *Háttatal* and C. S. Lewis's "The Alliterative Metre." By establishing a metrical baseline of knowledge for poets and critics alike, such guides serve a vital literary function. Nonetheless, poets in the Modern Revival vary widely in how they choose to engage the major alliterative traditions, and one of the stronger arguments for impressionism lies in how greatly Modern English differs linguistically from its older, cognate Germanic languages. Impressionists tend to indulge these differences, while purists tend to minimize them. Yet styles always differ, and even hard purists never share the same exact tendencies. As a result, rather than judging modern poems strictly by their metrical fidelity, readers might better engage this appendix by generating theories or explanations for why a revivalist might adhere or stray from a particular tradition. At the same time, several metrical trends *are* readily observable within the Modern Revival. They will be noted as we move along.

THE OLD ENGLISH TRADITION

Historically, poets in all known medieval Germanic languages used an alliterative meter. Because Germanic languages customarily put lexical stresses on the initial syllable of words, alliteration or "front-rhyme" became more natural than end-rhyme. Notably, early Celtic bards also made alliteration a prominent metrical feature of their verse, but, as Donka Minkova observes, little evidence exists for any direct influence on Old English practice (10n15). Instead, the meter used by Old English *scopas* came from those Germanic tribes—the Angles, the Saxons, the Jutes—who migrated to the British Isles in the fifth and sixth centuries after Rome abandoned the island. For anyone curious as to why *Beowulf*'s central events happen not in England but in

Scandinavia, these migrations explain why. Like the alliterative meter itself, the stories and historical legends that inform *Beowulf* came from over the sea.

Although nothing rigidly separates the Old English period from the Middle English period, linguists sometimes suggest the year 1150 as a practical cut-off point. According to Elly van Gelderen, the Peterborough version of the *Anglo-Saxon Chronicle* from around this time has several texts with undeniably "modern" grammatical features such as function words and reduced inflected endings (10). However, alliterative poetry *in* Old English meter seems to have faded about a century earlier. Granted, prior to the Norman Conquest, linguistic change had already begun to affect Old English texts such as *The Battle of Maldon,* composed no earlier than 991, but the last alliterative poem surviving from before the Conquest, *The Death of Edward* in 1065, scans as perfectly metrical according to classical rules in nearly all verses; in contrast, the first surviving alliterative poem from after the Conquest, *Durham* in c. 1100, fails to conform in more than half its verses (Cable, *English* 54–55). For us, then, the year 1066 serves as a convenient endpoint for alliterative poetry in Old English style. Some historians also tag 1066 as the end to the Viking Era. Just three weeks prior to William of Normandy's victory at Hastings, England's King Harold Godwinson himself bested Harald Hardrada of Norway at Stamford Bridge, although the Norse alliterative tradition would nevertheless continue up through the thirteenth century.

Unlike this Norse tradition, though, the Old English tradition conveniently employs just one main form of alliterative meter. As most readers might guess, the most obvious feature of this meter is alliteration, yet the term is misleading. By etymology alone, "alliteration" privileges spelling over sound, which directly reverses what Old English audiences—largely illiterate—would have privileged. Yet, following Russom, we can define the core concept behind alliteration as the phonological equivalence between any two stressed syllabic onsets. That is to say, the consonant sounds that begin any pair of words must match. Although vowel-initial words technically lack an onset, they still alliterate with one another because they all have matching "empty" onsets (Russom 64). In addition, Old English poets considered *sp-*, *st-*, and *sk-* to be unique clusters that alliterate only with themselves. For any given line of verse, primary alliteration follows one of two patterns: *ax/ax* and *aa/ax*. These letters track the four lifts—the heavily stressed long syllables—within every line. So, according to our two patterns, the first and third lifts *always* alliterate; the second lift *sometimes* alliterates (in *aa/ax*); but the fourth lift never alliterates.[2] Some permissible patterns incorporate secondary alliteration as well. Examples include crossed alliteration (*ab/ab*), transverse alliteration (*ab/ba*), and delayed alliteration (*xa/ax*). Alliteration, moreover, always coincides with semantic importance. Alliteration thus not only organizes the structure of every line but marks each line's most meaningful content. If unstressed syllables in a line happen to alliterate, they count for nothing formally. Such instances are either accidental or sheer ornament.

Besides emphasizing semantic content, another function for alliteration lies in uniting lines across their medial caesuras. These midline pauses are marked by the backslashes in *ax/ax* and *aa/ax* and lend a certain "swing" to each line, a sense of ebb and a flow. One major metrical breakthrough by Eduard Sievers, the nineteenth-century German philologist who created our most influential model of Old English metrics, is his four-position principle, which holds that every non-hypermetric verse must contain four—and only four—metrical positions. Lifts comprise two positions; dips comprise the other two. Whereas lifts, as mentioned, bear heavy stress and contain just one syllable, dips can have one unstressed syllable or many. Because lines can thus vary widely in length, front-rhyme helps listeners track the line's rhythm. This device also comes in handy because, in Old English poetry, metrical breaks infrequently coincide with sense breaks. That is to say, Old English poets loved enjambment, so punctuation often follows the *a*-verse, not the *b*-verse—a feature that helps distinguish Old English poetics from their Old Norse counterpart.

For a brief summary, the classic alliterative meter in Old English therefore requires

(a) structural primary alliteration across an *ax/ax* or *aa/ax* pattern;
(b) two lifts and two dips in each verse; and
(c) a medial caesura.

For the complete picture, however, we need one more major metrical element: the *way* Old English poets arranged their lifts and dips. Notably, *scopas* seem to have forbidden some possible rhythmic arrangements, but what arrangements they did permit can still bewilder modern audiences raised on the metronomic regularity of iambic and trochaic verse. This apparent inconstancy certainly confounded older antiquarians. As late as 1865, William Francis Collier could claim that "Saxon" poetry lacked meter or rhyme entirely, having only alliteration (38). Besides Sievers's four-position principle, though, another of his legacies is his five-types theory. I take my following examples from Tolkien's essay "On Translating *Beowulf*." Lifts appear as capital letters, and half-lifts, which affect only the final two types, appear in smaller capitals:

A	falling-falling	:	KNIGHTS in | ARmour
B	rising-rising	:	the ROAR | ing SEA
C	clashing	:	on HIGH | MOUNtains
Da	falling by stages	:	BRIGHT | ARCH-Angels
Db	broken fall	:	BOLD | BRAZen-FACED
E	fall and rise	:	HIGH-CREST-ed | HELMS (62)

The letters A, B, C, D, and E indicate the relative frequency of each verse type. Strange as it may sound, these Sieversian patterns—*not* alliteration itself—arguably constitute the core of Old English alliterative poetics. Lewis's own essay on the meter, for example, acknowledges that Old English has a "metrical structure, which could stand alone, and which would then be to this system as blank verse is to the syllabic" (15), and Tolkien makes a virtually identical claim in "On Translating *Beowulf*" (p. 66). Although neither Inkling ever in fact wrote a "blank" alliterative poem, good examples exist within the Modern Revival. One belongs to Edwin Morgan and his 1962 translation of *Beowulf*, a text that uses a four-beat accentual meter without alliteration, which Morgan considered distracting. An honorable mention also goes to Canadian poet P. K. Page for her book-length memoir *Hand Luggage* (2006).

Old English poets typically alternated between these Sievers types. For example, let us examine the opening to Lewis's *The Nameless Isle*:

C (xxSSx)	in a SPRING SEAson | i SAILED aWAY	B (xSxS)
A (SxxSx)	EARly at EVEning | of an A-pril NIGHT	B (xxSxS)
A (SxSx)	MASter *MARI*ner | of the MEN was I	B (xxSxS)
Db (SSxs)	EIGH-TEEN in ALL | and EVE-ry DAY	B (xSxS)

Except for alliterating on different *s*-initial consonant clusters in his first line (a prohibition he rarely follows), Lewis otherwise renders Old English rhythm perfectly. Each verse has two lifts and two dips arranged according to a valid Sievers type, and he employs short dips (a single unstressed syllable) as well as long dips (two or more unstressed syllables). The first three lines track an *aa/ax* alliterative pattern; the fourth is *ax/ax*. Some readers, knowing that vowel-initial words always alliterate, might be tempted to scan Lewis's fourth line as *aa/ax*, too, but since *all* is a half-lift, not a full one, it cannot formally participate in the line's alliterative structure.[3]

Some readers may also wonder why the first-person pronoun in *The Nameless Isle* receives stress in the third line but not the first. Unfortunately, scanning alliterative poetry is more art than science. Normally, Old English poets apportioned stress according to a word's grammatical class. Although nouns, adjectives, and non-finite verbs all bear strong stress, demonstratives, prepositions, and possessives (a class of words normally called "proclitics") almost never do. Falling somewhere in the middle are particles. These words—finite verbs, demonstrative adverbs, and personal pronouns—do not *usually* receive stress. Accordingly, most personal pronouns in *The Nameless Isle* belong within dips. However, positionality and semantic weight matter too. In verse 3b, the first lift, *men,* is obvious, but what about the second lift? Problematically, both *was* and *I* are particles—the former a finite verb, the latter a personal pronoun. The first-person pronoun, though, appears at a place of natural emphasis, and it bears more semantic content as well. Since there are no better options, we must promote this final pronoun to full-lift status.

Occasionally, Old English poets required special licenses to achieve their permitted rhythms. One common license, anacrusis, formally discounts an unstressed syllable from the meter if it occurs prior to the first lift in types A and D. Although usually limited to the *a*-verse, this license enables higher frequencies of types A and D. Another license is resolution, arguably the "central rule of Sieversian metrics" (Goering, "Sievers" 141). Resolution permits the merging of two syllables—the first stressed but short, the second unstressed—into a single one-syllable lift. We have seen one example already: *MARI*-ner. Since Old English poets never concluded A-types or C-types with a long dip, resolving "mari-" eliminates for Lewis an unhistorical long-dip ending. Likewise, Old English poets discouraged long dips in the third metrical position of types B. So, if someone pronounced "every" from verse 4b with three syllables rather than two, resolving *ever-* would remove an unwanted long dip. Finally, as a language, Modern English tends to encourage several rhythms forbidden within Old English practice. One such rhythm is SxxS. This pattern technically only contains three metrical positions, not four, since the unstressed syllables merge into a single long dip, but in the Modern Revival such variations appear with some frequency, especially among impressionists. Poul Anderson, for instance, has no qualms about opening "The Elf-woman's Curse" as follows:

x (SxxS)   SAILing the SEA   or SEEKing the LAND   B (xSxxS)

Although Anderson's *b*-verse forms a valid B-type (despite its long second dip, which is undesirable but not forbidden), his *a*-verse falls one metrical position shy of the full complement. An Old English *scop* would have rejected it.

Nonetheless, as this last example indicates, modern revivalists replicate some features of Old English prosody more regularly than others. While some medievalists—especially ones mindful of tradition—might consider Sievers's five types as foundational to Old English meter, contemporary poets are instead far likelier to retain alliteration, oftentimes in excess. Even purists cannot avoid the temptation. Both Tolkien and Lewis, for instance, use double alliteration (the *aa/ax* pattern) much more frequently than occurs in real Old English poetry. But this anomaly should surprise no one. After all, alliteration is easy to recognize. Most native speakers learn about alliteration quite early on, almost with their mother's milk, and the concept is culturally intuitive on a level unmatched by caesuras, the five types, or a four-beat accentual meter. Even within the Modern Alliterative Revival, however, there are exceptions to this alliterative excess. An interesting outlier is James Dorr's *The West-farer*. Since this poem employs caesuras, it grants Dorr's lines that classic Old English "swing," but he otherwise eliminates every major feature of alliterative poetics, including alliteration itself.

Yet the principle revivalists most often abandon is quantity: the duration of a syllable's pronunciation time. Unlike classical Greek or Roman poets, poets who compose in Modern English—a language with heavier stress patterns—have never managed consistently to use quantity for structural purposes. Nor is quantity normally taught to students at school. As a result, unless a contemporary poet has had classical training, the principle of syllable duration is dauntingly obscure. Intriguingly, Tolkien forebears from mentioning quantity in "On Translating *Beowulf*," but Lewis allots the principle significant space in "The Alliterative Metre." According to him, syllables are long if they contain:

(a) a long vowel (*fame, seek, pile, home*) or diphthong (*chair, tool, fear*); or
(b) a short vowel followed by multiple consonants (*punt, wind, helm, pelt*).
    (16)

A pithy example occurs in line 113 of "The Planets":

STOOP'D and STUMbling with STAFF GROPing

Here, Lewis's four lifts are *stoop'd* (diphthong), *stumbling* and *staff gr-* (short vowels followed by multiple consonants), and *groping* (long vowel). Notably, *staff* acquires length only by virtue of its subsequent word. Otherwise, *staff* would be considered short despite its spelling because speakers pronounce the final -*f* only once. Trained in the classics himself, Lewis firmly believed that contemporary revivalists must attend to quantity (Lewis 23). Some revivalists like Rahul Gupta and Paul Douglas Deane strongly agree, yet W. H. Auden confesses that, when writing *The Age of Anxiety*, he found the rules for quantity nearly impossible to follow (Jacobs, "Appendix" 109). Most revivalists, it seems, have taken a similar line, although this may be due more to the general obscurity of quantity than to any conscious decision-making.

THE MIDDLE ENGLISH TRADITION

One oddity about the Modern Revival is how, despite far more alliterative poetry surviving from the later Middle Ages than from its earlier half, the Old English tradition attracts far more revivalists. I suspect the Old English meter's greater antiquity mainly accounts for this. Many revivalists already have a strong predisposition toward antiquarianism, and it's telling that *Ars Poetica Societatis*, the SCA-produced guide on older verse forms, includes a section on Old English meter but none on its Middle English descendant. This disparity, though, grants literary critics one undeniable boon: scansion becomes *much* simpler. As my previous section demonstrated, Old English meter has a reassuringly concrete set of rules. In contrast, Middle English meter seemingly revels in metrical anarchy. In a famous description by W. K. Wimsatt Jr. and Monroe C. Beardsley, two New Critics better known for authoring "The Intentional Fallacy," they flat-out deny any structural purpose or utility to non-stressed syllables in the meter of *Piers Plowman*: "The gabble of weaker syllables, now more, now fewer, between the major stresses obscures all the minor stresses and relieves them of any structural duty" (592). Beyond those heavily stressed touchstones, in other words, no real rules apply. Accordingly, contemporary revivalists seem to feel less challenge or thrill when composing this younger, more amorphous Middle English form. To adapt a well-known remark by Robert Frost, writing a poem in Middle English style is somewhat like playing tennis without a net.

Still, medievalists have always known some concrete facts about this late medieval meter. Like its historical predecessor, Middle English alliterative poetry has a medial caesura and a pair of half-lines (the *a*-verse and *b*-verse) constituted by two lifts and two dips apiece. Sometimes, an additional half-lift—called by some a third full lift—elongates the *a*-verse and can participate in alliteration. For instance, "**S**iþen þe **s**ege and þe as**s**aut | watz **s**esed at Troye." In both traditions the same sounds alliterate except in a few cases. Middle English has a stronger tendency to alliterate on the same vowels; reduces the prohibition against alliterating *sp-, st-, sk-*, and *s-*; and has more dialectal alliterative pairings such as *s-/z-* and *f-/v-*. Moreover, although the Middle English line retains a dominant *aa/ax* alliterative pattern, other patterns appear as well, not only *ax/ax* but also delayed alliteration (*xa/ax*) and even two patterns impermissible within classic style: *aa/xa* and *aa/aa*. The opening to *Piers Plowman* demonstrates this last one: "In a **s**omer **s**esun, | whon **s**ofte was the **s**onne." Writing in 1977, Thorlac Turville-Petre contends that, despite variations, these basic principles underlie the "meter of every unrhymed alliterative poem" in Middle English (52).

Notably, Turville-Petre declines to include Sievers types in his description of Middle English meter. Within late medieval alliterative scholarship, these Sievers types have had a patchy history. Through the 1970s most medievalists assumed that Middle English meter derived directly from Old English meter and, accordingly, believed that the Sievers types still applied—or, at least, the A-, B-, and C-types still applied, plus a new combination "BA"-

type. Today, however, this scansion model has fallen out of favor. One advantage to Sievers's typology is its apparent universality, but in Middle English style there are so many exceptions that this universality takes a substantial hit. Yet, following Turville-Petre's thesis on discontinuity (see Part 1, section II of the Introduction), a paradigm shift has occurred. If the fourteenth century's Alliterative Revival *did* represent a new literary tradition entirely unconnected to Old English practice, as Turville-Petre claims, then metrists naturally needed new ways of scanning the irregular rhythms of this poetry. This new way of thinking has now become the norm. Although the continuity thesis challenged by Turville-Petre has seen a comeback in recent years, Sieversian scansions remain rare.

In the absence of any simple model of scansion, though, metrists have fallen back on thick description, particularly insofar as Middle English poets differ in comparison to their Old English predecessors. Overall, late medieval poets preferred end-stopped lines to enjambment, and they wrote in stanzaic (rather than stichic or continuous) style. Resolution disappeared. The most common feature of Old English poetic diction, creative compounding, which includes kennings, also declined drastically, and the reason involved a massive influx of new vocabulary.[4] In the years after the Norman Conquest, about "10,000 Romance words [were] added to English before the middle of the fifteenth century" (Minkova 13). These new borrowings—mostly from French and Latin—tended, unlike Germanic words, to lay stress-accent on non-initial syllables, and this accentual shift made the classic trochaic or A-type rhythms of Old English meter significantly harder to reproduce. Even more noticeably, Old English was an analytic language, but many inflected word endings dropped away as the language evolved toward prepositions, auxiliary verbs, and definite and indefinite articles. Accordingly, word order in Middle English became less flexible, and, on average, more grammatical words mean more length. Old English poets, in contrast, prized compactness and density.

Since the 1980s, though, another paradigm shift has arisen that has challenged the alleged shapelessness of Middle English alliterative poetry. Medievalists have already long recognized that more rules constrain the *b*-verse than the *a*-verse, but, during the 1980s, Hoyt N. Duggan and Thomas Cable independently discovered that actual, concrete, and *stable* rules do in fact govern the Middle English *b*-verse. According to one recent summary, *b*-verses in Middle English style participate in one of two possible shapes:

1. (x)Sx . . . xSx
2. X . . . xS(x)Sx
      (Cornelius 14)

In other words, every *b*-verse must contain two lifts; a long dip that follows or precedes the initial lift; and a short dip in the final metrical position. On this last point Yakovlev adds an even stronger claim: his "non-schwa" principle. Schwas are the final -*e*'s on some Middle English words, and Yakovlev's principle claims that the "alliterative long line cannot end on a syllable containing a non-schwa vowel" (Cable, "Progress" 246). At the same time, this research on Middle English *b*-verses impacts how we understand the Middle English *a*-verse. Although medievalists continue to debate whether "asymmetry" is more principle or preference, many scholars now agree that the *a*-verse can follow any metrical pattern *except* for the two allotted to the *b*-verse. Cable thus suggests a new "common template" for alliterative poetry in Middle English. All verses must possess two lifts and one long dip, and the *b*-verse, furthermore, must end on an extra weak schwa syllable. The *a*-verse can follow any "pattern not allowed within the *b*-verse" and can sometimes bear three lifts ("Progress" 262).

These advances have lent new elegance and simplicity to scanning late medieval alliterative poetry. Unfortunately, few of these insights have yet entered the Modern Revival, partly due to research lag. Because most revivalists are not academics, they must rely on older but more easily accessible metrical guides. Fantasy poets in particular seem to rely heavily on Tolkien's "Appendix on Verse-forms," a text included in his posthumously published series of translations, *Sir Gawain and the Green Knight, Pearl, and Sir Orfeo* (1975). For obvious reasons, this guide conveys an older state of metrical knowledge. It originated as a series of drafts for a planned introductory talk by Tolkien in the BBC's 1953 broadcast of his *Gawain* translation (C. Tolkien, Preface x), and it thus reflects his knowledge of *Gawain's* meter at that time. Accordingly, Tolkien states that unstressed syllables were "not counted, nor in this medieval form was their placing strictly ordered" ("Appendix" 200–01), a view that clashes with Cable's common template. Nevertheless, Tolkien's view is the one most familiar to fantasy poets in the Modern Revival.

Curiously, one element missing from Tolkien's "Appendix on Verse-forms" are Sievers types. Although he mentions "clashing stresses" in his essay, Tolkien neither names these clashing stresses as types C nor conveys their general importance within Sievers's five-types theory. Still, Tolkien firmly believed that a Sieversian typology was applicable to Middle English style. In 1925, he and colleague E. V. Gordon co-edited an influential scholarly edition of *Gawain*, and their section on meter, reprinted several times since, includes both the Sievers types and their belief—then quite common—that Middle English alliterative poetics descended directly from the Old English meter. Although Gordon probably wrote this section on meter himself—Tolkien did the editing and the glossary—it seems quite likely that Tolkien would have agreed with his junior colleague, friend, and former student. Tellingly, when Norman Davis (another former student of Tolkien and his as Merton Professor of English Language and Literature at Oxford) revised *Gawain* for its second edition in 1967, he retained their theories on direct metrical descent and the Sievers types despite otherwise revising Tolkien and Gordon's section on meter heavily (Davis 147–52). So it seems more probable that Tolkien, rather than abandoning the traditional (and still consensus) view about Sievers types for his draft notes in "Appendix on Verse-forms," simply thought them unnecessarily technical for a radio broadcast. Although this excision fortuitously anticipated later scholarship, Tolkien's most accessible essay on Middle English poetics ironically excludes a major part of his actual practice in this meter.

In any event, alliterative poetry from the late medieval period varies widely enough from poem to poem that, for the Modern Revival, if we want to assess a poet's degree of purism, we should turn first to their specific medieval model. For instance, when writing "The Worm in the Wood," James Dorr admits to having *Gawain* at the back of his mind, and Daniel Marsh reports analyzing and translating the *Alliterative Morte Arthure* while composing "Snowberg at the Bridge." Likewise, the bob-and-wheel technique in "Aislin's Ride" obviously derives from *Gawain*, but, like most revivalists, Paul Douglas Deane allows significant room for personal innovation. According to several short metrical essays on Deane's website, *Forgotten Ground Regained*, he developed his style partly by studying early work by medievalists such as Hoyt Duggan, Geoffrey Russom, R. D. Fulk, and especially Thomas Cable—a situation that flavors Deane's poetics with elements of post-1980s metrical research. Nonetheless, as a trained linguist, Deane also lets the unique rhythms of Modern English guide his ear. He accepts quantity, for one thing, and that long dips differ noticeably in feel from short dips. At the same time, Deane makes no use of Sievers types, which puts his practice at odds with Tolkien's, or the structural necessity of long dips, which puts him at odds with contemporary metrists.

As a final caution, critics might feel tempted to categorize any revivalist with impressionist leanings as composing in a Middle English style. The logic is simple. If a poem is in neither Old English meter nor Old Norse meter, the only option remaining is Middle English. But while certainly sometimes true, this temptation risks failing to credit revivalists with adapting or innovating on their chosen historical tradition, which is one reason I prefer the "purist–impressionist" spectrum rather than a simple tripartite division between revivalists in Old English, Middle English, or Old Norse meters. After all, impressionists like Auden, Heath-Stubbs, and even Jo Walton have literary or thematic goals that go well beyond strict metrical fidelity, and they are partly attempting to devise an alliterative style uniquely adapted to Modern English. In contrast, purists always consider metrical fidelity an important part of their literary project. And nothing, of course, prevents individual poets from swinging back and forth between purism and impressionism on a poem-to-poem basis.

THE OLD NORSE TRADITION: EDDIC POETRY

As readers may have noticed, the Old and Middle English alliterative meters—two traditions separated by a gap of several centuries—have had an unusual history. Worse, everything we know about these traditions stems from scholarship that long postdates the Middle Ages. For Old Norse meters the situation is otherwise. For one thing, Snorri's *Prose Edda* provides an authoritative medieval guide that helps mitigate one quirk of Norse literary history: the lateness of our surviving texts. In contrast to Old English poetry whose earliest attested text, *Cædmon's Hymn*, hails from the early eighth century, most Norse manuscripts, including both Snorri's and the *Poetic Edda*, hail from the thirteenth century or later (Gade 856–57). Nonetheless, we know Old Norse alliterative poetry existed long before this because archaeologists have uncovered several famous runic inscriptions in the Elder Futhark, including the Gallehus horn (c. 400 AD) and the Rök stone in Sweden (ninth century). To the ninth century also belongs Bragi Boddason, the semi-divine first skald from Norse legend, and scholars originally date many surviving manuscript poems to the ninth century as well.

Although not always holding firm in practice, Norse poetry traditionally divides into two groups, eddic and skaldic. Whereas skaldic poetry typically focuses on contemporary subjects and people, eddic poetry handles myth and heroic legend. Given this subject matter, the most common eddic meter is understandably called *fornyrðislag*, "old lore meter." The rules for this classic Norse meter resemble Old English meter quite closely. Caesuras separate lines into *a*-verses and *b*-verses, and each line follows an *ax/ax* or *aa/ax* pattern of alliteration. All vowels alliterate, and *sk-*, *sp-*, and *st-* continue to be considered unique sounds. Both *fornyrðislag* and Old English meter follow Sievers's four-position principle. In fact, one massively detailed recent study has authoritatively concluded that the "four-position principle was strictly obeyed in the Norse meter" (Suzuki 777). As a result, the metrics of *fornyrðislag* require the same principles of resolution, anacrusis, and quantity as Old English poetry, and Sievers's five types remain equally relevant.

Nonetheless, despite this closeness, *fornyrðislag* and Old English meter differ in slight but measurable ways. Norse poets strongly preferred to end verses on a trochaic cadence, which increases types A and C at the expense of types B, D, and E. Resolution occurs only on the initial lift of a verse. Anacrusis is rarer. Furthermore, Norse poems are stanzaic, not stichic—a formal technique that lends them a clipped quality filled with breaks and pauses. Rather than unfolding slowly through a continuous narrative such as *Beowulf*, eddic poetry is conveyed through a "series of impressions, reflections, or short bursts of dialogue" (Schorn 276)—a narrative technique, observes Nelson Goering, not unlike the one independently "developed by writers of comic books and graphic novels" with their panel-by-panel structure (*The Fall* 42n30). Moreover, Norse poets championed terseness even more ardently than their Old English counterparts. Although English poets placed no theoretical limits on the length of their dips, *fornyrðislag* forbids dips longer than two syllables. Such compression leaves little room for dawdling, and Tolkien, for one, imitates this terseness in his own revivalism. The following chart by Goering indicates the syllable counts for *The Fall of Arthur*, Tolkien's long poem in Old English meter, and "Völsungakviða," his long poem in *fornyrðislag*:

SYLLABLES PER VERSE	3	4	5	6	7
"Völsungakviða"	.04%	72.5%	25.3%	1.6%	0.2%
The Fall of Arthur	0.00%	57.7%	36.5%	5.6%	0.2%

(*The Fall* 33)

In other words, Tolkien's Norse poem has 4% fewer verses with six syllables than *The Fall of Arthur*, yet 15% more verses with the four-syllable minimum. This leads to a sparser overall text. As also indicated by this chart, eddic poets sometimes composed catalectic verses with just three syllables. A non-Tolkienian modern example occurs in "The Changeling's *Fornyrðislag*" by Marcie Lynn Tentchoff. From an Old English standpoint, her second *a*-verse ("crying soft") is blatantly unmetrical, but from an Old Norse standpoint it works just fine: type A (SxSx) with the final dip dropped. Additionally, Norse poets preferred end-stopped lines to enjambment.

Two other major meters appear within the eddic corpus: *málaháttr* and *ljóðaháttr*. For the former, *málaháttr* ("speech meter") resembles *fornyrðislag* except for having five metrical positions, not four. It suspends resolution more often, and it permits anacrusis more frequently. Within *ljóðaháttr* ("song meter"), this form deploys six verses across four lines. Odd lines retain the traditional *a*-verse and *b*-verse found in *fornyrðislag*, but even lines contain a single hypermetric verse. This "long" verse has three lifts, not two, and six metrical positions rather than four. Alliteration can occur across all three lifts or just two. Most unusually, at least within the Norse tradition, these hypermetric lines often end on a heavy monosyllable, leading to frequent xSxS (or type B) cadences in the final four metrical positions. Examples of modern poems in *ljóðaháttr* include Michael McAfee's "The Nine of Swords" and Jere Fleck's two Markland oaths.

THE OLD NORSE TRADITION: *DRÓTTKVÆTT*

Like *málaháttr* and *ljóðaháttr*, skaldic meters arose from *fornyrðislag*—a development, Tolkien suggests, spurred by northern kings in the ninth century becoming "rich enough or powerful enough to hold splendid court" ("Introduction" 20). Skaldic poetry is a court poetry. It deals with contemporary subjects, often praises of kings, but rarely retells myth or heroic legend at length despite requiring lightning-fast familiarity with such material for its notoriously complex kennings. Unlike the names of eddic poets, most skalds' names survive. Over time, these court poets developed several different but related meters, including *kviðuháttr* and *hrynhent*, but the most prestigious by far is *dróttkvætt*. Unlike the other alliterative meters discussed here, *dróttkvætt* counts syllables, an inheritance (some have argued) from early contact with Irish bardic poetry. Far more than its kindred alliterative meters, though, *dróttkvætt* entails a highly intricate prosody that makes the form one of the most complex and inflexible in Western literature. If writing alliterative verse in Middle English style is like playing tennis without a net, then composing skaldic poetry is akin to playing tennis with a bowling ball.

Every *dróttkvætt* stanza contains eight lines. All lines bear six syllables. The first four syllables must correspond to *fornyrðislag* and follow a Sieversian rhythm, but the final two syllables must conclude on a trochaic cadence. Three syllables in every line are lifts that are quantitatively long. In odd lines, the *a*-verses, two syllables must alliterate, but in even lines, the *b*-verses, only the first syllable or "head-stave" can alliterate. Roberta Frank provides a wonderfully mathematical description:

> Of the forty-eight syllables in a full stanza, normally twenty-four are stressed, twelve bear alliteration, eight form full rhyme, and eight form half-rhyme. There is no choice in the placement of eight rhyming and four alliterating syllables. (393–94)

Beyond the rigidity of alliterative placement and syllable counts, the full- and half-rhymes cited by Frank are what make *dróttkvætt* so challenging. For modern audiences, we already grasp the concept of full-rhyme easily enough. For any two words, the main vowels and subsequent consonant(s) must match: *bear* and *care*, or *pain* and *complain*. These full-rhymes always fall within the *b*-verse. Skaldic half-rhymes, however, are a far stranger beast for modern audiences. In half-rhymes, a similar consonant must follow a dissimilar main vowel: *cat/hot*. Such half-rhymes belong only to the *a*-verse, but they pose special hurdles for revivalists because modern readers aren't equipped to recognize them readily. For instance, when Math Jones was training himself to write *dróttkvætt* by studying Richard North's bilingual edition of *The Haustlǫng of Þjóðólfr of Hvinir* (1997), he explains that, while he noticed the form's full-rhymes in *b*-verses quickly enough, he initially missed the half-rhymes completely ("Re: Modern"). Only after finishing "Lencten-long" did Jones realize his oversight.

For a modern *dróttkvætt*, a good example comes from the "excrements" stanza in "An Army of Hallowe'en Toadstools" by Rahul Gupta. The first two lines should suffice:

Dirts steam. Dritt of foxes,
deer-turds. Merd and fewmet,

Each line has the mandatory six syllables, and the first four metrical positions correspond to a Sievers type—type A in the *a*-verse, type Da in the *b*-verse. A trochaic cadence concludes each line. Alliterating lifts (on *d*-initial words) appear in their proper places, including the head-stave. A full-rhyme on *turd* and *merd* graces the even line, and a deft half-rhyme variation, *dirt* and *dritt*, graces the odd line. This last word pair, *dirt/dritt*, performs double metrical duty by bearing alliteration as well. Still, despite Gupta's meticulousness, even these two lines fall just shy of historical perfection. With four stressed syllables apiece, each line slightly exceeds Frank's requirement of three—although, technically, Gupta is following a four-stress variation called *sextánmæltr* also employed within the third stanza of "Straubhaar's *Háttatal*." Nonetheless, for every word-pair that participates in full-rhyme and half-rhyme, *dróttkvætt* de-mands one word occur in the fifth metrical position, which here isn't the case. Another committed purist, Jere Fleck, requires this deviation as well—a sign of the sheer impossibility of composing perfect *dróttkvætt* in Modern English. For example, describing a hall in "Coronation Ode," Fleck writes:

Oft its rafters rang with
roaring horns to Oðin,

Neither rhyme appears on the penultimate syllable, but otherwise Fleck dem-onstrates due technical diligence. In the *a*-verse, he pairs *oft* and *raft* as half-rhymes, and in the *b*-verse he creatively rhymes *roar-* with *horns*, something quite easy for readers to miss if they're instinctively paying more attention to spelling than sound.

In terms of popularity, eddic meters seem to attract more Pagan poets, and skaldic meters seem to attract more historical reenactors. On Michaela Ma-cha's website *Odin's Gift*, for example, which contains the largest collection of Pagan verse on the internet, eddic-style poems outnumber skaldic poems by a fair margin, probably because eddic meters are more strongly associ-ated with mythic and legendary material that bear deep spiritual significance. In contrast, skaldic-style poetry flourishes within the Society for Creative Anachronism (SCA). As a predominantly social group, not a religious one, the SCA holds poems of praise, celebration, or lamentation—the traditional bread and butter of the skalds—in high esteem. Sometimes poets will adopt eddic meters for traditionally skaldic subjects, such as Sandra B. Straubhaar in "Bjorn's *Drápa*," a poem in *fornyrðislag* despite *drápur* being historically set in *dróttkvætt*, but otherwise SCA poets overwhelmingly choose skaldic meters for their longest and most ambitious works. Just in this anthology alone, Ron Snow, Robert Cuthbert, Beth Morris Tanner, Frida Westford, and Jere Fleck all chose skaldic meters for their long-form poetry.

Intriguingly, my spectrum between purists and impressionists rarely applies to contemporary skalds. Outright impressionists are few. One example is Poul Anderson—a poet who, in *The Broken Sword,* imitates skaldic court poetry by using alliteration and six-syllable lines but who disregards every other metrical feature of *dróttkvætt*. Otherwise, most revivalists seek an asymptotic ideal of historical fidelity, and part of the appeal of skaldic poetry, it seems, lies in the pure challenge of writing it. Even arch-purists, however, seem reluctant to compromise basic intelligibility. As Anthony Faulkes observes, Norse skalds wrote in a way unnatural in terms of diction, word-order, and grammar, and their texts convey an evident "aesthetic preference for complexity and puzzlement" (30). In order to fit language to an inflexible prosody, skalds relied on grammatical distortions and convoluted word orders enabled by such techniques as intercalary clauses, incomplete syntactic units, and tmesis. The rich semantic density of such poetry, in other words, is matched only by its dazzlingly obscurity. To illustrate historical Norse practice, let's examine one poem by Egil Skallagrímsson, a tenth-century skald, and its accompanying translation by Roberta Frank:

Gekk, sá's óðisk ekki,	Strode he, who feared nothing,
jarlmanns bani, snarla,	the earl's slayer—quickly—
(þreklundaðr fell) Þundar	the bold one fell—of Óðinn
—Þórólfr—í gný stórum;	—Þórólfr—in the great din;
jörð grœr, en vér verðum,	earth grows—and I have to—
Vínu nær, of mínum,	near Vína—over my—
(helnauð es þat) hylja	deadly agony is it—hide—
harm, ágætum barma.	sorrow—noble brother. (Frank 394)

As anyone can see from Frank's translation, she uses a syntax and grammar that comes nowhere close to matching Modern English norms, yet she reflects the semantic nuances and complex interruptions of Skallagrímsson's original. In the Modern Revival, I've yet to discover any skaldic texts that replicate these same disruptions to their same historical degree. For contemporary audiences, although contemporary skaldic verse is never exactly easy, modern-day skalds nevertheless make as many concessions as possible by limiting the circumvention of normal sense and syntax.

NOTES

1. For an extremely pellucid account of these two theories, see "Appendix E: Metrical Theories" in Nelson Goering's *Prosody in Medieval English and Norse* (2023).

2. In rare cases, some surviving Old English manuscripts show alliteration on the final lift, but medievalists usually attribute this discrepancy to scribal error.

3. To give a sense of how complicated scansion can become, it's worth discussing verse 4a in particular. My "Db" scansion follows a note made by Lewis in a posthumously discovered metrical preface to *The Nameless Isle*. However, this unpublished guide inexplicably excludes type E, so its reliability is open to question. Personally, I would scan verse 4a as a type E since if we pronounce *-teen* as a half-lift and *all* as a full lift, we maintain Lewis's customary *aa/ax* pattern. In addition, the second lift in any pair of consecutive lifts tends naturally to take reduced stress.

4. For kennings, the canonical example is a phrase referring to *sea*, "whale-road." Formally, kennings are poetic circumlocutions that involve two or more nouns to describe a third. Medievalists often describe kennings as consisting of a head-word modified by a determinant. One complex example—technically, two genitival kennings—is *Mary's son's speakers* in "An Old English Chronicle Praise Poem"; Keveney's referent is *priests*, since only priests speak for the Son of Mary (Christ). Besides kennings, Old English poets also combined nouns creatively to form new compounds. Analogues in Modern English might include *Spear-Danes* (for the Danes), *shield-warrior* (for warriors), and even words like *speedboat* and *highway*. Metrically, such compounds help poets fill Sieversian rhythms while clearing away extraneous grammatical words and unstressed syllables.

WORKS CITED

Cable, Thomas. *The English Alliterative Tradition*. U of Pennsylvania P, 1991.

———. "Progress in Middle English Alliterative Metrics." *The Yearbook of Langland Studies*, vol. 23, 2009, pp. 243–64.

Collier, William Francis. *A History of English Literature in a Series of Biographical Sketches*. Thomas Nelson and Sons, 1868. *GoogleBooks*, www.google.com/books /edition/A_History_of_English_Literature/SPwdAAAAMAAJ. Accessed 12 Aug. 2022.

Cornelius, Ian. *Reconstructing Alliterative Verse: The Pursuit of a Medieval Meter*. Cambridge UP, 2017.

Davis, Norman, editor. *Sir Gawain and the Green Knight*. Edited by J. R. R. Tolkien and E. V. Gordon, revised by Norman Davis, 2nd ed., Clarendon Press, 1967.

Faulkes, Anthony. *Poetical Inspiration in Old Norse and Old English Poetry*. The Dorothea Coke Memorial Lecture, 28 Nov. 1997, Viking Society for Northern Research, University College London. Published lecture.

Frank, Roberta. "Dróttkvætt." *New Literary History*, vol. 50, no. 3, 2019, pp. 393–98.

Gade, Kari Ellen. "History of Old Nordic Meters." *The Nordic Languages: An International Handbook of the History of the North Germanic Languages*, edited by Oscar Bandle et al., vol. 1, de Gruyter, 2002, pp. 856–70.

Goering, Nelson. "Eduard Sievers' *Altgermanisch Metrik* 125 years on." *Of Ye Olde Englisch Langage and Textes: New Perspectives on Old and Middle English Language and Literature*, edited by Carlos Prado Alonso, Rodrigo Pérez Lorido, and Paula Rodríguez-Puente, Peter Lang, 2020, pp. 139–62.

———. "*The Fall of Arthur* and *The Legend of Sigurd and Gudrún*: A Metrical Review of Three Modern English Alliterative Poems." *Journal of Inklings Studies*, vol. 5, no. 2, 2015, pp. 3–56.

———. *Prosody in Medieval English and Norse*. Oxford UP, 2023.

Jacobs, Alan. "Appendix: Two Letters on Metrical Matters." *The Age of Anxiety: A Baroque Eclogue*, by W. H. Auden, edited by Jacobs, Princeton UP, 2011, pp. 109–12.

Jones, Math. "Re: Modern Alliterative Poetry." Received by Dennis Wise, 29 May 2021. E-mail.

Lewis, C. S. "The Alliterative Metre." *Selected Literary Essays*, edited by Walter Hooper. 1969. Cambridge UP, 1980, pp. 15–26.

Minkova, Donka. *Alliteration and Sound Change in Early English*. Cambridge UP, 2003.

Morris, Elizabeth [Beth Morris Tanner], editor. *Ars Poetica Societatis. The Compleat Anachronist*, vol. 67, Society for Creative Anachronism, 1993.

O'Donoghue, Heather. "The Reception of Eddic Poetry." *A Handbook to Eddic Poetry*, edited by Carolyne Larrington, Judy Quinn, and Brittany Schorn, Cambridge UP, 2016, pp. 349–65.

Russom, Geoffrey. *Beowulf and Old Germanic Metre*. Cambridge UP, 1998.

Schorn, Brittany. "Eddic Style." *A Handbook to Eddic Poetry*, edited by Carolyne Larrington, Judy Quinn, and Brittany Schorn, Cambridge UP, 2016, pp. 271–87.

Suzuki, Seiichi. *The Meters of Old Norse Eddic Poetry: Common Germanic Inheritance and North Germanic Innovation*. De Gruyter, 2013.

Tolkien, Christopher. Preface. *Sir Gawain and the Green Knight, Pearl, and Sir Orfeo*, by J. R. R. Tolkien, Ballantine, 1975, pp. vii–x.

Tolkien, J. R. R. "Appendix on Verse-forms." *Sir Gawain and the Green Knight, Pearl, and Sir Orfeo*, translated by J. R. R. Tolkien, edited by Christopher Tolkien, Ballantine, 1975, pp. 199–212.

———. "Introduction to the 'Elder Edda.'" *The Legend of Sigurd & Gudrún*, edited by Christopher Tolkien, HarperCollins*Publishers*, 2009, pp. 16–32.

———. "On Translating *Beowulf*." *The Monsters and the Critics and Other Essays*, edited by Christopher Tolkien. 1983. HarperCollins*Publishers*, 2006, pp. 49–71.

Turville-Petre, Thorlac. *The Alliterative Revival*. D. S. Brewer, 1977.

Van Gelderen, Elly. *A History of the English Language*. John Benjamins Publishing, 2006.

Wimsatt, Jr., W. K., and Monroe C. Beardsley. "The Concept of Meter: An Exercise in Abstraction." *PMLA*, vol. 74, no. 5, Dec. 1959, pp. 585–98. *JSTOR*, www.jstor.org/stable/460509. Accessed 4 Nov. 2021.

Appendix C

"The True Critics" by Paul Edwin Zimmer

Aesthetic theories come and go
With ebb and flow of changing times:
Now rhyme is out, free verse is in—
Has been since I was young,
When they sung the best minds of that generation, starving, hysterical,
    running through the negro streets—
That's right, the Beats! I remember well those days,
Lazing in the library in High School,
Fooling around, reading about that scene
In magazine articles on abstract expressionism
And espresso: Ginsberg, Kandinsky and Jack Kerouac—   10
Back in the Fifties they were all the rage.
The age was bland and they seemed raw.
(I saw the best minds of *this* generation—
Plump, well-dressed, and into meditation,
Running through the street negroes at rush hour,
Looking for a horny fox.)
A paradox: Futurism is part of History.
A Mystery: How is a man on an operating table
Able to pass himself off as an evening?
Sing Goddess, of the *hubris* of Pound,   20
Bound overseas to teach Yeats how to write
The right way in his old age; the *new* way.
Oh say, have you seen Walt Whitman on the Ave.?
Have you not heard his very rhythms and themes
Echoed in reams in the Poetry Bars,
The Avant-Gard of 1855?
Strive to be new in the same old ways,
And praise from the Critics you'll earn.

395

Learn to follow the originality formula:
Form you'll avoid, for you'll have been told   30
Old styles are bad; imitation is sin.
Yet in Alexander Pope's olden time—
Rhyme then was still in fashion—
Passion and newness were faults declared:
Men cared for wit and reason: Artifice!
Nice Poets learned by imitation:
A generation passed, and in a while
The style called "Romantic" took the stage,
To rage for passion, newness—a revolt
Against older styles and older men.   40
When in the course of human events,
The present style has been "in" too long;
A strong aversion grows up in the young,
And tongue and pen new theories form and hold:
The old order changeth, and having writ,
Its wit and work are left to ruthless time.
Neither crime nor virtue in "fashion's" eye
Will buy it free from time's unbiased trust.
Rust and moth are the only true Critics:
Although Aesthetic Theories come and go.

Appendix D
A Selected Bibliography

For readers wishing to dive more deeply into alliterative poetics and metrical history, the following three categories may help. The first list, which comprises work by professional medievalists, can grow quite technical; these scholars generally assume some familiarity with medieval literature in the original language. Since there is a vast amount of work on medieval alliterative poetics though, I've limited this first list to only the more obvious or useful secondary sources. In contrast, the next two lists about research on contemporary alliterative poetry is relatively exhaustive. The third list in particular, which focuses on scholarship about speculative poets, is mainly constituted by articles on Tolkien. It excludes, however, some of the less relevant source studies and more superficial treatments.

WORK ON MEDIEVAL ALLITERATIVE POETRY— ENGLISH AND NORSE

Bliss, A. J. *The Metre of Beowulf.* Basil Blackwell, 1958.
Cable, Thomas. *The English Alliterative Tradition.* U of Pennsylvania P, 1991.
———. "Progress in Middle English Alliterative Metrics." *The Yearbook of Langland Studies*, vol. 23, 2009, pp. 243–64.
Chism, Christine. *Alliterative Revivals.* U of Pennsylvania P, 2002.
Clunies Ross, Margaret. *A History of Old Norse Poetry and Poetics.* D. S. Brewer, 2005.
Cornelius, Ian. *Reconstructing Alliterative Verse: The Pursuit of a Medieval Meter.* Cambridge UP, 2017.
Duggan, Hoyt N. "The Shape of the B-Verse in Middle English Alliterative Poetry." *Speculum*, vol. 61, no. 3, July 1986, pp. 564–92.

Frank, Roberta. *Old Norse Court Poetry: The* Dróttkvætt *Stanza*. Cornell UP, 1978.

Fulk, R. D. "Eddic Metres." *A Handbook to Eddic Poetry*, edited by Carolyne Larrington, Judy Quinn, and Brittany Schorn, Cambridge UP, 2016, pp. 252–70.

———. *A History of Old English Meter*. U of Pennsylvania P, 1992.

Gade, Kari Ellen. "History of Old Nordic Meters." *The Nordic Languages: An International Handbook of the History of the North Germanic Languages*, edited by Oscar Bandle et al., vol. 1, de Gruyter, 2002, pp. 856–70.

———. *The Structure of Old Norse Dróttkvætt Poetry*. Cornell UP, 1995.

Goering, Nelson. "Eduard Sievers' *Altgermanisch Metrik* 125 years on." *Of Ye Olde Englisch Langage and Textes: New Perspectives on Old and Middle English Language and Literature*, edited by Carlos Prado Alonso, Rodrigo Pérez Lorido, and Paula Rodríguez-Puente, Peter Lang, 2020, pp. 139–62.

———. *Prosody in Medieval English and Norse*. Oxford UP, 2023.

Minkova, Donka. *Alliteration and Sound Change in Early English*. Cambridge UP, 2003.

Myrvoll, Klaus Johan. "The Constitutive Features of the *Dróttkvætt* Metre." *Approaches to Nordic and Germanic Poetry*, edited by Kristján Árnason et al., Háskólaútgáfan, 2016, pp. 229–56.

Putter, Ad, Judith Jefferson, and Myra Stokes. *Studies in the Metre of Alliterative Verse*. (Medium Aevum Monographs, n.s., 25.) Oxford: Society for the Study of Medieval Languages and Literature, 2007.

Russom, Geoffrey. *Beowulf and Old Germanic Meter*. Cambridge UP, 1998.

Suzuki, Seiichi. *The Meters of Old Norse Eddic Poetry: Common Germanic Inheritance and North Germanic Innovation*. De Gruyter, 2013.

Terasawa, Jun. *Old English Metre: An Introduction*. U of Toronto P, 2011.

Tolkien, J. R. R. "Appendix: Old English Verse." *The Fall of Arthur*, by J. R. R. Tolkien, edited by Christopher Tolkien, Mariner, 2014, pp. 223–33.

———. "Appendix on Verse-forms." *Sir Gawain and the Green Knight, Pearl, and Sir Orfeo*, Del Rey, 1975, pp. 199–212.

———. "On Translating *Beowulf*." *The Monsters and the Critics and Other Essays*, edited by Christopher Tolkien. 1983. HarperCollins*Publishers*, 2006, pp. 49–71.

Turville-Petre, E. O. G. *Scaldic Poetry*. Oxford UP, 1976.

Turville-Petre, Thorlac. *The Alliterative Revival*. D. S. Brewer, 1977.

Weiskott, Eric. "Alliterative Meter and English Literary History, 1700–2000." *ELH*, vol. 84, no. 1, Spring 2017, 259–85. *Project Muse*, doi.org/10.1353/elh.2017.0009.

———. *English Alliterative Verse: Poetic Tradition and Literary Tradition*. Cambridge, UP, 2016.

WORK ON MODERN ALLITERATIVE POETRY— NON-SPECULATIVE

Alexander, M. J. "Old English Poetry into Modern English Verse." *Translation and Literature*, vol. 3, 1994, pp. 69–75.

Frank, Roberta. "Dróttkvætt." *New Literary History*, vol. 50, no. 3, 2019, pp. 393–98.

Howe, Nicholas. "Praise and Lament: The Afterlife of Old English Poetry in Auden, Hill, and Gunn." *Words and Works: Studies in Medieval English Language and Literature in Honour of Fred C. Robinson*, edited by Peter S. Baker and Nicholas Howe, U of Toronto P, 1998, pp. 293–310.

Jones, Chris. "Anglo-Saxonism in Nineteenth-Century Poetry." *Literature Compass*, vol. 7, no. 5, 2010, pp. 358–69, doi: 10.1111/j.1741-4113.2010.00704.x.

———. "New Old English: The Place of Old English in Twentieth and Twenty-first-Century Poetry." *Literature Compass*, vol. 7, no. 11, 2010, pp. 1009–19, doi: 10.1111/j.1741-4113.2010.00760.x.

———. *Strange Likeness: The Use of Old English in Twentieth-century Poetry*. Oxford UP, 2006.

Magennis, Hugh. "Some Modern Writers and Their *Fontes Anglo-Saxonici*." *The Old English Newsletter*, vol. 24, 1991, pp. 14–18.

Morgan, Edwin. Introduction. *Beowulf: A Verse Translation into Modern English*, translated by Morgan. 1952. Carcanet, 2002.

O'Donoghue, Heather. *English Poetry and Old Norse Myth: A History*. Oxford UP, 2014.

Phelan, Joseph. "Native Traditions: Anglo-Saxon and Alliterative Verse." *The Music of Verse: Metrical Experiment in Nineteenth-Century Poetry*, Palgrave Macmillan, 2012, pp. 88–133.

Robinson, Fred C. "Part V: Old English in the Twentieth Century." *The Tomb of Beowulf and Other Essays on Old English*. Blackwell, 1993, pp. 239–315.

Toswell, M. J. "Two New Letters by Auden on Anglo-Saxon Metre and *The Age of Anxiety*." *The Year's Work in Medievalism for 2000*, vol. 15, 2001, pp. 57–72.

Wawn, Andrew, editor. *Northern Antiquity: The Post-Medieval Reception of Edda and Saga*. Hisarlik Press, 1994.

WORK ON MODERN ALLITERATIVE POETRY— SPECULATIVE

Fisher, Jason. "Horns of Dawn: The Tradition of Alliterative Verse in Rohan." *Middle-earth Minstrel: Essays on Music in Tolkien*, edited by Bradford Lee Eden, McFarland, 2010, pp. 7–25.

Goering, Nelson. "*The Fall of Arthur* and *The Legend of Sigurd and Gudrún*: A Metrical Review of Three Modern English Alliterative Poems." *Journal of Inklings Studies*, vol. 5, no. 2, 2015, pp. 3–56.

Hall, Mark F. "The Theory and Practice of Alliterative Verse in the Work of J. R. R. Tolkien." *Mythlore*, vol. 25, no. 1/2 (#95/96), 2006, pp. 41–52.

Honegger, Thomas. "*The Homecoming of Beorhtnoth*: Philology and the Literary Muse." *Tolkien Studies*, vol. 4, 2007, pp. 189–99.

King, Don W. "*Narrative Poems*: The Grand Tradition." *C. S. Lewis, Poet: The Legacy of his Poetic Impulse*, by King, Kent State UP, 2001, pp. 137–68.

Lee, Stuart D., and Elizabeth Solopova. "Alliterative Verse and Tolkien's Verse." *The Keys of Middle-Earth: Discovering Medieval Literature Through the Fiction of J. R. R. Tolkien*, Palgrave MacMillan, 2005, pp. 39–49.

Lee, Stuart D. "*Lagustreamas:* The Changing Waters Surrounding J. R. R. Tolkien and *The Battle of Maldon.*" *The Wisdom of Exeter: Anglo-Saxon Studies in Honor of Patrick W. Conner*, edited by E. J. Christie, de Gruyter, 2020, pp. 157–76.

Lewis, C. S. "The Alliterative Metre." *Selected Literary Essays*, edited by Walter Hooper. Cambridge UP, 1969, pp. 15–26.

Morris, Elizabeth [Beth Morris Tanner], editor. *Ars Poetica Societatis. The Compleat Anachronist*, vol. 67, Society for Creative Anachronism, 1993.

Niles, John D. "The Old Alliterative Verse Form as a Medium for Poetry." *Mosaic: An Interdisciplinary Critical Journal*, vol. 11, no. 4, Summer 1978, pp. 19–33

Phelpstead, Carl. "Auden and the Inklings: An Alliterative Revival." *The Journal of English and Germanic Philology*, vol. 103, no. 4, 2004, pp. 433–57.

———. "'For W. H. A.': Tolkien's Poem in Praise of Auden." *Tolkien's Poetry,* edited by Julian Eilmann and Allan Turner, Walking Tree Publishers, 2013, pp. 45–58.

Shippey, Tom. Review of *The Legend of Sigurd and Gudrún*, by J. R. R. Tolkien, edited by Christopher Tolkien. *Tolkien Studies*, vol. 7, 2010, pp. 291–324.

———. "Tolkien's Development as a Writer of Alliterative Poetry in Modern English." *Tolkien's Poetry*, edited by Julian Eilmann and Allan Turner, Walking Tree, 2013, pp. 11–28.

Smol, Anna, and Rebecca Foster. "J. R. R. Tolkien's 'Homecoming' and Modern Alliterative Metre." *Journal of Tolkien Research*, vol. 12, no. 1, 2021, pp. 1–21.

Sudell, T. S. "The Alliterative Verse of *The Fall of Arthur.*" *Tolkien Studies,* vol. 13, 2016, pp. 71–100.

Wise, Dennis Wilson. "Antiquarianism Underground: The Twentieth-century Alliterative Revival in American Genre Poetry." *Studies in the Fantastic*, vol. 11, Summer 2021, pp. 22–54, doi:10.1353/sif.2021.0001.

———. "Carved in Granite: C. S. Lewis's Revivalism in *The Nameless Isle.*" *Journal of Inklings Studies*, vol. 13, no. 2, 2023, pp. 151–79.

———. "Dating 'Sweet Desire': C. S. Lewis's Education in Alliterative Poetics." *English Text Construction*, vol. 16, no. 1, 2023, pp. 83–109.

———. "Paul Edwin Zimmer's Alliterative Style: A Metrical Legacy of J. R. R. Tolkien and Poul Anderson." *Mythlore*, vol. 37, no. 1, 2018, pp. 183–201.

———. "Poul Anderson and the American Alliterative Revival." *Extrapolation*, vol. 62, no. 2, Summer 2021, pp. 157–80, doi:10.3828/extr.2021.9.

Zimmer, Paul Edwin. "Another Opinion of 'The Verse of J. R. R. Tolkien.'" *Mythlore*, vol. 19, no. 2 (#72), 1993, pp. 16–23.

Credit Lines

Poems by C. S. Lewis, copyright © C. S. Lewis Pte. Ltd. Reprinted by permission.

"Night Out" and "Fair Day" were both originally published by John D. Niles in "The Old Alliterative Verse Form as a Medium for Poetry," *Mosaic: An Interdisciplinary Critical Journal*, 1978.

"I say to the Gods and the Sons of Gods" was originally published by Fletcher Pratt and L. Sprague de Camp in "The Roaring Trumpet," *Unknown Fantasy Fiction*, May 1940.

"The Death of Bowie Gizzardsbane" was originally published by John Myers Myers in *Silverlock*, 1949.

"Epigraph to 'Chain of Logic'" appeared in *Twilight World* by Poul Anderson, Tor, 1961; and is published by permission of The Trigonier Trust c/o The Lotts Agency, Ltd.

"The Scothan Queen" appeared in "Tiger by the Tail" by Poul Anderson, in *Planet Stories*, January 1951; and is published by permission of The Trigonier Trust c/o The Lotts Agency, Ltd.

Poems from *The Broken Sword* first appeared in *The Broken Sword* by Poul Anderson, Abelard-Schuman, 1954; and are published by permission of The Trigonier Trust c/o The Lotts Agency, Ltd.

"High Stood Our Helmets" appeared in *The Golden Slave* by Poul Anderson, Avon, 1960; and is published by permission of The Trigonier Trust c/o The Lotts Agency, Ltd.

"The First Love" by Poul Anderson appeared in *Amra*, Sept. 1960; and is published by permission of The Trigonier Trust c/o The Lotts Agency, Ltd.

"Route Song of the Winged Folk" appeared in *The People of the Wind* by Poul Anderson, Signet, 1973; and is published by permission of The Trigonier Trust c/o The Lotts Agency, Ltd.

Poems from *The Merman's Children* appeared in *The Merman's Children* by Poul Anderson, Berkley Publishing Co., 1979; and are published by permission of The Trigonier Trust c/o The Lotts Agency, Ltd.

"Starkadh's Offering" and "Autumn" both appeared in *The Boat of a Million Years* by Poul Anderson, Tor, 1989; and are published by permission of The Trigonier Trust c/o The Lotts Agency, Ltd.

"Veleda Speaks" appeared in "The Star of the Sea" in *The Time Patrol* by Poul Anderson, Tor, 1991; and is published by permission of The Trigonier Trust c/o The Lotts Agency, Ltd.

Poems from *War of the Gods* appeared in *War of the Gods* by Poul Anderson, Tor, 1997; and is published by permission of The Trigonier Trust c/o The Lotts Agency, Ltd.

"Give to Me Your Silence" appeared in *Mother of Kings* by Poul Anderson, Tor, 2001; and is published by permission of The Trigonier Trust c/o The Lotts Agency, Ltd.

"Lines Written By, or To, or For, or maybe Against, that Ignoble Old Viking, Harald Hardass, King of the Coney and Orkney Islands" was originally published by Avram Davidson in *Amra*, 1961.

"Heldendämmerung" was originally published by L. Sprague de Camp in *Amra*, 1964.

"The Outcast" was originally published by Darrell Schweitzer in *Eerie Country #4*, in 1980.

"Invocation," "Prayer," "Odin's Other Eye," and "The Skald's Appeal" were originally privately printed without titles in *The Wine of Kvasir* by Paul Edwin Zimmer, 1979.

"Logan" was originally published by Paul Edwin Zimmer in *Wyrd*, 1977.

"The Complaint of Agni" was originally published by Paul Edwin Zimmer in *Star*Line*, 1981.

"The True Critics" was originally published by Paul Edwin Zimmer in *Star*Line*, vol. 8, no. 5, 1985, p. 14.

"The Son of Harold's Hoarfrost" was originally published by Paul Edwin Zimmer (as Edwin Bersark) in *Tournaments Illuminated*, 1976.

"Gundohar's Death Song" was originally published by Diana L. Paxson in *The Lord of Horses*, AvoNova, 1996.

"For the Goddess Freyja" was originally published by Diana L. Paxson in *Brisingamen*, Berkeley Books, 1984.

"Beltane" was originally published by Diana L. Paxson in *Master of Earth and Water*, co-written with Adrienne Martine-Barnes, AvoNova, 1993.

"To Idunna" was originally published by Diana L. Paxson in the journal *Idunna*, vol. 63, 2005, p. 17.

"Poem for a Heathen Funeral, in Honor of Paul Edwin Zimmer" was originally published by Diana L. Paxson in *Odin: Ecstasy, Runes & Norse Magic*, WeiserBooks, 2017.

All poems by Jere Fleck originally published in *Tournaments Illuminated*, 1976–1978.

"The Witan of Markland" was originally published without a title by Peter N. Schweitzer (as TþB) in *Sword in the Sludge*, circa. 1976, p. 4.

"Mark Well, Men of Markland" was originally published by Barchan the Kipchak in *Sword in the Sludge*, 1979, p. 5.

"Hildebrandslied" was originally published by David Friedman in *Cariadoc's Miscellany*, 1988, 1990, 1992.

"In Praise of Geirr Bassi" was originally published by David Friedman in *Tournaments Illuminated*, 1978.

"Lady of Cats" (©1984) was originally published by Christie Ward in *Forgotten Ground Regained*, www.alliteration.net.

"An Old English Chronicle Praise Poem" was originally published by Ana Keveney (as Ana Areces) in *Tournaments Illuminated*, no. 157, 2006.

"An Anglo-Saxon Praise Poem" was originally published by Leigh Ann Hussey in *Tournaments Illuminated*, Fall 1994.

"Olaf Konungr's *Drápa*" was partially published by Beth Morris Tanner (as Elizabeth Morris) in *Ars Poetica Societatis,* 1993; stanzas 1–4 and 27–30 only.

"A Lausavísa for Rowan Dróttning," "An Alliterative Acrostic Poem," and "Sea Wars, A.S. xxiii" were all originally published by Beth Morris Tanner (as Elizabeth Morris) in *Ars Poetica Societatis*, 1993.

"Quest for Valhalla" (2015) and "Finnsvísur" (2017) were originally published by Robert Cuthbert on his website, http://ronanfionn.com/.

"Guðrinc's Lament" was originally published by M. Wendy Hennequin in *New Crops from Old Fields*, edited by Oz Hardwick, Stairwell Books, 2015.

"The Deed of Snigli" was originally published by Marcie Lynn Tentchoff in *Weird Tales*, summer 2001.

"The Song of the Dragon-Prowed Ships" was originally published by Marcie Lynn Tentchoff in *Illumen*, autumn 2007.

"The Changeling's Fornyrðislag" was originally published by Marcie Lynn Tentchoff in *Aoife's Kiss*, December 2011.

"The Westfarer" was originally published by James Dorr (as James S. Dorr) in *Dark Destiny: Proprietors of Fate* (White Wolf, 1995).

"The Worm in the Wood" was originally published by James Dorr (as James S. Dorr) in *Star*line*, May/June 2001.

"Lew Rosson's Hall" was originally published by Jo Walton in *The King's Peace*, 2000.

"In Death's Dark Halls, a Dog Howls" was originally published by Jo Walton on the website *Dark Planet*, 1996–1997.

"Still Odin" was originally published by Jo Walton on Patreon, November 2018.

"Grendel's Mother," "DCCXCIII—A Fragment," and "Riddle" were all originally published by Michael R. Collings in *Dark Designs: Forms and Fantasies—Speculative Poetry*, 2016.

"Grettir's Battle with Glám" was originally published by Frank Coffman in *The Coven's Hornbook &Other Poems*, Bold Venture Press, 2019.

"The Birth of Freolaf" and "Freolaf at the Bridge" were both originally published by Frank Coffman in *Black Flames & Gleaming Shadows*, Bold Venture Press, 2020.

"A Cry to Heaven (after Psalm 6)" (1999) and "Freeway Dawn" (2000) were both originally published by Paul Douglas Deane in *Forgotten Ground Regained*, www.alliteration.net.

"The Nine of Swords" was originally published by Michael McAfee in *Tarot Poems,* 2016.

"As one who wanders . . ." from *Selected Poems*, by C. Day-Lewis, reprinted by permission of Peters Fraser & Dunlop (www.petersfraserdunlop.com) on behalf of the Estate of C. Day-Lewis.

Excerpt from "Artorius" from *Collected Poems 1942–1987*, by John Heath-Stubbs (Carcanet Press), reproduced by permission by David Higham Associates.

"The Birch Canoe" is originally from *An Eagle Nation* by Carter Revard. © 1993 Carter C. Revard. Reprinted by permission of the University of Arizona Press.

"My Grandfather's Church Goes Up" was originally published by Fred Chappell in *Midquest: A Poem*, Louisiana State University Press, 1981.

"Ulestan's Lament" was originally published by Matthew Dickerson in *The Rood and the Torc*, Wings Press, 2014.

"Letter to the Editor" was originally published by Steve Rasnic Tem (as Steve Rasnic) in a letter to the editor in *Star*Line*, vol. 1, no. 5, May 1978.

About the Editor

Dennis Wilson Wise is a professor of practice at the University of Arizona, where he also serves as the English Department's director of undergraduate studies. His research focuses mainly on epic fantasy, Tolkien in particular, and his work has appeared in *Tolkien Studies*, *Law & Literature*, *Journal of the Fantastic in the Arts*, *Gothic Studies*, *Extrapolation*, *English Text Construction*, and more. In 2019, Wise received a R. D. Mullen Postdoctoral Fellowship from *Science Fiction Studies* to help support archival research into modern alliterative poetry. He has also earned awards for his teaching and research alike, including the SFRA's Mary Kay Bray Award in 2023, and Wise was the reviews editor for *Fafnir: Nordic Journal of SFF Research* when it became the first academic journal to ever win a World Fantasy Award.